Grand Strategy and

MW01255898

Alliances have shaped grand strategy and warfare since the dawn of civilization. Indeed, it is doubtful that the United States of America would have gained its independence without its Revolutionary War alliance with France. Such alliances may prove even more important to international security in the twenty-first century. Economic and financial difficulties alone will ensure that policy makers attempt to spread the burden of securing vital interests onto other nations through alliances, both formal organizations such as NATO and informal alliances of convenience as developed to wage the Gulf War in 1991. A team of leading historians examine the problems inherent in alliance politics and relationships in the framework of grand strategy through the lens of history. Aimed at not just the military aspects of alliances, the book uncovers the myriad factors that have made such coalitions succeed or fail in the past.

Peter R. Mansoor is the General Raymond E. Mason Jr. Chair of Military History at The Ohio State University. He assumed this position in 2008 after a 26-year career in the United States Army that culminated in his service in Iraq as the executive officer to General David Petraeus, the commanding general of Multi-National Force-Iraq. He is the author of *The GI Offensive in Europe: The Triumph of American Infantry Divisions, 1941–1945* (1999), which was awarded the Society for Military History's distinguished book award and the Army Historical Society's distinguished book award. He is also the author of two books on the Iraq War: *Baghdad at Sunrise: A Brigade Commander's War in Iraq* (2008), which was awarded the Ohioana Library Association distinguished book award, and *Surge: My Journey with General David Petraeus and the Remaking of the Iraq War* (2013), a finalist for the inaugural Guggenheim-Lehrman Prize in Military History.

Williamson Murray is Professor Emeritus in the Department of History at The Ohio State University and the Ambassador Anthony D. Marshall Chair of Strategic Studies at Marine Corps University, as well as a defense consultant and commentator on historical and military subjects in Washington, DC. His most recent books are *Successful Strategies* (edited with Richard Hart Sinnreich) and *The Iran–Iraq War* (written with Kevin Woods), both published by Cambridge in 2014, and *War, Strategy, and Military Effectiveness* and *Military Adaptation in War*, both published by Cambridge in 2011. He is co-editor of numerous books of military and international history, including *Hybrid Warfare* (with Peter Mansoor, Cambridge, 2012), *The Shaping of Grand Strategy* (with Richard Hart Sinnreich and James Lacey, Cambridge, 2011), *The Making of Peace* (with James Lacey, Cambridge, 2008), *The Past as Prologue* (with Richard Hart Sinnreich, Cambridge, 2006), *The Dynamics of Military Revolution, 1300–2050* (with MacGregor Knox, Cambridge, 2001), *Military Innovation in the Interwar Period* (with Allan R. Millett, Cambridge, 1996), and *The Making of Strategy* (with Alvin Bernstein and MacGregor Knox, Cambridge, 1994).

Grand Strategy and Military Alliances

Edited by

Peter R. Mansoor

General Raymond E. Mason Jr. Chair of Military History,
The Ohio State University

and

Williamson Murray

The Ohio State University, Emeritus

CAMBRIDGE
UNIVERSITY PRESS

CAMBRIDGE
UNIVERSITY PRESS

University Printing House, Cambridge CB2 8BS, United Kingdom

One Liberty Plaza, 20th Floor, New York, NY 10006, USA

477 Williamstown Road, Port Melbourne, VIC 3207, Australia

314-321, 3rd Floor, Plot 3, Splendor Forum, Jasola District Centre, New Delhi - 110025, India

79 Anson Road, #06-04/06, Singapore 079906

Cambridge University Press is part of the University of Cambridge.

It furthers the University's mission by disseminating knowledge in the pursuit of education, learning and research at the highest international levels of excellence.

www.cambridge.org
Information on this title: www.cambridge.org/9781316501726

First published 2016
First paperback edition 2018

A catalogue record for this publication is available from the British Library

Library of Congress Cataloging in Publication data
Names: Mansoor, Peter R., 1960- editor. | Murray, Williamson, editor.
Title: Grand strategy and military alliances / edited by Peter R. Mansoor and Williamson Murray.
Description: Cambridge ; New York : Cambridge University Press, 2016. | Includes bibliographical references and index.
Identifiers: LCCN 2015028654 | ISBN 9781107136021 (hardback)
Subjects: LCSH: Alliances—History—Case studies. | Strategy—History—Case studies. | BISAC: HISTORY / Military / General.
Classification: LCC JZ1314 .G73 2016 | DDC 355/.031—dc23 LC record available at http://lccn.loc.gov/2015028654

ISBN 978-1-107-13602-1 Hardback
ISBN 978-1-316-50172-6 Paperback

Contents

Maps

Contributors

DAVID L. BERKEY, HOOVER INSTITUTION

MARK GRIMSLEY, THE OHIO STATE UNIVERSITY

VICTOR DAVIS HANSON, HOOVER INSTITUTION

PAUL HARRIS, ROYAL MILITARY ACADEMY SANDHURST

MARCUS JONES, UNITED STATES NAVAL ACADEMY

PETER R. MANSOOR, THE OHIO STATE UNIVERSITY

WILLIAMSON MURRAY, THE OHIO STATE UNIVERSITY (EMERITUS)

CLIFFORD J. ROGERS, UNITED STATES MILITARY ACADEMY

DENNIS SHOWALTER, COLORADO COLLEGE

RICHARD HART SINNREICH, INDEPENDENT SCHOLAR

MARK A. STOLER, UNIVERSITY OF VERMONT (EMERITUS)

RICHARD SWAIN, INDEPENDENT SCHOLAR

INGO TRAUSCHWEIZER, OHIO UNIVERSITY

Acknowledgment

The editors wish to acknowledge the generous assistance of the Mershon Center for International Security Studies at The Ohio State University, whose grant made possible the conference in April 2013 in Columbus, Ohio, from which these chapters originated.

1   Introduction: Grand strategy and alliances

Peter R. Mansoor and Williamson Murray

In 2003, one of the editors of this volume attended a conference in Sandhurst on the importance of history to the military profession.[1] Surprisingly, he discovered that some of the British officers with whom he talked acidly noted that a number of their American colleagues during the invasion of Iraq had questioned what foreign officers were doing in what to them was an almost wholly American operation. Moreover, they commented with some sharpness on the unwillingness of many American officers to share information, much less intelligence, with their allies. In one case, a British officer recounted the refusal of Americans to share intelligence that the British had originally provided because of its new US security classification, which prohibited sharing of that information to foreigners! This ludicrous situation did little to cement inter-alliance harmony.[2]

During the same period the other editor was taking command of the 1st Brigade of the 1st Armored Division in downtown Baghdad three months after the overthrow of Saddam's regime.[3] During subsequent operations in spring 2004 in Karbala, the 1st Brigade Combat Team worked closely with a brigade of Polish soldiers, a contribution to Operation Iraqi Freedom by one of America's most steadfast allies in Eastern Europe. The Poles lacked many of the technological capabilities of similar US units. Nevertheless, they possessed a wide spectrum of combat and intelligence skills, made accessible by the interoperability procedures honed by the NATO alliance, which he folded into his brigade's overall mission. Despite different rules of engagement that precluded its use in offensive

---

1 Out of that conference came a book edited by Williamson Murray and Richard Hart Sinnreich, *The Past as Prologue: The Importance of History to the Military Profession* (Cambridge, 2005).
2 The US security classification SECNOFORN (secret no foreign) indicates that an item is not to be shared with foreign officers under any circumstances, including those officers assigned to coalition headquarters.
3 See Peter Mansoor, *Baghdad at Sunrise: A Brigade Commander's War in Iraq* (New Haven, CT, 2008).

combat, this allied Polish unit proved immensely useful in operations to eject the Jaish al-Mahdi, the Shi'ite militia beholden to the fiery cleric Muqtada al-Sadr, from Karbala. Unfortunately, this close working relationship between an American unit and one of its coalition partners was an anomaly in the early years of the war in Iraq. All too often American commanders marginalized non-US units rather than incorporating them in the conduct of operations. Part of this shortcoming was the result of lukewarm allied political (and therefore military) commitment to the war, which resulted in restrictive rules of engagement, but part of it was caused by hubris. Why take the time and expend mental energy to deal with allies when you are a representative of the world's sole remaining superpower?

Such attitudes reflected the final stage of the brief, blissful, but ultimately counterproductive unipolar moment enjoyed by the United States after the end of the Cold War. During this period many US military officers posited a revolution in military affairs based on a combination of superior intelligence, surveillance, and reconnaissance systems coupled with precision guided munitions that would render US military forces invulnerable to challenges by foreign militaries.[4] Not only were American military and intelligence capabilities going to eliminate fog and friction from the battlefield, but US forces would be able to accomplish their missions without significant help from allies.[5] Events in Iraq and Afghanistan soon ended such nonsense. Instead, the United States found itself conducting complex and difficult operations with less than ideal international support in counterinsurgency environments for which its military forces had insufficiently prepared in the decade before 2001.

This volume is predicated on the belief that in the future the United States will need alliance and coalition partners to achieve its strategic goals. It is also in part a response to the arrogance of some American leaders in the recent past that all too casually dismissed the importance of allies, other than as convenient political window dressing for American aims. It addresses the relationship between alliances and the conduct of grand strategy. By doing so it hopes to contribute to the larger understanding among policy makers, military officers, academia, and the

---

4 The decade immediately before the 2003 invasion of Iraq was, of course, the period of so-called rapid decisive operations, predicated on information dominance and associated command and control capabilities that would theoretically allow American military forces to see all enemy forces in their battle space and thus be in a position to destroy them.

5 For the claims of future war being dominated entirely by technological advances, see particularly Admiral William A. Owens with Ed Offley, *Lifting the Fog of War* (New York, 2001). For a rejoinder discussing the actual parameters within which revolutions in military affairs have occurred in the past, see MacGregor Knox and Williamson Murray, *The Dynamics of Military Revolution, 1300–2050* (Cambridge, 2000).

general public of the crucial importance that alliances and coalitions have played in the conduct of strategy in peace and in war over the centuries.[6] The contributors have focused their chapters on periods of history in which alliances or coalitions have played a major role in the articulation and conduct of grand strategy as well as military strategy in periods of peace as well as war. It not only deals with alliances and coalitions that have succeeded, but with those that have failed as well.

For the purpose of this study we have defined alliances as inter–state groupings formally constituted by treaty, while coalitions represent more informal groupings, brought together by a common interest.[7] Nevertheless, one needs to be careful even with such simple definitions. In the end it does not matter whether one talks of alliances or coalitions. What matters is how well or how badly such groupings function in the real world. The Anglo-American alliance of 1941–1945 during World War II was much more than a formal relationship bound by a treaty that both nations had signed on the dotted line. On the other hand, one really wonders whether the connection between the Anglo-American powers and the Soviet Union was truly an alliance, considering the consistent mistrust that Stalin's Soviet Union exhibited toward its "allies" even during the war's darkest days with the Germans on the outskirts of Moscow. In the latter case, of course, all three nations had signed numerous agreements on the dotted line, many of which were quickly breached once hostilities ceased.

There are, of course, alliances and coalitions that consist of the willing, the more or less willing, and the not so willing.[8] In the end, the degree to which the aims of the various nations are congruent is the crucial determinant of success or failure. The glue holding alliance or coalition partners together often may be no more than the agreed upon aim of destroying a common opponent. Such was the case particularly in World War II with regard to Nazi Germany, a state which had proven itself to be an enemy to all. Yet, even then the Western allies had reason to worry about whether Josef Stalin might make peace with Adolf Hitler given

---

6 For other volumes dealing with the issue of strategy in history see Williamson Murray, MacGregor Knox, and Alvin Bernstein (eds.), *The Making of Strategy: Rulers, States, and War* (Cambridge, 1992); Williamson Murray and Richard Hart Sinnreich (eds.), *The Shaping of Grand Strategy: Policy, Diplomacy, and War* (Cambridge, 2011); and Williamson Murray and Richard Hart Sinnreich (eds.), *Successful Strategies: Triumphing in War and Peace from Antiquity to the Present* (Cambridge, 2014).

7 Throughout this volume we will use the terms alliance and coalition within this defining framework. Unless explicitly stated, we use the terms alliance and coalition interchange-ably when discussing issues that affect both types of politico-military groupings.

8 The Athenian alliance during the Peloponnesian War was to a considerable degree an alliance of the unwilling, although Thucydides may have exaggerated the unhappiness of some of the allies.

their inability until 1944 to open a second front to take some of the pressure off of the hard-pressed Red Army.[9]

In fact, such a peace was never in the cards, largely because of the ideological nature of the war on the Eastern Front. But at the time this certainty was clouded with doubt. What held the Grand Alliance together was the quite correct belief that there could be no peace until the Allies had utterly and completely crushed the Third Reich. In fact, the demand for unconditional surrender, articulated by President Franklin Roosevelt at Casablanca in January 1943, represented recognition of that reality. Similarly, Napoleon's intransigent refusal to recognize that the political nature of the war had changed with his defeat in Russia in 1812 and subsequent operations in Central Europe in 1813 led the major powers in the Sixth Coalition to recognize that they had no choice but to crush the *Grande Armée* and remove the emperor from power. As Clausewitz suggested: "Not until statesmen had at last perceived the nature of the forces that had emerged in France, and had grasped that new political conditions now obtained in Europe, could they foresee the broad effect all this would have on war, and only in that way could they appreciate the scale of the means that would have to be employed."[10] Napoleon steadfastly refused to recognize that war had changed, and so finally even the Austrians realized that there was no choice but to fight the war to finish, depose Napoleon, and place Louis XVI on the throne of France.

In the end, the glue that has kept alliances and coalitions together has been the political cohesion of common aims. Regarding war, Clausewitz suggests: "We maintain ... that war is simply a continuation of political intercourse, with the addition of other means."[11] What is true for the relationship between states at war is equally true for coalitions of states in peace and war. If politics and political aims drive the conduct of war by nations and their military forces, then politics lies at the heart of alliances and coalitions as well.[12] The creation of alliances sometimes

---

9 The Soviet Union had signed a non-aggression pact with Nazi Germany in late August 1939, which suggested that such a possibility might occur again should Stalin waver.
10 Clausewitz, *On War*, ed. and trans. Michael Howard and Peter Paret (Princeton, NJ, 1976), p. 609.
11 Clausewitz, *On War*, p. 605.
12 Disastrously, the German military came to believe in the run up to World War I that what they termed "military necessity" should determine the conduct of the Reich's grand strategy as well as its military operations. The result was a disastrous series of political and strategic decisions, the most egregious of which were the Schlieffen Plan, which resulted in a massive invasion of Belgium guaranteeing that Great Britain would enter the war at its beginning, and the decision to resume unrestricted submarine warfare in early 1917, which guaranteed that the United States would enter the war. In this regard see particularly Isabel V. Hull, *Absolute Destruction: Military Culture and the Practices of War in Imperial Germany* (Ithaca, NY, 2006).

expands the goals of the belligerents, making shared negotiating space with the enemy harder to create. Roosevelt's policy of unconditional surrender was meant to keep the allies fighting towards a common goal rather than risk the alliance disintegrating over political disagreements concerning the contours of the postwar world. World War II is an anomaly in certain respects, for total victory over one's opponent is a rarity in military history. Enduring peace usually requires alliance partners to settle for less than optimal individual outcomes at the negotiating table. In this regard, alliances can also act as a brake on broader ambitions of great powers, as was the case with the United Nations command during the Korean War, in which the majority of the alliance members sought a return to the *status quo ante bellum* and threatened to withdraw their forces from the conflict if the United States and South Korea sought more ambitious aims.[13]

Moreover, in thinking through the complexities of the politics that influence alliance members, one should understand that alliance powers are influenced by differing historical experiences, geographies, political systems, and economic circumstances.[14] The nightmarish casualties of World War I pushed British strategy in the period from 1941 through to the end of World War II in quite different directions than those of their American allies, who not only possessed far greater economic and manpower resources, but who had not experienced the great killing grounds of World War I's first three years. On the other hand, from the British perspective on their island base the defeat in northern France and the Low Countries in spring 1940 represented only the opening battle in the war with Nazi Germany, while to the French it represented the end of both the war and the alliance.[15]

Equally important in the *Weltanschauungen* (world views) of those responsible for guiding states and military forces is the deep influence of geography. In the example above, the French – as did the Germans – regarded the shore of the English Channel as representing a geographical dead end where military operations ceased. But for the British the Channel and the ocean to which it leads represented a great highway,

---

13 Thomas A. Keaney, "The United States and its Allies: A Historical Perspective," in Barry Rubin and Thomas A. Keaney (eds.), *US Allies in a Changing World* (London, 2001), p. 14.
14 For a discussion of the influence such factors exercise on the making of strategy, see Williamson Murray and Mark Grimsley, "Introduction: On Strategy," in Murray, Knox, and Bernstein (eds.), *The Making of Strategy: Rulers, States, and War*.
15 The French General Maxime Weygand is reputed to have commented after the armistice with Germany that Britain would have its neck wrung like a chicken. Churchill, in addressing the Canadian parliament at the end of December 1941 commented, "some neck, some chicken."

over which they would be able to conduct future military operations against the Germans and Italians. It is not surprising then that the British were intellectually prepared to make the enormous and imaginative effort that led to the evacuation at Dunkirk, which saved the heart of the British Army and tens of thousands of French troops as well.[16] On the other hand, their French allies dithered and only late in the game joined in the great escape.[17] In the historical memory of the British there existed the example of the successful withdrawal from Corunna in Spain in January 1809 and the escape from Walcheren Island later that year.[18] On the other hand, the French had no such happy memories of the sea as a highway. Rather the sea was only a reminder of some of their worst defeats – Quiberon Bay and Trafalgar spring to mind – while their greatest strategic naval success, the Battle of the Virginia Capes, had at best helped others, namely the American colonists.

In the larger sense the wild card in the politics of alliance partners lies in the fact that each state will inevitably possess different aims. The more closely those aims align, the more effective in the long run will be alliance cooperation against its enemies. But inevitably those aims to one extent or another will diverge, and the farther they diverge, the more difficult it will prove to harmonize alliance military operations. Even if the war aims of the allies are relatively congruent, each alliance member will view the conduct of operations from quite differing perspectives. This was certainly true of the Americans and the British throughout World War II.

Moreover, one of the major factors that keeps a coalition working effectively has to do with the degree that each member feels threatened by an external opponent. Thus, what Churchill termed the "Grand Alliance" worked best in 1942, when German military forces were enjoying their greatest battlefield successes. By fall 1944 that alliance was fraying considerably due to the fact that the Germans and their Japanese allies were clearly on the brink of complete defeat (the Italians having already succumbed a year earlier). Similarly, in 1814 what kept the Sixth Coalition against Napoleon from collapsing was the fact that when Napoleon and the French rallied in early February of that year, the coalition members

16 The possibility exists that the British were preparing to make a similar withdrawal in the face of the massive German Michael Offensive in spring 1918.

17 And one might also note that the British had had a long experience of making major withdrawals of their ground forces from the continent. Dunkirk was occasioned not only by British geography, but by British historical experience as well.

18 For British strategy in this period see Richard Hart Sinnreich, "Victory by Trial and Error: Britain's Struggle against Napoleon," in Murray and Sinnreich (eds.), *Successful Strategies*.

remembered how extraordinarily dangerous the emperor had proven to be in the past.[19] Even more to the point was the fact that in March 1815, with the peace conference in Vienna about to collapse and the victorious allies on the brink of war with one another, Napoleon's return from Elba reunited the powers due to the military threat the emperor represented. The result was a renewed alliance and military effort that led to victory at Waterloo and finally ended the Napoleonic wars by shipping their author off to St. Helena.

Yet, one should also note that while desperate circumstances may well keep alliances together, they may also cause an alliance to splinter as its members attempt to salvage something from the wreckage of defeat. In late May and early June 1940, as Hitler's panzer divisions sliced across northern France and then after taking Dunkirk turned south, the Anglo-French alliance rapidly disintegrated in spite of Churchill's desperate efforts to persuade the French to stay the course.[20] Its sorry end came with Marshal Philippe Pétain's government signing an armistice on 22 June at Compiégne and dropping out of the war. Eleven days later the Royal Navy attacked the French fleet at Mers-el-Kébir and sank one battleship and damaged five other vessels with the loss of 1,300 French sailors, underlining just how differently the political leaders of the two former allies viewed the strategic balance.

We might also note that alliances tend to weaken as well when the moment of victory approaches. This is particularly true when coalitions have thrown together powers whose ideological world views and aims are fundamentally different. The most obvious case in this regard was the unsurprising collapse of the Grand Alliance as the victory in Europe approached. With Nazi Germany's rapid spiral downward to defeat in early 1945, there was little to keep the Anglo-American powers and the Soviet Union together and a great deal to separate them.[21] A less obvious case, but equally important, came with the Anglo-French alliance after World War I; peace quickly resulted in the dissolving of what had been a close wartime connection, but one that, absent the pressure of the Imperial German Army, splintered over the division of the spoils. That divorce was to be a major contributing factor in Hitler's ability to overthrow

19 For Napoleon's military prowess see particularly David G. Chandler, *The Campaigns of Napoleon* (New York, 1973).
20 Churchill even suggested a union of the two nations.
21 A whole generation of American diplomatic historians in the 1960s, 70s, and 80s created a cottage industry that argued that the United States was fundamentally at fault for the outbreak of the Cold War in the late 1940s. The collapse of the Soviet Union and the increasing availability of Soviet documents has served to underline how completely flawed such arguments were.

the Versailles settlement. Only in spring 1939, after the Germans had trashed the Munich Agreement by occupying Czechoslovakia, did the British and French begin to patch the alliance back together again in a desperate attempt to defend Europe against the threat represented by the Third Reich. Regrettably for Europe's fate, by then it was too late to make up for what Churchill quite correctly termed the "locust years."[22]

Finally, above all alliances and coalitions are matters of the present and the immediate future. They rarely live much past the crisis or crises that have occasioned their creation. In the fifth century BC, the Athenians and their allies celebrated their alliance by swearing oaths and then dropping lumps of iron, symbolizing those oaths, to sink to the bottom of the sea as an indication that the alliance would last forever.[23] Of course, it did not – the Spartans and the Peloponnesian League had something to say about its length. Defeat of the Athenian fleet at Aegospotomi in 404 BC ended the Athenian alliance, while at the same time terminating the Peloponnesian War. Even as tight an alliance as the Anglo-American alliance in World War II dissolved in the immediate aftermath of the conflict, only to resurrect with the creation in the late 1940s of the North Atlantic Treaty Organization, an alliance that the perceived threat of Soviet power did so much to create. Thus, one must remember that alliances and coalitions for the most part are largely the result of the exigencies of the present and their existence is largely a matter of external factors.

When those external factors disappear, for the most part so do alliances and certainly coalitions.[24] The crucial question, then, is how do political and military leaders keep an alliance together when it matters most. As the collapse of the Anglo-French entente in the aftermath of World War I underlines, such a collapse can have a disastrous impact on the course of events in the international arena.[25] Yet the difficulties that the Anglo-French relationship encountered in the aftermath of World War I partially reflected the problems that the two powers had

22 For the sorry story of Anglo-French relations in the late 1930s see Williamson Murray, *The Change in the European Balance of Power, 1938–1939: The Path to Ruin* (Princeton, NJ, 1984).

23 Aristotle, *The Constitution of Athens*, ch. 23 (www.amazon.com/Aristotle-Politics-Constitution-Cambridge-Political/dp/0521484006/ref=sr_1_1?s=books&ie=UTF8&qid=1438976222&sr=1-1&keywords=the+constitution+of+athens).

24 The exception being NATO which has, of course, continued to exist after the collapse of the Soviet Union. The coalition that the United States assembled in 1990 to liberate Kuwait after Saddam's military had invaded and occupied that country terminated almost immediately after the accomplishment of its military mission.

25 In this case the failure of the two nations to cooperate in confronting the rise of Nazi Germany until 1939 was to have disastrous results for both nations. See Murray, *The Change in the European Balance of Power*.

in dealing with the security problem that a still united Germany represented. For the French the solution was a truncated Reich, which was absolutely unacceptable to the British. In the end the French settled for considerably less, the peace supposedly cemented by a British guarantee to uphold the Versailles Treaty. Unfortunately for all concerned, the British guarantee proved completely worthless for much of the thirties and only came into play again when it was much too late.

The ingredients for successful alliances

One might then ask what makes an effective alliance beyond simply the politico-military threat that its members seek to address. Perhaps the most important requirement for participating in a successful alliance has to do with extending Sun Tzu's admonition that one should know oneself and one's enemies to include a deep understanding of one's allies, their aims, their strategic culture, their military capabilities, and their geography and history.[26] What this understanding demands is astute political and military leadership with a considerable degree of sophistication and the ability to work with the leaders of other nations and their military organizations, which inevitably possess quite different views of the world. Such leadership must be willing to compromise its goals and approach at times in order to accommodate the quite different views and goals of its more important allies. As one of the leading historians of British strategy in the eighteenth century has noted about the failure of British grand strategy during the 1770s in the war against the American colonials, "At times it seemed as if British statesmen would have to relearn the idea that they might have to do for others something that they might not want to do, in order to persuade somebody else to do something for Britain that they did not want to do."[27]

Here we are back to the most fundamental requirement for success in human affairs, but one of the rarest attributes, namely the need for competent, imaginative leadership. Some of the attributes of such leadership can be acquired through study – a knowledge of history, for example.

---

26 One might note that military historians have done little work on the subject of military cultures, including service cultures. Yet it is increasingly clear that military effectiveness depends to a great extent on military organizational culture. Such cultures are built up over decades if not centuries, and they rest on historical experience, the peculiarities of geography, the nature of government, the influence of tradition, and the inherent contradiction between the need for discipline and the requirement for innovation, adaptation, and initiative on the battlefield.

27 Brendan Simms, *Three Victories and a Defeat: The Rise and Fall of the First British Empire* (New York, 2007), p. 518.

But in the end who leads is more often than not a matter of chance. Two examples from the interwar period underline this point. In 1931 had Winston Churchill stepped off the curb in New York City during a lecture tour a second earlier, he might well have died rather than have received a glancing blow from the motor vehicle barreling toward him.[28] Similarly, Franklin Roosevelt, exposed to the polio virus, only suffered the loss of the use of his legs; had the disease been slightly more critical, he might have died or lost the use of most of the rest of his body. Can anyone doubt but that the history of the remainder of the twentieth century would have been affected in a disastrous fashion by the death or incapacitation of one or both of these leaders? The most important ingredient in success or failure of alliances has to do with the abilities of the political and military leaders responsible for developing strategy, but in considering this reality, one is dealing to a considerable extent with the accidents of life.

In this regard, ideological regimes have proven particularly incapable of understanding and working with allies. Nazi Germany is a good example of this weakness. Given Hitler's ideology and megalomania, there never was and never could be successful strategic cooperation among the Axis powers, which, combined with the failure of their leaders to understand the nature of their opponents, proved to be a disastrous mix in the long run in spite of considerable operational successes up through 1941. Similarly, the failure of Soviet leaders to understand their Chinese allies resulted in the collapse of the Sino-Soviet alliance in the late 1960s and early 1970s. The result was nearly a disastrous war between those two nuclear powers.[29] Similarly, the failure of the Western powers to understand the nature of Stalin's tyranny led to flawed decisions in their attempts to shape the war's outcome through an overestimation of the Soviet Union's willingness to cooperate with them in the postwar period.

Another point that needs emphasis is the need for transparency among alliance or coalition members. In this regard, the clearest example of the importance of this factor in building a level of trust between states during the initial stages of alliance creation came in the first meeting between British scientists and intelligence officers and their American counterparts in September 1940 at the height of the Battle of Britain. At that time Churchill had sent over the "Tizard Mission" under one of Britain's leading scientists, Sir Henry Tizard, to make contact with the Americans and pass along to their future allies some of the most important British technological advances. But, of course, that effort aimed at much more

---

28 Used to the British system where vehicular traffic moves on the left side of the road, Churchill looked the wrong way.
29 See Henry Kissinger, *Diplomacy* (New York, 1994), pp. 721–22.

than simply passing along British scientific advances to the Americans. Rather, it aimed to establish Britain's bona fides as a power worthy of America's trust and support.

In that meeting with leading US scientists, the British revealed that they had developed the cavity magnetron, one of the most important technological advances of World War II. With more resources available to them than their British colleagues, the Americans were then able to significantly leverage the device's capabilities.[30] The historian of the American scientific effort in World War II would note, perhaps with some exaggeration, that the cavity magnetron was "the most valuable cargo ever brought to our shores."[31] Among other items, the British also revealed their progress with the development of the jet engine. The developments that flowed from that openness were to provide the Allies with an immense advantage in the electronic war that would characterize much of the conflict through to its end in 1945.

The scientific cooperation moved into other areas beyond just technological cooperation. R. V. Jones, a major player in British scientific intelligence, notes: "Beside our co-operation in scientific and technical matters, where the superiority of American production engineering was often a powerful – even vital – aid, we also shared our experiences in Operational Research."[32] It was this symbiosis that made Anglo-American scientific input into the war effort such a major contributor to the eventual Allied victory.

In their immediate contacts with the Americans, the British failed to inform their future allies as to the full extent of their successes thus far in breaking the Enigma machine cipher on which the highest-level German communications depended, an effort (code-named Ultra) which was to prove to be the most important intelligence success of the war.[33] But they would soon inform the Americans of their successes and the combined Anglo-American code-breaking efforts thereafter would play a crucial role

---

30 The cavity magnetron would provide the Anglo-American powers with a significant technological edge in the use of radar throughout World War II. The device would prove crucial in the refinement of radar, particularly airborne radars, both to identify aircraft in flight and submarines at sea. It would also significantly improve the capabilities of surface escort vessels in identifying the nearby presence of U-boats.

31 Quoted in Stephen Budiansky, *Blackett's War: The Men Who Defeated the Nazi U-boats and Brought Science to the Art of Warfare* (New York, 2013), p. 127.

32 R. V. Jones, *The Wizard War: British Scientific Intelligence, 1939–1945* (New York, 1978), p. 377.

33 Likewise, the Americans failed to inform the British at this initial meeting of their success in breaking the Japanese "Purple" diplomatic cipher. The breaking of the Enigma machine cipher provided crucial intelligence to Allied commanders throughout the war, but there were distinct limits to what the Allies could discover both because there were days when Allied efforts were less than successful and other days when the information provided by Ultra was uncertain or lacked clarity.

in achieving victory in World War II, particularly in the Battle of the Atlantic (although at the beginning of their participation in the war, US naval commanders would prove slow on the uptake). The disastrous conduct of the anti-submarine war off the east coast of the United States for the first six months of America's participation in the war reflected an unwillingness of American naval commanders to use intelligence effectively, as well as their stubborn refusal to listen to the advice of Royal Navy officers, who had been fighting the U-boat menace for more than two years.[34]

Nevertheless, the openness of the British to their American counterparts at the start of their association set the standard for the relations between the two allies and their military and scientific communities for the remainder of the war. Ultra would prove to be particularly important for the conduct of military operations by the Western powers, although there has been some tendency among historians to exaggerate its importance.[35] The joint development of weapons systems was likewise of great importance, although in this realm there was to a certain extent the "not-invented-here" syndrome that inhibited allied adoption of one another's designs. Allied coordination of production, particularly in the maritime dimension, allowed a maximum use of their economies in support of the overall war effort.[36]

Nothing better underlines the importance of alliance transparency than the issue of command. For some alliances, the dominant power runs matters with little or no input from or discussion with its allies. Pericles's Athenian alliance represents an excellent example of this in the ancient world. Athens's allies had virtually no input into the making of strategy; on the other hand, Sparta's allies had considerable input into the decision-making processes of the Peloponnesian alliance. In neither case did the system necessarily work to the advantage of the leading state.

---

34 The naval commander of the American effort, Admiral Adolphus Andrews, displayed a consistent inability to adapt to the actual conditions that his forces confronted in fighting the German U-boats or to learn from British experiences in anti-submarine warfare. Interestingly, Andrews had performed with a singular lack of imagination in one of the last fleet exercises the US navy had run before American entrance into the war. For Andrews's prewar failure see Alfred F. Nolfi, *To Train a Fleet for War: The U.S. Navy Fleet Problems* (Newport, RI, 2010). For the general failure of the anti-submarine effort and its causes see Eliot A. Cohen and John Gooch, *Military Misfortunes: The Anatomy of Failure in War* (New York, 2005).
35 For the connection of Ultra to the conduct of ground operations see the outstanding work by Ralph Bennett, *Ultra in the West* (London, 1980). For the naval side of the story see Patrick Beesley, *Very Special Intelligence* (London, 1981).
36 The foremost example was the P-51 fighter escort, which possessed an American air frame and a British Rolls Royce engine. For a discussion of the P-51's design and development, as well as the backsliding by those not happy with the fact that the plane was a hybrid, see Paul Kennedy, *Engineers of Victory: The Problem Solvers Who Turned the Tide in the Second World War* (New York, 2013), ch. 2.

In World War II the Germans managed their alliances with neither subtly nor openness.[37] The Axis alliance was at most a slight improvement on the German alliance with Austro-Hungary in World War I, when there was likewise no real harmonization of military strategy. This lack of alliance coordination was to have disastrous consequences in 1916, when the Austro-Hungarians weakened their forces on the Eastern Front to launch an offensive against the Italians without bothering to inform their German allies. The direct result was the collapse of the Austro-Hungarian front during the Brusilov offensive, which in turn forced the Germans to shut down their offensive against Verdun just when it was on the brink of success.[38]

The difficulties of alliance management even in successful cases suggest the extent of the problem in creating some form of unity of command. Political leaders rightly value the independence of their armed forces in war, for their actions on the battlefield create political capital that leaders can use in follow-on peace negotiations. But independent forces within a coalition are often not the most militarily effective. The bitter arguments over the amalgamation of US combat forces into French and British forces on the Western Front during World War I is an excellent example of this conundrum in practice. Despite the pressure placed on the allies by the German spring offensives of 1918, American General John J. Pershing held fast to his goal of creating independent US armies that could play a decisive role in winning the war, and therefore potentially winning concessions at the peace table afterwards.[39] On the other side of the World War I front line, the dysfunctional nature of the alliance between Germany and Austria-Hungary resulted in coordination that was so bad that even major strategic decisions, such as the prioritization of the main effort in any given year, were often not discussed. The Axis powers in World War II did no better. Mussolini's "parallel war" in the Balkans and North Africa in 1940, for example, was uncoordinated with his German ally's operations to the north. The end result was disaster for Italy and the enmeshing of the *Wehrmacht* in military operations in a peripheral theater of operations in the Mediterranean.[40] In practice, most coalitions seek unity of command in order to employ forces most

---

37 The Finns, of course, refused to be the handmaiden of German desires, much to Hitler's annoyance, but the Germans had no real opportunity to pressure the Finns, except by occasionally denying them arms shipments.

38 See Alistair Horne, *The Price of Glory, Verdun 1916* (London, 1962).

39 Keaney, "The United States and its Allies," pp. 6–8.

40 For an excellent examination of Italy's failures in this regard, see MacGregor Knox, *Mussolini Unleashed, 1939–1941: Politics and Strategy in Fascist Italy's Last War* (Cambridge, 1982).

effectively, but settle on unity of effort created by shared goals while allowing national forces a certain degree of independence in military operations.

The case of Anglo-American relations during World War II is perhaps the best example of where unity of command at nearly every level resulted in the articulation of an effective grand strategy, as well as effective military strategies to realize those goals. In retrospect, British objections in 1942 to a landing on the northern French coast in either that year or 1943 were entirely correct. At the same time, Roosevelt's recognition of the importance of keeping the American people engaged in defeating the Axis in Europe resulted in his overruling his military advisers and ordering them to carry out Operation Torch, the landing in North Africa, an operation championed by America's British allies.[41] And when push came to shove, when Anglo-American forces at last had the military capabilities to make a landing on the northern coast of France by 1944, the Americans (and Soviets, one might add) pushed the British onto the continent in spite of considerable efforts by Churchill and the Chief of the Imperial General Staff, Field Marshal Alan Brooke, to delay that effort. In all of this the creation of the combined chiefs of staff that met regularly, and when not meeting passed important information back and forth, represented as effective a coordination of military strategy by two major powers as history has ever seen.[42]

General Dwight D. Eisenhower's tenure as commander of Supreme Headquarters Allied Expeditionary Forces underlines the difficulties involved in commanding in an alliance, even a successful one. After World War II a number of British historians argued that Eisenhower should have placed the great bulk of allied troops and resources under Field Marshal Bernard Montgomery's command for a massive push through

41 In his order in July 1942 instructing his senior military leaders to coordinate joint action with British forces in Europe by the end of the year (which would lead to the invasion of North Africa), and for the only time in the war, Roosevelt appended the title "commander-in-chief" to his signature to make clear his intent.
42 One can gather the impact of the combined chiefs of staff on alliance harmony by the fact that General George C. Marshall authorized the burial of Lieutenant General Sir John Dill, the British permanent representative on the combined chiefs of staff in Washington, DC, in Arlington National Cemetery after his untimely death in 1944. The manifest effectiveness of the Grand Alliance, of course, has not prevented historians from pointing to its supposed disunity because of the extended and sometimes bitter arguments that took place. But these arguments strengthened the resulting strategic decisions, which resulted from serious debate and deliberation within Allied councils of war. Even the Soviet Union, which had a separate command structure, cooperated on the macro level, for instance by timing its summer 1944 offensive to coincide with the Allied landings in Normandy, or by entering the war against Japan ninety days after the defeat of Nazi Germany.

Holland and across the Rhine onto the north German plain, the military strategy that Montgomery, commander of the British Twenty-first Army Group, had vociferously proposed in September 1944.[43] The British military commentator and historian, Basil Liddell Hart, argued that the idea of a single thrust was correct, but that Montgomery was not the general who possessed the ability to have led such a drive.[44] Rather, he suggested that the troops and resources should have been given to Lieutenant General George S. Patton Jr., commander of the US Third Army. All of this made great sense in military terms, but not in political calculation, and as suggested above, politics should always drive the decision-making processes in alliances.

Eisenhower understood the primacy of politics over military operations. Thus, his broad-front strategy represented recognition that any emphasis on a British push into northern Germany at the expense of the US effort would receive howls of protest from the American media, while an emphasis on an American drive would have elicited equal outrage from the British press. Even if the broad-front strategy was not the most effective military strategy (although it probably was the best option available, given the significant logistical challenges and enemy opposition a single thrust would have encountered), political ends should in all cases trump military strategy.[45] What made Eisenhower such a superb alliance commander was the fact that he understood the importance of alliance harmony and was willing to take the harsh barbs aimed at him at the time not only by his British subordinates, particularly Montgomery, but his American subordinates as well, including Patton and General Omar Bradley, the latter the commander of the US Twelfth Army Group. Ike's recognition of the criticality of keeping the Anglo-American alliance together would eventually pay enormous dividends when it became necessary to reknit the alliance at the onset of the Cold War in the late 1940s.

In the post-world War II period the willingness of the United States to cooperate and compromise in the development and articulation of an overall alliance strategy in meeting the political and military threat that the Warsaw Pact represented was a major factor in victory in the Cold War. There were, of course, considerable differences among the various nations that made up the NATO alliance, but while each found itself occasionally in the position of having to sacrifice on issues it felt were important,

---

43 Chester Wilmott, *The Struggle for Europe* (London, 1952).
44 See B. H. Liddell Hart, *History of the Second World War* (London, 1970).
45 Here one might note that Montgomery's failure to open up the Scheldt Estuary after Antwerp had fallen into Allied hands in virtually undamaged condition was the real cause of the Allied failure to mount a sufficiently powerful attack to break into the Third Reich in the latter half of 1944.

the overall result was greater than the sum of its parts. The fact that the United States often was willing to compromise to assuage the needs of smaller powers worked to the advantage of the entire alliance. In the long run the willingness of all to compromise gave NATO a far deeper and longer run than has been the case with most alliances in history.

Conclusion

One of the major points that occurred to both the editors and to the various authors who participated in the conference in April 2013 at the Mershon Center for International Security Studies at The Ohio State University from which this volume originated is how essential alliances have been to successful grand strategies throughout history. As we shall see, they have been particularly important in the conduct of grand strategy by maritime powers. Yet, inevitably given the quite considerable differences in culture, historical perspective, aims, and perception of the nature of the threat, the conduct of alliance politics has inevitably been difficult, annoying to its members, and as with all things in life, confronted with uncertainty, chance, and friction. As Churchill once commented, "There is only one thing worse than fighting with allies, and that is fighting without them."[46] It is the purpose then of the chapters in this volume to lay out for its readers the nature of the relationship between grand strategy and the conduct of alliances and to discern what has made them succeed or fail in the harsh arbitration of war.

---

46 Attributed to Lord Alanbrooke's diary, 1 April 1945.

Part I

Maritime powers and the continental commitment

2 Grand strategy, alliances, and the Anglo-American way of war

Williamson Murray

Alliances have proven to be an essential and integral element in the approach to grand strategy for maritime/island powers. Since such powers do not find themselves directly threatened by ground invasion, they do not have to engage continental powers and their armies unless they choose to do so. Moreover, maritime/island powers can find alliances with continental powers particularly useful.[1] While maritime/island states can use sea and air power to defend themselves from attack, they cannot afford to allow a hostile hegemonic continental rival to arise, one that could potentially isolate and then challenge them for dominion of the seas through control of the continental domain, either through alliances or conquest.

Nevertheless, within maritime/island powers historically there has arisen considerable tension between those who have advocated alliances with continental land powers, along with a concomitant commitment of not only financial and economic support but ground forces as well, and those who have strongly urged a "blue water" strategy of isolation from continental commitments to focus almost exclusively on control of the maritime dimension. Because of this tension, maritime/island powers

---

1 One of the reviewers of this volume argued that our description of maritime/island powers did not discuss Japan and that had we done so, our argument would have been far weaker. However, what the reviewer missed is the geographical context within which the Japanese polity emerged and then interacted with its external environment was far different than the situations that the Athenians, British, and Americans found themselves in. Unlike the British Isles, Japan was far enough removed from the Asian mainland so that threats only occasionally appeared on the horizon. When they did, in almost every case from China, there were no allies to be had. Moreover, the Japanese response in the seventeenth century to their strategic environment was to pull out of international competition both in trade and military affairs. They managed to escape the consequences of that isolationism for a time, but in the end found themselves in an extraordinarily dangerous strategic situation when American warships appeared in the mid-nineteenth century, followed soon after by those of the European powers. In the twentieth century, the Japanese sought to go it alone in fighting on the Chinese mainland. The results speak for themselves in a catastrophic strategic and political defeat. As is the case with all historical case studies that are used as examples to discuss theories of international relations, the context matters.

are a particularly good example of the role that grand strategy plays in the complex nature of alliances and their impact on the global strategic balance of power. Moreover, because the United States is in effect a maritime/island power, an examination of this debate should represent a useful guide for thinking about the future strategy that American leaders might pursue.[2]

Over the centuries the pattern of that debate among those responsible for articulating grand strategy in maritime/island nations or city states whose power has largely rested on the sea has remained constant in spite of what might seem the consistency of potential lessons from the past.[3] This debate has occurred not only in the early modern and modern eras in Britain and the United States, but as early as the ancient Greek world of Thucydides and the city state of Athens. In the latter case, the construction of the long walls down to Piraeus from the inland location of the polis made Athens to all intents and purposes a maritime/island power. Its military weight rested on its "wooden walls," in other words its ships, as well as the economic power derived from its maritime trade.[4] In particular, this debate about how to engage in military competition with land powers has remained central to the development of the grand strategies and military strategies conducted by maritime/island maritime powers that the seas and oceans protect from direct land threats.

The nature of the debate is of considerable importance to this volume on strategy and alliances, because the key piece in the strategic puzzle confronting maritime/island powers has been the willingness of such nations to ally with and support continental allies with money, resources, and supporting ground forces. The geography of island powers allows them to decide how much military, economic, and financial aid they should supply their continental allies, or even whether they need to support those allies at all, in the latter case relying entirely on a pure "blue water" strategy to achieve national security aims.[5] The strategic debate has thus revolved around what Michael Howard termed "the continental

2 While the United States is a continental as well as a maritime/island power, it confronts no real land threat in the Western hemisphere.

3 I am indebted to Brendan Simms for his outstanding study of British strategy in the eighteenth century on which much of the argument and research for this chapter rests. See Brendan Simms, *Three Victories and a Defeat: The Rise and Fall of the First British Empire* (New York, 2007).

4 The Delphic oracle used this phrase in reply to an Athenian query as to what Athens should do when confronted by the massive Persian invasion of 480 BC. Themistocles, the great Athenian statesman, then persuaded his countrymen that the oracle was referring to the Athenian navy and not to wooden walls around the city of Athens.

5 To a certain extent the writings of Alfred Thayer Mahan and Julian Corbett have framed this debate.

commitment," but one inherently tied to an alliance system. Simply put, the debate has been between those advocating the primacy of sea power with relatively minor support for a continental commitment or no allies at all versus those who have argued that a commitment of ground forces to support allies in a war against a land power is the *sine qua non* for realizing the strategic advantages of sea power.[6]

In fact, in most successful cases, it has not been a matter of either/or; the maritime/island power in question has had to support its allies with both its own ground forces and substantial funds or other resources for allied armies, while at the same time ensuring its continued dominance over the maritime environment. But the continued reoccurrence of the debate suggests that what may seem historically obvious is rarely obvious in the real world where blood, treasure, myths, and hope inevitably influence the choices made by political and military leaders and those few strategists among them.

Those patterns of debate have repeated themselves throughout history whenever island/naval powers have confronted the problem of devising grand strategy given the difficulties of waging war against land powers. Significantly, the willingness to recognize or to ignore the connection between operations on land, allies, and maritime supremacy has played a major role in the successes, and failures, that British and American statesmen have enjoyed over the past 300 years.[7] In one form or another it has dominated strategic debate in both great maritime/island nations since the Nine Years War at the end of the seventeenth century.[8] It finds its echo in current debates about a pure naval–air strategy in the western Pacific, in other words over America's future grand strategy as the wars spawned by 9/11 wind down.

Echo of the past: the Peloponnesian War

The debate over the reliance on sea power versus land power and allies was present in the great war in the fifth century BC between the Athenian

6 This former argument was the basis of the theory of sea power that the British naval thinker Sir Julian Corbett developed in the early twentieth century.
7 Japan clearly fits into the definition of a maritime power, but it confronted a hegemonic power in China which already dominated the Asian land mass. Thus, it was never in a position to embark on a similar strategy to that followed by Britain. And then when the Chinese Empire collapsed at the end of the nineteenth century, the Japanese attempted to conquer the wreckage. But in effect there were no powers on the Asian continent with whom the Japanese could ally themselves.
8 For the purpose of this chapter, the United States needs to be considered an island power, for while it lies on a continent, it has never been directly threatened by foreign armies on its territory since the War of 1812.

Empire and the Peloponnesian League, well before the British and Americans appeared on the scene. While wars pitting sea powers against continental powers played less of a role in the ancient world than in the wars of the modern era, the Peloponnesian War was one such conflict, which is undoubtedly one of the reasons why its history still speaks to us today. That greatest of all strategic historians, Thucydides, recounted its course and outcome in terms that examine the most fundamental issues of war and strategy.[9] Here the conundrum raised by a great naval power confronting a great land power makes its appearance for the first time. Like Britain (and England before 1700) and the United States from the sixteenth century to the present, to all intents and purposes, Athens was a maritime power, protected as it was by the great walls that ran down to Piraeus from the inland city. In Thucydides's account the debate remains somewhat mute, a subtext if you will. Whatever the brilliance of his account, as Donald Kagan has pointed out, there are events and strategic arguments to which Thucydides does not give full voice, given his strongly held views on the crucial factors he believed determined the war's course and the eventual defeat of the Athenians at the hands of the Spartans.[10]

In the first two books of his *The History of the Peloponnesian War*, Thucydides argues forcefully in favor of the strictly maritime strategy that Pericles, the Athenian statesman, advocated for Athens in the upcoming war with Sparta and from which Thucydides argued the Athenians then deviated after the great statesman's death. "Then, with regard to the present situation, [Pericles] gave just the same advice as he had given before," Thucydides relates. "This was that they were to prepare for war and bring into the city their property in the country. They were not to go out and offer battle, but were to come inside the city and guide it. Their navy, in which their strength lay, was to be brought up to the highest state of efficiency."[11]

Thus, the Athenians at Pericles's urging were to refuse to engage their opponents directly on land. Instead they were to rely on control of the seas and utilize their superior economic position to wear the Peloponnesians down, while raids around the periphery of the Peloponnesus would

---

9 See among a host of other commentaries on Thucydides my own examination of what makes him a historian who speaks so perceptively to our age as well as his: "Thucydides: Theorist of War," *Naval War College Review*, Fall 2013.

10 Among others see Donald Kagan, *The Peloponnesian War* (New York, 2004); *The Outbreak of the Peloponnesian War* (Ithaca, NY, 1989); *The Archidamnian War* (Ithaca, NY, 1990); *The Peace of Nicias and the Sicilian Expedition* (Ithaca, 1991); and *The Fall of the Athenian Empire* (Ithaca, NY, 1991).

11 Thucydides, *History of the Peloponnesian War*, trans. Rex Warner (London, 1954), p. 132.

further discourage the willingness of the Spartans and their allies to continue the conflict. In the end, Pericles's strategy represented war on the cheap, a strategy to preserve the resources and manpower of Athens, while imposing the cost of the war on Sparta and particularly its allies. It was also a "blue water" strategic approach to the problems of a great maritime power at war with a great land power.

However, at times Thucydides refuses to give voice to alternative strategies, which surely some in the assembly must have voiced. We do know that when the Peloponnesian army appeared in Attica, there were a significant number of Athenians who desired to leave the safety of their city's walls and go out to meet the invading Peloponnesian army head-to-head. Thucydides admits as much when he records the fact that Pericles refused to call an assembly during that period, because he realized full well that there was a good chance his countrymen would vote to do precisely that. This fact certainly suggests that Pericles did not receive unanimous support from the Assembly when proposing his strategy before the war began.

An even clearer example of Thucydides's willingness to choose the evidence in favor of his line of argument comes during the period immediately after the Athenians and Spartans had agreed to the Peace of Nicias in 421 BC. Shortly after the signing of the peace, the Argives declared war on the Spartans with the aim of destroying the Spartan hegemony over the Peloponnesus. However, Thucydides provides us with no substantial account of what then transpired in the Assembly. But surely some of the Athenians must have argued in favor of sending a substantial ground force to aid the Argives in their war against the Spartans.

The fact that Socrates's star pupil, Alcibiades, then led approximately 1,000 Athenian hoplites to support the Argives in the Battle of Mantinea in spite of the Peace of Nicias underlines that there must have been a serious debate in Athens about whether or not to abide by the peace. What is particularly interesting here is the fact that the Athenians had at their disposal a significant hoplite army on the Peloponnesus, ready and prepared to take on the Spartans, but chose not to risk supporting the Argives to the fullest extent with the means available. The result was that Athenian strategy fell between two stools, to the detriment of both. Undoubtedly, the presence of Athenian hoplites alongside the Argives must have infuriated the Spartans. But at the same time there were too few Athenians to deal the Spartans a mortal blow, which was almost achieved despite Athenian unwillingness to commit themselves fully to supporting the Argive army.

In the end, the Spartans followed the advice their king, Archidamnus, had provided them before the onset of war. Using Persian money and augmented by allies with naval forces, they eventually defeated the Athenians at sea. Nevertheless, considerable incompetence on the part of the Athenians aided that victory.[12] The Peloponnesian War was indeed a case of the elephant defeating the whale. For our purposes in examining the strategic parameters of the conduct of war, strategy, and continental commitments by maritime/island powers, the Spartans never confronted throughout the conflict a serious challenge on land, with the brief exception of that mounted by the Argives in 418 BC. Athenian reluctance to find and support allies that could challenge Sparta on land cost the city state dearly.

Following the Peloponnesian War and the eventual collapse of the Greek city states before the overweening power of first Macedonia and then Rome, the problem of alliance politics, naval power, and grand strategy disappeared almost entirely from the Mediterranean world in the great wars that engulfed the area for the next three centuries. All-conquering Alexander destroyed whatever naval forces or armies the Persians threw at him. He had no need for allies. In the case of the Punic Wars, Rome and Carthage, two relatively equally matched powers, slugged it out in the central Mediterranean. While Carthage made some half-hearted efforts to acquire allies from the Greek world of Alexander's successors and a more determined effort to woo Latin states from Rome's orbit, they were not particularly successful. After the fall of Carthage, the Romans simply gobbled up the rest of the Mediterranean basin, and much else as well, but while they were not comfortable at sea, they were capable of using it when needed. As for allies, the Romans made it clear what their proper role was to be – namely to follow orders. There was, as a result, no true maritime/island power capable of debating and/or choosing a "blue water" strategy at the expense of a continental strategy throughout the remaining course of ancient history.

The wars for empire

At the beginning of the eighteenth century the strategic debate resumed, this time in respect to the choices available to English and then British leaders.[13] Should the proper focus for their strategy be that of supporting

---

12 That incompetence at the strategic level lay in choosing to launch a great expedition to Sicily, which depleted Athenian resources for no gain, and at the tactical level lay in failing to protect their fleet at Aegospotomi, which led to their final defeat.

13 The act of Union in 1707 united the crowns of England and Scotland; before that date one must speak of English strategy and after of British strategy. It is also worth noting that in the sixteenth century Queen Elizabeth had supported the Dutch rebels against the Spanish with money and soldiers, while at the same time engaging in a *guerre de course* against Spanish commerce and treasure fleets.

major allies on the continent with financial resources and troops, or should it be on the Royal Navy and a war against the enemy at sea, its colonies, and its trade? As James Wolfe, the British commander at Quebec commented, strategy, like war, "is an option of difficulties."[14] In strategy there are no easy choices, no silver bullets that provide a ready or obvious guide to those who make the critical decision as to how one might best divide up what are always scarce military and financial resources in the face of complex strategic conundrums.

The first of these global wars with its attendant choices came with the war against Louis XIV's France in the War of Spanish Succession (1701–1714).[15] That conflict broke out shortly after the Nine Years War (1688–1697) had concluded. Immediately after the conclusion of peace in 1697, a significant strategic debate emerged. William of Orange, the Stadtholder of the Netherlands as well as the king of England as a result of the Glorious Revolution of 1688, and his advisors pushed for a major continental commitment to hold the line against French encroachments in the Spanish Netherlands as well as a major effort at sea against the French. In opposition the country squires, characterized by the party label of "Tories," pushed for a naval strategy that would emphasize the war at sea, particularly in the Caribbean against the colonial possessions of the French and Spanish.

This debate over England's potential strategy partially revolved around the financial burden the nation would have to bear. The Nine Years War had heralded England's appearance on the European stage as a major power. Nevertheless, the war against France had also proven immensely costly, while at the same time gaining little more than a stalemate.[16] Thus, a substantial body of opinion among the Tories argued that England need not commit financial support and ground forces to the continent, but rather should rely on its naval power and let others do the fighting on land. In other words, they were advocating what we would today call a "blue water" strategy. The Stadtholder-king, on the other hand, still

---

14 Quoted in Williamson Murray, *War, Strategy, and Military Effectiveness* (Cambridge, 2011), p. 58.
15 The idea for this chapter partially comes out of a paper written for the "Successful Strategies" project that the Office of Net Assessment sponsored in spring 2013. See Jamel Ostwald, "Creating the British Way of War: English Strategy in the War of Spanish Succession," in Williamson Murray and Richard Hart Sinnreich (eds.), *Successful Strategies: Triumphing in War and Peace from Antiquity to the Present* (Cambridge, 2014).
16 What is particularly interesting is the fact that during this period the English and then the British developed a financial system that revolutionized the ability of the government to mobilize the financial resources of the kingdom. It rested on not only effective taxation but a modern system of borrowing. For the revolution in financial affairs see particularly: D. W. Jones, *War and the Economy in the Age of William III and Marlborough* (New York, 1988); and John Brewer, *The Sinews of Power, Money and the English State, 1688–1783* (New York, 1988).

firmly believed that his English kingdom needed to support his provinces in the Netherlands as well as the Hapsburgs in southern Germany.

In the aftermath of the Nine Years War, it appeared to most in England that another major conflict was not in the cards. Thus, parliamentary support and funding for the army almost entirely dried up. However, Parliament could not have been more wrong. In 1701 the king of Spain died without an heir and left his entire kingdom to Louis XIV's grandson. The "Sun King" then exacerbated matters by declaring in favor of the Stuart pretender to the English throne. That decision ended whatever possibility might have existed for the English committing only a small ground force to the continent. War began once French troops moved into the Spanish Netherlands against the Hapsburgs and the Dutch – a move that suggested to France's enemies the Sun King's unlimited aims.[17] Thus, in 1701, another war had broken out, barely three years after the Nine Years War concluded.

Almost immediately a debate began between the Tories, the supporters of the "blue water" school of strategy, and the Whigs, who for the most part supported a continental commitment. The debate would continue throughout the lengthy conflict and become increasingly bitter as the cost of the war increased. Initially, given William's position, those supporting a continental commitment won out.[18] William's death in 1702 did not change English strategy, because Anne, the new queen, initially supported the continental strategy that the Duke of Marlborough, William's successor as England's military leader, advocated. For the first eight years of her reign, Anne supported Marlborough and a major continental commitment to Holland and Austria. The English provided a 40,000-man army to fight at the side of their allies on the continent as well as mounting major campaigns at sea, on the Iberian Peninsula, and in the Mediterranean.[19] Marlborough's three great victories over the French at Blenheim, Ramilles, and Oudenarde seemed to validate the continental commitment. Nevertheless, Anne's political preferences lay with the Tories, and the war's costs as well as the failure to achieve a reasonable peace, largely the fault of excessive demands on the part of the allies, led to growing unhappiness back home in the British Isles.

Moreover, after the years of Marlborough's great successes, the allies ran into difficulties. In 1709 in the massive Battle of Malplaquet, the

17 My rather brief discussion of British strategic arguments rests to a great extent on Ostwald's essay, "Creating the British Way of War."
18 For a discussion of this debate and its implications see ibid.
19 The latter effort would lead to the capture of Gibraltar, a major strategic gain for England.

French fought Marlborough and his Austrian co-general, Prince Eugene, to a draw, bought at the cost of over 20,000 allied casualties. Those military difficulties only exacerbated the attacks on the war by the Tories, the most effective being Jonathan Swift's scurrilous *On the Conduct of the Allies*. Beginning in 1710 Anne moved increasingly toward the Tory position that some compromise needed to be made to end the war. With the Tories in power, the result was the Treaty of Utrecht in which England abandoned her Dutch and Austrian Allies. While the Whigs, who returned to power in 1715 after Anne's death and her replacement by George I (the first of the Hanoverian line), would attack the peace as a sellout, the overall result was most favorable to Britain's strategic position in the world. But the crucial point here is that the War of Spanish Succession had set the framework for the debate between those who favored a major commitment of ground forces and financial resources to support allies on the continent and those who urged a straight "blue water" strategy with a minimal commitment of troops and money on the continent.

In the wars that followed in the mid-eighteenth century – the War of Austrian Succession (1740–1748) and the Seven Years War (1756–1763) – the same pattern of debate emerged, in each case with those supporting a continental commitment dominating the conduct of the wars. In the first conflict, George II drove British strategy along the lines of supporting Austria with considerable subsidies against the French and Prussians, while at the same time deploying British troops and financial support to the Dutch and to the Electorate of Hanover, of which he was also the ruler. In strategic terms the war gained the British relatively little, but in military terms the Royal Navy achieved a domination over its French opponent that would carry over with considerable impact into the next war.

Significantly, after the Second Battle of Cape Finisterre (October 1747), in which the French lost six out of their eight ships of the line, they abandoned their naval efforts because of the costs of the continental war, a war they had to fight given that their enemies could threaten France directly on land. On the other hand, the British could supply significant financial support to their Dutch and Austrian allies, as well as troops to defend the Dutch barrier fortresses and Hanover, but those commitments never threatened the support the Royal Navy needed to dominate at sea. Nevertheless, the war brought the British few significant gains, thus making its costs more painful to bear. At the war's outset, Britain's national debt had stood at £49,000,000; by the war's close it had reached £76,100,000, an increase of over 50 percent.[20] Not surprisingly, the debate continued

---

20 Simms, *Three Victories and a Defeat*, p. 361.

throughout the conflict as to how extensively Britain should provide financial support and troops to support its continental allies in the fighting taking place in Germany and the Spanish Netherlands. Nevertheless, the king still had a major voice in the making of strategy, although he did have to rely on Parliament for the financial resources required to support the war. Thus George II with his close connections to Germany as Elector of Hanover was a strong supporter of the continental commitment, and Britain's strategy remained focused on supporting its continental allies.

The Seven Years War was to be Britain's most significant conflict in the eighteenth century; its results determined the outcome of what one might term the "war for empire" between the British and the French. In the long run, Britain's victories led to the dominance of English as the global language of choice in the twentieth century and beyond, among other ramifications. During the conflict British Prime Minister William Pitt handled the conduct of British strategy in masterful fashion. He supported the war on the continent with a major British effort in manpower and resources; at the same time, understanding the American colonists as no other British ruler was to do throughout the eighteenth century, he provided the financial resources and political savvy that mobilized the colonial manpower and resources essential to the decisive defeat of the French in North America.[21]

Those whom Pitt chose for high command rewarded Britain with an astonishing series of victories that fundamentally cemented Britain as the premier global power. The victories of 1759, the *annus mirabilis* (Year of Miracles), included a victory on the Plains of Abraham that effectively ended French rule in Canada and the destruction of the French fleet at Quiberon Bay, when the British admiral, Edward Hawke, pursued the French over unchartered reefs and captured or sank most of their fleet in the midst of a howling gale. Matters went no better for the French in India. Moreover, during that same year a combined allied army with 10,000 British soldiers and 50,000 Hanoverians and Germans, the latter financed by British subsidies, crushed the French at the Battle of Minden, thereby thwarting the French invasion of Hanover and covering Fredrick the Great's western flank.[22]

21 For an outstanding examination of the war's course in North America see Fred Anderson, *Crucible of War: The Seven Years' War and the Fate of Empire in British North America, 1754–1764* (New York, 1961). It also provided the training for the middle-level leadership of the colonial militia that would make it such a major factor in the coming Revolutionary War.
22 The Battle of Minden was also to become infamous for the refusal of Lord George Sackville, the commander of the British contingent, to obey an order to have his cavalry charge the collapsing French army. As the politically rehabilitated Lord George Germain, Sackville would direct the British effort during the American Revolutionary War and bear a major share of the blame for the British defeat.

During the Year of Miracles the British deployed 30,000 soldiers on the British Isles and 20,000 in North America, with a further 25,000 American militia paid for by the British treasury. Moreover, three times during the year Pitt would send reinforcements to the continent. Thus, the ratio of deployed and subsidized troops between Britain's European and its global commitments was approximately 60/40.[23] In the following year the British would have approximately as many of their troops on the continent as in North America. And by pinning the French down on the continent, Pitt ensured they lacked the resources to maintain their fleet, thus turning control of the world's oceans over to the Royal Navy.

Thus, the significant continental commitment reinforced Britain's strategic position at sea. As a historian of this period notes:

Pitt had co-opted and refined a strategic tradition which went back to the glorious revolution. He created – for the time being at least – the perfect strategic virtuous circle, in which Germany was defended in America, and America was won in Germany. He turned Hanover from a liability back into a geopolitical asset. He created a Protestant hero [Frederick the Great] to replace the "old system." He rallied a motley collection of radicals, planters, Tories, and orthodox Whigs.[24]

Pitt was that rare combination of capable politician and brilliant strategist.

The problem was that Pitt was almost too successful for Britain's run of victories to continue. George II had consistently supported Pitt and the strategy of major aid in troops and money for Britain's continental ally Prussia. Thus, the most significance blow to the great statesman's strategy of supporting the allies on the continent came with the king's death in the fall of 1760 and the accession of his grandson, George III, to the throne. The new king had little interest in Hanover and even less interest in supporting Frederick the Great. From the first George III supported the "blue water" school. Contributing to the new king's conception of British strategy was the support he received from those many Britons, especially among the Tories, who waxed enthusiastic about the extent of Britain's global victories, while complaining about the cost of the continental war. In fact, in a virtual replica of the broadsides launched by the media on the continental strategy during the latter stages of the War of Spanish Succession, a host of pamphleteers attacked the commitments to the war against the French in Central Europe. As for the new monarch, not only did he support such views, but he was eager to get rid

23 Simms, *Three Victories and a Defeat*, p. 451.
24 Ibid., p. 462.

of Pitt, who showed too little deference to the new monarch, at the first opportunity.

In October 1761, to the king's delight, Pitt resigned. His departure removed the central advocate of a continental commitment as essential to British strategy. Almost immediately his successors overruled Pitt's urging that the British directly aid the Prussians with an auxiliary force.[25] Not only were those around George III deeply suspicious of what a later American president would term "entangling alliances,"[26] but the extent of Britain's successes in the war thus far misled them as to the nature of the strategy and support that had laid the foundation for those gains. At the same time the king and too many British politicians had drunk deep of that dangerous cup, *hubris*.[27]

The result was to be a lamentable alteration, at least for the British, in the strategic culture that had driven them to success in the previous decades of the eighteenth century. A British broadsheet of the time could not have made that contrast more sharply: "Mr. Pitt thinks that we ought, by well chosen alliances, to prevent the approach of danger, weaken the connections of France, and maintain the balance of power in our hands. Mr. Grenville [the chief minister of George III] disclaims all knowledge of foreign affairs; and thinks no alliance worth the money paid."[28] In bailing out of the Seven Years War, the British made an even more egregious exit than they had in abandoning their allies at the end of the War of Spanish Succession. If the term "perfidious Albion" had yet to make its appearance, it represented an entirely apt description of how most European policy makers at the time felt about the British.

George III's ministerial choices during the first decades of his reign remind one of the comment made about the successor Cabinet to David Lloyd George's government in 1922, that it was difficult to make a bunch of empty sacks stand upright. Admittedly the government faced considerable difficulties, particularly with regards to the debt incurred in achieving victory in the Seven Years War. But it now charted a course that cut back defense spending, including substantial cuts in the Royal Navy,

---

25 Ibid., p. 483.
26 The words of President Thomas Jefferson, often mistakenly attributed to George Washington.
27 Oliver Goldsmith would comment that "Britain is stronger fighting by herself and for herself, than if half Europe were her Allies." Quoted in Simms, *Three Victories and a Defeat*, p. 515. There is among the British a troglodytic streak that revels in the picture of Britain standing alone. King George VI would note after the fall of France in June 1940 that "Personally, I feel happier now that we have no allies to be polite to and to pamper." Quoted in A. D. Harvey, *Collision of Empires: Britain in Three World Wars, 1793–1945* (London, 1992), p. 731.
28 Quoted in Simms, *Three Victories and a Defeat*, p. 501.

raised taxes in the colonies as well in the mother country, exacerbated the frictions inherent in the relations with the colonists, eliminated any and all subsidies for allies on the continent, and followed a policy that was to all intents and purposes isolationist. Ignorance rendered the new strategic course even more dangerous. Neither the new ministers nor the king knew much about continental affairs, and they understood even less about the American colonies, since none of them had ever visited North America.[29]

There was, not surprisingly, continued debate in Parliament and in the country in general about the policies George III and his ministers were pursuing. The Whigs continued to warn against the government's strategy, which largely ignored Britain's need for allies on the continent, just as they were less than enthralled with the treatment the king's ministers were dealing out to the American colonists. But the mood of the country was simply unwilling to recognize the dangers of the government's course, especially since a return to the policies that had characterized Britain's strategy through to 1763 involved considerable and inevitable expenditures.

That disaster came in 1775 is not surprising. Arrogantly contemptuous of the colonists, sure of their superiority at sea, unwilling to engage diplomatically with the continental powers, and with the navy still on a meager financial diet, Britain went to war unprepared for the complexity and difficulty of the conflict in North America. Moreover, British leaders remained oblivious to the fact that their many enemies on the continent, especially the French and Spanish, would be delighted at the opportunity to pay Britain back for its many successes during the Seven Years War.[30] When war in North America erupted, Lord North and his ministers, having sought a confrontation with the colonists in the midst of major retrenchments in defense spending, found themselves reduced to the expedient of hiring mercenaries from the German principalities to cobble together sufficient troops to conduct military operations in the colonies. Frederick the Great displayed his contempt for his former allies by making those detachments of German troops pay a cattle tax as they marched across Prussian territory to the ports in northern Germany from which they would depart. The cost, length, and battlefield failures in a war of continental distances soon showed how deeply British political and military leaders had underestimated the colonists. Defeat at

29 The ignorance about the colonies was, nevertheless, understandable, given the distances and the difficulties of an Atlantic crossing in the eighteenth century. The ignorance of European politics was less excusable.
30 For a strategic history of the Revolutionary War from the British point of view see particularly Piers Mackesy, *The War for America, 1775–1783* (London, 1964).

Saratoga in October 1777 brought the French into the war, a war that now became a global, maritime conflict, in which Britain had no allies.

The surrender of Lord Cornwallis's army at Yorktown ended British pretensions about the wisdom of embarking on a war without continental allies. It also destroyed the North Cabinet, which had guided the nation's policies for well over a decade. In defending his failed efforts to keep the Royal Navy in a position of dominance, Lord Sandwich, First Lord of the Admiralty, admitted that "we are now engaged in a war with the House of Bourbon [Spain as well as France, since both had members of the House of Bourbon on their thrones], closely united and their naval force unbroken." He then admitted, to make matters worse, that Britain's enemies "have no Continental struggles to draw their attention and to exhaust their finances, so that they are able to point their whole efforts to their naval departments."[31] Indeed, the opposition Whigs could not have articulated more clearly the case against a period of arrogant strategic policies that had isolated Britain among the continental powers and generated hostility among even neutrals such as Prussia, Russia, and Sweden.[32] In every respect, the "blue water," isolationist policy of George III and his ministers could not have placed Britain in a more dangerous situation, and the British paid for their short-sightedness and arrogance with the loss of their North American colonies.

The great wars against the French and Germans

The wars that began with the French Revolution presented the British with a set of challenges that exceeded any they had faced thus far in the eighteenth century. The British had certainly learned the lesson of the disastrous war they had waged against the American colonists and their Bourbon allies. Without continental allies, Britain's naval power had proved incapable of defeating its opponents. Now confronting a twenty-five-year long war, British strategic policy swung in the opposite direction, attempting to defeat the French on the continent with the aid of allies, all supported by major subsidies and occasionally with the intervention of British land forces. Although the development and articulation of British grand strategy never ran smoothly, over the long term it eventually was to play a major role in defeating the French threat to

---

31 Simms, *Three Victories and a Defeat*, pp. 665–67.
32 The British confronted considerable hostilities among the other major European powers including Prussia, Russia, Holland, Denmark, and Sweden – a not surprising situation, given the arrogance with which they had treated everyone on the continent in the aftermath of the Seven Years War.

the balance of power in Europe. Against Napoleon the various coalitions collapsed almost as fast as the British were able to cobble them together despite the payment of vast sums of money and supplies, while British military expeditions to the continent did no better until finally Sir Arthur Wellesley, soon to be the Duke of Wellington, arrived in Spain in 1808. In the short term, Admiral Lord Nelson's great victory over the French fleet at Trafalgar in 1805 was not decisive, but in the long term it had a crucial impact on the war because its outcome provided a secure political and economic base from which the British could project military power directly (via the Peninsular campaign) and indirectly (via financial subsidies to allies) onto the continent of Europe.

Britain and the other European powers faced a unique strategic challenge, as a massive political revolution in France overthrew the entire framework of the European political and military system.[33] As Clausewitz noted:

in 1793 a force appeared that beggared all imagination. Suddenly war again became the business of the people – a people of thirty millions, all of whom considered themselves to be citizens ... The people became a participant in war; instead of governments and armies as heretofore, the full weight of the nation was thrown into the balance. The resources and efforts now available for use surpassed all conventional limits; nothing now impeded the vigor with which war could be waged, and consequently the opponents of France faced the utmost peril.[34]

The seizure of power in France in 1800 by one of the greatest military geniuses in history only served to exacerbate the strategic problems raised by the French Revolution. Not until the *ancien regimes* of Europe were willing to address the French Revolution and the military genius it spawned on their own terms by mobilizing their resources and populations to a similar extent was the Corsican ogre finally tamed. For the British, the expenditure of vast sums of cash as well as the products of the first stages of the Industrial Revolution on coalitions that consistently collapsed did little to encourage those making strategic policy in London.[35]

---

33 For the place of that revolution in the course of Western military history see the opening chapter in MacGregor Knox and Williamson Murray, *The Dynamics of Military Revolution, 1300–2050* (Cambridge, 2000).

34 Carl von Clausewitz, *On War*, ed. and trans. Michael Howard and Peter Paret (Princeton, NJ, 1976), pp. 591–92.

35 In this respect see particularly "Richard Hart Sinnreich, "Victory by Trial and Error: Britain's Struggle against Napoleon," in Williamson Murray and Richard Hart Sinnreich (eds.), *Successful Strategies: Triumphing in War and Peace from Antiquity to the Present* (Cambridge, 2014).

The consistent failures on the continent aroused great angst in London and, at times, led to ill-fated and irrelevant departures from the basic strategy of continental commitment, such as the Buenos Aires expedition of 1806. But the British entertained few illusions that they could win the war anywhere other than on the continent. In the end, massive subsidies as well as a major commitment of military forces to the continent – first in Portugal and Spain and then in 1815 in the Low Countries – were necessary to crush Napoleon. Control of the world's maritime environment through great naval victories at the Battles of the Nile, Copenhagen, and Trafalgar provided the strategic framework within which the British could influence political and strategic events on the continent, but they could not by themselves secure eventual victory.

The exhaustion of Europe after nearly twenty-five years of almost uninterrupted conflict resulted in a period of sustained peace that lasted nearly a century. Fifty years later, Bismarck's brilliant strategy allowed the Prussian military to reunify Germany without causing a disastrous pan-European war, despite the unleashing of the dogs of nationalism during the Franco-Prussian War. Thus, for most of the nineteenth century the British enjoyed a period during which they pursued a grand strategy of "splendid isolation." They did not separate themselves from the affairs of the continent but, with the exception of the quickly concluded Crimean conflict, remained unfettered by alliances and commitments to support the continental powers. Thus, they maintained a massive naval superiority at relatively low cost, while at the same time enjoying the fruits of the first industrial revolution that brought unparalleled prosperity to their nation.

But at the turn of the century, Bismarck's successors raised a new challenge that the British had not seen since Trafalgar. Kaiser Wilhelm II and his naval advisor, Admiral Alfred von Tirpitz, with help from a supporting cast of what passed for strategic thinkers in the Second Reich, decided to challenge the Royal Navy in the belief that a rapidly industrializing Germany could in the long run out-build the British in a battleship competition.[36] Among a host of ill-founded assumptions was the belief that Britain would neither abandon her splendid isolation from continental affairs, nor match the Reich in a massive naval building

---

36 For the best account see Holger H. Herwig, *The Luxury Fleet: The Imperial German Navy, 1888–1918* (London, 1987). Perhaps most astonishingly, the Germans paid no attention to the fact that a simple look at the map would have indicated that the Reich was in a much more unfavorable geographic position in the case of a naval competition with the British than the French had been in the eighteenth century. But the Germans paid no attention to that reality.

program.[37] Moreover, the Germans ignored entirely, as had the French a century earlier, the fact that they confronted continental threats that would inevitably limit the resources they could devote to their naval forces.

In fact, the British were more than willing and able financially to meet the threat to their maritime superiority. Churchill remarked about the 1909 budget for the Royal Navy, "The Admiralty had demanded six [battleships]: the [Treasury] offered four, and we compromised on eight."[38] In the long run, the Germans could not win the competition, given the strategic realities they confronted in Europe. But the threat certainly drove the British to take strategic actions that the Germans had regarded as impossible. First in 1904, British statesmen settled all the major colonial differences they had with the French, in what was at the time called the *Entente Cordiale* between the two powers; an Anglo-Russian entente followed three years later. These agreements were not strictly speaking alliances, but rather represented a signal of close cooperation among the three powers.[39] Behind the scenes, the British were drawing ever closer to a continental commitment in some form. Staff talks with the French actually began as early as 1905 on the commitment of the British Army to the defense of France. Nevertheless, outside an inner circle of politicians, the Cabinet was not informed of such discussions until November 1911.[40] Even then, despite the threatening international situation, the Cabinet made its approval contingent on the understanding that there would be no binding commitment to support the French in case of war.

Even more of a commitment occurred in 1912 with the Anglo-French Naval Agreement, which allowed the British to redeploy warships from the Mediterranean to concentrate their entire battleship strength in the North Sea against the German High Seas Fleet. At the same time the French moved their battleships in the Atlantic squadron to the Mediterranean to cover the future movement of French troops from North Africa to France. Again, there was no binding commitment, but that agreement uncovered the French Atlantic coast in the event war broke out and the British did not join in. Still, the British government

---

37 Fundamental to German thinking was the assumption that it would be impossible for the British to form any kind of coalition with either France or Russia, the former because of the historical rivalry between the two nations, and the latter because of their vastly different forms of governments. This belief runs counter to our findings in this volume, that the political bases of alliances rest on the realities of the present and the future rather than on the past.

38 Quoted in Richard Holmes, *In the Footsteps of Churchill* (London, 2003), p. 80.

39 The French and the Russians, of course, were tied together by a formal alliance.

40 The best resource remains Samuel Williamson's superb study, *The Politics of Grand Strategy: Britain and France Prepare for War, 1904–1914* (New York, 1969).

refused to make any kind of specific commitment to deploy troops to the continent. In fact, it would not make that commitment firm until two days after it had declared war on Germany as a result of the invasion of Belgium in 1914.

What followed after the outbreak of war and the ruthless German invasion of Belgium and northern France was the commitment of a rapidly expanding expeditionary force to the continent. Initially four infantry and one cavalry divisions (two divisions were held back) went to France to form up on the left flank of the French armies. By 1918 the British Expeditionary Force (BEF), including dominion divisions, had expanded to well over fifty divisions. The losses for the British in the fighting on the Western Front were horrific – but less horrific than those suffered by other major European powers.[41] Without the aid of the BEF, the French would undoubtedly have collapsed, as did the Russian Empire, thus leaving the Germans in control of the entire continent and free to challenge the British on the high seas.

Three years later the American Expeditionary Force followed the BEF onto the continent. Initially, the Americans had had no intention of participating in a war far from their shores. But egregious German behavior slowly but steadily led to a growing realization that the United States could not tolerate either morally or politically a German victory that would provide the Reich with a general hegemony over the European continent and the ability to impede shipping on the high seas. Yet, the eventual victory failed to solve the German problem. The Versailles settlement was the best peace obtainable at the time, given the battlefield bloodletting and the resulting constraints on the statesmen of the victorious powers.[42] That said, Britain and the new maritime/island power on the scene, the United States, triumphed as a result of their willingness to support their allies on the continent not only with massive injections of financial support, but great armies as well. Thus, the strategic approaches of both maritime nations fell within the traditions of a strategy that rested

41 The assault by British historians, novelists, and others on the necessity of committing the British army to the continent in August 1914 has continued from the moment several Cabinet members resigned in early August 1914 through to the present. For one of the more recent arguments in this genre see Naill Ferguson, *The Pity of War: Explaining World War I* (London, 2000). Casualties were nevertheless heavy; the Thiepval memorial on the Somme carries the names of more than 72,000 Commonwealth soldiers whose bodies were never recovered, while at Ypres the Menin Gate and the Tyne Cot memorial respectively list the names of a further 54,896 and 34,984 missing soldiers.

42 For an examination of the Treaty of Versailles in the context of the time see Williamson Murray, "Versailles: The Peace Without a Chance," in Willliamson Murray and James Lacey (eds.), *The Making of Peace: Rulers, States, and the Aftermath of War* (Cambridge, 2008).

on continental allies and the commitment of major military forces to support those allies.

Liddell Hart and the "British way of war"

Neither the British nor their American cousins were willing to recognize that the war's cost was a burden that their populations had to bear, given the extent of the threat. Instead the argument about their nations not needing to send ground forces abroad – except to protect the possessions of empire – re-emerged as it had in the wake of the Seven Years War. The casualties suffered by the BEF soon led to a growing sense among the educated in Britain that the war had been a terrible mistake – a conflict in which Britain should not have participated. The vote at the Oxford Union in February 1933 that its members resolved to fight for neither king nor country pretty much summed up the national mood. The novels and literature of the time, particularly from the late 1920s on, reinforced such attitudes.[43]

The Americans were even more vociferous in their belief that they should not have, and would never again, commit resources and military forces to support allies on the European continent. A growing swell of isolationist opinion denounced the participation of the United States in the Great War as the result of the machinations of Wall Street bankers, the supplying of arms and raw materials to the Entente powers by the so-called "merchants of death," and the callous manipulation of American public opinion by the Machiavellian British. In the mid 1930s, Congress passed the Neutrality Acts, which forbade the export of any war materials to countries that were involved in armed conflict. Even as late as summer 1941, the House of Representatives renewed the draft by a single vote, underlining the fact that at the same time that German panzer divisions were overrunning Smolensk on their way to Moscow, a considerable number of Americans believed that their nation remained secure behind the moat of two oceans protected by their navy. Nor should one forget that the senior American military officers opposed President Franklin Roosevelt's efforts to supply the British in summer 1940 with desperately needed arms.

The consequences of the belief that island powers could exist independently of allies and continental commitments are clearest in British appeasement policies of the 1930s. In the mid thirties the British military pundit, Basil Liddell Hart, promoted a strategic assessment, supposedly

---

43 See among others the works of Siegfried Sassoon, Fredrick Manning, Robert Graves, and Wifred Owen.

based on history, to support the position that Britain did not, nor had she ever, required a major continental commitment to win its wars. He argued in the mid 1930s that Britain had in the eighteenth century developed a particular national grand strategy that had rested on its geographic position and the increasing dominance of the Royal Navy over the world's oceans.[44] Thus, according to Liddell Hart, throughout the great European wars in which the British had found themselves involved – the War of Spanish Succession, the War of Austrian Succession, the Seven Years War, the War of American Independence, and the French Revolutionary and Napoleonic Wars – they had been able to use their naval power to eliminate their European rivals, particularly the French, in the global arena to create the British Empire. At the same time as they were achieving this success, he argued, British governments had committed minimal troops, resources, and support to the great European wars in which the continental powers wallowed.

In effect, Liddell Hart, as a World War I veteran and severe critic of the generalship displayed by the leaders of the British Expeditionary Force (BEF), was using created history to attack what he regarded as the faulty strategic decisions the British government had made in the Great War.[45] These mistakes were: first, in committing the relatively small professional army the nation possessed to a continental war; and second, in building the BEF into what became a great continental army that had taken such terrible casualties on the Somme, at Passchendaele, and during the battles of 1918. Instead, he argued Britain should have used its naval power to engage the Central Powers along the periphery and abroad, while providing the financial and industrial support that its allies required in their battles with the Germans. In the aftermath of three-quarters of a million dead suffered by the British and Dominion armies, Liddell Hart's argument made a deep impression on the British public, especially the politicians. Yet, however unwilling he was to recognize the criticality of Britain's commitment of substantial British forces to the continent, Liddell Hart's strategic arguments retained an essential element: namely, that Britain had depended on continental allies to achieve victory.

44 A more sophisticated version of this argument is Sir Julian Corbett's *Some Principles of Maritime Strategy* (London, 1911), but because it appeared before the war it had less impact on debates in Britain over strategy.
45 Liddell Hart had been badly gassed on the Somme, but he had as a junior officer spent only a relatively short time in combat. The damage his lungs suffered from the gassing, however, prevented him from being committed to combat again. As for his criticism of British generalship, his voice was one among many. David Lloyd George, the former prime minister during the last two years of the conflict, described Field Marshal Douglas Haig as "brilliant to the top of his boots."

Liddell Hart's strategic argument was to have a profound and disastrous impact on British preparations to meet the German threat in the late 1930s. Moreover, no matter how persuasive it may have sounded, it was in fact a use of history that distorted significantly the reality of British strategy in the eighteenth and early nineteenth centuries. In a devastating critique of Liddell Hart's theory, Michael Howard emphasized how different the context between World War I and the wars of the eighteenth century had been:

It was ... precisely the failure of German power to find an outlet and its consequent concentration in Europe, its lack of any significant possessions overseas, that made it so particularly menacing to the sprawling British Empire in two world wars and which make so misleading all arguments about "traditional" British strategy drawn from earlier conflicts against the Spanish and French Empires, with all the colonial hostages they had to offer to fortune and the Royal Navy.[46]

In the mid-to-late 1930s, the German threat grew ever more menacing, as rearmament increasingly augmented the *Wehrmacht*'s capabilities and strength.[47] For British governments that were desperate to keep a lid on British defense expenditures, Liddell Hart's theory of Britain's traditional strategy appeared to be a Godsend. It provided an intellectual justification for minimal spending on the army, the role of which the government confined to the defense of the empire's borders, particularly India's Northwest Frontier, and its contribution to the anti-aircraft defenses of the British Isles. As Neville Chamberlain argued in the Cabinet in May 1937 at the beginning of his term as prime minister:

He could not accept the question at issue as being a purely military matter. Other considerations entered into it. He himself definitely did challenge the policy of their [the Cabinet's] military advisers. The country was being asked to maintain a larger army than had been the case for very many years; a great air force, which was a new arm altogether; and, in addition, an army for use on the Continent; as well as facilities for producing munitions which would be required not only for our forces but also for our allies.[48]

---

46 Michael Howard, *The Continental Commitment* (London, 1972), p. 32. Howard's title is apt to the discussions in this paper because as late as the 1938–1939 period, the British government was again arguing about the need for a continental commitment to support the French against the rising military power of Nazi Germany.
47 Ironically, the British overestimated German capabilities in 1937 and 1938 and then underestimated those capabilities in 1939. For a discussion of these issues see Williamson Murray, *The Change in the European Balance of Power, 1938–1939: The Path to Ruin* (Princeton, NJ, 1984).
48 PRO CAB 23/88, Cab 20 (37), Meeting of the Cabinet, 5.5.37.

By the time that Chamberlain had become prime minister, such British attitudes, minimizing both a continental commitment as well as support for potential allies across the Channel, had already altered the strategic situation of the Western powers. In May 1936 the Belgians had attempted to place an order for arms with British manufacturers. When the British failed to respond, another request arrived two months later. The Foreign Office then passed the request on to the War Department, which in turn passed the request on to the Committee of Imperial Defense. Not until January 1937 did the British agree in principal, but the Belgians then placed such a large order that the War Office suggested that the government examine the political implications. Not until February 1938 did the Cabinet authorize a favorable response, which was not passed on to the Belgians until July.[49] Even more serious was the Belgian retreat into neutrality from their alliance with France as a result of the remilitarization of the Rhineland in March 1936. Here the failure of the British to offer any support to the French in opposing the remilitarization was as responsible for that abandonment by the Belgians of the French alliance as were internal Belgian fears about French domination of their country.[50]

In their treatment of their French ally, British leaders in the late 1930s displayed not only condescension but considerable contempt. At least Liddell Hart in his arguments for a British "way in war" had displayed some sense of the importance of continental allies to future British strategy. Churchill gave great voice to the importance of supporting the French militarily on the continent, but until the collapse of support for appeasement in March 1939, few paid him much heed.

Such arguments fazed the Chamberlain government not in the least. The great crisis of 1938 over the fate of Czechoslovakia crystallized the worst in Britain's strategic misreading of the European situation.[51] In a meeting with leading French politicians in late April 1938, the British suggested staff talks but only between the respective air staffs. Lord Halifax, the Foreign Secretary, indicated to the French that should war break out, Britain's wartime contribution would be largely limited to air and naval forces. But the larger message throughout the discussions, in spite of French objections, was that there was no need for a detailed examination of the overall strategic situation that confronted the Western

---

49 David O. Kieft, *Belgian's Return to Neutrality* (Oxford, 1972), pp. 164–66.
50 Ibid., p. 157.
51 Not that the French were much better. French policy largely seems to have been driven by a desire to use British appeasement of Nazi Germany over Czechoslovakia as a front so that they could escape the consequences of their mutual security treaty with that nation and not have to honor their obligations to go to war in defense of the Czechs.

powers at the time. Chamberlain also added that his government was unwilling even to commit its two under-strength and under-equipped divisions to the continent.[52]

As the crisis spiraled out of control toward the end of September 1938, it became apparent that the British had no desire to support the French in any conflict that occurred over Czechoslovakia. On 12 September, Halifax summed up British intentions in instructions he sent to the British ambassador in Paris. While His Majesty's Government would never allow France's security to be threatened, "they were unable to make precise statements on the character of their future action, or the time at which it would be taken in circumstances that they cannot at present foresee."[53]

In fact, so unwilling was the Cabinet to address the issue of supporting the French should war break out over Czechoslovakia that on 25 September it instructed Chamberlain to tell the French that Britain refused to commit itself to declaring war on Germany.[54] On the next day the French commander in chief General Maurice Gamelin arrived in London to be greeted by the refusal of the British chiefs of staff to discuss their plans in case of war.[55] Four days later, Britain, leading, and France, trailing, surrendered Czechoslovakia with its thirty-plus divisions to the tender mercies of the Nazis. Chamberlain returned home to the plaudits of a public immensely delighted at the outcome. The prime minister announced that he had brought "peace in our time."[56] He then planted his government's defense policy on the position that there would be no significant rise in defense expenditures. Thus, Britain would make no effort to rebuild its army to buttress the French. Moreover, even the Royal Air Force received only minimal additional funding. The government announced that it was increasing the number of fighters on order by 50 percent, but it did so by extending the two-year contract for a third year.

The ramifications of the Munich agreement became apparent during the winter of 1938–1939. During the run up to the Munich surrender only one member of the Cabinet had at the last moment raised the issue

---

52 *Documents on British Foreign Policy (DBFP)*, 3rd Series, vol. I, Doc. 164, "Record of Anglo-French Conversations, held at No. 10 Downing Street, on April 28 and 29, 1938."
53 *DBFP*, 3rd Series, vol. II, Doc. 843, 26.9.38., Halifax to Phipps.
54 PRO CAB 23/95, Cab 43 (38), Meeting of the Cabinet, 25.9.38, p. 227.
55 *Documents Diplomatiques Français*, 2nd Ser., vol. XI, Doc 376, 26.9.38, "Compte rendu des conversations techniques de Général Gamelin au Cabinet Office 26 septembre 1938."
56 A phrase that President Obama used in his second inauguration speech, albeit not in the same context.

of what the strategic balance would look like were the Western powers to surrender Czechoslovakia and its army. It now appears that German opposition to Hitler began spreading rumors throughout Europe that Hitler was about to invade Holland and use the bases in the Netherlands to launch air and sea attacks on the British Isles. When the British queried the French as what their response might be, they gloomily replied that without the Czech divisions or a British commitment of a major army to the continent there was nothing they could do. That was not the answer the British wanted to hear, but it finally brought home to them the strategic consequences of their decision to surrender the Czechs at Munich.

The result of the long-drawn out arguments was that Chamberlain "with some reluctance ... saw no alternative," but to increase substantially the size of the British Army to support Britain's continental ally. Thus ended British efforts to pursue a naval strategy, buttressed by air power, that would allow them to place minimal ground forces, if any at all, on the continent. It was a policy that had undermined fundamentally the Anglo-French alliance and if it did not directly cause the disastrous defeats of May–June 1940, it certainly contributed to them.[57] Nor should we ignore the responsibility of the Americans for the disaster of 1940 by their eschewing of any cooperation with the European democracies and their pursuit of irresponsible isolation from ongoing events in Europe and to a lesser extent Asia. The great irony of their participation in the coming war was the fact that Hitler by his invasion of the Soviet Union provided both Britain and the United States with a great ally to Germany's east, which would bear the human cost of much of the fighting on the continent. Likewise, the Japanese attack on Pearl Harbor and the German declaration of war on the United States brought a united nation into the great struggle by destroying isolationism as a political force overnight.

Setting the strategic parameters of the Cold War and after

In the immediate postwar world the US navy dominated the world's oceans to a degree never before seen in history while with its possession of the atomic bomb, the United States appeared able to dominate the world. In this regard, the immediate massive demobilization of US military forces at the end of World War II reflected two main strategic

57 The disastrous attitude that so many of the French who supported the Vichy regime displayed resulted at least in part from the anger they felt at the behavior of perfidious Albion throughout the 1930s.

assumptions. The first was that American naval superiority assured the invulnerability of the United States from ground attack. The second was that the possession of the atomic bomb provided the United States with unchallenged offensive destructive power. Unfortunately for the Americans, the Soviet Union had a vote in the strategic balance of power. Initially, the Truman administration hoped that its control of the world's oceans along with the atomic bomb would be sufficient to prevent further Soviet advances beyond what they had gained as a result of their military operations in World War II. The Berlin blockade suggested otherwise, but even with the warnings contained in NSC-68 that the United States needed to rearm and support it allies on the continent beyond economic aid, the Truman White House continued along its path of minimizing American military forces in an attempt to balance the national budget.

The North Korean attack on South Korea put paid to the administration's hopes. In one of the wisest strategic decisions the Truman administration would make, the United States fought the Korean War, while at the same time supporting a major buildup of its forces in Europe to support the newly created North Atlantic Treaty Organization, which now became a true military as well as political alliance. The American commitment of ground forces to NATO fell within the same tradition that had marked Britain's support of its continental allies in the eighteenth, nineteenth, and first two decades of the twentieth centuries.

Despite considerable ups and downs in the relationship between the Americans and the Europeans, the American commitment of ground forces on the European continent provided a clear signal that any Soviet military drive to the west would mean war between the nuclear armed powers. This strategic situation held until the fall of the Berlin Wall in 1989, followed shortly thereafter by the disintegration of the Soviet Union and the advent of America's "unipolar moment." Reinforcing the arrogance and overconfidence of American policy makers was the ease with which US military forces had crushed the much-vaunted Iraqi Army, a victory the unequalled decisiveness of which caught most military analysts by surprise.[58] Given this manifest military superiority, would the United States need close allies in the twenty-first century and a continued continental commitment? Such questions represented a replay of the centuries old strategic debate in maritime/island powers.

---

58 This author remembers visiting Marine Corps University in early January 1991, where he ran into a number of instructors who were seriously worried about the heavy casualties US ground forces would suffer against the Iraqis should a land war occur.

Conclusion

The pattern of continental commitments to allies by maritime powers
could not be clearer. The conflicts discussed above break down as follows:

Nation	War	Major continental ally	Commitment	Result
Athens	Peloponnesian War	No	No	Lost
Britain	War of Sp. Succession	Yes	Yes	Won
Britain	War of Aus. Succession	Yes	Yes	Tie
Britain	Seven Years War	Yes	Yes	Won
Britain	American Revolution	No	No	Lost
Britain	Napoleonic Wars	Yes	Yes	Won
Britain	World War I	Yes	Yes	Won
Britain	France 1940	Yes	Too late	Lost
Britain	World War II	Yes	Yes	Won
US	World War II	Yes	Yes	Won
US	Cold War	Yes	Yes	Won

The historical record clearly shows that every time a maritime power
attempts to fight a major war without continental allies and without a
ground force commitment, it loses.

One might also note that all too many Anglo-American theorists
believe that the peculiar characteristics of air and naval forces remove
the need for ground forces and a commitment to continental allies. In
Alfred Thayer Mahan's view, "those far-distant, storm-tossed ships upon
which the Grand Army had never looked" were largely responsible for
Napoleon's defeat. The British theorist Julian Corbett argued in the early
twentieth century that naval power was a crucial enabler which allowed
the island power of Britain to attack its continental opponents on the
periphery with relatively small armies, which he termed "disposable
forces," hardly a ringing endorsement of a continental commitment.

Air power theorists have been even more explicit as to the ability of
aircraft to achieve victory without the use of armies or, for that matter,
navies. Secure in the belief that their bases could not be threatened, the
Billy Mitchells and Hugh Trenchards of the interwar period argued for
an air strategy that would minimize, if not entirely remove, the need for
a continental commitment. Their contempt for naval power and their
refusal to recognize the crucial importance of the sea lines of communications to providing the petroleum, armaments, and spare parts necessary

to support the Combined Bomber Offensive delayed the deployment of long-range aircraft to the Battle of the Atlantic and caused the loss of millions of tons of shipping. Nor were they willing to recognize the political implications of having no ground forces on the continent to occupy the ruins of Nazi Germany.[59] German air-power theorists living on the land mass of Eurasia, however, who lacked the luxury of national territory and air bases that were relatively immune to attack by anything other than other aircraft, developed theories of air power that were much more closely integrated into a larger, joint strategic picture.

What does the historical pattern suggest regarding how American political and military leaders need to think about alliances and coalitions in the coming decades, as well as the commitment of US ground forces to the defense of those allies and our common interests? In terms of the costs of major wars, there is no doubt that war on the ground is the most expensive in terms of lives and resources, both because of the demands of combat as well as the expenses involved in occupying and administering conquered territories. In the late 1990s the American military focused on developing concepts such as "rapid decisive operations" and "effects based operations" with the aim of making war technologically sophisticated and thus quick, painless (at least to Americans), and decisive. Such concepts proved attractive not only among those who passed for military thinkers, but also among civilians. This was particularly true in the case of George W. Bush's Secretary of Defense Donald Rumsfeld and his chief deputy Paul Wolfowitz, and they exercised a baleful influence over the conduct of the wars that the United States has waged in response to 9/11.

In fact, as too many airmen and naval strategists forget, what matters in the end are the political results that persist when military operations cease. Inevitably, boots on the ground largely determine the political and strategic results of war.[60] Yet ground war through the ages has proven excessively expensive. Continental powers are inevitably forced to fight ground wars. One of the major factors that led the *Luftwaffe* in the interwar period to focus on a far wider application of air power beyond just strategic bombing, as was the case with the Royal Air Force and the US Army Air Corps,

---

59 Nothing underlines more clearly the bankruptcy of such theories of air power than the construction of the air bases on mainland China to attack Japan with B-29s. The Japanese response, given the miserable state of the Chinese armies, was not hard to predict. Once they recognized what the Americans and Chinese were up to, they simply launched an offensive in the summer of 1944 that overran the airfields.

60 One should not forget that one of the major failures that resulted from the outcome of World War I had to do with the fact that on 11 November 1918 not a single Allied soldier, except for prisoners of war, stood on German territory, allowing German apologists (among them Hitler) to claim that the German army remained undefeated in the field as it was "stabbed in the back" by communists, socialists, and Jews at home.

was the reality that bombing of enemy population centers and/or industry would count for little if Germany were at the same time to lose Silesia or the Saar.[61] Again, the geography of a continental power resulted in a very different view of naval and air power in the calculus of a future war.

Maritime/island powers have more strategic choices. They do not have to commit ground forces to a continental war. Nor do they necessarily require allies. As long as they manage to control their maritime environment, they remain relatively safe, at least from enemy armies. Yet, in effect they are isolated in a strategic dead end. They cannot win a war on land with naval or air power alone. Nelson's devastating victory at Trafalgar over French and Spanish navies represented a long-term advantage: it guaranteed Britain's security from amphibious assault. But it had no impact on the continental balance of power, as Napoleon's devastating victories over the Austrians and Russians at Ulm and Austerlitz underlined. William Pitt the younger accurately commented after news of Austerlitz arrived in London: "Roll up the map of Europe; it will not be wanted these ten years."[62] Nevertheless, Trafalgar was the enabler that allowed Britain the security from which she could utilize her financial and industrial resources to support continental allies and eventually project Wellington's army into the Peninsular War to aid in the destruction of Napoleon's empire. Michael Howard, as usual, expressed it best when he noted: "A commitment of support to a Continental Ally in the nearest theater, on the largest scale that contemporary forces could afford, so far from being alien to the traditional British strategy, was central to it."[63]

Thus, if maritime/island powers refuse to commit their troops to fighting on the continent, they place themselves at risk of finding themselves without allies. And while allies may not appear to be essential to those willing to ignore history, in the end they do matter. The great advantage that maritime/island powers enjoy is their far wider spectrum of strategic choices. They can put off the dangers of today until tomorrow. But in the end they must develop a grand strategy that utilizes the maritime dimension to establish an alliance or coalition that allows the projection of ground power to defeat their opponents. Inevitably such a strategy will prove costly in lives and resources. Not to do so, however, is to court the destruction suffered by Athens in the fifth century BC or the defeat inflicted on Britain and France nearly two and a half millennia later.

---

61 For an examination of the various factors that influenced the development of the *Luftwaffe*'s doctrine between the wars see Williamson Murray, *Luftwaffe* (Baltimore, MD, 19985), ch. 1.

62 Quoted in Charles Esdaile, *Napoleon's Wars: An International History* (London, 2007).

63 Michael Howard, *The Causes of War and Other Essays* (London, 1983), pp. 193–94.

3 The Anglo-Prussian alliance and the Seven Years War

Dennis Showalter

Even obscure diplomatic relationships have consequences. The Convention of Westminster, concluded in January 1756, appears to be on its face a relatively innocuous document. Great Britain and Prussia agreed not to attack each other's possessions and to protect the German states from any other power. But if the Diplomatic Revolution structured the Seven Years War, the Convention of Westminster ignited it. For that reason the antecedents of the Anglo-Prussian alliance are as important as its consequences.[1]

Alliances, like marriages, tend towards the *longue durée*. Like marriages, they be enerated by passion, affinity, or necessity. The Anglo-Prussian alliance of 1756 was companionate: a relationship of convenience that lasted only six years. A familiar proverb says that a bird and a fish may fall in love – but where will they make a home? The same can be said for a wolf and a shark. Prussia had its strategic focus solidly on the continent; it was a military power with definite and circumscribed aims. Britain was a dominant maritime player with an expanding global empire that was becoming an end in itself. The genesis, nature, and history of their brief and tempestuous association offer useful insights into why states come together – and why they break apart.

The Convention of Westminster did not represent a formal alliance; the two partners never formalized it. The connection it established was *de facto* rather than *de jure*. Its realities reflected four characteristics. The alliance was reactive: a last-choice consequence of diplomatic and military factors outside the immediate, direct control of either party. The alliance was negative. It had no fundamental, significant joint aims corresponding to, for example, the defeat of the Axis that created and sustained the Anglo-American grand alliance of World War II. The alliance was mutually exploitative. Britain saw Prussia as a client, the hiring of

---

1 The standard general works on the alliance are Karl Schweizer, *England, Prussia, and the Seven Years War: Studies in Alliance Politics and Diplomacy* (Lewiston, NY, 1989); and *Frederick the Great, William Pitt, and Lord Bute: The Anglo-Prussian Alliance, 1756–1763* (New York, 1991).

48   Dennis Showalter

which had been characteristic of the wars against Louis XIV. Admittedly, British statesmen did believe Prussia merited special handling because it was more powerful and more expensive than the usual middle-ranked German power, but subaltern nevertheless.

Frederick II of Prussia considered Britain a long-term source of the hard currency and diplomatic support he required to sustain Prussia's increasingly vulnerable position – not to say its existence. Finally, the Anglo-Prussian alliance was minimalist. At its beginning, Britain believed the agreement secured Austria from a renewed Prussian attack. Frederick reasoned he had done his then-ally France a service by limiting Britain's presence on the continent. Once hostilities began, neither partner did more than absolutely necessary to sustain the alliance, and then for as short a time as possible.

The background

The remote cause of this odd-couple connection was the strategic shrinking of Europe in the seventeenth century. England had been historically at best a demi-island. The English Channel could be and was regularly crossed in force. As for the "Celtic fringe," Scotland was a constant major threat, Ireland a persistent running sore, and both were ever willing to assist England's continental enemies. From at least the time of the Tudors, English policy accepted as a given that England's first line of defense was across the Channel. Flanders and the emerging Dutch Republic offered the most threatening bases for an invasion. They were best kept in friendly hands by a "forward policy." The optimal glacis was initially modest in terms of territory and influence. Its scope was extended, however, by warfare's expanding scale. By the last quarter of the 1600s, it was clear that the long-term security of the Low Countries, a fundamental basis for securing British interest, depended ultimately on stability in northern and western Germany.[2]

Obtaining and sustaining that kind of forward position required continuing levels of military and financial commitment no British government could hope to obtain from a generally fractious Parliament. The alternative was securing continental allies, and that required continental involvement on a continuing basis. For three-quarters of a century Britain's preferred connection was Austria. Specifically, British statesmen structured their European policies to support Habsburg power in the Holy Roman Empire and the southern Netherlands. Generally, that

2 This is the theme of Brendan Simms's seminal *Three Victories and a Defeat: The Rise and Fall of the First British Empire* (London, 2007).

strategy involved sustaining coalitions against France, the persistent chal-
lenger of the status quo. The ultimate objective was maintaining the continental balance of power that underwrote Britain's liberty and security.[3]

In the aftermath of the Peace of Utrecht in 1713, two developments
destabilized this policy. One was the expansion of British influence and
power outside of Europe – a process that generated comprehensive
and consistent friction with a France doing approximately the same
thing. Throughout the period, their respective North American colonies
were in a state of escalating low-level war, declared and undeclared. In
south Asia, economic rivalry segued into armed conflict even before the
formal Carnatic Wars that began in the 1740s. The Eurocentric Anglo-
French treaty of alliance negotiated in 1716 correspondingly devolved
into a dead letter.[4]

Far more significant, however, was the accession to the British throne
in 1714 of the Elector of Hanover. Both George I and his son and successor saw their British and German interests in a dynastic context, with
no essential difference between them. Aged 54 at an accession by default,
made possible more by his Protestant faith than any directly secular considerations, George I's Anglicization was limited. He accepted the British
crown in the expectation of expanding Hanover's position in Germany –
somewhat along the similar line being pursued by Prussia. He spent as
much time in the Electorate as possible, even dying there. George II was
educated in Germany; his English remained German-accented throughout his life; and he too divided his time between London and Hanover.

Predictably, support for the Georges' Hanoverian interests had a great
deal to do with which British politicians enjoyed royal favor – a major consideration at a time when the party system was still embryonic. In practice
British diplomacy tended to coordinate with that of Hanover, confirm-
ing the unconsidered consequence of accepting the Hanoverian dynasty:
Britain had become a German power with ongoing European interests.[5]

The details of that segue in Britain's diplomatic policies and domestic
politics in general are outside the scope of this chapter. Highly relevant,
however, is the impact of the Hanoverian connections on Anglo-Prussian

---

3 Useful here is Jeremy Black, *A System of Ambition? British Foreign Policy, 1688–1793*
   (Stroud, 2001). Derek McKay, *Allies of Convenience: Diplomatic Relations between Great
   Britain and Austria, 1714–1719* (New York, 1986) demonstrates the relationship's under-
   lying contingent nature.
4 Still the best overview of this process is Patrice Higonnet, "The Origins of the Seven
   Years War, "*Journal of Modern History*, 40 (1968), 57–90. Cf. as well Jeremy Black, *The
   Collapse of the French Alliance, 1727–1733* (Gloucester and New York, 1987).
5 Cf. Jeremy Black, *The Continental Commitment: Britain, Hanover, and Interventionism,
   1714–1793* (Abingdon, 2005); and the anthology *The Hanoverian Dimension in British
   History, 1714–1837*, ed. T. Riotte and B. Simms (Cambridge, 2007).

relations. In principle Prussia's King Frederick William I (1713–1740) believed European stability best served Prussia's interests. He took pains to alienate no one directly, deferring to Austria in particular. When in 1725 he accepted the Treaty of Hanover with France and Britain, it was to balance a previous Spanish–Austrian connection. He abandoned that treaty a year later, and was subsequently fatally cool to suggestions of marrying his son and daughter into the British royal family. The fact that Prussian recruiters began crossing into Hanover to seize prospective soldiers for Frederick William's regiment of giant grenadiers further exacerbated British concerns. George II, new to his thrones, fulminated. Frederick William mobilized. Britain marshaled diplomatic support and even guaranteed to send troops.[6]

The crisis – or better the *kerfuffle* – eventually faded away. But the memories remained, particularly as what for decades had seemed the "natural alliance" of Britain and Austria began eroding and France, recovering from the worst effects of the wars of Louis XIV, reasserted itself continentally and globally.[7] Hanover was a hostage to fortune or a diplomatic opportunity, depending on where one stood in the increasingly acrimonious parliamentary debates on the subject. When the War of Austrian Succession began in 1740, George II negotiated – or, more accurately, manipulated – an agreement with France guaranteeing that the French would not occupy Hanover and guaranteeing it as well against any other threat – meaning France's newly minted ally Prussia.[8]

The immediate price was neutrality: Hanover's, but not Britain's. Austria's fortunes waned, however, as the war progressed. The imperial crown fell to the Elector of Bavaria. Prussia seemed in a position to orchestrate and broker the breakup of the empire – perhaps Austria itself. But above all, Parliament took Britain to war in 1742 in order to preserve the glacis of the Low Countries protecting British security. A "Pragmatic Army" financed from London, built around German, Dutch, and Austrian components with a British core, held France in check and sustained Hanover – despite a run of French victories in 1745–47, and the resulting objections in Parliament that the continental tail was wagging the British dog.[9]

---

6 Simms, *Three Victories and a Defeat*, pp. 211–12.
7 Jeremy Black, "When 'Natural Allies' Fall Out: Anglo-Austrian Relations, 1735–1740," *Mitteilungen des oseterreichischen Staatsarchivs*, 36 (1983), 120–49.
8 Simms, *Three Victories and a Defeat*, p. 296; Uriel Daun, *Hanover and Great Britain, 1740–1760* (Leicester, 1991), pp. 35–39.
9 Reed Browning, *The War of the Austrian Succession* (New York, 1993), is an outstanding overview. Wolfgang Handrick, *Die Pragmatische Armee* (Oldenbourg, 1990), focuses on its nature and performance.

Initially, Prussia's specific challenge to Britain's strategic glacis was interpreted in the context of its war with Austria. But in 1744 Frederick's troops occupied the port of Emden, potentially both a threat to Hanover from the northeast and a harbinger of maritime commercial ambitions. Neither of these possibilities carried any particular weight with Frederick at the time. In 1752 he established a trading company to China – based in Emden. Its half-dozen ships never amounted to much.[10] But in conjunction with Frederick's open support of the Jacobite cause in the late 1740s and his refusal to pay loans against Silesian assets that the Hapsburgs had originally incurred but which Prussia now owned, Frederick's actions gave him the image of a loose cannon in London, who by no means had repented of his ways with the formal end of the War of Austrian Succession in 1748.[11]

The emerging Diplomatic Revolution

Morally as well as diplomatically, Maria Theresa's Austria saw itself unable to accept Prussia's new position in Central Europe and in the great power system. To Vienna, Frederick's Prussia represented a predator and an outlaw state, making and breaking treaties with frightening confidence. Austria had been its primary victim, and sought revenge. As its global rivalry with Britain had again escalated to shooting war in India and North America, France considered the British presence in Hanover as an unacceptable challenge and an inviting vulnerability. Further complicating the situation, Russia's permanent emergence on the European strategic scene in the 1740s brought to the table its long-standing fear of a strong Prussia on its western frontier – a fear Austria skillfully nurtured with bribes and promises that resulted in an alliance, concluded in 1746, built around a provision for common action against a Prussian attack.[12] The resulting games of bluff and double bluff, the interaction of mutual suspicion and mutual self-doubt, absorbed almost a decade. The outcome was the Diplomatic Revolution. But well before the treaties were signed, straws were blowing in the wind.

One should not exaggerate Austria's alienation from Britain at this point. Count Wenzel Kaunitz, Austria's chancellor and foreign minister

---

10 Florian Schui, "Prussia's 'Trans-Oceanic Moment': The Creation of the Prussian Asiatic Trade Company in 1750," *The Historical Journal*, 49 (2006), 1143–60.

11 Simms, *Three Victories and a Defeat*, pp. 361–63.

12 W. J. McGill, "The Roots of Policy: Kaunitz in Vienna and Versailles, 1749–1753," *Journal of Modern History*, 43 (1971), 229–35; and Reiner Pommerin, "Buendnispolitik und Maechtesystem: Oesterreich und der Aufsteig Russlands im 18. Jahrhundert," in J. Kunish (ed.), *Expansion und Gleichgewicht: Studien zur Europaeischen Machtpolitik des ancient regime* (Berlin, 1986), pp. 113–64.

after 1753, saw the worth of entente with the British and hoped to secure the island nation's participation in the anti-Prussian coalition that he worked for nearly a decade to create. Britain, however, was more concerned with its French connection – or the absence thereof. Pressure from the parliamentary opposition impelled the British government to send a small force to North America, the nucleus of an operation against French traders in the Ohio Valley. The French responded by reinforcing their North American garrison with metropolitan regulars. Even after Braddock's disaster along the Monongahela on 9 July 1755, war was not inevitable. Neither state was anxious for a colonial imbroglio. But both parties had ample justification for war, and no prospects of meaningful external interventions in the cause of peace.[13]

For the British, impending war meant looking to Hanover's security. Distancing relations with the electorate was not an option with George II on the throne. That generalization was affirmed in 1753, when the Hanoverian government noted with alarm what it considered to be threatening Prussian troop movements on its frontier. Though Frederick repeatedly denied any hostile intentions against the electorate, Parliament and public opinion accepted, at least for the moment, the synergy between the colonial and continental aspects of Britain's foreign policy. The British Cabinet accepted Hanover's recommendations that Britain improve its Austrian relations and pursue a treaty with Russia with surprisingly limited criticism. But the long-standing Anglo-Austrian entente could not be considered as a given in the face of Austria's obvious reluctance to become involved in a colonial struggle so remote from its own interests. The Austrian initiative foundered primarily, however, on Kaunitz's emphasis on Britain's adhering to the Russian treaty of 1746. Britain's goal was to deter a Prussian threat to Hanover, not commit its resources *a priori* to a general war in central Europe.[14]

An Anglo-Russian connection was a different matter. The two states' relations had been historically cordial. The Royal Navy depended heavily on the Russian Baltic for naval stores. Russia's ambitions in Poland and

---

13 T. R. Clayton, "The Duke of Newcastle, the Earl of Halifax, and the American Origins of the Seven Years War," *The Historical Journal*, 24 (1981), 571–603. Fred Anderson, *Crucible of War: The Seven Years War and the Fate of Empires in British North America, 1754–1766* (New York, 2001) and Daniel Baugh, *The Global Seven Years War, 1754–1763* (Harlow, 2011) are distinguished general histories incorporating solid discussions of this bitter undeclared conflict.

14 W. Mediger, "Great Britain, Hanover, and the Rise of Prussia," in Ragnhild Marie Hatton and Matthew Smith Anderson (eds.), *Studies in Diplomatic History. Essays in Honor of David Bayne Horn* (Hamden, CT, 1970), pp. 199–213; Reed Browning, "The British Orientation of Austrian Foreign Policy, 1749–1754," *Central European History*, 1 (1968), 299–323.

the Ottoman Empire generated regular friction with France. An alliance would be as stern a warning to Prussia as could be given short of war. A Russian government perpetually short of money was correspondingly ready to court British diplomats and bankers. In this hand, in contrast to the others being played in Europe, Britain seemed to hold the high cards. To modify a familiar aphorism, everybody knew that Empress Elizabeth could be bought. It was just a matter of fixing the price.[15]

A diplomatic initiative at this level depended on more than suspicion of Frederick's intentions and integrity. It also manifested the British desire to tap into Russia's seemingly inexhaustible resources on favorable terms. Public hostility to standing armies was a social, cultural, and political given in Britain. Whigs and Tories alike denounced even limited efforts to improve the British Army in the aftermath of the War of Austrian Succession as a preliminary to introducing continental-style despotism.[16] British governments had historically responded to this conundrum by leasing soldiers on the continent. Middle-sized German states like Hesse-Kassel and Brunswick, along with lesser powers like Denmark and Holland, had willingly accepted British treaties and British specie – not least because such treaties served their own diplomatic and domestic interests. In simpler times, the Elector of Prussia himself had not been too proud to conclude subsidy treaties with London.

By the mid-eighteenth century, however, the limits of this policy were clearer than its advantages. The military capacity of small states, no matter how efficient their armies, was diminishing significantly relative to the capabilities of the major powers. Britain was correspondingly likely to have to rely on a mixed bag of client troops from every state with men for hire. Cohesion and efficiency of this polyglot force were likely to be minimal and time to improve them was unlikely to be forthcoming given the new standards for striking quick and hard set by Prussia in 1740. In contrast, Russia appeared a source of effective, homogeneous expeditionary forces the size of which only Parliament's willingness to vote funds and the treasury's ability to find the money would limit.[17]

Russia for its part was neither passive, nor a catspaw. The tsarist empire had the longest, most exposed borders in Europe – and in good part for that reason favored an assertive foreign policy. Prussia was its focal point: a potential dangerous enemy; a potential source of territory; a potential

15 D. B. Horn, Sir Charles Hanbury, *William's and European Diplomacy, 1747–1758* (London, 1930), pp. 179ff.
16 Lois G. Schwoerer, *"No Standing Armies!" The Antiarmy Ideal in Seventeenth-Century England* (Baltimore, 1974).
17 D. B. Horn, "The Cabinet Controversy on Subsidy Treaties in Time of Peace, 1749–1750," English Historical Review, 45 (1930), 463–66.

loss to the eastern position of its ally France. British funds would stabilize the Russian treasury and make possible the concentration of a strong army close to Prussia's frontiers: a simultaneous threat and deterrent.

Negotiations continued into the summer of 1755. Britain and France severed diplomatic relations in July, making war a virtual certainty – and an unpopular one. Calls for neutrality, even for alliance with France, were emerging in the Dutch Republic. Russia correspondingly saw the balance shifting in its favor; now Britain was the party needing an agreement. St. Petersburg temporized. London began to question what a Russian alliance might be worth in the context of a shrinking time frame. Pressed by Britain, Kaunitz offered good will, but refused to authorize reinforcement of the Austrian Netherlands. This was precisely the kind of opportunity he sought to bring Britain into his anti-Prussian alliance, even if only from lack of an alternative.[18]

The final steps to war

The ongoing game of thrones was disrupted by a player that up to now had been passive. Frederick the Great was aware of the outlines of Kaunitz's grand design, but considered it more pipe dream than prospect. Of greater concern to him was the Austro-Russian treaty of 1746. Prussian intelligence had secured a copy of the document, and Prussia's king was aware of the clauses aimed at his state. He was also aware of Kaunitz's specific efforts to secure alliances with the small German states. And he increasingly recognized Russian hostility, both as a general trope and in particular contexts, as a risk that bade fair to rival that posed by Austria.

To date Frederick had countered with, and counted on, his French connection. In 1752 he described France and Prussia as having married sisters, Silesia and Lorraine, with that provincial connection committing them to a common policy. In a wider context France's historic rivalry with Austria was a better guarantor of the connection than Prussia's behavior. And indeed the relationship was solid enough to withstand Kaunitz's blandishments during his tenure as ambassador to Paris between 1750 and 1753. Prussia's military performance in the War of Austrian Succession had established it as a useful ally in the pattern of France's German clients: a successor to Bavaria as Austria's principal rival in Germany. Louis XV and his diplomats saw no reason to resign their Central European position for the sake of a relationship with a state that had no history of wishing

---

18 Cf. Walther Mediger, *Moskaus Weg nach Europa: Der Aufstieg Russlands zum Europaeischen Mschtstaat im Zeitalter Friedrichs des Grossen* (Berlin, 1952); and Herbert Kaplan, *Russia and the Outbreak of the Seven Years War* (Berkeley, 1968).

France well, and less reason to do so should the German balance shift decisively in its favor.

Frederick did his best to cultivate at least stable relations with Britain while avoiding the risk of seeming too friendly from a Parisian perspective. He encouraged France to consider Prussia a mediator in future contretemps with the island kingdom. But as North America edged towards war, that prospect took second place to Frederick's concern that the transatlantic conflict would spread to Europe.[19] In that the king had ample company. Unique to Prussia's situation, however, was Britain's opening of obviously broad-gauged negotiations with Russia. The latter state's lack of hard money had previously minimized the consequences of Russia's clumsily veiled antagonism to Prussia. However, British subsidies might be all Russia needed to realize the actualization of its 1746 treaty with Austria. In summer 1755 Frederick contacted London in a series of dispatches expressing his interest in discussing the current crisis – with the discussions including the possibility of neutralizing Germany in a war that now seemed all but certain.

The Duke of Newcastle, Britain's prime minister, responded promptly and favorably. The Russian negotiations were moving slowly. Austria's position was uncertain. An agreement with Prussia, unexpected though it might be, offered fresh prospects. If Frederick could make good on his offer and secure German neutrality under Prussian auspices, Hanover's security would be assured. Britain in turn could fight the war with maritime and financial power while keeping land forces and engagements to a politically safe minimum. However, an Anglo-Prussian rapprochement would not come easily or cheaply. The subsidy on which it hinged could, however, be defended as an exchange between equals. Payment actualizing common vital interests, made to a monarch of Frederick's standing, seemed far less grubby than doling out money to minor powers for obviously self-serving purposes.

There seemed, moreover, no immediate reason to choose between Prussia and Russia. Properly negotiated and managed, subsidies to Russia would give Britain leverage in Russia's policy-making. Subsidized guarantees to Prussia would secure Hanover. These gains would not come cheaply. But considering the cost in money, lives, and prestige that had resulted from previous British experiences of being drawn into

---

19 The Franco-Prussian relationship is surveyed in Dennis E Showalter, *The Wars of Frederick the Great*, rev. edn. (Barnsley, 2012), pp. 124–35; and presented in detail in R. N. Middleton, "French Policy and Prussia after the Peace of Aix-la-Chapelle: A Study of the Prehistory of the Diplomatic Revolution of 1756," PhD dissertation, Columbia University, 1958.

continental wars by stages as a consequence of making policy incrementally, the expense seemed well worth the effort. In August 1755, Newcastle agreed to direct negotiations with Prussia. Frederick was flattered by the duke's insistence that he was the key to peace in Germany. He was, however, reluctant to guarantee anything without more information on the progress of the Anglo-Russian negotiations. He was even more reluctant to act in any way that might risk an open break with France, despite his concern over French policies he saw as weak and indecisive.[20]

That indecision reflected growing French awareness that their North American strategic position was permanently and irrevocably unfavorable. In contrast to the burgeoning colonies along the British-governed coast, New France had remained a commercial outpost. The sustaining of a war on any scale in North America required regular reinforcement from home, the security of which the French navy could not guarantee, while the potential for maritime allies was currently nonexistent.[21] There was, however, a possibility of winning a transatlantic war by extending it. Frederick, always ready to help, had suggested the prospects of overrunning Hanover in a quick campaign, as he had done with Silesia in 1740. The long-term consequences of that initiative were, however, unlikely to encourage Paris to repeat it. Nor did Frederick's conduct in the War of Austrian Succession indicate a pattern of loyalty and reliability.[22]

As for other prospects of international support, Spain, preoccupied with domestic reform, showed no interest in risking war with Britain. A tentative approach to Vienna stalled on mutually exclusive expectations. Kaunitz sought an alliance as a step towards restructuring the balance of power in Europe by putting Prussia in its place. France wanted peace on the continent in order to free its resources for a struggle in North America and for strengthening its navy. Negotiations remained predictably static over the fall and winter of 1755.[23] Direct contact with London, aimed at defusing the situation even at this late date, still seemed the most promising approach, despite increasing pressure from elements in Newcastle's own Whig party, which advocated fundamental

---

20 Reed Browning, *The Duke of Newcastle* (New Haven, 1975), pp. 228–30; Showalter, *Wars of Frederick*, pp. 125–26.
21 Jonathan Dull, *The French Navy in the Seven Years War* (Lincoln, NE, 2005), pp. 9–30.
22 Stephen Skalweit, *Frankreich und Friedrich der Grosse: der Aufstieg Preussens in der öffentlichen Meinung des "ancien régime"* (Bonn, 1952).
23 Walter G. Roedel, "Eine geheime franzoesische Initiative als Ausloeser fuer die Renversement des Alliances?" in J. Kunish (ed.), *Expansion und Gleichgewicht: Studien zur Europaeischen Machtpolitik des ancient regime* (Berlin, 1986), pp. 97–112.

reorientation of Britain's foreign policy away from Eurocentric schemes and subsidies and towards sea power in general, and towards North America in particular.[24]

Meanwhile, Russia was recalculating risks and options. Since the turn of the century its leaders had found themselves simultaneously concerned with enlarging their holdings and defending their position in Central Europe. Sweden remained a force to be reckoned with in the Baltic – and its queen was Frederick the Great's sister. Poland was a wild card; the unpredictability alike of its magnates and its government remained proverbial. The Prussian king had to date demonstrated little interest in an east he regarded as barbaric. But Frederick had shown himself almost as unpredictable as Poland, and Prussia represented a force stronger than Sweden.[25] In September 1755 the Russians had agreed on terms with the British: a large Russian force deployed on Prussia's eastern frontier as an objective guarantee of Hanover's neutrality, in exchange for a substantial subsidy, substantial enough that Parliament never ratified the treaty. In November, Russian diplomats raised to their Austrian counterparts the possibility of joint direct action for the recovery of Silesia. Vienna responded with a mix of promises and offers of bribes sufficiently attractive to block a decision on Newcastle's proposals.[26]

At the same time Newcastle was using Britain's Russian negotiations to put pressure on Frederick. In November the Prussian resident secretary in London was informed of the details of the Anglo-Russian alliance with accompanying reassurances of its defensive nature, but presented as a virtual *fait accompli*. Simultaneously, Britain offered to settle all its outstanding disputes with Prussia, the Silesian loans included. Suddenly Frederick found himself on the horns of a dilemma. He faced disaster in the west should the Franco-Austrian negotiations bring results. Paris had made no secret to Berlin of its Vienna initiative. And should Austrian blandishments or British gold underwrite Russian assertiveness in Central Europe, Prussia had nothing with which to bargain in St. Petersburg, except Silesia. That agreement, unlikely in itself, would depend on Vienna's acquiescence without setting further, wider conditions affecting Prussia's status.

For neither the first nor the last time, Frederick took the initiative: a "flight forward," based as much on faith as reason. He believed in the venality of the Russian court and the incompetence of its empress.

24 Simms, *Three Victories and a Defeat*, pp. 397–400.
25 Klaus Zernack, "Preussen-Polen-Russland," in Otto Buesch (ed.), *Preussen und das Ausland* (Berlin, 1982), pp. 106–25.
26 Pommerin, "Buendnispolitik und Maechtesystem," pp. 141–42. The most detailed modern study is John Charles Batzel, "Austria and the First Three Treaties of Versailles, 1755–1758," PhD dissertation, Brown University, 1974.

Enough pounds sterling and Russia would heed instructions from London to abandon hostile intentions towards Prussia. As for France, the formal Anglo-Prussian agreement to neutralize Germany currently being negotiated would enable concentration of British effort in North America. It would warn Paris against taking Prussia for granted. And the final draft included a British guarantee of Silesia. Moreover, though the agreement under discussion did not incorporate subsidies, Britain's previous diplomatic history established such financial inducements as a likely future consideration.

When the French ambassador informed Frederick that Paris wished to continue the alliance, the king showed him a copy of the Convention of Westminster and informed him that the document was in the process of being signed. Not surprisingly, the Frenchman responded by denouncing Prussia for concluding such an agreement with a Britain already at war with France. Frederick declared his behavior as within the limits of international law and was sufficiently confident of his position to try to persuade the French that the Convention did them a favor. Its exclusion of the Austrian Netherlands offered a potential theater of continental operations should that policy be considered. But in Paris the slight remained unpardonable. France was already *de facto* at war. Its foreign policy seemed stymied everywhere. Now its one ally had abandoned it; abandoned it, moreover, in a public and insulting fashion. Nor was wounded pride the only grievance. Louis XIV had spent blood, money, and influence to secure French rights of intervention in Germany. How dare Prussia seek to determine French policy in what remained a vital sphere of interest, whatever might be happening across the Atlantic?[27]

In February 1756, the French council of state formally refused to renew the Prussian alliance. At the same time France began seriously and openly considering its Austrian option. Now it was Kaunitz's turn to temporize. He had no interest in blindly committing Austria's painstakingly restored military and financial resources as long as France still opposed giving Austria hegemony in Germany by the destruction or emasculation of Prussia. Nevertheless, after two month of diplomatic fencing the two powers concluded the Treaty of Versailles on 1 May 1756. Like the Convention of Westminster, it was ostensibly a defensive alliance; each state promised the other 24,000 men in case of an attack by a third party. Britain was specifically excluded, a fact reflecting Kaunitz's specific doubts about France's commitment and Austria's general reluctance to sever completely the London–Vienna axis.

---

27 Showalter, *Frederick the Great*, pp. 127–28.

Limited on the surface, the agreement satisfied both parties. France could reasonably consider its European position secured. The Bourbon monarchs of Italy and Spain were not expected to protest. The United Netherlands, Britain's other long-time continental ally, was more than ever determined to maintain its neutrality. For Frederick to repeat his initiative of 1740 would pit him against both France and Austria – nor were there any obvious options in lieu of such a move. With the decks seemingly cleared on both sides, in May 1756 France and Britain mutually and formally declared war.

Austria for its part had added a key piece to the diplomatic puzzle Kaunitz had long sought to assemble. France had backed away from its historic pretensions in Germany. Sweden and Saxony were making claims for Prussian territory. Prussia was isolated on the continent. When during the summer of 1756 a still-cautious France continued to refuse direct cooperation in a war against Prussia, Kaunitz was confident that something would happen to force Paris's hand.[28]

St. Petersburg obliged. Russia considered Britain had acted in bad faith by concluding the Convention of Westminster. Perfidious Albion was now in position to choose between partners according to circumstances. Britain's stock shrank at court; by March Russia was openly planning a full-scale war against Prussia with Austrian and now French assistance.[29] Now it was Kaunitz's turn to temporize. More diplomat than warrior, he questioned whether even in combination Russia and Austria, on the front lines of the projected war, could crush Frederick's formidable army quickly and decisively enough for his still gossamer-fragile triad to cohere in success, as opposed to showing its fault lines under stress. Instead, Kaunitz argued for delaying the offensives against Prussia for a year, thus providing the alliance time to move its diplomatic and military pieces into position, while forcing Frederick to initiate the conflict from sheer desperation, a possibility Kaunitz considered likely. That would give Austria a final edge: the moral high ground.[30]

The Treaty of Versailles came as a surprise and a shock to Britain. Newcastle described it as "unnatural" and "to all intents and purposes offensive": a repudiation of the balance of power and a leap into the diplomatic dark.[31] That judgment did not improve when in the course of the summer, alarmist reports from Vienna described Austria as willing

---

28 Showalter, *Frederick the Great*, pp. 129–30.
29 L. J. Oliva, *Misalliance: A Study of French Policy in Russia during the Seven Years War* (New York, 1964), pp. 14 ff.; Kaplan, *Russia and the Outbreak of the Seven Years War*, pp. 47ff.
30 Pommerin, "Buendnispolitik und Maechtesystem," p. 144.
31 Simms, *Three Victories and a Defeat*, p. 410.

to trade the Austrian Netherlands for Silesia. Whether directly in French hands or under a Parisian puppet, that realignment would put Britain's strategic glacis at unacceptable risk. In North America the French, under a new commander, Louis-Joseph de Montcalm, were inflicting defeats on the British and their colonial allies. And in May a French squadron bluffed a British one into abandoning an attempt to relieve the strategic Mediterranean island of Minorca. Executing the disgraced Admiral Byng only divided public and Parliament further. An invasion scare during the summer and fall found the army so attenuated that the government had to hire Hanoverian and Hessian mercenaries – "auxiliaries" imported to provide sufficient ground forces for the defense of the British Isles.[32]

For Frederick, Britain's difficulties represented little more than a backdrop for events on the continent. In July Russia proposed to send a contingent of troops into Saxony, ostensibly to shore up Austria's flank. The force was no mere tripwire, but between 30.000 and 35,000 men.[33] This was at sufficient right angles to Kaunitz's approach that the Austrian ambassador quashed the project. But the Russian Grand Chancellor achieved much the same results by leaking information to the Dutch ambassador of the project in strictest confidence, with the expectation he would pass on the intelligence, an expectation that was quickly fulfilled.

Frederick's response was clear enough, although his motives remain opaque. A "patriotic/realist" school describes the Prussian king as a man without alternatives. Russian troops were concentrating in the Baltic. Austria was mobilizing forces for deployment into Bohemia. France was unlikely to do more than protest briefly should its new allies reduce Prussia to a badly carved rump. Thus, his only option was to seize the strategic initiative in order to structure the decisive battles on which Prussian diplomacy, and Prussia's survival, depended.

An alternative perspective depicts Frederick as a predator, ready to initiate a preventative war to forestall aggression based, as his foreign minister, suggested, essentially on rumors. Russian preparations were hardly models of logistical effectiveness or operational readiness. Austrian implementation on the ground lagged significantly behind written orders. But when Heinrich von Podewils urged delay, Frederick rejected "timid politics." He had, moreover, an objective. Frederick understood war as a means of gaining territory, and his reflections on possible concrete benefits from the current crisis increasingly focused on Saxony. The electorate was an ally/client of Austria. It posed objective geographic threats.

---

32 Ibid., pp. 410–19; Browning, *Newcastle*, pp. 231–38.
33 Mediger, *Moskaus Weg nach Europa*, pp. 626–27.

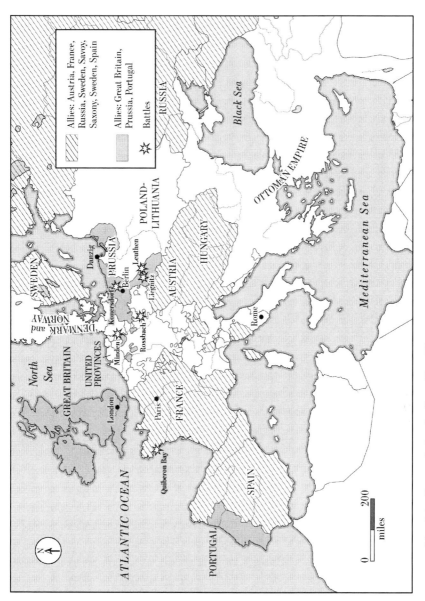

Map 3.1   Europe during the Seven Years War

Berlin and Potsdam were exposed to attack across the nearby border, while the Elbe River could transport men and supplies deep into the heart of Brandenburg. On the other side of the balance sheet, Saxony had a well-developed economy and an efficient army, both tempting lures for a state perpetually working on narrow margins.[34]

Whether Frederick intended to absorb the electorate or exploit it, his most trusted general, Hans von Winterfeldt, had travelled throughout Saxony, evaluating terrain, defenses, and possible routes of advance. He predicted an easy victory, if the king acted promptly.[35] Britain's ambassador to Prussia, Andrew Mitchell, urged restraint. With what was already on his country's plate, the last thing it needed was a full-scale continental war. Frederick's responses were reassuring.[36] But in the back of his mind lay the comforting prospect that the Convention of Westminster would be a first step to subsidies underwriting the kind of sudden, overwhelming offensive in which Prussia's army specialized. Frederick began preparing for such an operation in June. On 29 August 1756, after the obligatory final diplomatic fencing between Vienna and Berlin, Prussian troops crossed the Saxon border and the Seven Years War had begun.

The war and alliance

Frederick's rapid occupation of Saxony against no more than token resistance did not lessen the shock in London. Not only was Britain caught in an unwanted war in Europe, but Hanover's strategic position was worse off than ever. The historic French approach to fighting Britain on the continent had involved attacking the Low Countries' provinces of Britain's usual ally, Austria. The new Franco-Austrian alliance voided that option, but facilitated a French initiative against Hanover. The electorate was a valuable bargaining chip to exchange for overseas advantages in the next peace settlement. It also offered an opportunity to lure British forces onto a European killing ground, against a French army greatly superior in numbers and quality to anything it might encounter in north Germany.[37]

---

34 Showalter, *Frederick the Great*, pp. 131–32. Franz Szabo, *The Seven Years War in Europe, 1756–1763* (Harlow, 2008), makes an eloquent and continuing argument for the "predator" school; Johannes Kunisch, *Friedrich der Grosse. Der Koenig und seine Zeit* (Munich, 2004), is a measured presentation of the "realist " case.

35 Christopher Duffy, *Frederick the Great: A Military Life* (London, 1985), p. 87.

36 Patrick F. Doran, *Andrew Mitchell and Prussian Diplomatic Relations during the Seven Years War* (New York, 1986), pp. 50ff.

37 For the background of French preparation and execution see Lee Kennett, *The French Armies in the Seven Years War: A Study in Military Organization and Administration* (Durham, NC, 1967).

There existed the possibility of declaring neutrality, on the grounds that Prussia had violated the Convention of Westminster's terms. King George vigorously supported that option. Newcastle regarded it as a dead end, but his position was compromised by the foreign policy debacle for which many considered him responsible. He resigned in November. For the next five years, William Pitt would dominate Britain's politics and diplomacy.[38]

Pitt and Frederick shared two qualities: self-confidence not always justified by events, and a belief in forcing events rather than reacting to circumstances. A long-standing and vociferous critic of a European commitment in general and subsidy treaties in particular, Pitt understood the necessity of fighting the war he inherited as opposed to the one he might have preferred. He obtained parliamentary funding for an "Army of Observation" to defend Hanover: forces hired from the medium-sized north German states plus 10,000 never-delivered Prussians, the whole commanded by George II's son, the Duke of Cumberland. He explained and justified this action in the context of Britain's security.[39] But Pitt's affirmation of the long-standing point that French domination of the continent was unacceptable also incorporated a global dimension. That hegemony, Pitt argued, would enable France to challenge on even terms the "command of the ocean," on which British prosperity, security, and liberty depended. British liberty, in other words, ultimately depended on the "public liberty" of Europe. And the front-line defender of that liberty was a most unlikely candidate: Frederick the Great of Prussia.[40]

Two primary requisites for a successful grand-strategic alliance are common aims and common enemies. In 1757 Britain and Prussia had neither. Britain's immediate objective was the security of Hanover; its ultimate concern was France's extra-European challenge. Frederick was indifferent to both. Above all he feared Austrian revanchism, specifically its desire to recover Silesia, and more generally its goal of reducing Prussia to second-rank status in Germany and Europe. And neither of those had any priority in British councils of state.

---

38 Manfred Schlenke, *England und das friderizianisce Preussen 1760–1763. Ein Beitrag zum Verhaeltnis von Politik und oeffentlicher Meinung im England des 18, Jahrhunderts* (Freiburg, 1963), pp. 227–34n.

39 Brendan Simms, "Pitt and Hanover," in T. Riotte and B. Simms (eds.), *The Hanoverian Dimension in British History, 1714–1837* (Cambridge, 2007), pp. 28–57.

40 There is a Pitt, as there is a Frederick, for every intellectual and ideological taste. Simms, *Three Victories and a Defeat*, pp. 432 passim, presents a world-historical statesman and war leader. Marie Peters, *The Elder Pitt* (London, 1998), counters by arguing for Pitt's improvised strategy and his indifference to cost. Jeremy Black, *Pitt the Elder* (Cambridge, 1992), stresses the disconnects Pitt's policies fostered between Britain's continental commitment and its global ambitions.

What brought this diplomatic odd couple together was less a common enemy than their parallel strategic needs. During the first half of 1757, Pitt increased Britain's financial and military commitment on the continent, but not enough to counter the 75,000 French troops that crossed the Rhine in March. As the French advanced into Hanover, Cumberland fell back, fought an indecisive action at Hastenbeck, and retreated again. The Army of Observation unraveled. On 8 September Cumberland agreed to evacuate Hanover and disband his forces.[41] Pitt's support in Parliament grew so unstable that in July Newcastle resumed the office of prime minister with Pitt as secretary of state: an unlikely pairing given their long-standing rivalry. As the British war effort unraveled, Frederick came to Britain's rescue.

Prussia's king had not suddenly embraced altruism. His plans for carrying on the war once his troops had overrun Saxony were vague. Eight months of fighting had resulted not in a decisive battle, but in an empty treasury, an exhausted army, and stalemate in Bohemia. Moreover, more than 100,000 Russians menaced East Prussia with another 60,000 French and Imperials, Austrian allies from the Holy Roman Empire, advancing against Prussia from the Rhine. Desperately needing a victory to buy time, Frederick scraped together a scratch army, turned west, and on 5 November 1757, crushed the Franco-Imperials at Rossbach.[42]

In the battle's aftermath, the British raised the stakes. Rossbach was the first good news to come out of the war. Not since the days of William of Orange and the Glorious Revolution of 1688 had a continental connection been so popular. Frederick became a "Protestant hero" with taverns, hotels, and entire villages named after him as far away as Pennsylvania.[43] On 11 April 1768, British and Prussian representatives revised the Convention of Westminster into a formal alliance based on the mutual agreement not to negotiate a separate peace and underwritten by an annual subsidy to Prussia of £670,000.

The subsidy represented a goodly amount, larger than any ever paid by Britain. But in the aftermath of Rossbach, Britain and Prussia still lacked common aims and enemies. It took approximately £2 million to keep 40,000 Prussians in the field for a campaigning season, with rations, forage, and pay included. From Frederick's perspective Britain was getting a bargain, especially compared to the £1.2 million cost of the abortive Army of Observation. Pitt essentially agreed. The sums forwarded to Berlin were

41 Reginald Savory, *His Britannic Majesty's Army in Germany during the Seven Years War* (Oxford, 1966), pp. 14–46.
42 Showalter, *Frederick the Great*, pp. 177–92; Duffy, *Military Life*, pp. 138–45.
43 Schlenke, *England und das friderizianische Preussen*, pp. 236–48.

from his perspective an investment in a strategy conceptually far broader than the mere underwriting of Hanover's security. It was a strategy synergizing the German and American theaters of war, the continental balance of power, and British commercial expansion.[44]

Pitt did not exactly take Frederick for granted, but he correctly believed it safe to ignore such irritants as Frederick's repeated recommendations on how best to deploy British troops in Europe and his repeated requests to send a squadron to the Baltic to counter regional naval forces.[45] Pitt understood Machiavelli's aphorism that gold will not always get you good soldiers was not entirely correct. Enough gold, and you can lease very good soldiers, especially if the state they served had nowhere else to turn. And Prussia was fighting for survival, as a power if not necessarily a state.

The Army of Observation was revived under a more than competent Prussian commander, Ferdinand of Brunswick and renamed "His Britannic Majesty's Army in Germany," eventually to be reinforced with a substantial British contingent. The second front was in place again, and the British made clear that it would be financed and supplied only if it were operationally active. Frederick's contributions to the western theater were tokens: a dozen squadrons of cavalry (admittedly first-rate) and eventually a locally raised infantry battalion.[46] To Pitt, however, what mattered was Prussia's willingness to continue its own war.

That conflict bade fair to become a war of mutual exhaustion. In December 1757 Frederick won another impressive victory at Leuthen. In the next eighteen months the king and his army stabilized the situation in Central Europe. But as the war progressed, mutually steep, interacting learning curves created an increasing symmetry among the combatants. The result was a series of campaigns and battles the outcomes of which brought no decisive strategic or diplomatic results.[47] The anti-Prussian coalition stayed in the field despite increasing internal friction. Frederick privileged hope over experience, using his army as collateral for the next round. Britain celebrated Prussia's victories, but saw them as laying the groundwork for the end of an alliance that was becoming more burden than support.

The slow-motion dissolution began when the old-fashioned commander of an army of British-paid contingents from a half-dozen German

---

44 Schweizer, *Frederick, Pitt, and Bute*, pp. 60ff.
45 Richard Middleton, *The Bells of Victory: The Pitt-Newcastle Ministry and the Conduct of the Seven Years War, 1757–1762* (Cambridge, 1985), pp. 58–59.
46 Savory, *Army in Germany*, pp. 451–52.
47 Showalter, *Frederick the Great*, pp. 207–59; Duffy, *Military Life*, pp. 155–96.

states with a hard British core fought an old-fashioned campaign across Westphalia and Hesse. In the summer and fall of 1758, Ferdinand of Brunswick and his revitalized command executed a deft campaign of maneuver across northern Germany that maneuvered the French back to the Rhine and in the process covered Frederick's western strategic flank. During the next spring the French advanced again and with more success until the Battle of Minden on 1 August. At Minden, six British battalions deployed in line broke three successive French cavalry charges with volley fire at point-blank range, and then drove the horsemen from the field at bayonet point.[48]

Success in Britain's strategic backyard more than compensated for the failure of a series of "descents" on the French coast.[49] Even better news came from overseas. In North America the capture of Louisbourg in July 1758 was the preliminary to the next year's successful attack on Quebec. Further west the British overran the Ohio country and captured the fortress of Ticonderoga. The sugar island of Guadeloupe fell after six disease-ridden months to a joint army–navy operation. In India, Madras withstood a French siege. Best of all because closest to home were the naval victories of Lagos in August and Quiberon Bay in November. Between them they ended any prospects of a French invasion and established the Royal Navy's superiority at sea for almost two centuries. The Pitt-Newcastle team, a "broad-bottom government" in British political parlance, was on a roll.[50]

All of this in a single year! Seventeen fifty-nine was for Britain an *annus mirabilis* indeed. For France it was the *annus miserabilis*. The government, anticipating a quick and positive decision, had decided to finance its war through loans instead of taxes. Inefficient military and civil administration drove costs ever higher. By 1759 France's ability to pay for its war was seriously challenged. The duc de Choiseul, appointed foreign minister in October 1758, responded with an offensive strategy, global in scope but one that failed on a global scale in 1759. By fall an emptying treasury made peace doubly desirable in Paris.[51]

---

48 Savory, *Army in Germany*, pp. 51–201. Piers Mackesy, *The Coward of Minden: The Affair of Lord George Sackville* (London, 1979), includes a detailed account of the battle and a perceptive depiction of Brunswick's army on its best day.
49 W. K. Hackmann, "English Military Expeditions to the French Coast, 1757–1761," dissertation, University of Michigan, 1969.
50 Frank Mc Lynn, *1759: The Year that Britain Became Master of the World* (London, 2005), is more balanced in tone than its title suggests. Baugh, *Seven Years War*, pp. 319–452, is operationally focused.
51 James C. Riley, *The Seven Years' War and the Old Regime in France: The Economic and Financial Toll* (Princeton, 1986).

The war's end

But not just the French were eager for peace. After the disintegration of a Prussian army at Kunersdorf on 12 August, Frederick too was amenable, at least temporarily, to a general congress to discuss ending the war. Nothing came of the attempt, except to increase a growing sense in London that the Prussian alliance was a liability. Frederick for his part quickly recovered his confidence, declaring his intention to dictate peace in Vienna and entertaining an ephemeral project of bringing the Ottoman Empire into play on the Austro-Russian eastern frontier.[52]

Frederick's optimism was underwritten when Britain renewed Prussia's subsidy. Pitt, riding the wave of victory, had no intention of making peace on any terms but his own. The British Army's budget was increased by £2.5 million; Ferdinand's numbers were raised to just short of 100,000 men. Choiseul responded by sending 140,000 men into north Germany in 1760. But logistical problems exacerbated by the deepening financial crisis hampered French movements. Brunswick kept the French in difficulty. His army had developed into a battle-seasoned, tactically competent force confident in its leader and flexible enough to rebound from a crisis in morale and discipline, the result of logistical failures in the first months of 1761. It simultaneously became the major objective of a desperate French strategic move: to impel Britain to the negotiating table by destroying His Britannic Majesty's Army in Germany. The commitment of 160,000 men to the enterprise invites the suggestion that the forces committed were too large either to move freely in, or be sustained by, north Germany. As the French got in each other's way, Brunswick enmeshed them in a campaign of skirmishes and maneuvers, feints, raids, and foraging expeditions.[53]

By this time the conflict was looking like a "forever war" in London. In August 1761 Spain concluded an alliance with France. Denied a declaration of war against Madrid, Pitt resigned in October. Newcastle, however, failed to avert the war with Spain that broke out in January. In May he was replaced by the Tory Earl of Bute – not for reasons of policy but because of the personal animosity of the new king, George III.[54] No pacifist, Bute was nevertheless peace-minded. The financial burden of sustaining a fully mobilized navy along with extensive campaigns in North America and the indecisive fencing in northwest Germany had escalated to a point where Britain's war expenses were more than double those of France. Bute had also inherited a new theater of war.

---

52 Szabo, *Seven Years War*, p. 268; Showalter, *Frederick the Great*, p. 267.
53 Savory, *Army in Germany*, pp. 283–359.
54 Schweizer, *Frederick, Pitt, and Bute*, pp. 99ff.

When Spain invaded Portugal, the British found themselves constrained for economic and strategic reasons by how large an expeditionary force they could send to the Iberian peninsula. The result was just enough operational success to produce strategic stalemate – an all too familiar situation for British continental commitments.[55]

Bute began his term in office by re-examining Britain's relationship with Prussia. The stalemate in Central Europe had existed through 1761, but Prussia's army was worn thin. Frederick was debasing his own state's coinage, while his administrators had to exert extreme pressure for contributions from still-occupied regions like Saxony and Mecklenburg.[56] Nevertheless, the king seemed ready to fight on indefinitely. From Bute's perspective Britain was financing a war without end and for limited strategic gain. This sense was reinforced when in December he received a request to support Prussia's interests until they were satisfied, even in the event of an Anglo-French peace.[57]

Marriage without love is possible, but it depends on a realistic assessment of the relationship's terms. The same holds for alliances. Bute promptly informed Frederick that Britain, should it conclude peace with France, would guarantee nothing. The subsidy treaty would not be renewed; the coming year's amount would instead be paid by a special grant of Parliament. Frederick should adjust his terms of peace to those he could compel by a realistic use of force. Bute urged him to seek peace with Austria, even at the price of significant territorial concessions. Silesia was not specified, but the implication was unmistakable. Finally, Bute demanded a report on Prussia's military resources and intentions.[58]

For Frederick, Bute's position boded catastrophe. As the final episode of the summer campaign, the Russians had captured the Baltic port of Kolberg, enabling them to move reinforcements and supplies almost at will across a Baltic that had become a Russian lake. Austria had taken the fortress of Schweidnitz and established most of its winter camps in Silesia. Kolberg had fallen to a *coup de main*, Schweidnitz to a combined-arms siege. Both operations indicated the continuing improvement of the Russian and Austrian armies. Both showed the allies' developing ability to hit hard where Frederick was not present. And both highlighted Prussia's overstretch. The civil and military administrations were so disorganized that company captains were not receiving the money needed to purchase

55 A. D. Francis, "The Campaign in Portugal, 1762," Journal of the Society for Army Historical Research, 59 (1961), 25–43.
56 Showalter, *Frederick the Great*, pp. 299–302.
57 Baugh, *Seven Years War*, p. 566.
58 Schweizer, *Frederick, Pitt, and Bute*, pp. 142ff.

supplies for the coming year. The heart of the state, Brandenburg and Pomerania, lay open to raiding and invasion. Even if the allies might be unable to overrun the kingdom, they were in a good position to make it ungovernable.[59]

One of history's most unlikely and most significant coincidences restored Frederick's position. Elizabeth of Russia died on 6 January 1762. Her nephew and successor, Peter III, was a German prince who barely spoke Russian, despised his aunt, and admired Frederick. None of these things made him a fool. Whatever its initial wisdom, the policy reducing Prussia to a middle-ranking power was draining Russia's resources as the empire found itself drawn into conflict on its east and south: in Poland, in the Caucasus, in Persia and Siberia, with the Ottoman Empire, and even against the Chinese. And would Austrian hegemony in Germany really serve Russia's long-term interests? Peter had no difficulty deciding to open negotiations with a grateful and delighted Frederick.[60]

Bute perceived this as a heaven-sent opportunity. He sought to facil-itate the process by informing Frederick that no more money would be forthcoming for continuing the war. If, however, the subsidy should be devoted to securing peace, the Crown would immediately request it of Parliament. At the same time, Bute informed the Russian ambassador of his hope for Russia's continued participation in the war until Frederick listened to reason. In return, Russia could expect the Prussian king to make reasonable sacrifices. When pressed, the ambassador reported, Bute mentioned East Prussia.

The ambassador, who favored continuing the war, also misrepre-sented, not to say falsified, what were after all tentative soundings by a man new to the office. Peter, perhaps too new on his throne to be appro-priately suspicious of such intelligence, responded by sending Frederick a summary of the report, accompanied by his offer to entertain peace proposals immediately.[61] Frederick reacted by suggesting that Bute deserved to be broken on the wheel and then telling his entourage what he *really* thought of the British minister. And that was only the beginning. Newcastle still believed in the worth and the prospects of an Austrian connection. During his final weeks in office he sent Kaunitz a carefully worded note suggesting Britain might assist in negotiating a solution of the Silesian question satisfactory to Austria. Kaunitz rejected the trial

---

59 Showalter, *Frederick the Great*, pp. 309–11; Duffy, *Military Life*, pp. 229–34.
60 Carol S. Leonard, *Reform and Regicide: The Reign of Peter III of Russia* (Bloomington, IN, 1993), pp. 123 passim has the details; John P. Le Donne, *The Grand Strategy of the Russian Empire 1650–1831* (New York, 2004), provides the matrix.
61 Karl W. Schweizer and Carol S. Leonard. "Britain, Prussia, Russia, and the Galitzin Letter: A Reassessment," The Historical Journal, 26 (September 1983), pp. 531–56.

balloon, but the Prussian minister in London learned of the contact and informed Frederick.[62]

Although one should understand one's allies as well as oneself and one's enemies, sometimes allies can understand each other's motives all too well. A less trusting man than Frederick of Prussia might have been pardoned for believing he was about to be comprehensively betrayed by his ostensible ally. A more reflective one might have remembered his own cavalier approach to alliances in the War of Austrian Succession. Frederick authorized his ambassador in St. Petersburg to sign anything Peter put in front of him.[63]

The actual terms were more than generous, restoring all occupied Prussian territory and concluding not only peace, but an alliance promising the dispatch of 20,000 Russian troops to Silesia. Frederick responded by promptly undertaking a campaign against Austria. After Peter's deposition and assassination in July definitively removed the promised Russian contingent from the equation, there was as much bluff as substance to the operation. This time, finally, it was just enough. Left to her own devices, Peter's wife and successor Catherine might have returned Russia to the conflict, if only from spousal spite. But the new tsarina was feeling her way into power. The treaty stood. Austria counted its cards, and Empress Maria Theresia decided to cut her losses. The Peace of Hubertusburg, concluded on 18 February 1763, amounted to a mutual acceptance of the *status quo ante bellum*.[64]

After the break with Prussia, the British continentalists who, like Newcastle, continued to support direct engagement in Europe were overshadowed by the globalists and the Americanists. George III spoke English as his native language and never visited Hanover. Across the Channel, France faced the complete collapse of its positions in North America and India, along with a looming, overwhelming threat to its West Indian sugar islands – vital to a stumbling economy and an empty treasury. The resulting Treaty of Paris, signed in February 1763, restored Hanover's independence and ended France's status as a power in North America and India. The global bits and pieces obtained as concessions were fig leaves that did little to conceal the fact that France had lost a war and paid a heavy price for defeat.[65]

---

62 Karl W. Schweizer, "Lord Bute, Newcastle, Prussia, and the Hague Overtures: A Re-Examination," *Albion*, 9 (1977), 72–97, highlights Frederick's attempt to force Bute from office by a propaganda offensive in England, but concluded that even without this incident the alliance would not have endured.

63 Schweizer, *Frederick, Pitt, and Bute*, pp. 142–321, and Doran, *Mitchell*, pp. 295–341, give the details from the perspectives of London and Berlin, respectively.

64 Showalter, *Frederick the Great*, pp. 311–20, and Szabo, *Seven Years War*, pp. 413–423, are a useful survey of peacemaking in Central Europe.

65 Baugh, *Seven Years War*, pp. 613–19; Zenab Esmat Rashed, *The Peace of Paris, 1763* (Liverpool, 1951), remains a useful narrative.

Conclusion

The Anglo-Prussian alliance brought its contracting parties success. Prussia was confirmed as a great power beyond question, if not beyond challenge. Britain was confirmed as a global power, also not beyond challenge. The partners' responses were, however, fundamentally different. Britain for its part suffered from a slow-acting version of victory disease. It rested (1) on insularity: a focus on self-defined virtues and qualities; (2) on expansionism: in North America, in India, and commercially in East Asia as well; (3) on navalism: sea power became less a deterrent than a first-use instrument of intimidation; and (4) on withdrawal: a leaving of Europe to its own devices that in turn produced isolation. Yet when Britain paid for its errors between 1776 and 1783 in the War of American Independence, the cost was ultimately moderate, because the bill was presented everywhere in the world but Europe.[66]

That war spared the continent owed much to Prussia. After 1763 Frederick proceeded on the principle that the readiness and the capacity to make war were more important than its waging. He showcased the Prussian army as a deterrent. Frederick cultivated an image as one of history's greatest generals. Anything encouraging belief in the unacceptable risks of trying conclusions with Old Fritz and his faithful grenadiers was welcome in a state strategy assigning force the role of intimidation rather than implementation. From being the disturber of Germany's and the continent's peace, Frederick became a staunch defender of the sovereign rights established in 1648 by the Peace of Westphalia, and of the international order confirmed at such cost during the Seven Years War. Prussia's king, state, and army became key participants in a Europe whose crises for more than a quarter century were resolved by concession, compromise, and negotiation. When in 1778 Britain, on the brink of war with France, made overtures for an alliance, Frederick's response is best described as "dusty." Grievances taste best when marinated over time.[67]

Considered at long range and second hand, the Anglo-Prussian alliance of the Seven Years War stands in this anthology as the outstanding example of a relationship of convenience, maintained *in extremis* and terminated *ad libitum*. It ended in fury on one side and indifference

---

66 Simms, *Three Victories and a Defeat*, pp. 501–661; and for background Linda Colley, *Britons: Forging the Nation, 1707–1837* (London, 1992).

67 H. M. Scott, "Aping the Great Powers: Frederick the Great and the Defense of Prussia's International Position, 1763–1786," *German History*, 12 (1994), 286–307; and in more detail Frank Althoff, *Untersuchungen zum Gleichgewicht der Maechte in der Aussenpolitik Friedrichs des Greossn nach dem Siebenjaehrigen Krieg* (Berlin, 1995). Christopher Clark sums it up best in *Iron Kingdom* (Cambridge, MA, 2006), p. 217: "The poacher had become a gamekeeper."

on the other. It functioned at arm's length. Its successes and its defeats alike were solo performances. Each partner consistently privileged interests over commitments. Each single-mindedly sought its own advantage. Each viewed the other as a useful instrument, nothing more. In the terms of what makes a successful alliance, this one was a disaster waiting to happen. Yet the Anglo-Prussian alliance of the Seven Years War suggests that a first-rate army and a dominant navy, underwritten by an iron kingdom and Europe's most successful fiscal-military state[68] and guided by two gifted war lords, were able to produce results even in an alliance of mutual desperation. Clio indeed has a sardonic sense of humor.

68 See P. G. M. Dickson, *The Financial Revolution in England: A Study in the Development of Public Credit, 1688–1756* (London, 1967).

4   Preserved by friend and foe alike
The Sixth Coalition against Revolutionary France

Richard Hart Sinnreich

> There is only one thing worse than fighting with allies, and that is fighting without them.[1]

On 26 June 1813, at the Mercolini Palace[2] in Dresden, capital of the Kingdom of Saxony, a fateful meeting took place between Napoleon Bonaparte, self-proclaimed emperor of the French, and Prince Clemens von Metternich, minister plenipotentiary of Bonaparte's nominal ally and father-in-law, Francis I, emperor of Austria.[3] The purpose of the meeting was to discuss terms by which peace might be made between France and its adversaries, at the time comprising Russia, Prussia, Sweden, and Great Britain.

We do not know precisely what took place during the nearly nine hours of discussion. Both participants later described what occurred, but not surprisingly those recollections fail to agree, and no third party was present who might have reconciled the disagreement.[4] What we do know is what resulted. Presented with an ultimatum requiring him to surrender the lion's share of his European conquests in return for the possibility, but by no means the assurance, of peace, Bonaparte stubbornly rejected Metternich's terms. His intransigence enabled Metternich to convince his reluctant monarch to abandon neutrality for outright belligerence, and the allies' resulting augmentation by Austria's 300,000 troops radically transformed the military force balance, in the end decisively. As

---

1 Winston Churchill to Sir Alan Brooke, Chief of the Imperial General Staff, April 1945, quoted in Arthur Bryant, *Triumph in the West, 1943–1946* (London, 1986), p. 445.
2 Also known as Elsterwiese Castle.
3 As Francis II, he had ruled as Holy Roman Emperor until Austria's defeat at Austerlitz in August, 1806, after which, as Francis I, he reverted to his second title, emperor of Austria, created two years earlier.
4 Frank McLynn, *Napoleon: A Biography* (Arcade Publishing, 2011), ch. 24. Metternich's *Memoirs* were published in English translation 1880 (London, 1980). Volume 1, ch. 8 records his famous account of the conversation. Napoleon's *Memoirs* were published in English translation in 1891.

Metternich later claimed to have declared on leaving Napoleon's presence, "Sire, you are lost."

Not quite a year later, in February 1814, another meeting took place at Troyes on the Seine, 90 miles southeast of Paris. As with the Dresden meeting, this one resulted in an ultimatum to Napoleon. But in this case, the vital dispute was among the allies themselves, and especially with Russia's Tsar Alexander, whose intentions threatened to shatter the coalition at the very moment when its triumph seemed assured. As he had at Dresden, Bonaparte disdained the peace terms the allies offered, terms no one expected him to accept in any case. But the real achievement of what became known as the Treaty of Chaumont, engineered largely by British Foreign Minister Robert Cecil Lord Castlereagh, was to commit the allies – including Russia – to defer reconciliation of incompatible postwar visions until the allies had achieved victory, without which none would be realized.

Chaumont guaranteed that victory, but not the peace that followed. Eight months later, with Napoleon exiled to Elba and a Bourbon king once more on the throne of France, war threatened again, this time not between France and the allies – that tragedy would not recur until Bonaparte's escape and the Hundred Days that followed – but instead between Prussia on one side and Austria and Britain on the other, the latter two supported, ironically, by erstwhile enemy France. In the event, war was averted, and a settlement achieved that would produce Europe's longest period of great power peace since the fall of Rome. It was a record of success unequaled even in our own time.

The making of a coalition

The cohesion of any wartime coalition confronts two opposite dangers. The first is military defeat or its threat, which crystallizes the differing vulnerability of the coalition's partners to its potential consequences. The second is military victory or its imminence, which tends to rekindle the inevitable political disagreements that fear of defeat papers over. Both conditions risk at least disaffection and at worst the outright defection of one or more of the coalition partners.

The history of the Sixth Coalition is above all the story of how the statesmen involved surmounted these two dangers. At the heart of the story were three crises, one prompted by the common enemy, the other two by the allies themselves. Successful resolution of the first helped produce a military victory that otherwise would not have been possible. Resolution of the second assured the translation of that victory into war termination without which it might never have proved decisive. As for successful resolution of the third, it allowed the coalition and the peace it had achieved to survive the war that it had won. Each crisis was surmounted only at the risk of the coalition's collapse. And in each case but the last, the essential accomplice in preventing that collapse was Napoleon himself, who proved total victory necessary by demonstrating the impossibility of accommodation, and allied unity essential by demonstrating the inability of anything less to achieve and cement that victory.

Historians generally consider the Sixth Coalition to have been among history's most successful wartime alliances. In addition to defeating one of the world's great captains – not once, but twice – the coalition also managed to achieve a political settlement that, to paraphrase Henry Kissinger, restored a shattered world.[5] But success was neither preordained nor easily achieved. Rather, notes one historian: "All of the thorny problems with which Western statesmen have wrestled during World War II, the Korean conflict, and the troubled history of NATO can be found, in hardly altered form, within the anti-Napoleonic coalition, a fact that suggests that certain problems are endemic to military alliances, which may or may not be comforting."[6] America's repeated reliance on formal and informal coalitions to prosecute its wars argues for a continuing effort better to understand those problems. Apart from intrinsic historical interest, that aim alone justifies revisiting the successful and remarkably durable final alliance against Napoleon.[7]

The Sixth Coalition's numerical designation tells a depressing story from the point of view of the nations that opposed Revolutionary

5 Henry A. Kissinger, *A World Restored* (New York, 1973).
6 Gordon A. Craig, "Problems of Coalition Warfare: The Military Alliance against Napoleon, 1813–1814," US Air Force Academy: USAFA Harmon Memorial Lecture #7, 1965 (www.usafa.edu/df/dfh/docs/Harmon07.pdf), p. 1. This superb lecture should be mandatory reading for anyone interested in the subject.
7 So much has been written about the Napoleonic wars in English alone, never mind other languages, that a topical essayist's preeminent narrative challenge is simply to summarize relevant events comprehensibly. Readers interested in examining the War of the Sixth Coalition in greater depth than offered here can choose from an abundance of sources. For alliance politics, one scarcely can do better than Kissinger's *A World Restored* and Harold Nicolson's *The Congress of Vienna* (London, 1946). Gregory Fremont-Barnes offers a readable short history of the campaigns of 1813–1815 in *The Napoleonic Wars*, IV: *The Fall of the French Empire 1813–1815* (London, 2002). A much more detailed examination of the Allied invasion of France itself is Michael V. Leggiere's *The Fall of Napoleon* (Cambridge, 2007), vol. I. Rory Muir's *Britain and the Defeat of Napoleon 1807–1815* (New Haven, CT, 1996) is a pleasure to read and uniformly insightful. And of course, David G. Chandler's *The Campaigns of Napoleon* (London, 1966) remains perhaps the definitive history of Napoleon's military operations.

France from 1792 to 1812.[8] During that twenty-year span, five successive coalitions foundered on the rocks of French nationalism and Bonaparte's incandescent military genius. Throughout, only Great Britain remained undefeated and undaunted, protected by the Channel and the matchless Royal Navy, but compelled to watch in impotent dismay as one British-subsidized coalition after another collapsed in military defeat or political exhaustion, and as French hegemony expanded across the European continent. The toll of French victories tells the tale: Marengo, Ulm, Austerlitz, Jena-Auerstädt, Friedland, Wagram – over a decade of nearly unbroken triumph on land over every power daring to challenge French military prowess. Only at sea, and against France's colonies and those of allies Holland and Spain, could Britain claim limited success. But while naval and colonial defeats might annoy Bonaparte, they did little to weaken his grip on the European mainland. As one British First Lord of Admiralty complained to his Cabinet colleagues in 1806, "While we are acquiring colonies, the enemy is subjugating the Continent."[9]

It was Bonaparte's own unbridled ambition that finally began to shake that grip. In 1808, his armies invaded France's former ally Spain, deposed and imprisoned its Bourbon rulers, and enthroned Napoleon's elder brother Joseph in their place. Expecting a still largely feudal nation rent by internal schism to welcome more enlightened French rule, Napoleon instead found his invading forces embroiled in bitter hybrid warfare, assailed simultaneously by rarely victorious but nevertheless irrepressible regular Spanish armies, the proliferating irregular partisans who endowed military history with the term "guerilla," and increasingly capable Anglo-Portuguese forces led by an aristocratic Anglo-Irish general named Arthur Wellesley who, if he lacked Napoleon's operational brilliance, more than compensated with cold-blooded calculation and iron determination.[10]

---

8 Historians differ in the way they name anti-French coalitions, the first of which formed in 1792 and the second in 1798, both in response to the French Revolution. Because the Peace of Amiens briefly intervened between these two and their successors, and because Bonaparte declared himself emperor only thereafter, some (principally British) historians denote as the Fourth Coalition what most call the Sixth. Similarly, some writers attribute to a Seventh Coalition operations from Bonaparte's escape from Elba in March, 1815 through the second Treaty of Paris following his defeat at Waterloo and second abdication. Inasmuch as its membership differed little from that of the Sixth, this chapter ignores that distinction.

9 A. D. Harvey, *Collision of Empires: Britain in Three World Wars, 1793–1945* (London, 1992), p. 25

10 For a brief account of the Peninsular War, see the author's "That Accursed Spanish War," in Williamson Murray and Peter R. Mansoor (eds.), *Hybrid Warfare: Fighting Complex Opponents from the Ancient World to the Present* (Cambridge, 2012), pp. 104–50.

During the next four years, battle raged throughout the Iberian Peninsula, neither side able to secure a decisive advantage in what Bonaparte began calling his "Spanish ulcer." Meanwhile, in January 1812, to punish Sweden for its failure to enforce his economic blockade against Britain, the so-called "continental system," and anticipating renewed war with a similarly uncooperative Russia, Bonaparte invaded Swedish Pomerania, confiscating Swedish estates and occupying key cities. In response, Sweden's Prince Bernadotte, himself a former French field marshal, declared Sweden neutral with respect to Britain and France, simultaneously opening negotiations with Russia's Tsar Alexander to repair relations ruptured by their war of 1808–1809 and Russia's resulting annexation of Finland. On 5 April 1812 the two sovereigns signed a secret treaty at St. Petersburg reconciling their differences and committing themselves to oppose France and its ally, Denmark-Norway. Although it helped to midwife the agreement, Britain refused to subsidize the new allies with money and arms unless and until they committed themselves openly against Napoleon.[11] That moment was not long in coming. On 23 June 1812, Bonaparte crossed the River Niemen from Poland into Russia with an army of more than half a million men.[12] One month later, the Treaties of Orebro formally ended hostilities between Britain and both Sweden and Russia, opening the floodgates of British financial and material support.[13]

In Russia itself, while the main French army under Napoleon headed for Moscow, a separate wing commanded by Marshal Jacques MacDonald and composed heavily of Prussian auxiliaries moved against the Baltic port city of Riga. Unable to breach the city's defenses, and learning of Alexander's stubborn refusal to capitulate and Bonaparte's subsequent retreat, MacDonald likewise retired, assigning his Prussian contingent under General Ludwig Yorck to cover his withdrawal. Instead, Yorck's Russian opposite number, General Hans von Diebitsch, persuaded him to agree to an armistice.[14] Although quickly repudiated by Prussia's weak-willed King Frederick William, who feared Napoleon's wrath, the Convention of Tauroggen, as it became known,

---

11 For the British government, lending assistance to Russia presented domestic political problems stemming from lingering liberal anger at Alexander's 1808 annexation of Finland. Only outright Russian opposition to Napoleon promised to overcome it.

12 The army included 20,000-odd troops withdrawn from Spain, further straining an already overburdened occupation.

13 The Foreign Office, *British and Foreign State Papers 1812–1814* (London, 1841), vol. I, pp. 13–17.

14 Aided by then-Colonel Carl von Clausewitz, who had resigned from the Prussian army to take up arms with its enemy when Prussia's King Frederick William agreed to join in the invasion of Russia in spring 1812.

unleashed a long-building wave of Prussian nationalism and anti-French revanchism that the king ultimately dared not resist.[15] Accordingly, in February 1813, after further negotiation between the two former allies-turned-enemies, the Treaty of Kalisch once again united them. The Sixth Coalition thus fairly could be said to have germinated in the insubordination of a previously obscure Prussian general.

But while the Kalisch Agreement helped launch the Sixth Coalition, it also sowed the seeds of eventual allied disaffection. The problem was Poland, partitioned since 1795 among Prussia, Russia, and Austria, until Napoleon defeated all three and erected the Duchy of Warsaw as a satellite state in nominal union with the Kingdom of Saxony. At Kalisch, Prussia agreed to cede to Russia all claims to Poland apart from Silesia in return for Prussian annexation of Saxony and parts of the Rhineland. Implemented as agreed – which of course presumed Bonaparte's expulsion from Germany – Kalisch thus would extend Russian power well to the west and Prussia's well to the south, both at the expense of Hapsburg Austria. No strategic knot ultimately would prove harder for the allies to untie.

The first crisis: Lützen and Bautzen

On 14 December 1812, fewer than 25,000 tattered survivors of Bonaparte's *Grande Armée* escaped Russian territory hours ahead of their vengeful pursuers. The magnitude of the disaster and its revelation of Napoleon's vulnerability shook chancelleries throughout Europe. Nevertheless, as 1813 dawned, it was far from clear that Bonaparte's strategic position was irredeemable. Returning to Paris in haste after temporarily delegating command of his remaining forces in Eastern Europe to Marshal Joachim Murat, he immediately began creating a new *Grande Armée*. With Russia's generals reluctant to venture beyond their own frontiers, Prussia's reviving military capabilities still to be tested, Sweden's commitment to offensive operations uncertain, and Britain's renewed support conditional on convincing evidence of allied military commitment, whether the new coalition would be any more enduring than its predecessors remained to be seen.

Considered solely in terms of the force balance in Eastern Europe, Bonaparte's position at the beginning of 1813 certainly was perilous.

---

15 Notes Fremont-Barnes, "For Prussia and for a number of other German states, this new struggle was to have an ideological component which had been absent from her war of 1806–1807: the campaign of 1813 was to become known by its patriotic title: the 'War of German Liberation.'" Gregory Fremont-Barnes, *The Napoleonic Wars*, IV, p. 8.

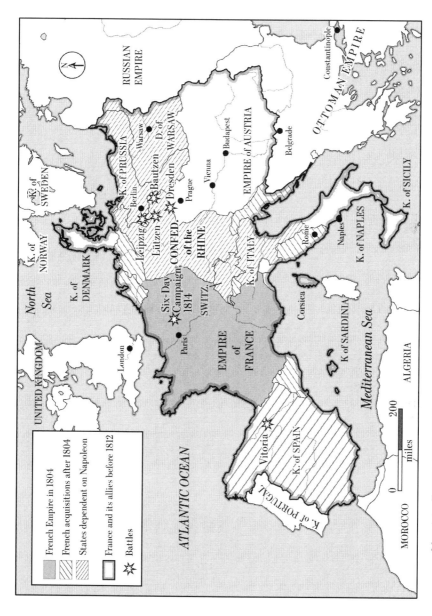

Map 4.1 Europe, 1813–1814

Apart from the exhausted survivors of the Russian campaign, French troops east of the Rhine were scattered in garrisons along a 700-mile front from the Baltic to Bavaria. Ordered by Napoleon to hold the line of the Vistula, Murat could not even begin to comply. Instead, leaving a substantial garrison at Danzig and smaller contingents at the northern Polish towns of Thorn and Modlin, Murat evacuated Warsaw and withdrew toward Posen, today's Poznan, upon reaching which he shamefully abandoned his responsibilities to his second-in-command, Prince Eugène de Beauharnais,[16] and decamped to his throne in Naples.[17] On 7 February 1813, Marshal Michael Kutusov's Russians entered Warsaw unopposed.

Eugène's tactical situation was of course no improvement on Murat's. Grudgingly acknowledging reality, Bonaparte authorized him to withdraw to the Oder, but even that river proved indefensible. By the time Eugène reached Frankfurt and linked up with additional French troops under Marshal Gouvion St. Cyr, Russian forces already had forced the Oder to his north. He therefore retired further to the Elbe at Wittenberg, only to conclude that the northern Elbe similarly was too long to defend with the troops available. Accordingly, on 12 March he ordered Hamburg evacuated. A week later, with Berlin now secure, Prussia fulfilled the terms of the Kalisch agreement and declared war on France.

Prussia's defection enlarged the forces immediately available to the allies to nearly 150,000, including 28,000 Swedes under Bernadotte in Pomerania and 9,000 Anglo-Hanoverians in nearby Stralsund. With fewer than 40,000 disposable troops of his own,[18] Eugène was at a massive numerical disadvantage; and although he managed to check Marshal Peter Wittgenstein's advancing Russians at Möckern on 3 April, he could not prevent them from linking up with Blücher's Prussians at Dresden.[19] Until the French could organize, equip, and deploy the fresh levies Bonaparte was frantically raising, the French could not hope to recover the Elbe. Instead, following the engagement at Möckern, Eugène withdrew to the Saale 50 miles further west, which promised a defensible position.

16 Napoleon's stepson by Josephine, and among his better commanders.
17 On which he had been installed by Napoleon in 1808. Bonaparte's reaction to his great cavalry commander's shirking was to complain bitterly to his sister Caroline, Murat's wife, that "Your husband is very brave on the battlefield, but weaker than a woman or a monk when out of sight of the enemy." Robert Harvey, *The War of Wars* (Basic Books, 2006), p. 822.
18 As noted earlier, additional French forces were present in the theater, but were isolated in garrisons bypassed by the advancing Russian armies.
19 Wittgenstein was chosen to succeed Kutusov when the latter, age 67, fell ill (he died on 28 April).

Even so, a concerted allied offensive at that point might well have brushed Eugène aside and penetrated all the way to the Rhine. But the allies' superiority was more apparent than real, for they too labored under significant difficulties. For the Russians' part, in seeing the French off Russian soil, Alexander's troops and "General Winter" had effectively destroyed the *Grande Armée*, but at a price nearly as great as the French themselves had paid. Historians estimate that the Russian campaign killed or crippled as many as 300,000 Russian soldiers.[20] Reflecting those losses, and with their supply lines already extending hundreds of miles, Russian generals, including Kutusov, were not eager to carry the war deeper into Germany. Only the tsar's determination to avenge the burning of Moscow and his romantic ambition, fed by mentor and former Russian Foreign Minister Adam Czartoryski, to be hailed as Germany's liberator and the restorer of Polish nationhood induced them to do so.

Prussia similarly remained an uncertain quantity. Although Frederick William had promised at Kalisch to furnish 150,000 men to the combined Russo-Prussian effort, until the French fell back to the Elbe, uncovering Berlin, he had continued to dither, and when he finally declared war, fewer than 80,000 Prussian troops were available to take the field. Thanks to Gerhard Scharnhorst's *Krumpersystem*, that number soon would grow, but in the meantime, Prussia's troop contribution, though not its generals' enthusiasm, would be limited.[21] As for Sweden, no one knew how far Bernadotte's commitment would extend past recovering Pomerania and furthering his long-standing ambitions toward Denmark and Norway.

Finally, there was the problem of command-and-control. As the prime mover of the allied effort, initially its largest troop contributor, and with its reputation burnished by Bonaparte's expulsion from its soil – the first continental power to manage the feat – Russia could lay fair claim to leadership of the combined military effort. Even so, Kutusov's appointment as allied commander in chief was not undisputed even among his compatriots, and his death from illness only weeks into the campaign prompted additional confusion. While competent, his successor Wittgenstein was relatively junior. Resentment of his appointment by more senior Russian generals compelled Alexander to limit his authority and invited the tsar's repeated interference in operational matters. The Möckern engagement further undermined allied confidence in Wittgenstein, and while Eugène's

20 See, for instance, Chandler, *The Campaigns of Napoleon*, p. 853.
21 A method devised by Scharnhorst to circumvent the 42,000-troop limitation imposed on the Prussian army by the Treaty of Tilsit, by which recruits were cycled through the active force to furnish a growing pool of trained reserves.

subsequent withdrawal to the Saale enabled the Russian commander to claim a victory, it did little to encourage acceptance of his leadership, particularly among the Prussians, who had a more experienced candidate of their own in Marshal Gebhard Blücher. Accordingly, one history records, "Orders were often transmitted from headquarters to the armies by the monarchs [themselves], who also were prone to issuing threats to withdraw or redirect their contingents when it suited them."[22]

Given these problems, having driven the French from Poland and Lithuania and after largely liberated Prussia, the allies advanced cautiously. They soon were confirmed in that caution by Bonaparte, who had not been idle since reaching Paris. By recalling discharged veterans, expanding conscription, recalling more troops from Spain, and mobilizing national guardsmen and gendarmes – even French seamen left unemployed by Britain's blockade – Bonaparte succeeded by April 1813 in reconstituting a field army of some 200,000 men.[23] Through similarly heroic efforts, French foundries and manufactories managed to re-equip the new levies with everything from uniforms to artillery.[24] In only one respect did that prove impossible: there were no replacements available for the tens of thousands of horses lost or consumed in Russia's snows. Merely to remount the cavalry of the Imperial Guard forced Napoleon to disband several of his cherished Polish and Lithuanian cavalry regiments and to purloin additional cavalry from Spain.[25]

Nevertheless, with the arrival of spring, Bonaparte was ready to fight, and in early April he began deploying 120,000 fresh soldiers to the Main River. Together with Eugène's 58,000 men at the Saale, Marshal Louis-Nicholas Davout with 20,000 troops west of Hamburg, and 14,000 men under General Horace Sébastiani deployed along the lower Elbe, he now disposed of more than 200,000 effectives, outnumbering Wittgenstein's 56,000 Russians and Blücher's 37,000 Prussians combined. On 2 May, the armies collided outside the town of Lützen, 12 miles southwest of Leipzig. The fighting was intense, but by the end of the second day the allies were in full retreat. While the shortage of cavalry and his own heavy losses prevented Bonaparte from pursuing, Lützen was a powerful

---

22 J. P. Riley, *Napoleon and the World War of 1813: Lessons in Coalition Warfighting* (London, 2000), p. 121.

23 The withdrawals from Spain had a serious impact on Napoleon's brother Joseph's already overstretched French forces. See Sinnreich, "That Accursed Spanish War," pp. 135–36.

24 As the Marquis de Caulincourt, Napoleon's grand marshal and later foreign minister noted, "France is become one vast workshop." Armand-Augustin-Louis de Caulaincourt, *Memoirs* (London, 1950), vol. II, p. 345.

25 George Nafziger, *Lutzen & Bautzen: Napoleon's Spring Campaign of 1813* (Lakewood, OH, 1993), p. 9.

reminder that, even weakened, the emperor remained a dangerous and self-confident foe. On the following day, he detached Marshal Michel Ney with 85,000 men to regain the Elbe crossings at Torgau and Wittenberg in preparation for attacking Berlin to punish Frederick William for his betrayal, while he himself advanced with the rest of his troops toward Dresden.

Lützen shook the allies, who had accepted battle confident that their combined forces, even though outnumbered, would be more than a match for Napoleon's unblooded levies.[26] Ney's detachment, and the confidence it reflected and threat it presented to Berlin, shook them even more. Disputes accordingly arose, Russian generals urging retirement of the combined armies back to the Oder, while fears for Berlin urged the Prussians to recall their troops north. At that crucial moment, with the coalition's cohesion in the balance, Alexander's personal intervention saved the day. Forbidding his own army to withdraw further east than Bautzen on the River Spree, some 30 miles east of Dresden, he also convinced Frederick William to keep the bulk of the Prussian army in company, detaching only a single corps under General Friedrich von Bülow to cover Berlin.

Alexander's stubbornness probably preserved the coalition. Two weeks later, having finally located the allies' concentration at Bautzen, Napoleon recalled Ney and attacked. Forewarned, but outnumbered 115,000 to 96,000, the allies mounted a stubborn defense in the hills and villages on the banks of the Spree. Although eventually overwhelmed and forced to retreat, they were able by virtue of French tactical errors to escape envelopment and annihilation.[27] Not surprisingly given that failure, Bautzen cost Napoleon more dearly than his enemies, inflicting more than 20,000 French casualties. One can only speculate about what might have happened instead had Frederick William withdrawn the bulk of his army north after Lützen, leaving Wittgenstein's Russians to face Bonaparte alone.

26 The battle's ferocity and his enemies' stubbornness also shook Bonaparte, who remarked of his opponents, "These animals have learned something." Alastair Horne, *How Far From Austerlitz?* (London, 1998), p. 334. Among Lützen's other costs was the loss of Marshal Jean-Baptiste Bessières, killed during a reconnaissance. For their part, the Prussians mourned the loss of General Gerhard von Scharnhorst, Blücher's chief of staff and a prime mover of the Prussian army's post-Jena revival. Blücher himself was wounded and command of Prussia's troops assumed temporarily by Yorck.
27 Notes Fremont-Barnes, "With marshals constantly shifted from command of one corps to another and corps changing in composition as circumstances seemed to require … errors were inevitable, and at no time in [Bonaparte's] military career were those errors as glaring as in 1813–15." Fremont-Barnes, *The Napoleonic Wars*, IV, p. 9.

After two defeats in a row, however, even Alexander could not prevent the allied armies from recoiling across the Oder into Silesia; but once again, his own losses and lack of cavalry prevented Bonaparte from mounting a vigorous pursuit. Meanwhile, as it had after Lützen, defeat prompted renewed inter-allied disputes, this time focused on Wittgenstein's generalship. When the retreating allies reached the Polish fortress of Schweidnitz, 30 miles southwest of Breslau, Wittgenstein resigned in favor of the more experienced Barclay de Tolly. However, friction with Prussian generals, particularly Blücher, persisted. When at last Napoleon was able to resume his advance, the allies suffered two further setbacks, Davout reoccupying Hamburg and the emperor himself retaking Breslau on 1 June. Only Bülow's defeat of Marshal Nicolas Oudinot at Luckau on 6 June, assuring the continued safety of Berlin, convinced the Prussians to remain united with their allies.

After Bautzen, it was evident to both Bonaparte and his adversaries that neither could continue the contest without reorganization and reconstitution. Accordingly, when on 2 June, Metternich on behalf of Austria proposed a 36-hour local ceasefire, followed on 4 June with the signing of a general armistice at Pläswitz, both sides were more than ready to accept. That neither expected the armistice to endure was apparent to all concerned.[28] Meanwhile, Prussia and Russia having demonstrated their resolve to the British government's satisfaction, on 14 and 15 June Britain formally joined the coalition in the Treaty of Reichenbach, promising subsidies of some £2 million in cash and materiel to the allied effort. For his part, Bonaparte used the respite to replenish his depleted regiments, calling forward additional levies from France and pulling together scattered detachments from the northern Elbe to Bavaria.

Interlude: Bonaparte versus Metternich

Whatever else they had or had not accomplished, allied operations during the spring of 1813 demonstrated that even a wounded Bonaparte remained more than a match for any single adversary or collection of adversaries lacking both a significant preponderance in forces and the politico-military leadership to make effective use of it. The key to both was Austria. Ruling over the polyglot remnant of a once-powerful

---

28 Many historians have wondered why Napoleon agreed to an armistice when, as one put it, "by a final effort, he could certainly have nipped the Fourth Coalition [sic] in the bud." Nicholson, *The Congress of Vienna*, p. 34. He himself wrote at the time that "Two considerations have made up my mind; my shortage of cavalry, which prevents me from striking great blows, and the hostile attitude of Austria." Chandler, *The Campaigns of Napoleon*, p. 898.

Hapsburg Empire, and having unsuccessfully tried conclusions with Napoleon at Marengo, Ulm, Austerlitz, and Wagram, Austria's Francis I had at last bowed to circumstance, and in March 1810 allied Austria to France, marrying his daughter Marie-Louise to Bonaparte. In consequence of that alliance, and relying more heavily on Hapsburg familial loyalties than events were to prove wise, Napoleon permitted Austria to rebuild its army. With both sides momentarily deadlocked after Bautzen, the moment had come when that army could tip the strategic balance.

Austria's fortunes, however, were in the grip of one of the more enigmatic and controversial figures of the early nineteenth century. Clemens von Metternich had assumed the office of Austrian foreign minister in October 1809 following Austria's defeat in the Battle of Wagram. Described by Henry Kissinger as a "rococo figure," the man who eventually would become both celebrated and vilified as the "prime minister of Europe" was a master manipulator, of whom Napoleon once allegedly commented that "he confused policy with intrigue."[29] Convinced that Austria could not afford another contest with Bonaparte (and, in the view of some detractors, privately Bonaparte's reluctant but compulsive admirer), Metternich had engineered Napoleon's marriage to Marie-Louise, Francis's eldest child.[30] Playing on the confidence engendered by that dynastic alliance, he convinced Napoleon to allow the defeated Austrian army to retain an active force of 150,000, more than three times the number permitted the Prussians after Tilsit. Then, when Bonaparte launched his fatal lunge into Russia, in addition to furnishing an auxiliary corps operating under French command, but that managed through skillful maneuver to avoid serious losses, Metternich convinced Napoleon to authorize raising an additional Austrian "corps of observation," carefully ensuring, however, that the troops in question never left Austria.[31]

The French disaster in Russia shocked Metternich, but also presented him with both an opportunity and a dilemma. Bonaparte's weakness offered Austria the chance to regain strategic flexibility, but how to exploit that flexibility safely remained unclear. Almost certainly aware of and concerned by the Kalisch agreement, Metternich considered an unrestrained Alexander to be potentially as dangerous to the restoration of a Central European balance, and hence to Austria, as an unrestrained

29 Kissinger, *A World Restored*, p. 11.
30 "Metternich, in his momentary role of continental mediator, preferred in his heart of hearts the discipline and order of the Napoleonic system to the liberalism of the British, the sentimental intuitions of Alexander, or the rabid German nationalism of the Tugendbund and Stein." Nicholson, *The Congress of Vienna*, p. 58.
31 The Austrians achieved this maneuver by secretly arranging for the Russians to deploy a military presence in Galicia sufficient to justify the corps' immobility.

Bonaparte. "Everything depended, therefore, not only on the defeat of Napoleon but on the manner in which it was achieved, not only on the creation of a coalition but also on the principle in the name of which it was to fight."[32] For Metternich, the only such principle that would safeguard Hapsburg Austria was sovereign legitimacy, and he remained convinced that its expression required restoring the Central European territorial *status quo ante Napoleon*. The challenge was how to bring that about.

What followed was a delicate diplomatic ballet in which Metternich first convinced Bonaparte to allow him to mediate with the allies with a view to achieving a general peace, in effect repositioning Austria from ally to neutral; then used Napoleon's own intransigence to justify shifting from neutrality into an outright reversal of allegiance.[33] Along the way, with the connivance of the Russians, Metternich managed to redeploy Austrian Marshal Karl Philip von Schwarzenberg's auxiliary corps southward toward Cracow. Together with its corps of observation, the result was to give Austria the largest undamaged army in the theater, while also removing Austrian forces from the Russian army's path into Germany.

Examining these events in hindsight, the mystery is why Napoleon allowed Austria so easily to regain its military strength and political freedom of action. The answer lay partly in Bonaparte's military weakness after his Russian debacle, and partly in his overconfidence in the adhesive power of his marriage to Marie-Louise.[34] Both induced him to indulge Austria in the expectation that, when fighting resumed, he could persuade or intimidate Francis into contributing Austria's undiluted military strength to a renewed campaign against Russia and Prussia. That the allies cherished precisely the obverse hope is a fair measure of how successfully Metternich maneuvered between the two contestants, neither of which, still less Britain, believed for a moment in the possibility of a negotiated peace leaving Napoleon in power, an aim toward which Metternich had directed his diplomacy.

There remained the task of completing Austria's shift from armed mediator to outright belligerent. On 19 June Metternich met with the tsar at Opotschna, and a week later, Austria and the allies signed the

---

32 Kissinger, *A World Restored*, p. 25.
33 Metternich's justification was aimed at Francis as well as the world at large. Notes Kissinger, "Austria, united to France by marriage and by a treaty signed with the appearance of freedom, could not simply change sides without offending the dignity of its ruler. Austria's task must be to regain its freedom with the consent of Napoleon, to *be released from its bonds by France itself*." Kissinger, *A World Restored*, p. 50.
34 "Why was [Napoleon] not certain of a treachery which was so evidently predetermined? It was simply because he never believed that the Emperor of Austria would proceed to extremities against the husband of his daughter." Col. G. B. Malleson, C.S.I., *Life of Prince Metternich* (London, 1888), p. 106.

Reichenbach Convention, by which Austria agree to join the coalition if, within a month, Napoleon refused to accept four conditions preliminary to convening a formal peace congress at Prague.[35] These were the dissolution of the Duchy of Warsaw, return of Prussian territory surrendered at Tilsit, return of Illyria to Austria, and restoration of the independence of the Hanseatic cities of Hamburg, Lübeck, Bremen, and Danzig.[36]

Those conditions by no means satisfied all the allies, least of all Britain, whose maritime concerns, opposition to French control of Antwerp, and alliance with Spain they entirely neglected.[37] Nor did they satisfy Prussian and Russian territorial ambitions. But Metternich reminded the allies that the conditions were merely preliminary: accepted, they promised nothing more than a further negotiation to settle the terms of a permanent peace. In effect, they would require Bonaparte to divest himself of his German conquests merely to obtain the privilege of negotiating with the powers that he had just twice defeated. Hence it was scarcely surprising that Metternich urged them on the allies confident that Bonaparte would refuse them. More important, as he had earlier warned his chief negotiator, Count Johann Stadion, Francis would never take Austria to war once again unless first shown that Napoleon would refuse even such moderate terms.[38]

There followed on 26 June the famous meeting already described between the emperor of the French and Austria's master manipulator, beginning, according to the former, with Bonaparte challenging Metternich's good faith, and ending, according to the latter, with his parting declaration, "Sire, you are lost," but with an agreement to resume negotiations at Prague. Two weeks later, on 7 July, news of Wellington's defeat of Joseph Bonaparte at Vitoria having reached the allies, Bernadotte finally agreed to postpone invading Denmark in favor of combined operations in north Germany. On 12 August, the peace congress at Prague never really having met, Austria formally declared war on France. And with the subsequent signing on 9 September of the Treaty of Teplitz, the Sixth Coalition was at last complete.

---

35 Opotschna is currently Opočno in the Czech Republic, 120 miles southeast of Dresden.
36 Illyria is today's Slovenia.
37 The problem went a good deal deeper. Britain's *bête noire* was Bonaparte himself, whose removal it viewed as essential, while for Austria, as noted earlier, a vacuum in Central Europe threatened to replace French with Russian domination. Metternich thus was careful to exclude British diplomats from the Reichenbach negotiations.
38 Kissinger, p. *A World Restored*, p. 75. He later writes (p. 80) that Francis "entered what came to be known as the 'War of Liberation' with all the resolution of a shopkeeper defending himself against a competitor who cannot be brought to see that splitting up the market is the best insurance for mutual harmony."

Dresden to Leipzig

Now the question was, how should the coalition apply its combined military strength and under whose direction? When allied operations resumed on 13 August 1813 that strength was divided among four separate armies: Bernadotte's 110,000 Prussians and Swedes near Berlin; Blücher's 95,000 Prussians and Russians south of Breslau; Schwarzenberg's 230,000 Austrians near the upper Elbe; and an additional 60,000 Russians under General Count Levin von Bennigsen still in the process of forming in Poland. The question was who would command this vast and dispersed assemblage?

Nominally, the answer could only be Schwarzenberg. As Metternich famously argued, "The power that puts 300,000 men in the field is the first power, all the others only auxiliaries."[39] Just as by default Metternich had become the coalition's sole interlocutor with Bonaparte, so Schwarzenberg, by virtue of the Austrian army's size and location, was the obvious commander in chief. In one distinguished military historian's view, he was "far from the ideal supreme commander, lacking confidence and tending to be over-cautious."[40] But no candidate more acceptable to all the allies presented himself. In any case, afflicted with the presence of three monarchs and their advisers at his headquarters, Schwarzenberg was anything but a free agent. "Life at General Headquarters was one continual war council, in which all of these royal advisers subjected operational plans to niggling criticism or proposed substitutes of their own." The constant bickering led Schwarzenberg to complain bitterly, "It really is inhuman what I must tolerate, surrounded as I am by feeble-minded people, fools of every description, eccentric project makers, intriguers, asses, babblers, criticasters; I often think I'm going to collapse under their weight."[41]

In part reflecting that internal dissension, the plan of operations eventually agreed by the allies reflected caution bordering on timidity. Lützen

---

39 Michael V. Leggiere, *Napoleon and Berlin: The Franco-Prussian War in North Germany, 1813* (Norman, OK, 2002), p. 128.

40 Chandler, *The Campaigns of Napoleon*, p. 901. Notes Craig, "The new supreme commander's talents were, to be sure, more diplomatic than strictly military, and it was probably a good thing that this was so. Like Dwight D. Eisenhower in another great coalition a hundred and thirty years later, his great gift was his ability, by patience and the arts of ingratiation, to hold together a military alliance which before Napoleon was finally defeated comprised fourteen members, and to persuade the quarrelling monarchs and their field commanders to give more than lip service to the alliance's strategical plan." Alexander preferred Archduke Charles, victor at Aspern-Essling, but Metternich considered him too likely to bend to the tsar. Craig, "Problems of Coalition Warfare," p. 3.

41 Craig, "Problems of Coalition Warfare," p. 4.

and Bautzen had confirmed the continued danger of confronting Bonaparte in a pitched battle on his own ground. Instead, the allies adopted what became known as the Trachenberg plan.[42] In mute acknowledgment of Bonaparte's continued moral dominance, they agreed that, until attrition could dissipate the emperor's strength, they would engage only detached French forces, avoiding a decisive battle with Bonaparte himself. As Schwarzenberg reportedly put it, "When these losses have sufficiently weakened the enemy, we will be able to push him back from the Elbe and against the Saale and here, possibly in the area of Leipzig, we can offer him battle with our united forces and fate will take care of the rest."[43]

He turned out to be remarkably prescient. Instead of concentrating on what Clausewitz later would call the center-of-gravity of the coalition – Schwarzenberg's Austro-Russian forces in southern Poland (possibly because he still cherished hope of recovering Austria's allegiance) – Napoleon divided his 700,000 troops into two wings, deploying the larger in defensive positions in the vicinity of Dresden, while launching the smaller under Oudinot northward toward Berlin. Then he uncharacteristically dithered, first ordering an attack against Blücher, whom he feared was about to receive reinforcements; then changing his mind and ordering an attack against Wittgenstein's Russian reinforcements; then, learning that Blücher was advancing against his flank, reverting to his earlier intention and massing against the Prussians, who, in accordance with the Trachenberg plan, immediately backpedaled. Meanwhile, with Napoleon thus preoccupied, Schwarzenberg launched his Army of Bohemia at Dresden, momentarily defended only by St. Cyr's corps.

Learning of Schwarzenberg's advance, Napoleon left MacDonald with 100,000 men to deal with Blücher and prepared to envelop the allied force, only to learn of Oudinot's defeat by Bernadotte at Grossbeeren on 23 August. With St. Cyr about to collapse, there was no further time for clever maneuver, and leaving 30,000-odd troops under General Dominique-Joseph Vandamme to cover his flank, Bonaparte countermarched his remaining 70,000 to St. Cyr's relief. The threat of his arrival prompted another debate among allied leaders.[44] This time, however, it

---

42 So-called because it was devised at Trachenberg Castle, 40 miles north of Breslau, where the allied sovereigns had assembled in late July to consider whether to extend the Pläswitz armistice into August.

43 Digby Smith, *1813 Leipzig: Napoleon and the Battle of the Nations* (Barnsley, UK, 2006), p. 13.

44 Writes Harold Nicolson, "Throughout the autumn campaign of 1813 the strategy of the allies was hampered by uncertainty of purpose and division of counsel." Nicolson, *The Congress of Vienna*, p. 49.

was the tsar who argued for breaking off the offensive and retiring in accordance with the Trachenberg plan, while Prussia's normally timid Frederick William, egged on by his generals, urged exploiting the allies' still significant numerical superiority. The debate dragged on through the morning of 26 August, and while Schwarzenberg was ordered to suspend operations until it could be resolved, by the time the orders reached him, the allied attack already had begun.

It had been delayed, however, just long enough for Bonaparte to reinforce St. Cyr, and for the rest of the day, the allies battered fruitlessly against well-prepared French defenses, until late in the afternoon, when, sensing their exhaustion, Bonaparte counterattacked, regaining nearly all the ground lost during the day. Then, on the following morning, after a rain-drenched night during which Murat arrived with another 50,000 men, Napoleon managed to turn the allies' left; and with a significant part of their army trapped by the flooded Weisseritz River, and a French cannonball having nearly decapitated Alexander, the allies hastily abandoned the field and sought the protection of Bohemia's mountains.

Dresden cost the allies 38,000 casualties to Napoleon's 10,000, but Bonaparte once more lacked the wherewithal to exploit his success. Meanwhile, allied morale was at least partly restored by Blücher's defeat of MacDonald on 28 August.[45] Vandamme's virtual annihilation by combined Prussian and Russian forces at Kulm two days later further encouraged the allies, both successes enabling Schwarzenberg to retire undisturbed. To complete Bonaparte's discomfiture, a week later Ney, who had resumed the march on Berlin after Oudinot's defeat, blundered into a meeting engagement with Bernadotte's Prussians near the village of Dennewitz.[46] After a back-and-forth fight, Swedish reinforcements arrived to envelop Ney, routing him with a loss of 10,000 men. Together, these defeats largely offset the Battle of Dresden's moral and material damage. Instead, "Dresden joined Lützen and Bautzen on the growing list of practically valueless French victories."[47]

While these events were occurring in Central Europe, Wellington had not been idle in Spain. Furious at Joseph's defeat at Vitoria, Napoleon stripped both him and his principal subordinate, Marshal Jean-Baptiste Jourdan, of their positions and replaced them with Marshal Nicolas

---

45 Ignoring Bonaparte's instructions not to pursue Blücher beyond the River Bober, MacDonald allowed himself to be trapped on the far side of the Katzbach River and defeated in detail, suffering more than 15,000 casualties to Blücher's 4,000 and losing a third of his precious artillery.

46 Once again, resulting in large measure from the French lack of sufficient cavalry with which to reconnoiter.

47 Chandler, *The Campaigns of Napoleon*, p. 912.

Soult (in the process depriving his own army of one of its most reliable commanders). Soult immediately counterattacked Wellington, but in a series of battles from 25 July through 2 August, known collectively as the Battle of the Pyrenees, was soundly defeated, escaping across the French frontier with fewer than 50,000 effectives out of an army that once had counted more than five times that number.

While Wellington's success contributed an undeniable boost to allied morale, of more immediate importance to the allies were Britain's financial and material contributions to their own efforts. During the remainder of 1813 and into 1814, Britain supplied its allies with hundreds of cannon, tens of thousands of small arms, millions of rounds of ammunition, and supplies and equipment ranging from uniforms to rations – including some 28,000 gallons of brandy and rum – along with financial subsidies exceeding £11 million.[48] Not until World War II would a single nation once again contribute so overwhelmingly to its allies' material ability to wage war.

The Battle of the Nations

By the beginning of September, allied operations had had Schwarzenberg's desired effect of seriously depleting Napoleon's effective strength. Between battle losses and mounting desertions, French forces had been reduced during the previous two months by more than 200,000 troops, while supplies of food and ammunition were becoming critically short. During the next two weeks, Napoleon's frustrations mounted as the allied armies repeatedly lunged, then withdrew, forcing the French into a tiring and pointless series of marches and countermarches. "The Allied strategy of refusing to fight the Emperor in person but of maintaining ceaseless pressure on his subordinates was clearly paying dividends. Its net result was to keep Napoleon off balance, as again and again he had been compelled to rush from one sector to another to reinforce his marshals."[49] Meanwhile, Bennigsen's 60,000-strong Army of Poland had finally finished its organization and soon would be available to reinforce Schwarzenberg, allowing him in turn to shift Blücher's Prussians north to reinforce Bernadotte's Swedes.

On 24 September Bonaparte finally acknowledged failure and withdrew all French field forces west of the Elbe, abandoning to their fate

---

48 Fremont-Barnes, *The Napoleonic Wars*, IV, p. 27. See also John M. Sherwig, *Guineas and Gunpowder: British Foreign Aid in the Wars with France, 1793–1815* (Cambridge, MA, 1969), pp. 309–14.
49 Chandler, *The Campaigns of Napoleon*, p. 915.

such garrisons as could not be relieved. Even as he did so, Bernadotte was crossing the Elbe in the north, and when augmented by Blücher, would be driving south with 140,000 men. Learning of that threat on 5 October and aware that Schwarzenberg was once again advancing on Leipzig, Napoleon left 45,000 men under Murat to cover the city and moved the rest of his army north with a view to defeating Bernadotte and Blücher before the allied armies could converge. But the allies once again frustrated that effort by withdrawing west to the Saale; and with Schwarzenberg approaching Leipzig from the south with 180,000 troops and Bennigsen with 60,000 more from the east, Napoleon could no longer avoid battle with the combined allied armies.

The Battle of Leipzig began on 16 October.[50] Involving more than 600,000 men on both sides, it was the largest battle fought on European soil prior to World War I. After a day of bloody but inconclusive combat followed by a day-long pause, it climaxed on 18 October in six massive allied attacks by more than 300,000 troops supported by nearly 1,500 guns. The battle raged in Leipzig's eastern suburbs throughout the day and into the following morning. By noon on 19 October, Allied forces had driven the French back into the city itself, from which they were evacuating when premature demolition of the only bridge over the Elster River trapped 20,000 men of the French rear guard. Bonaparte's Italian and German contingents promptly deserted to the allies, joining the Saxons and Würtembergers, who had already turned their coats; and while the remaining French and Polish troops fought desperately, they soon were overwhelmed. On 20 October the allied sovereigns marched triumphantly into the city. The battle had cost Bonaparte 70,000 men with nearly all their equipment and supplies. It left him little alternative but to retreat to the Rhine, where reinforcement and resupply awaited.

Leipzig's political fallout exceeded even its military costs. Bavaria had already defected from Napoleon's Confederation of the Rhine. Now Saxony followed, with other German states not far behind.[51] Meanwhile, on 7 October, Wellington crossed the Bidassoa River into France, ending what Bonaparte had called "that accursed Spanish war." To cap matters off, in January 1814, Murat would defect to the allies on their promise that he would be allowed to keep his Neapolitan throne provided

50 Actually several battles, among them Markkleeberg, Liebertwolkwitz, and Möckern on 16 October, what amounted to a pause on 17 October, the battle of the suburbs on 18 October, and the final assault on Leipzig and French retreat on 19 October.
51 Its king, Frederick Augustus, formerly the Elector of Saxony, having changed sides too late, was imprisoned in Berlin and his former domain occupied by Russia and governed *pro tem* by a Russian general. He was later restored to the throne of a much reduced rump state.

that he furnish 30,000 troops to Austrian operations in Italy. In short, as J. F. C. Fuller commented, defeat at Leipzig accomplished on land what Trafalgar had achieved at sea: it robbed Napoleon of any further strategic initiative.[52]

That, however, did not mean that the strategic initiative automatically reverted to the allies. On their side, Leipzig had been marked by the same bickering and political interference with tactical operations that had characterized the campaign from the outset. Now, with Bonaparte decisively defeated, the squabbling among sovereigns and generals intensified. At an allied council of war on the morning of the 19 October, Alexander, dissatisfied as usual with Schwarzenberg's performance, proposed that he himself should assume command of the combined armies with the assistance of a military council to advise him, a proposal to which, Metternich warned him, Austria would never consent. It was scarcely the first such intervention from a man whose emotionalism and excitability had become legendary. As Napoleon said of Alexander, "he had great abilities but 'something' was always missing in whatever he did. And since one could never foresee which particular piece would be missing in any given instance, he was totally unpredictable."[53]

At any rate, between the allies' internal disagreements and their own need to rest and refit after Leipzig's carnage, it was several days before they managed to mount an effective pursuit. By then Napoleon was well away. After pausing briefly to replenish his depleted logistics at Erfurt on 23 October, he directed his battered forces through Frankfurt toward Mainz, crossing the Rhine on 6 November after brushing aside General Karl Philipp von Wrede's 40,000 Austrians and Bavarians at Hanau on 30 and 31 October. Five days later, St. Cyr surrendered at Dresden, and the French were behind their own frontiers for the first time in two decades.

Interlude: Metternich and Castlereagh

The question now before the allies was whether to pursue the French across the Rhine into France itself. Once again, sovereigns and soldiers were at odds both among themselves and with each other. Russian troops far from home were eager to return to their native soil, their commanders little happier than they with Alexander's continued obsession to occupy Paris. Precisely the reverse disagreement afflicted the Prussians, whose sovereign shared little of his generals' burning hatred of the French, and

---

52 J. F. C. Fuller, *A Military History of the Western World* (Avon, CT, 1955), vol. II, p. 485.
53 Kissinger, *A World Restored*, p. 90

moreover could not quite shake the fear that, for all Bonaparte's apparent weakness, what the Corsican had done before, he might well do again. Bernadotte similarly preferred to turn his attention back to Denmark-Norway and, some suspected, cherished the secret hope that his native land might one day welcome him back in Napoleon's place.[54] As for Metternich, a France under the rule of a weakened Napoleon bound to Austria by marriage continued to offer the best assurance against replacement of France's domination of Central Europe with Russia's. Only Britain, Bonaparte's most remorseless foe, remained unbending in its conviction that British interests would never be secure while he remained in power. But Britain was represented in allied councils by emissaries who were no match for either Alexander's stubbornness or Metternich's cunning, and its concerns had thus far largely been ignored.[55]

Accordingly, when, in the first week of November, the French minister at Weimar, released from Russian captivity at Metternich's request, arrived at allied headquarters at Frankfurt, Metternich seized the opportunity to offer Napoleon still another chance to preserve his throne and, in the process, continue to furnish a strategic counterweight to both an unrestrained Russia and an over-ambitious Prussia. Peace with Napoleon might be possible, he suggested, with a France satisfied to remain within its "natural boundaries." Just what those would be was left somewhat ambiguous. They certainly would include the Rhine, the Alps, and the Pyrenees on the west and south, and Holland on the north. But the latter's southern boundary, as well as the status of Belgium, might be negotiable.

That offer, and the possibility that the war might end, not only with Bonaparte still in power, but also with Antwerp still in French hands, and without formal acknowledgment of Britain's "maritime rights," was enough to persuade Castlereagh to repair to allied headquarters himself, the first British foreign secretary to travel abroad.[56] By the time he arrived at allied headquarters, then at Basel, the immediate danger had passed. Stalling for time to reconstitute his depleted formations, Napoleon ignored Metternich's offer, proposing instead still another peace conference at Mannheim. That ploy failing, and the allies continuing to

---

54 Chandler, *The Campaigns of Napoleon*, p. 947.
55 General William Viscount Cathcart, ambassador to Russia, and after Austria's change of allegiance, the Earl of Aberdeen, ambassador to Austria, then only 29 years old.
56 Britain was chiefly concerned with the right to enforce a blockade by stopping and searching neutral as well as belligerent merchant vessels, which in large part precipitated the War of 1812 with the United States. For a contemporary British defense of the claim, see Sir Frederick Morton Eden, *Address on the Maritime Rights of Great Britain* (London, 1808).

advance, he authorized his new foreign minister, Armand Caulaincourt, to accept the Frankfurt proposals as a basis for negotiation. By then it was too late. With both Britain and Russia opposed for different reasons to Metternich's terms, the allies replied that negotiations could proceed only on the basis of a France restricted within her "ancient limits," excluding much of the Rhineland and the entirety of the Low Countries. On 22 December, even while these terms were being conveyed, the first Russian forces crossed the Rhine at Hunigen, and a week later, Blücher began crossing at Mannheim.

Even so, the entire episode had reconfirmed that the allies were by no means of one mind about what conditions would justify making peace. "The coalition had formed, but it was barely held together by the consciousness of a common danger. As the enemy was reduced in power, the centrifugal elements in the Alliance were becoming increasingly evident."[57] Only Napoleon's own stubbornness had prevented a situation that might and probably would have fractured the coalition at the moment when it seemed poised for success. In the next few weeks, that fragility would only become more apparent.

The second crisis: Châtillon and Chaumont

At the beginning of 1814, with the allies poised to invade France, though far from agreed on their ultimate aims, their military situation looked promising. In the north, positioned around Hamburg, Bernadotte commanded a combined force of more than 80,000 men, comprising contingents from Sweden, Britain, Prussia, Russia, and even 10,000 Dutch troops. From Silesia, Blücher was advancing with another 110,000 Prussians and Russians. The largest allied force, Schwartzenberg's 210,000-strong Austro-Russian Army of Bohemia, was poised to attack northwest out of Bavaria.[58] To oppose this massive three-pronged assault, Napoleon was disposed of fewer than 100,000 troops from the Belgian coast to Switzerland. Meanwhile, further south, Eugène struggled to defend northern Italy against Austrian General Heinrich Bellegarde and Napoleon's turncoat brother-in-law Joachim Murat, while Soult fought desperately to bar Wellington from Toulouse and the heart of southern France.

During the first few weeks of January, allied armies poured into France. In the north, Bülow's Prussians overran Belgium and marched

---

57 Kissinger, *A World Restored*, p. 105.
58 Numbers shown are approximate, since no two histories entirely agree on either the strengths of allied armies or their national compositions.

south. In the center, after forcing Marshal Auguste Marmont back on Metz, Blücher's Army of Silesia crossed the Meuse; while further south, confronted with Schwartzenberg's overwhelming strength, Marshal Claude Victor evacuated Strasbourg and Nancy without even attempting to fight. As Napoleon's military situation deteriorated, so too did his political position. Having returned Spain's deposed king to Madrid on the promise of peace, he could only watch in impotent fury as Ferdinand renounced the agreement the moment he found himself safely back on Spanish soil, precluding redeployment of any part of the French forces defending France's southern provinces. Murat's Kingdom of Naples formally joined the alliance on 11 January, similarly increasing the pressure on Eugène, followed three days later by Denmark. Meanwhile, in Paris, even Bonaparte's supporters were beginning secretly to talk among themselves of a Bourbon restoration.[59] Threatened as a result with a vote of no confidence by France's heretofore supine Chamber of Deputies, Napoleon promptly disbanded it.

That accomplished, on 25 January the emperor left Paris to assume personal command of his reconstituted forces. Using his interior lines and logistical freedom of action in a series of brilliant maneuvers during the second and third weeks of February, Napoleon attacked separate allied forces in turn, reminding them how he had achieved his reputation for military genius in the first place. While successful in slowing the allied advance, however, what became known as the Six-Day Campaign cost Bonaparte casualties and desertions that he could not replace, and his resources thus steadily dwindled.

Meanwhile, the allies once again were at loggerheads: Metternich pressing to reopen negotiations based on Bonaparte's belated agreement in principle with the Frankfurt proposals, Alexander determined to dictate peace terms from Paris, Prussia's generals hell-bent on vengeance, and Castlereagh unwilling to sanction any discussion that failed to deal with the status of Antwerp and Britain's maritime rights. But now the very military success that Austria's contribution had made possible eroded Metternich's power to manage events. "The result was one of those specious compromises by which coalitions maintain the façade of unity and obscure the fact that a shift in the balance within the alliance has occurred."[60] Negotiation would be reopened, but its

---

59 Among them Napoleon's erstwhile foreign minister Charles Maurice de Talleyrand, who thus managed without the slightest embarrassment to complete his extraordinary transformation from aristocrat and ordained bishop to defrocked revolutionary to Napoleonic foreign minister to, most astonishingly, foreign minister of Louis XVIII.
60 Kissinger, *A World Restored*, p 118. Comparison with the similar shift among the allies at Yalta 130 years later is unavoidable.

terms would remain undefined. In the meantime, offensive operations would continue.

The Congress of Châtillon began on 3 February and was doomed from the outset, as much by Bonaparte's intransigence as by the allies' disunity. On 7 February the latter renewed their offer of a peace restoring France to its "ancient limits," terms provisionally accepted by Caulaincourt on 9 February, but immediately rebuffed by Bonaparte, to whom Caulaincourt was obliged to refer them. The allies in any case could not agree among themselves on whether to accept Caulaincourt's acceptance, the tsar in particular demanding that it be ignored altogether on the grounds that the road to Paris lay open. His intransigence nearly fractured the alliance. In what history knows as the "Crisis of Troyes," Metternich demanded that his allies spell out what they would accept as a basis for peace. When the tsar replied that Bonaparte must be deposed and France ruled by a Russian general pending a decision on its future governance by an "assembly of notables," and subsequently implied that he might support Bernadotte's unspoken desire for the French throne, Metternich threatened to withdraw Austrian troops from further operations and conclude a separate peace. To forestall that disaster, and convinced that Alexander's solution would incite prolonged civil war in France, Castlereagh remonstrated with the tsar, for the first time aligning himself with Metternich and Britain with Austria.

In the event, "the Coalition was saved, not by Castlereagh, nor by Metternich, but by Napoleon."[61] At the very moment when dissolution threatened, Bonaparte launched his Six-Day Campaign, which precipitated immediate allied panic. Recorded Prussian chancellor Karl von Hardenberg in his diary: "The Czar has gone to pieces and the King [Frederick William] talks all the time like Cassandra."[62] Now it was Alexander's turn to propose an armistice, but Castlereagh insisted that the allies conduct negotiations and operations concurrently. Meanwhile, success had only emboldened Napoleon; and when on 17 February the allies once more offered peace based on the "ancient limits" formula, he angrily rejected the proposed terms and insisted on France's "natural frontiers." With that final rejection, Napoleon sealed his fate.

On 1 March the allied advance resumed. On the 9 March, Blücher defeated the French at Laon. On that same day, the allies signed the Treaty of Chaumont, by which the four major powers pledged "not to treat separately with the common Enemy, nor to sign Peace, Truce, nor Convention, but with common consent. They, moreover, engage not to

---

61 Muir, *Britain and the Defeat of Napoleon*, p. 316.
62 Nicolson, *The Congress of Vienna*, p. 79.

lay down their Arms until the object of the War, mutually understood and agreed upon, shall have been attained," further agreeing "to concert together, on the conclusion of a peace with France, as to the means best adapted to guarantee to Europe, and to themselves reciprocally, the continuance of the Peace."[63] In effect, Napoleon having refused the terms offered at Châtillon, the Treaty of Chaumont pledged the allies to continue the war until he capitulated, to suspend until that had been achieved their disagreements about France's future governance, and to keep what would become known as the Quadruple Alliance in place for twenty years thereafter to guarantee the peace thus secured.

The Coalition triumphant

Thereafter, Bonaparte's situation deteriorated rapidly. In the north, units under Bernadotte penetrated nearly to Reims, bypassing and isolating French coastal garrisons from Antwerp to Boulogne. In the southwest, on 27 February, Wellington defeated Soult at the Battle of Orthes and inflicted 4,000 casualties, while driving the survivors across the Gave de Pau River, opening the road to Toulouse. On 12 March, municipal authorities in Bordeaux pulled down the tricolor and declared for Louis XVIII. In Italy, Eugene was forced back nearly to the French border, while further east, after losing several engagements to a detached Austrian corps under General Ferdinand Bubna, Marshal Pierre Augureau abandoned Lyon.

With only 75,000 troops remaining under his direct command, Bonaparte attempted during the rest of March to repeat his signature tactic of attacking separated allied formations with his entire strength, and actually succeeded in defeating an isolated Prussian corps at Reims on the 13 March. But the allies by now were experienced in sidestepping his lunges, and his inexperienced conscripts were not the veterans of Austerlitz and Wagram. By the end of March, the allies were at the gates of Paris. Refusing to accept defeat, Napoleon proposed to continue the fight from Fontainebleau, but his marshals had had enough. Declared MacDonald after Napoleon reviewed his troops on 3 April, "We do not intend to expose Paris to the fate of Moscow."[64] There followed the famous exchange between Bonaparte and Ney, "the Bravest of the Brave," in which Napoleon insisted that the army would march despite his subordinates' opposition, to which Ney rejoined, "Sire, the

63 Frank Maloy Anderson, *The Constitution and Other Select Documents Illustrative of the History of France* (London, 1904), p. 441.
64 Fremont-Barnes, *The Napoleonic Wars*, IV, p. 59.

army will obey its generals." Three days later, having unsuccessfully attempted suicide, Napoleon abdicated and on 10 April, in the Treaty of Fontainebleau, grudgingly accepted exile to Elba, renouncing "for himself, his successors and descendants, as well as for all the members of his family, all right of sovereignty and dominion, as well to the French Empire and the Kingdom of Italy as to every other country."[65] A week later, accompanied by elements of his own Imperial Guard, he left Paris to embark into exile.

Who would succeed him remained unclear. Noted one historian, "We take it almost for granted that the Coalition were united in desiring the dethronement of Napoleon and the restoration of the Bourbons and that they executed this joint purpose with celerity and skill. These are incorrect assumptions."[66] On 1 April, with the tsar his houseguest, Talleyrand persuaded the French senate to appoint himself head of a provisional government and on 6 April convinced the French senate to accept a new constitution calling for the return of the House of Bourbon. A month later, however, after a less than cordial interview with the tsar at Compiègne upon arriving in France, Louis XVIII promptly disbanded the senate on the grounds that it had been complicit in Bonaparte's usurpation, then scrapped its constitution. It required all the pressure that Talleyrand and Castlereagh between them could muster to compel Louis to adopt a modified constitution – the Charter of 1814 – while assuaging Alexander's resentment sufficiently to convince him that a constitutional Bourbon monarchy offered the only hope of enduring peace. At the end of the day, the Treaty of Paris ratified on 30 May was extraordinarily generous.[67] It imposed no occupation or indemnity, actually added modestly to France's pre-revolution territory, and even allowed the Louvre to retain the priceless Italian artwork looted by Bonaparte.[68]

But while the events of April and May 1814 rid the allies of Bonaparte (or so they believed) and resolved the issue of France's territorial limits and governance, they left unresolved the problem, carefully deferred until now, of the future of that vast swath of Central European territory between the Vistula and the Rhine that Russia and Prussia had prospectively carved

---

65 Anderson, *The Constitution and Other Select Documents*, p. 450.

66 Nicolson, *The Congress of Vienna*, p. 84.

67 It was negotiated largely by Alexander, Castlereagh, and Metternich arriving in Paris ten days after the tsar, and none of his allies was entirely pleased with it, least of all Metternich, who warned that exiling Bonaparte so close to France would produce a renewed war within two years. Kissinger, *A World Restored*, p. 140.

68 The boundary adjustments included the retention of Avignon and the other "Papal Territories."

up in the Treaty of Kalisch, an agreement to which neither their allies nor the new French government were party. Now, with the common threat removed, the very agreement that had inaugurated the Sixth Coalition threatened to spark a new war, this time among its own members.

The final crisis: Poland and Saxony

In September 1814, the population of Vienna temporarily swelled by nearly half again, as rulers and diplomats from virtually every European state and principality, together with scores of other delegations representing everything from religious orders to commercial interests, converged on Austria's capital for the congress promised in the Treaty of Paris to settle the future of post-Napoleonic Europe.[69] The number and diversity of delegates presented a procedural problem for which the allies were totally unprepared. Clearly nothing would be accomplished without some division of labor. Noted Talleyrand to his master on arrival, "Not even the English, whom I thought more methodical than the others, have done any preparatory work on this subject."[70]

In the end, several *ad hoc* committees eventually formed to deal with important but strategically ancillary issues ranging from diplomatic precedence to the regulation of river commerce. However, the allies had no intention of submitting the resolution of territorial issues to so diverse and uncontrollable a throng. As Hardenberg sensibly insisted, "No plan could be considered which would give the minor princelings the right to interfere in the general arrangements of Europe."[71]

Instead, after some debate, the leading members of the coalition – Russia, Prussia, Austria, and Britain – declared themselves "great powers" and agreed that decisions reached among themselves would first be shared with French and Spanish delegates, and only then presented by all six to the full congress for ratification. That plan collapsed almost immediately when, at a contentious meeting on 30 September, Talleyrand disputed the allies' authority to exclude other affected states and threatened to publicize his objections.[72] Desperate to avoid so direct a challenge to

69 What follows relies heavily on the author's earlier essay, "In Search of Military Repose: The Congress of Vienna and the Making of Peace," in Williamson Murray and Jim Lacey (eds.), *The Making of Peace: Rulers, States, and the Aftermath of War* (Cambridge, 2009), pp. 131–59.
70 Nicolson, *The Congress of Vienna*, p. 137.
71 Sir Charles Webster, *The Congress of Vienna* (New York, 1963), p. 87.
72 Noted Metternich's adjoint in his diary, "Talleyrand protested against the procedure we have adopted and soundly rated us for two hours." Susan Mary Alsop, *The Congress Dances* (New York, 1984), p. 120.

the legitimacy of the congress even before it convened, the allies instead invited Talleyrand to join in their deliberations, thus tacitly acknowledging that no stable European balance was conceivable that excluded their former enemy.[73]

The key to any such arrangement, it was clear, would be resolution of the status of Napoleon's now defunct Duchy of Warsaw and German Confederation. In turn, that would require finding a way out of the political box in which the 1813 Russo-Prussian Treaty of Kalisch had put the coalition. As one writer put it: "On the question of Poland depended the fate of Saxony; and on the disposal of Saxony depended all the other arrangements in Germany, so that the frontier of almost every German State was likely to be affected."[74]

Kalisch, it will be recalled, proposed to resurrect a Polish kingdom under Russian guardianship, in effect annexing to Russia all of Poland minus Silesia, which would be returned to Prussia together with additional compensation for lost Prussian territory in the form of Saxony and parts of the upper Rhineland. The first agreement would extend Russian power well to the west, the second push Prussian power well to the south. The bill payer would be Austria, which, in addition to losing its own share of partitioned pre-Napoleonic Poland, would lose any buffer between itself and two uncomfortably powerful neighbors. Metternich, of course, was well aware of this arrangement and had intentionally allowed the Treaty of Teplitz following Bonaparte's rejection of the Reichenbach proposals to leave Poland's future vague. Now, however, the allies could no longer defer settling that issue.

For Metternich, of course, the solution was to restore the *status quo ante*, returning to each of the three Central European powers, with only minor adjustments, those territories of which Napoleon had stripped them. The principal obstacle was Alexander, whose combination of romantic idealism and volatility made him a difficult man with whom to deal and who insisted on acting as his own negotiator, repeatedly overriding or reversing agreements to which his foreign minister had tentatively acceded. Notes one historian, "[T]he tension between liberalism and autocracy [was] deeply rooted in Alexander's personality – his wish, to paraphrase Czartoryski, that the whole world should be free to do what he wanted."[75]

In this case, what Alexander wanted, whether from idealism or greed, was a unified Poland. Unable to penetrate his obstinacy, Metternich

---

73 Along with Spain's Don Pedro Labrador.
74 Webster, *The Congress of Vienna*, p. 75.
75 Paul W. Schroeder, *The Transformation of European Politics 1763–1848* (Oxford, 1994), p. 504.

attempted instead to bribe Prussia, offering over his generals' objections to accede to Prussia's annexation of Saxony in return for support in deflecting the tsar's Polish ambitions.[76] The attempt backfired. Furiously assailed by Alexander, Frederick William ordered Hardenberg to abort any further discussion with Metternich. Meanwhile, in London, opposition parliamentarians attacked the British government for failing to oppose the forced annexation of Saxony by Prussia.

With relations among the senior members of the coalition deteriorating rapidly, Talleyrand saw his opportunity. Rightly judging an expanded Prussia directly across the Rhine to be a greater threat to France than a distant Russia, he joined Castlereagh in opposing Kalisch's *quid pro quo*, accusing Russia of bad faith, Prussia of aggression, and both of ignoring the need to ensure that any settlement enjoyed international legitimacy. At the same time, anticipating the coming crisis, he convinced Louis to mobilize.[77]

The crisis came in December. Sensing that the tsar was beginning to falter under the pressure of his allies and his own advisers – the latter far from sanguine about the potential influence of revived Polish nationalism on Russia's own restless peasantry – Hardenberg abruptly threatened to annex Saxony unilaterally, if necessary by war. In response, ignoring guidance from London, on 3 January 1815 Castlereagh joined Metternich and Talleyrand in a "secret" agreement by which France and Austria each would commit 150,000 troops and Britain the equivalent in funds and mercenaries were Prussia to persist in its expansionist aims.

It was an extraordinary step, especially for Castlereagh, and it worked.[78] Leaked almost immediately, the agreement proved the last straw for Alexander, who grudgingly renounced the Kalisch agreement. In turn, diplomatically isolated and no more eager for another war than his allies, Frederick William reined in Hardenberg and his generals.[79] On

---

76 Austria could tolerate Prussian expansion, but not a unified Poland, even one under Russian influence. Poland's history threatened nationalism and revolution, the very things most dangerous to Austria's polyglot empire.

77 As he wrote presciently in October, "Who can calculate the results if a mass like the German, amalgamated into a single whole, should turn aggressive? Who can tell where such a movement would stop?" Hilde Spiel (ed.), *The Congress of Vienna: An Eyewitness Account*, trans. Richard H. Weber (London, 1968), p. 32.

78 Praising Castlereagh's courage in ignoring his own instructions, Schroeder writes, "The difference he made to British policy was as important as the difference it made that, in May 1940, Winston Churchill rather than Lord Halifax succeeded Neville Chamberlain." Schroeder, *The Transformation of European Politics*, p. 458.

79 As Austria's Archduke Johann confided to his diary, "No one will dare to start an unpopular war, exhausted as their lands are." Spiel, *The Congress of Vienna*, p. 23.

8 February the allies concluded a revised agreement surrendering nearly half of Saxony to Prussia, but neither of its two major cities, hence less than half its population. Further negotiations essentially repartitioned Poland, the south of which, minus Kracow, returned to the jurisdiction of a relieved Austria.

Three weeks later, Bonaparte escaped from Elba, inaugurating the Hundred Days. But while his return gave Europe a brief scare, he found himself confronted not by a coalition fractured by internal divisions, but instead by one united in its desire for military repose even at the price of compromising cherished but incompatible territorial aims. In proof of which, on 18 June the very Prussians who had nearly found themselves at war with Austria and Britain five months earlier instead arrived on Waterloo's bloody battlefield just in time to help their British comrades defeat the Little Corporal once and for all.

Managing alliance cohesion

In a monograph written some years ago for the Army's Command and General Staff College, Navy Lieutenant Commander John Kuehn attributed the success of the Sixth Coalition to application by the allies of four fundamental principles ignored in one way or another by its five failed predecessors: commonality of goal, unity of effort, agreement on an operational plan, and faithful adherence to the plan once adopted.[80] That appraisal has a certain validity, but must at least be qualified. To the extent that all the allies sought to deprive Bonaparte of his European conquests, they certainly could be said to have shared a common aim, although, as this chapter has argued, not defined identically by all of them, nor, especially by Britain, adjudged by itself to be sufficient inducement to peace. More important, agreement to end Napoleon's hegemony by no means implied agreement on what should replace it. And the allies' tacit decision from Teplitz through Chaumont to defer that question, while it undoubtedly helped to win the war, also came uncomfortably close to begetting another.

Unity of effort similarly must be qualified. Throughout the campaigns of 1813 and 1814, unity of command – the vital ingredient of unified effort – was at best honored in the breach. Where it prevailed at all, unity of command owed less to Schwartzenberg's nominal supreme authority than to the presence of the allied sovereigns at headquarters that

---

80 John Trost Kuehn, "The Reasons for the Success of the Sixth Coalition against Napoleon in 1813" (Fort Leavenworth, KS, 1997), www.dtic.mil/dtic/tr/fulltext/u2/a331849.pdf.

caused him such grief. Even then, the allies constantly quarreled. In the circumstances:

that the strategical task confronting the allies was carried out at all ... was doubt-less a tribute to the patience and forbearance of Schwarzenberg, but it was cer-tainly due more to the general fear of Napoleon and the common awareness that he was still far from being beaten. The divisive factors were always held in restraint by the common danger.[81]

Even the accretion of overwhelming manpower could not absolve the allies of wariness bordering on fear of Bonaparte's fading but still formidable military brilliance, a nervousness that lingered as late as the Six-Day Campaign. Viewed in that light, the Fabian character of the Trachenberg Plan was as much a concession to allied disunity and lack of self-confidence as a triumph of operational creativity. That it helped to produce the decisive allied victory at Leipzig is indisputable. But that victory owed nearly as much to Napoleon's own tactical blunders after Dresden, and to his failing sway over his own allies, as it did to the consistency with which the Trachenberg Plan governed allied decisions.

In short, viewed strictly from a military perspective, the success of the Sixth Coalition in 1813 and 1814 can be attributed largely to the gradual but ultimately insuperable shift in what the Russians later would call the correlation of forces, and the subsequent defection, first of Bonaparte's allies, then of his generals. As one writer comments, the Sixth Coalition "was the first time in the Napoleonic wars that [the] three major conti-nental powers opposed Napoleon at the same time ... Even the military genius of one of history's greatest captains could not overcome these tremendous odds indefinitely."[82]

But the crucial prerequisites to keeping the coalition together long enough to achieve that decisive military preponderance were as much political as military. Absent the Kalisch agreement, Russia and Prussia might have found themselves fighting independently, risking the same defeat in detail that had allowed Bonaparte to destroy earlier coalitions. Absent Reichenbach and Teplitz, neither Austria's army nor Britain's material and financial support would have been brought to bear. Absent Châtillon and Chaumont, the coalition might have foundered on the cusp of victory. And absent the Peace of Paris and the allies' tacit accept-ance of France's reentry into the ranks of the great powers, the Hundred Days might have ended with Bonaparte once again triumphant.

81 Craig, "Problems of Coalition Warfare," p. 5.
82 Kenneth A Turner, "Complexity in Coalition Operations: The Campaign of the Sixth Coalition against Napoleon" (US Army War College, 2003), p. 23, www.dtic.mil/cgi-bin/GetTRDoc?AD=ADA414581.

That these political achievements owed a great deal to the influence of Napoleon himself cannot be gainsaid. "The four great powers that signed the Treaty of Chaumont were reluctant allies, made to cooperate only in extreme need. They came together not to help each other but simply to defeat France after twenty years of largely unsuccessful wars in which the individual pursuit of separate aims had failed."[83] As late as Troyes, fear of a resurgent Bonaparte was the uninvited guest at every alliance debate. Even so, that it ended by increasing rather than eroding cohesion reflected extraordinary statesmanship. Indeed, the need for statesmanship only increased as the fear diminished, and as each ally began to see itself better able to pursue its own interests free of a common threat.

Any attempt to generalize from the experience of the Sixth Coalition to the alliance challenges of our own day should recall Nicolson's wise reminder, "Events are not affected by analogies; they are determined by the combinations of circumstance. And since circumstances vary from generation to generation, it is illusive to suppose that any pattern of history, however similar it may first appear, is likely to repeat itself exactly in the kaleidoscope of time."[84] Not the least of the circumstances distinguishing the Sixth Coalition from more recent successors was that the negotiations that created and sustained it were the very antithesis of "open covenants openly arrived at." The men who argued, cajoled, threatened, and ultimately agreed at each moment of crisis were either themselves autocrats, or else (excluding Castlereagh) the servants of autocrats. No pertinacious press hounded their deliberations; and in the one potentially critical case in which Britain's quasi-democratically elected government explicitly instructed him, Castlereagh ignored its instructions.

Conditions conducive to backroom diplomacy no longer exist, as recent events have demonstrated clearly. Today's diplomats operate in a far more transparent environment and under far more taxing political constraints. While complicating their task, however, those conditions cannot relieve them of the need to manage some of the same recurring diplomatic and military challenges that confronted their predecessors.

---

83 Tim Chapman, *The Congress of Vienna: Origins, Processes, and Results* (London, 1998), p. 31. The similarity to a more recent wartime alliance is inescapable. Writes Colin Gray of World War II's Grand Alliance, "The Anglo-Americans and the Soviets were not genuine allies; they were co-belligerents ... the Grand Alliance did not erode and break down in the 1945–1947 period because it could not. That alliance never existed except in words." Colin Gray, "Mission Improbable, Fear, Culture, and Interest: Peace Making, 1943–1949," in Williamson Murray and Jim Lacey (eds.), *The Making of Peace: Rulers, States, and the Aftermath of War* (Cambridge, 2009), p. 276.
84 Nicolson, *The Congress of Vienna*, p. viii.

One is the need to achieve and sustain mutual trust, and the inescapable contest that it introduces between the pressure for transparency and the urge to reticence in exchanges among allies. Too little transparency risks forfeiting the mutual confidence on which any concerted action depends. But too much transparency indulged too early risks straining alliance comity before shared military success accumulates to reinforce that confidence. Metternich could safely demand explicit articulation of allied war aims at Troyes only because military success and the reawakened fear of forfeiting it immunized the coalition against rupture. A similar insistence at Teplitz might have rendered Austria's transfer of allegiance impossible. On the other hand, Alexander saw Metternich's backdoor approach to Prussia at Vienna for the outright breach of trust that it was; and but for Castlereagh and Talleyrand, the result might have been tragic.

No formula can specify how much of one's intentions and concerns to share with one's co-belligerents and when. But while, as Teplitz suggested, permitting a certain ambiguity to prevail for a time probably is acceptable and may even be desirable, outright prevarication among allies is an invitation to mutual mistrust that, once permitted to flourish, may prove difficult to eradicate. In few situations is the short-term gain likely to justify the long-term cost.

Closely associated with the need for mutual trust is the need for mutual tolerance, especially when confronted with military setbacks. Not the least of the contributions of the Trachenberg Plan was the room it allowed for tactical defeat without penalty to allied cohesion. Unlike the situation after Lützen, when defeat threatened to send Prussian and Russian forces in opposite directions, or after Bautzen, when mutual recriminations cost Wittgenstein his job and nearly prompted an open split between Russian and Prussian generals, defeats after Trachenberg, while they may have retarded the resumption of offensive operations, never entirely derailed them. Nor, even after Dresden, were the allies again tempted each to go its own way. It helped enormously that every major allied force, from Bernadotte's Army of the North to Schwartzenberg's Army of Bohemia, was a multinational formation, so that no ally could be held uniquely responsible for any single tactical setback. Even when the Six-Day Campaign briefly panicked allied sovereigns, mutual recriminations among their generals were notably absent.

Finally, and perhaps most important, the cohesion of any coalition depends on each participating nation's self-restraint, above all that of the most powerful. Writing of Louis XIV's failure in the previous century to sustain the League of the Rhine erected by Cardinal Jules Mazarin, which had given France what one historian called "near-perfect security," one historian notes that due regard to one's allies' sensibilities is necessary, not just "because the quid pro quo of their participation requires that their views be taken seriously," but also because "the need to honor others' interests encourage[s] a wisdom that avoids self-deluded policy."[85]

That self-restraint is the more necessary the closer the coalition comes to achieving its military objectives, when the proximity of victory tempts the stronger power or powers to go it alone rather than accommodate the inconvenient preferences of weaker partners, as Alexander was briefly tempted to do as the allies approached Paris. In that case, Bonaparte once again saved the coalition from itself. But even when no such immediate penalty threatens to accrue from over-ambition, the long-term cost to alliance comity is likely to exceed any short-term policy advantage. Significantly Kissinger writes, "The test of a statesman … is his ability to recognize the real relationship of forces and to make this knowledge serve his ends … Statesmanship thus involves not only a problem of conception but also of implementation, an appreciation of the attainable as much as a vision of the desirable."[86]

In repeatedly subordinating the desirable to the attainable without forfeiting the central aim of a Europe free of domination by a single untrammeled will, the authors of the Sixth Coalition revealed statesmanship of a high order indeed, as much on the part of the sovereigns involved as on that of the remarkable diplomats and soldiers who served them. Replicating that feat should not be beyond current abilities. Speaking in the mid 1960s, when the North Atlantic Alliance was under mounting pressure, Gordon Craig reminded his listeners that "others have found it possible to live with administrative deficiencies and conflicts of interest and yet to be effective partners … [W]e may do so too, provided we remember why our alliance was established in the first place and provided we do not lose sight of the fact that our Bonapartes too are always in the near distance and that their menace is undiminished."[87]

Today's Bonapartes are different in appearance even from those that menaced America and its allies during the Cold War, let alone their nineteenth-century predecessors. But the need to create and rely on coalitions – and, derivatively, the need better to understand and practice their care and feeding – if anything has only increased as the political and cultural diversity of potential participants has multiplied. No aspect of foreign and military policy is more worthy of continued study.

---

85 John A. Lynn, "The Grand Strategy of the *Grand Siècle*: Learning from the Wars of Louis XIV," in Williamson Murray, Richard Sinnreich, and Jim Lacey (eds.), *The Shaping of Grand Strategy: Policy, Diplomacy, and War* (Cambridge, 2011), p. 52.
86 Kissinger, *A World Restored*, pp. 325–30.
87 Craig, "Problems of Coalition Warfare," p. 12.

5   The Franco-British military alliance during World War I

Paul Harris

The Franco-British alliance of 1914 to 1918 was critical in shaping the modern world.* Had such an alliance failed to emerge, or had it disintegrated under the stress of war before the arrival of sufficient help from the United States to tip the balance against Germany, the Hohenzollern Reich would surely have achieved the hegemonic status in Europe that many Germans considered to be their inherent right. Domination of the world's mightiest continent would have made it the twentieth century's first superpower and given it the resources to fulfil many of its Kaiser's most grandiose ambitions for naval and overseas imperial expansion. Indeed, the transfer to the Reich of French and Belgian overseas possessions as part of a peace settlement might already have put it on the road to *Weltmacht*. German victory at this time would have meant the European triumph of militaristic, illiberal, and anti-democratic forces. With such an outcome there is no certainty that liberal democracy and free-market capitalism would have achieved their present degree of global influence and prestige.

Given its pivotal importance in world history, the Franco-British alliance has inevitably attracted great scholarly attention. The literature is voluminous and some of it of the highest quality. A number of historians have made this alliance the focus of their professional lives.[1] In a chapter as short as this it is scarcely possible even to summarize their work.

---

* The author would like to thank Dr. Anthony Clayton, Professor William Philpott, and Professor Peter Simkins for reading this chapter in advance of publication and making valuable comments. For any mistakes of fact or interpretation that remain, however, he is solely responsible.

1 Historians who have made this alliance central to their academic lives include Elizabeth Greenhalgh, William Philpott, and Roy Prete. Their principal works include E. Greenhalgh, *Victory Through Coalition: Britain and France during the First World War* (Cambridge, 2005) and *Foch in Command: The Forging of a First World War General* (Cambridge, 2011); W. J. Philpott, *Anglo-French Relations and Strategy on the Western Front 1914–18* (London, 1996) and *Bloody Victory: The Sacrifice on the Somme and the Making of the 20th Century* (London 2009); and R. A. Prete, *Strategy and Command: The Anglo-French Coalition on the Western Front, 1914* (Montreal, 2009).

This chapter, therefore, will focus on the alliance from the British perspective and mainly with regard to operations on the Western Front. Alliance diplomacy with regard to the affairs of the extra-European world (the Sykes-Picot agreement, for example) will receive no attention here and naval aspects almost none. While it is clear that the financial, industrial, and broader economic aspects of the alliance were crucial (France having been doomed to defeat without British help in these areas), this chapter will pass them over with little comment, focusing instead largely on the military matters that confronted the alliance.

The Franco-British military cooperation of 1914–1918 was not totally unprecedented. England and France were co-belligerents against the Dutch in the 1670s and against the Russians in the 1850s.[2] Yet the observation that centuries of antagonism had characterized relations between the two nations remains broadly true.[3] Up to the beginning of the twentieth century it was indeed France and Russia, powers in a firm military alliance since 1894, which seemed to offer the greatest threats to Britain's global interests.[4] Though by 1904 the aggressive foreign policy of Wilhelmine Germany, amongst other factors, had led the British government to seek a settlement of outstanding differences with France, the resulting Entente could not immediately dispel centuries of accumulated mistrust. Initially intended to reduce friction over such matters as imperial spheres of influence and fishing rights, the Entente did not become a military alliance at any time before the British declaration of war on 4 August 1914. Admittedly, there were intermittent staff talks between the French and British general staffs from 1906, and these concerned the potential dispatch of a British field force to serve alongside the French army in the event of a German attack. It is also true that naval talks in 1912 suggested that in the event of war, the Royal Navy would deal with the Germans in the North Sea and the Channel, while the French navy would protect French and British interests in the Mediterranean. Yet however much the French may have wanted and felt entitled to a firm diplomatic and military commitment, none of these talks bound a British government to declare war in any set of circumstances. Nor did they compel Britain to deploy its armed forces in wartime in any manner contrary to its perception of national interests.[5]

2 O. Figes, *Crimea: The Last Crusade* (London, 2008), pp. 100–493.
3 For an exploration of Franco-British relations in the most general terms see R. and I. Tombs, *That Sweet Enemy: The French and The British: From the Sun King to the Present* (London, 2006).
4 Rene Albrecht-Carrié, *A Diplomatic History of Europe since the Congress of Vienna* (London 1970), pp. 208–14.
5 Prete, *Strategy and Command*, pp. 3–43. Greenhalgh, *Victory Through Coalition*, pp. 15–17.

The attitude of the bulk of H. H. Asquith's Liberal Cabinet was pacific. The British went to war only after the Germans had massively violated Belgian neutrality. Even then two ministers resigned. Others apparently went along with the intervention only because the Cabinet would otherwise have split, the government would have fallen, and they would have been out of office.[6] In the first week of the war, moreover, the British government's behaviour does not suggest that it felt bound by prewar staff talks. The Cabinet decided to withhold for defense against invasion and internal security two of the six infantry divisions that staff talks had earmarked for the continent. It was even not clear until a week into the war that the expeditionary force would go where the French wanted it.

Field Marshal Lord Kitchener, the late-Victorian military hero brought into the government as Secretary of State for War, had the gravest doubts about sending British forces to the Maubeuge area. Before the British expeditionary force (BEF) could be deployed there, he thought the area might be overrun by the massive enveloping sweep that he rightly perceived the Germans to be making north of the Meuse. Sir Henry Wilson, the intensely Francophile British staff officer who had played the largest role in the prewar talks, exploded in fury at what he saw as Kitchener's interfering obstructionism. But it was not until a meeting on 12 August with French staff officers and with Sir John French, commander of the BEF, and his staff that Kitchener finally relented and allowed the BEF to proceed to France.[7]

On 15 August French held talks with the French President, Raymond Poincaré, with the premier, René Viviani, and with other French political leaders. The following day he met the commander in chief, General Joseph Joffre and his deputy chief of staff, General Henri Berthelot, at their headquarters at Vitry-le-Francois. The British commander in chief declared himself impressed by his allies, admiring the calm, purposeful atmosphere of Joffre's headquarters. But he also felt it necessary to point out to Joffre the terms of his instructions from the British government. He was to do everything within reason to assist his allies but, ultimately, he alone was responsible to the British government for the fate of the British army. The BEF was, therefore, not under Joffre's command. Somewhat dismayed at the idea of having constantly to negotiate for British cooperation, Joffre recognized that he had no choice but to make the best of it. He explained to Sir John French the military situation on the Western Front as he saw it and requested that the BEF be ready to move forward

6 J. Joll, *The Origins of the First World War* (London, 1992), pp. 24–32.
7 K. Jeffery, *Field Marshal Sir Henry Wilson: Political Soldier* (Oxford, 2006), pp. 84–106, 131–34.

into Belgium on the left flank of General Charles Lanrezac's French Fifth Army on 21 August.[8]

Over the next few weeks the level of cooperation achieved between French and Lanrezac would prove crucial for the alliance. But given their personalities, the prospects of harmonious relations between them were not good. Sir John French initially had the best of intentions towards his allies, but he was subject to acute mood swings and did not easily forgive perceived slights, still less betrayals of trust. Lanrezac had acute anti-British prejudices and considered their army to be of minimal combat value. If Joffre was aware of Lanrezac's Anglophobia, he had apparently not taken it into account when arranging for the BEF to fight alongside the Fifth Army. The stage was set for an early crisis in the alliance so acute that it could have led to an irretrievable disaster.[9]

To be fair to Lanrezac, when French first came to meet him at his headquarters at Rethel on 17 August, he was deeply troubled. Like Kitchener, Lanrezac perceived that the Germans had weighted their right wing far more heavily than Joffre at this stage realized. Lanrezac visited Joffre's headquarters on 14 August and tried to point out the acute danger of envelopment faced by Fifth Army and, indeed, by the whole of the Allied left wing. He had failed to convince Joffre of this reality. The French commander in chief did not rescind his orders for Fifth Army to advance into Belgium. It did not help their first meeting that Sir John French spoke little French while Lanrezac apparently spoke no English. Though interpreters were available, French seemed slow to grasp Lanrezac's reading of the situation. The Fifth Army commander made no effort to conceal his contempt and the discourtesy was obvious to all except possibly Sir John French himself.[10]

On 21 August when the BEF advanced in accordance with Joffre's plan, Lanrezac held his army back behind the Sambre River, exposing the British right flank. Lanrezac failed to inform French of the Fifth Army's dispositions, and French only learned about his ally's failure to advance from the British liaison officer with Fifth Army, Lieutenant Edward Spears, on the evening of 21 August. On 23 August, when elements of the German First Army heavily attacked the British II Corps at Mons, Lanrezac, whose own army had been fighting a defensive battle

8 Prete, *Strategy and Command*, pp. 92–94; R. Holmes, *The Little Field Marshal: A Life of Sir John French* (London, 1981), pp. 200–208.
9 Prete, *Strategy and Command*, pp. 94–95; G. C. Cassar, *The Tragedy of Sir John French* (Newark, DE, 1985), pp. 81–95.
10 Cassar, *The Tragedy of Sir John French*, pp. 94–95. This, at least, is the traditional version. It is queried in W. Philpott, "Gone Fishing: The Meeting of Sir John French and Lanrezac in August 1914," *Journal of Army Historical Research*, 86 (Autumn 2006).

at Charleroi, now had clear proof that his fears of being overwhelmed by a massive German envelopment were correct. He ordered Fifth Army to retreat. Such a move was undoubtedly necessary. Lanrezac initiated it, however, without prior consultation with French and without giving the British due warning. Fifth Army's precipitate withdrawal left the BEF's right wing up "in the air" and presented the BEF with the risk of double envelopment. French found out about this danger only late at night on 23 August.

In terms of his operational understanding, Lanrezac was no fool. But his behaviour towards his country's newfound ally in the first days of active operations was as contemptible as it was contemptuous. Its consequences were potentially as catastrophic for France as they were for the BEF. Sir John French was soon contemplating pulling the BEF out of the line and falling back to Amiens, and then, perhaps, to Le Havre. Indeed, for a short time even the intensely Francophile Sir Henry Wilson, French's sub-chief of staff, considered that it might to be necessary to head for "Havre and home."[11]

Though French's mood fluctuated during the harrowing retreat from Mons, up to the end of August, the notion that he would soon need to pull the BEF out of the line to rest and refit never altogether left him. On 30 August he wrote to Kitchener indicating that he might shortly have to make such a move. But such a withdrawal had the potential to cause such a major crisis that it might have doomed the Allied cause. A British retreat would have made the general counteroffensive that Joffre was straining every nerve to organize impossible, and would have opened a dangerous gap in the Allied line of battle.[12]

Fortunately, the key decision-makers in the British government were already aware of French's desire to pull the BEF out of the line. The BEF's Inspector-General of Communications, Major-General Robb, had informed them of it a few days earlier. Aware through other channels that the French army was in the process of recovery from its initial disasters and was about to attempt to regain the initiative, the government decided to veto any such withdrawal. Instead, it insisted that Sir John French cooperate with Joffre's proposed counteroffensive. To impress upon him the vital importance of complying with these instructions, Lord Kitchener proceeded personally to Paris, where he met French on 1 September.

11 Prete, *Strategy and Command*, pp. 96–101; E. Spears, *Liaison 1914: A Narrative of the Great Retreat* (London, 1968), pp. 168–75; Philpott, *Anglo-French Relations*, pp. 20–23.
12 Prete, *Strategy and Command*, p. 106; R. Poincaré, *The Memoirs of Raymond Poincaré, 1914* (London, 1929), pp. 122–23.

Kitchener's position was unusual. As Secretary of State for War he held a political office. In that capacity it would be entirely proper to give a commander in the field general strategic direction, but overruling his military judgment as to measures necessary for his force's survival was questionable. Kitchener, however, was also a field marshal and in that rank senior to French. Presumably to indicate that he was issuing orders and not just offering political guidance, Kitchener met French wearing full uniform. French took umbrage. But Kitchener successfully enforced his authority, abating the most serious crisis of the alliance thus far.[13]

British participation in Joffre's proposed counteroffensive on the Marne was crucial. The BEF was the hinge between the French Fifth and Sixth Armies, the operations of which would largely determine the battle's outcome. Vitally important in securing this participation was General Louis-Felix Franchet d'Espèrey, the new Fifth Army commander, whom Joffre had ordered to replace the dispirited Lanrezac on 3 September. Franchet d'Espèrey was a hard-driving commander who combined a distinctly ruthless streak with a capacity for courtesy and consideration towards allies that had eluded his predecessor.[14] On 4 September he met Henry Wilson at a small town about halfway between the BEF's headquarters and that of Fifth Army. They agreed that their two armies would jointly comply with Joffre's demand for a counteroffensive on 6 September. Upon hearing of this meeting, Joffre experienced a profound sense of relief. He later wrote, "The role of Franchet d'Espèrey on September 4, 1914 merits being underlined in history: it is he who made the battle of the Marne possible."[15] Franchet d'Espèrey ("Desperate Frankie" as he was later known to British troops)[16] was, indeed, a true hero of the Franco-British alliance who both gained and reciprocated the respect of British officers.[17]

In addition, on 4 September Archibald Murray, French's chief of the general staff, met General Joseph Gallieni, who was planning the Sixth Army attack from the direction of Paris. Gallieni wanted the BEF in a somewhat different position on the morning of 6 September from where Franchet d'Espèrey wanted it, and Sir John French inclined more to

13 Cassar, *The Tragedy of Sir John French*, pp. 128–38; Prete, *Strategy and Command*, pp. 108–12; G. H. Cassar, *Kitchener: Architect of Victory* (London, 1977), pp. 236–40.

14 J. P. Harris, *Douglas Haig and the First World War* (Cambridge, 2008), pp. 84–85.

15 R. A. Doughty, *Pyrrhic Victory: French Strategy and Operations in the Great War* (Cambridge, 2005), pp. 85–90; J. Joffre, *Memoirs of Marshal Joffre* (London, 1932), vol. I, pp. 249–50.

16 Greenhalgh, *Victory Through Coalition*, pp. 144–45.

17 A. Wakefield and S. Moody, *Under the Devil's Eye: Britain's Forgotten Army at Salonika, 1915–1918* (Stroud, 2004), p. 196.

Gallieni's scheme. But the important thing was that, on the afternoon of 5 September, Joffre heard from Colonel Victor Huguet, his liaison officer with the British, that French did intend to join the offensive the following morning. Joffre personally went to see the British commander later the same afternoon, ostensibly to thank him for this decision, but actually to impress upon him the importance of the operation so that he did not change his distinctly mercurial mind. Outlining at some length what he intended as the decisive offensive of 1914, Joffre declared that history would judge the British harshly if they failed to play their part. Betraying the immense nervous strain he was experiencing, he banged his fist on the table and declared, "The honour of England is at stake, Marshal." The British commander tried to respond in French, but the pressure of the moment overwhelmed his limited linguistic prowess. Asking others to interpret he replied, "Damn it, I can't explain. Tell him that all that men can do our fellows will do."[18]

The BEF, however, had still not fully regained its equilibrium after the harrowing retreat from Mons. Its initial performance in Joffre's counteroffensive was tardy, hesitant, and somewhat lacking in aggressiveness. This was particularly the case with Sir Douglas Haig's I Corps, the BEF's most powerful, which was to lead the British attack.[19] Nevertheless, it soon became clear that the Allied counteroffensive had caught the Germans by surprise. On 9 September the BEF crossed the Marne and threatened to exploit a gap that had opened up between the German First Army and the German Second Army. By 12 September it was clear that the Battle of the Marne, as it became known, had been a major Allied victory.[20] The first major crisis of the alliance was over and, at least for a week or so, the armies of the Western allies tended to take a rather more charitable view of one another.

The rest of 1914, however, was by no means without strain. There were tensions over the British demand in late September that the entire BEF shift from the Aisne, where it had its first real taste of trench warfare, to the far left of the Allied line. Joffre eventually agreed, but the move greatly complicated Allied logistics, already under massive strain, as his headquarters used the French railway system to shift troops to a left flank the Germans seemed determined to envelop. Joffre's headquarters also disapproved, quite reasonably, of the despatch of British troops (largely at Winston Churchill's instigation) to Antwerp in a vain effort

---

18 Doughty, *Pyrrhic Victory*, pp. 90–91; Joffre, *Memoirs*, I, pp. 253–54.
19 Harris, *Douglas Haig*, pp. 85–87; H. H. Herwig, *The Marne, 1914: The Opening of World War I and the Battle that Changed the World* (New York, 2009), pp. 252–53.
20 Herwig, *The Marne, 1914*, pp. 266–306.

to prevent its fall. Having arrived on the Allied left flank the BEF found itself involved in intense fighting in Flanders, fighting later known as the First Battle of Ypres. In this fighting Ferdinand Foch, who commanded the French Northern Army Group, played a crucial role. He greatly assisted the BEF and established better relations with Sir John French than Joffre had achieved. Allied cooperation, however strained, frustrated a second German bid for decisive victory in 1914, the Germans failing to envelop and destroy the Allied left wing. By the end of the year there was a more or less continuous Western Front between the English Channel and the Swiss border.[21]

From August to December 1914 the alliance had achieved a good deal. In early September, immediately before the counteroffensive on the Marne, and at some points during the First Battle of Ypres, fortune had poised on a knife-edge. The effort that Joffre devoted to ensuring its compliance with his plans indicates that he considered the BEF's contribution critical. Though tiny by continental standards and, contrary to British legend, not especially skilled or efficient, it may indeed have been vital in preventing a French collapse.[22] Despite the stresses and the casualties (the BEF's minuscule in absolute terms compared with those of the French), the alliance had also served British interests.

At least for the time being, the Allies had prevented German dominance of the continent. Though nearly all of Belgium had fallen into German hands, the French Channel coast had not. Moreover, and most important, the Reich had been unable to escape the nightmare of a war on two fronts. Outside of Europe, the Royal Navy had swept the Germans off the seas and had imposed a crippling blockade on the Reich. With the British and the French able to draw on the resources of their overseas empires and having far better access to the wider world, Germany's long-term prospects, though by no means hopeless, did not look good.[23]

After the Battle of First Ypres, Joffre appears to have become somewhat more favorably disposed towards Sir John French. But the winter and the following spring did not exactly constitute an era of good feelings among the Allies. Faults on both sides contributed to continuing tensions.

---

21 Doughty, *Pyrrhic Victory*, pp. 97–104; Prete, *Strategy and Command*, pp. 120–48; Philpott, *Anglo-French Relations*, pp. 31–50; I. F. W. Beckett, *Ypres: The First Battle 1914* (Harlow, 2004), pp. 67–187.

22 On the mixed performance of the BEF in 1914 see, N. Gardner, *Command and the British Expeditionary Force in 1914* (Westport, CT, 2003), passim and T. Zuber, *The Mons Myth: A Reassessment of the Battle* (Stroud, Gloucestershire, 2010). Zuber perhaps pushes the case for British military incompetence in relation to German excellence too far, but his work is a useful corrective to earlier British writings that were excessively adulatory of the BEF of 1914.

23 D. Stevenson, *1914–1918: The History of the First World War* (London, 2004), pp. 80–92.

Though Kitchener had initiated efforts to create a mass army (on a voluntary basis) in the first weeks of the war, the British seemed desperately slow to make anything like an equal contribution to the military effort on the Western Front, and it was natural for French leaders to chafe at this gross inequality of sacrifice.[24]

A large part of the problem, however, lay with the French high command, especially Joffre. Preparation for large-scale continental warfare had been the peacetime stock in trade of French military planners to a degree that was not true of their British counterparts. France's prodigious losses in the Battles of the Frontiers were due to errors in French military doctrine and weaknesses in French army performance for which French leaders, including Joffre, had only themselves to blame. Joffre and his headquarters deserve great credit for the strategic rebalancing of the French army that made the Marne counteroffensive possible. But when stalemate set in at the end of First Ypres, Joffre failed adequately to adjust the tempo and method of operations for a war that was becoming a military marathon, not the sprint he had expected. From winter 1914 through to October 1915 he made unrealistic demands on both Allied armies on the Western Front, his own far more than the British.[25] One can surely attribute France's excessive expenditure of its lifeblood in 1914 and 1915 more to the impatience and reckless aggressiveness of its own high command (and to a degree of operational and tactical inefficiency relative to the Germans) than to the lack of readiness of the British to make equivalent sacrifices.

One could argue justifiably the necessity of mounting limited offensive operations to keep the Germans under a degree of pressure on the Western Front. The Central Powers, the alliance of Germany and Austria-Hungry, occupied a strategically "central position" and therefore enjoyed interior lines of operation, the potential strength of which had long been recognized in military theory. The Allies, including the Russians and the Serbs, were, in contrast, fighting on "exterior lines." While remaining on the defensive on some fronts, the Germans could potentially exploit their central position by throwing overwhelming strength against selected opponents successively, defeating their enemies in detail. On this logic the French and British needed to continue offensive operations in the west to prevent the Central Powers from inflicting decisive defeats on Russian and Serb forces.

24 P. Simkins, *Kitchener's Army: The Raising of the New Armies, 1914–16* (Manchester, 1988), pp. 31–48; G. C. Cassar, *Kitchener's War: British Strategy from 1914 to 1916* (Dulles, VA, 2004), pp. 30–33; Prete, *Strategy and Command*, p. 83.
25 Doughty, *Pyrrhic Victory*, pp. 104–52.

Grand Duke Nicholas, the Russian commander in chief, certainly found this logic compelling. In early December he warned Joffre that unless the Western allies increased the pressure on the Germans the Russians would have to cease conducting mobile offensive operations and "adopt the system of entrenchments used on the Franco-Belgian front."[26] In the aftermath of early defeats at German hands, a conscious transition to the defense accompanied by appropriate fortification of their front is exactly what the Russians should have done. But Joffre was not yet prepared to encourage them to adopt such a course.

The French commander in chief did recognize that a form of "siege warfare" had set in by mid October 1914 and that the French army was poorly equipped to conduct such a war. Indeed, when the stalemate began the French, like the British, had no grenades or mortars, little barbed wire, and few wire cutters. Having relied excessively on its excellent 75mm field gun, the French army also possessed little in the way of modern heavy artillery. But Joffre did not think it appropriate to suspend major offensive operations to gain the time necessary to make up for shortages in equipment. During the winter he continued to order a series of major attacks. It is not clear whether the true purpose of such offensives was primarily to "fix" German troops on the Western Front, as Joffre sometimes suggested, or to recapture vital ground in order to restore mobile warfare and "liberate completely the national territory," as his headquarters announced to French troops at the beginning of the Artois-Champagne offensive of mid December 1914. Certainly in late March 1915 Joffre told French ministers that his army would be ready at the end of April to take the offensive and chase the Germans out of France.[27] Events soon indicated that this was a serious misjudgment, compounding a whole series of others that Joffre had made since the onset of the war.

On the basis of its performance in 1914, Joffre judged that the British army had little capacity for the offensive. But he hoped that it would, at least, take over more of the front to release French troops for offensive operations. At the end of the First Battle of Ypres in November 1914 the British held 65 kilometres of the Western Front, the Belgians 27, and the French 700. The fighting of 1914 had severely depleted the BEF by the end of First Ypres and by February 1915 its sector had actually shrunk to approximately 50 kilometres. Moreover, while in February 1915 the French had seven times as many troops as the British on the Western Front, they held a front line fourteen times longer. It is true that long stretches of front the French held were quiet, whereas the whole

26 Ibid., p. 112.
27 Stevenson, *1914–1918*, pp. 156–58; Doughty, *Pyrrhic Victory*, pp. 105–52.

British front was active. Yet those bare statistics reinforced a French sense of disparity of effort within the alliance, a sense conveyed even more starkly by relative casualty figures. In an effort to create reserves for his planned spring offensives, Joffre wanted the British to take over the defense of the whole Ypres salient, thereby releasing two French corps. But the reinforcements from the United Kingdom that Sir John French deemed necessary to bring this about were slow to arrive. He thus stalled on the expansion of the British front. Frustrated, Joffre tried to appeal through the French government to Kitchener, over the British commander's head.[28]

Kitchener and the British War Council, however, did not accept that Joffre should have the last word on the employment of British troops. Kitchener's military judgment was that a decisive breakthrough on the Western Front was extremely unlikely – an opinion he appears to have held consistently until his death in June 1916. He believed Joffre's obsession with mounting frequent, large-scale offensives aimed at breakthrough ill-conceived. He considered (with remarkable prescience) that the war was likely to last another three years, and that it would ultimately be brought to an end by a process of attrition and not by a dramatic breakthrough.

Kitchener's military judgment in this respect was superior to Joffre's.[29] But French officers who believed that, while they suffered, the British kept an eye on their own long-term interests were by no means wrong. Kitchener, for one, did not want the British to consume all their resources in this war. He wanted them to be strong enough at war's end to shape the peace in their own interests and thought it possible that enmity, or at least rivalry, with France and Russia might revive once the war was over.[30]

Given limited British cooperation, Joffre had to modify his military plans for early 1915. He originally intended his February offensive to comprise converging efforts in Artois and Champagne directed at the shoulders of the Noyon salient. Eventually the French army attacked only in Champagne, where it suffered huge losses for little result. Joffre nevertheless continued mounting massive offensives on the Western Front. In so doing he hoped to take advantage of a French miracle of wartime industrial production, accomplished in the direst circumstances, that is comparable with the Soviet achievement in World War II. Yet, despite prodigious expenditure of artillery ammunition, none of Joffre's

28 Doughty, *Pyrrhic Victory*, pp. 135–39; Cassar, *The Tragedy of Sir John French*, 201–11.
29 D. French, *British Strategy*, pp. 71–72; Cassar, *Kitchener's War*, pp. 162–67; J. Charteris, *At GHQ* (London, 1931), p. 137.
30 Doughty, *Pyrrhic Victory*, p. 139.

1915 offensives gained much ground.[31] Furthermore, their human cost (together with that of the Battles of the Frontiers and of the Battle of Verdun in 1916) traumatized France for a generation.

While the British did not give Joffre all the cooperation he wanted, they can hardly be said to have turned their backs on their allies. The BEF expanded greatly in the course of 1915, becoming by far the largest army Britain had ever put in the field. Contrary to their traditions the British introduced progressively greater degrees of compulsion, mainly in order to raise troops to sustain and expand the army, and in early 1916 they introduced full-blown wartime conscription.[32] In addition to playing a major role in the defense of the Ypres salient against a German offensive April–May 1915, the BEF also undertook a series of offensive operations (Neuve Chapelle, Aubers Ridge, Givenchy, and Festubert). Though small by the standards of the war, most of these exceeded, in terms of numbers involved and casualties suffered, most battles in the previous history of the British army. After punishing losses at Festubert in May, however, both the First Army commander, Sir Douglas Haig, and Sir John French believed that the BEF needed to wait until increasing production at home had strengthened its artillery before launching further offensive operations.[33]

The Russians, however, were in crisis after the Austro-German May 1915 breakthrough at Gorlice-Tarnow precipitated a series of costly reverses and retreats in the east. Though he recognized that his own army was now weary, Joffre felt compelled to mount a further major offensive effort on the Western Front in September to help keep Russia in the war. He demanded British support with an offensive in the La Bassée area. The British not only regarded their army as under-equipped and inadequately trained for such an offensive but the ground chosen for them as most unsuitable, a point on which the Sir John French and Sir Douglas Haig, the commander chosen to execute the operation, agreed. French wanted to confine the British support to a demonstration, an artillery bombardment not followed by an infantry assault.

Kitchener, however, realized that holding the alliance together required a more substantial British effort. Kitchener seems to have viewed the offensive mounted near Loos on 25 September as little more than a regrettable blood sacrifice necessary to preserve the alliance. After being

31 For the French munitions miracle see Stevenson, *1914–1918*, pp. 229–30 and Greenhalgh, *Victory Through Coalition*, p. 109. On Joffre's offensives of 1915 see Doughty, *Pyrrhic Victory*, pp. 140–202.
32 D. French, *British Strategy and War Aims 1914–1916* (London, 1988) pp. 117–22 and 169–73. A. J. P. Taylor, *English History 1914–1945* (Oxford, 1976), pp. 52–55.
33 Harris, *Douglas Haig*, pp. 107–53; Cassar, *The Tragedy of Sir John French*, pp. 196–237.

pushed into action by Kitchener, Haig chose to conduct it as a real attempt at breakthrough. Especially on the offensive's disastrous second day, this decision arguably caused excessive British loss of life.[34]

During October all Allied offensive efforts on the Western Front ground to a miserable halt, capping off a bad year for the Allies. Huge casualties for little result on the Western Front accompanied military disaster on the Eastern Front. Italy's joining the Allies on 23 May 1915 did not, in the short run, pay the dividends hoped for. Bulgaria's intervention on the side of the Central Powers on 6 September, however, led to the virtual destruction of the Serbian state, while joint Franco-British endeavours away from the Western Front proved most disappointing.[35]

The establishment, by the end of 1914, of a continuous Western Front, which in the existing state of military technology looked extremely difficult to rupture, had led some policy makers in both Britain and France to look for opportunities to mount offensives elsewhere. Turkish entry into the war on the German side in November 1914 seriously concerned Winston Churchill, the First Lord of the Admiralty. He believed that that development offered a significant threat to the Russian Empire in the Caucasus and to the British position in Egypt. He took the lead in a substantial diversion of the naval and military effort of the British Empire to the Dardanelles, the idea being to put battleships in a position to bombard the Ottoman capital at Constantinople and thus force Turkey out of the war. The French too took part in both a failed naval assault on 18 March and an amphibious operation on 25 April. In the latter operation, French troops landed at Kum Kale in Asia Minor, while British, Australian, and New Zealand troops landed on the Gallipoli peninsula.

For the British Empire's forces the Dardanelles became the second bloodiest theater of operations during World War I, after the Western Front. The campaign also caused massive, probably much greater, losses for the Turks. But it was reasonably clear by the end of 1915 that there was no prospect of getting battleships to Constantinople and the Allies decided to withdraw their forces from Gallipoli early in 1916.[36] By May 1915 failure at the Dardanelles (coupled with a "shell shortage scandal") had forced Asquith, the British Liberal Prime Minister, to form a coalition with the Conservatives and remove Winston Churchill, discredited by the failure of the Dardanelles effort, from the Admiralty.[37]

34 Holmes, *The Little Field Marshal*, pp. 272–98; Harris, *Douglas Haig*, pp. 153–77.
35 Stevenson, *1914–1918*, pp. 106–26.
36 R. Prior, *Gallipoli: The End of the Myth* (New Haven, CT, 2009).
37 G. H. Cassar, *Asquith as War Leader* (London, 1994), pp. 90–110.

While the inspiration for operations at the Dardanelles was essentially British with the French going along as junior partners, the opposite was true of intervention in the Balkans. Amongst the early advocates of an expedition there was Franchet d'Espèrey, who, later in the war, was to command in that theater with remarkable success. But the French Council of Ministers, with Alexandre Millerand, the Minister of War playing a leading role, ultimately made the critical decisions. One could certainly have made a reasonable case for intervention. Given that decisive victory on the Western Front seemed a remote prospect, did it not make sense to help the Serbs survive the attacks of the Central Powers and perhaps ultimately strike north into Austria-Hungary, the soft underbelly of the Central Powers?

Yet, while the Greek government was prepared to allow the Allies to use Salonika as a base, it was not prepared to declare war or to participate with its own troops. The British authorities generally were far from certain that anything useful could be accomplished by this intervention and went along reluctantly, committing few troops to the enterprise. The landing of Allied forces at Salonika on 5 October came, indeed, too late to deter Bulgarian entry into the war and did not prevent Serbia's being overrun by Bulgarian, Austrian, and German troops. The Salonika base provided a refuge for some Serb troops. Otherwise it proved of little real value to the Allies until 1918.[38]

As we have noted, politicians were instrumental in the Allied interventions at the Dardanelles and at Salonika. The principal military figures in both Britain and France preferred to concentrate on the Western Front. Yet while historians tend to view the statesmen of the Grand Alliance during World War II as political colossi, dominating the events of their time, the British and French political leaders for much of World War I seem less substantial figures. President Raymond Poincaré of France, who served throughout hostilities, was a forceful personality.[39] But, under the Third Republic the presidency had relatively little power, political leadership depending principally on the premier. Historians seem to agree that René Viviani, the French premier in August 1914, was not a natural war leader, though, arguably, his task was made especially difficult by the French constitution and politics of the period. Despite efforts to establish a political truce – the *union sacrée* – France had five premiers in little more than four years of war and some of those led more than one ministry. Only the last, Georges Clemenceau, who took office in

38 Doughty, *Pyrrhic Victory*, pp. 214–28; C. Falls and A. F. Becke, *Military Operations: Macedonia from the Outbreak of War to the Spring of 1917* (London, 1933), pp. 29–50.
39 J. F. V. Keiger, *Raymond Poincaré* (Cambridge, 1997), pp. 145–239.

November 1917, is generally regarded as a first-rate war leader.[40] For much of the war instability and weakness at the top in France made the exertion of effective political control over the military difficult. This partly explains Joffre's retention long after he arguably should have been replaced.[41] Yet in some respects France managed remarkably well in spite of the frequent changes of ministry. French bureaucracy, entrepreneurship, management, and labour between them achieved, as we have noted, prodigies of war production.

The unwritten and flexible British constitution permitted rapid adaptation to war conditions, and the Asquith government was not slow to enact sweeping war powers. But the mechanics of government needed radical transformation to wage a war of this type and scale. Before 1914 British Cabinets had not even had secretaries or kept minutes. The Cabinet Office apparatus, which allows the operations of the various government departments to be coordinated, was largely a product of this war.[42] Asquith, however, was no more temperamentally suited to this kind of war than was his French counterpart, Viviani.[43] Kitchener could help the Asquith government exert control over its main army in the field. But Kitchener himself was so imperious and uncommunicative that he did not, to put it mildly, work well with civilian colleagues. He had lost much of his influence months before he died on 5 June 1916, after HMS *Hampshire*, on which he was travelling for talks in Russia, hit a German mine off the Orkneys.[44] By that stage Churchill, who arguably had the greatest natural talent for war leadership of any civilian minister, had his reputation severely damaged by failure at the Dardanelles.

Lloyd George, who became prime minister in November 1916, was a strong character, but untutored in military matters. However, as prime minister he was also in a bizarre political position. He was a radical Liberal who had revolted against his party leader (Asquith) and found himself leading a government largely backed by Conservative MPs. Lacking a dependable parliamentary majority (and reluctant to call a general election in wartime) he could not be the sort of leviathan that Winston Churchill became from 1940 to 1945. Particularly in the early months of his time in office he was essentially a political fixer, surviving on his wits from day to day.[45]

40 G. Dallas, *At the Heart of a Tiger: Clemenceau and his World, 1841–1929* (London, 1993), pp. 424–554.
41 A. Clayton, *Paths of Glory: The French Army, 1914–18* (London, 2003), pp. 81–82.
42 M. Hankey, *The Supreme Command 1914–18* (London, 1961), vol. I, pp. 223–67 and vol. II, pp. 575–96; S. Roskill, *Hankey: Man of Secrets* (London, 1970), vol. I, pp. 342–53.
43 Cassar, *Asquith as War Leader*, pp. 192–236.
44 Cassar, *Kitchener's War*, pp. 283–88.
45 Harris, *Douglas Haig*, pp. 294–97.

Allied heads of government were slow to meet face-to-face to coordinate strategy. Admittedly, in an age before air travel became routine, international summit conferences were much less common. Nevertheless, it still seems odd that Asquith and Viviani did not physically meet for nearly a year into the war. The year 1915 was crucial in the alliance's development. The first proper Franco-British politico-military summit was at Calais on 6 July.[46] British and French representatives met Russians and the Italians at an inter-Allied military conference held at Joffre's headquarters at Chantilly the following day. Though it is difficult to pinpoint any precise agreements made at either of these conferences, they started a trend. There were major multi-ally conferences at Chantilly (again) 6–8 December 1915, at Chantilly (yet again) 15 November 1916, at Rome 4–7 January 1917, in Petrograd in February 1917, in Paris 25–26 June 1917, at Rapallo 5–7 November 1917, and in London on 15 March 1918. Bilateral Franco-British conferences were considerably more common than this, the frequency of such interaction from mid 1915 making the Franco-British alliance seem a more modern, sophisticated affair. However, the French and British did not create in World War I the large number of highly integrated military staffs that would be a feature of the Anglo-American alliance of 1941–1945. Apart from anything else, the lack of appropriate language skills amongst officers would have made this well nigh impossible. But their civil servants formed effective joint committees for procurement and supply.[47]

Attempting to concert plans for 1916, at a conference held at Chantilly on 6 December 1915, the French, British, Russians, and Italians could only make a rather vague agreement that they would all mount major offensives on their fronts as soon as possible after the beginning of March – perhaps not much, but better than nothing. For the Western Front Joffre intended that, after a number of preliminary attacks to confuse the Germans and wear down their reserves, the main Allied attack would be mounted on the Somme, where the French and British sectors of the Western Front joined. Joffre initially intended that the Somme offensive would be organized and directed by the French, the larger, more experienced and better equipped of the two armies. But he also intended for the British to at last begin to bear their fair share of the fighting.

---

46 Hankey, *Supreme Command*, pp. 347–50; Greenhalgh, *Victory Through Coalition*, p. 9.
47 Hankey, *Supreme Command*, pp. 411, 533, 594, 606–12, 687–89, 720–29, 787, 791; Joffre, *Memoirs* (London, 1932), vol. II, p. 380. On Allied economic cooperation, especially in response to the German submarine threat, see Greenhalgh, *Victory Through Coalition*, pp. 102–32. Notable combined committees for coordinating purchase and supply included the Commission Internationale de Ravitaillement, the Inter-Ally Bureau of Munitions, and the Wheat Executive.

Joffre had disagreements with Haig – who had taken over from French as British commander in chief in France in December 1915 – about how big a role the British would play in preliminary "wearing out" attacks before the main offensive effort began. Haig had made clear that his preference was for the principal Allied offensive of 1916 on the Western Front to occur in Flanders. Nevertheless, a working Franco-British agreement was obtained for operations on the Western Front in 1916 with the Somme offensive as the main effort.[48]

The events of 1916 on the Western Front, however, perfectly illustrate the truth of the military maxim that in making plans "the enemy has a vote." On 21 February 1916 at Verdun, the Germans unleashed a massive offensive that seized the strategic initiative and pre-empted Allied arrangements. The German high command under General Erich von Falkenhayn, who had replaced General Helmuth von Moltke as chief of the Great General Staff in September 1914, concluded that the best hope of victory in 1916 lay in bleeding the French army white. French casualties in the Battle of the Frontiers and in Joffre's 1915 offensives had been so great that French morale seemed likely to collapse, if faced with further losses of that magnitude.

Falkenhayn thus consciously planned a battle of attrition at Verdun, a fortress of great emotional significance to the French nation. He intended to confine the battle to a narrow salient deluged by German artillery. The German offensive did create a crisis of morale for the French army and indeed the French nation. French losses were so extreme that it became vital to do something to relieve the pressure. The only practicable course seemed to be to go ahead with the Somme offensive as soon as possible.[49]

The defense of Verdun, however, absorbed so much of the French army that the Somme offensive became, of necessity, more a British that a French operation, though the French remained heavily involved. The more the operation became the responsibility of the weaker and less prepared of the two Allied armies on the Western Front, the more it was delayed. British delays in mounting the offensive seemed to the French, in their Verdun agony, callous and uncooperative, much in the way that British and American delays in opening a "second front" appeared to the Soviets in World War II. These tensions of spring and early summer of 1916 constituted another major crisis in the Franco-British alliance. But British losses of approximately 20,000 soldiers killed on the first

---

48 Philpott, *Anglo-French Relations*, pp. 112–21.
49 R. T. Foley, *German Strategy and the Path to Verdun: Erich von Falkenhayn and the Development of Attrition, 1870–1916* (Cambridge, 2002), pp. 181–208; Doughty, *Pyrrhic Victory*, pp. 250–83.

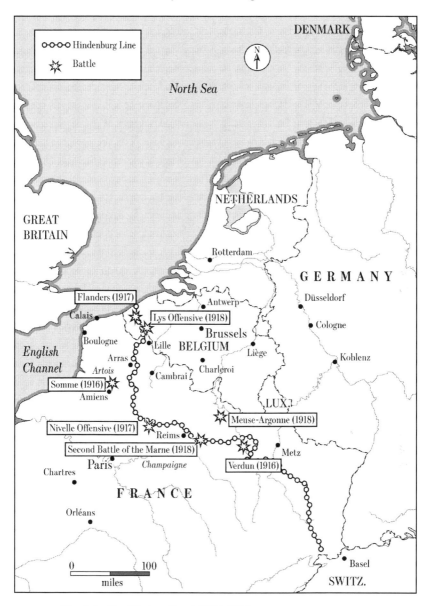

Map 5.1   The Western Front, 1916–1918

day, 1 July 1916, for gains that were almost nonexistent across much of the frontage of the attack, underlined just how unready they were to take the lead in an offensive on this scale. French forces attacking alongside the British achieved greater gains for significantly fewer casualties, indicating their greater experience, greater artillery firepower, and more cautious and systematic approach, as well as the weaker German defensive positions in their sector.[50]

It is, however, indicative of just how serious the British were about maintaining their alliance with the French and ultimately emerging triumphant in this war that, while modifying the focus of their attack after the disastrous first day, they continued to proceed energetically with the Somme offensive. On 14 July they achieved a major success, breaking into the German second-line position. Even before then, the Somme offensive and a Russian offensive on the Eastern Front relieved the pressure on the French at Verdun. Once again the Franco-British alliance had been saved. But neither Joffre nor Haig was satisfied with this; each hoped for a decisive victory. Though Haig tried, most conscientiously, to take regular French lessons from Captain Gemeau, a French ADC who lived in his chateau, communication between Haig and Joffre and their armies remained remarkably poor, the poverty of communication and cooperation becoming major factors in the ultimately disappointing result of the joint offensive on the Somme.[51]

One matter of crucial importance to the conduct of the offensive was the climate of this part of France. Joffre and his staff were aware that, given that it had started later than intended, time was of the essence. If the Allies had not cracked the main German defensive positions by mid September, it would probably be too late to do so, for the late autumn climate would make the conduct of operations all but impossible. But after its promising seizure of the German second-line position on 14 July 1916, the British Fourth Army became bogged down in fighting for a group of woods that the Germans turned into improvised but highly effective intermediate positions ahead of their third main line. Haig and Sir Henry Rawlinson, the British Fourth Army commander, became baffled by the problem of fighting through the wooded terrain. For several weeks they effectively lost control of the battle, rather as senior American commanders would lose control of the Hürtgen Forest fighting in 1944.[52]

Haig was acutely aware of French pressure to speed up the offensive. But it is indicative of the shockingly poor state of Franco-British liaison

50 Philpott, *Anglo-French Relations*, pp. 121–26; Harris, *Douglas Haig*, pp. 208–37.
51 Harris, *Douglas Haig*, pp. 238–54; Greenhalgh, *Victory Through Coalition*, pp. 83–84.
52 Harris, *Douglas Haig*, pp. 254–57.

(as well as, perhaps, Haig's limited intellect) that he and his staff seem to have supposed this a mere matter of impatience. In reality the French knew that low clouds and a major increase in rainfall would dominate the weather in the area in late autumn. The resulting conditions would dramatically reduce the accuracy of artillery fire and bog the infantry down in the mud. Haig seems to have grasped this critical point only after Poincaré, the President of the Republic, explained it to him at a meeting on 27 August.[53] That so elementary and vital a point was effectively communicated only so late in the day proved little short of disastrous. The poor state of liaison between the armies at this stage may, in part, be accounted for by Joffre's choice of General Pierre des Vallières as his main conduit to and from Haig. Des Vallières, though he spoke English fluently, intensely disliked the British and had repeatedly made it clear that he did not want the job. While polite to Haig's face, in communication with Joffre's headquarters he generally and often unfairly deprecated the BEF. Thus, he tended to undermine rather than consolidate the alliance.[54]

By the end of September the British Fourth Army had broken the third main line of German fortifications on the Somme. The Germans had constructed a fourth line but this was hastily built and much less powerful compared with those they had occupied earlier in the year. Had this situation arisen a month earlier, the Germans would have been in real trouble. In the face of increasingly powerful and accurate British artillery, now better coordinated with infantry action, they might well have been forced to make a major strategic withdrawal of the sort they actually did make early the following year but under much greater pressure and with far heavier attendant losses. In October, however, they gained the assistance of both atmospheric murk – which tended to blind British aviation and artillery – and a morass of glutinous mud in which attacking British infantry floundered. By mid November the offensive on the Somme had ground to a halt. The inter-Allied conference at Chantilly that month approved its renewal early in 1917, but this agreement fell into abeyance when Robert Nivelle replaced Joffre in December.[55]

Another crisis in Franco-British military relations occurred early in 1917. It is explicable only in terms of the growing frustration of both the French high command and David Lloyd George, the British prime

53 Haig's diary, Sunday 27 August 1916, in G. Sheffield and J. Bourne, *Douglas Haig: War Diaries and Letters 1914–1918* (London, 2005), p. 224.
54 Greenhalgh, *Victory Through Coalition*, pp. 94–101.
55 Harris, *Douglas Haig*, pp. 266–73; Greenhalgh, *Victory Through Coalition*, pp. 65–68; Doughty, *Pyrrhic Victory*, p. 325.

minister, with Haig. During the Somme battle, Lloyd George, who had replaced Kitchener in the War Office after his death, had been horrified by British losses and had come to believe that the French army was fighting more efficiently than the British. There was some truth in this, though the French had only gained their 1916 level of offensive efficiency after appalling losses in the 1914–1915 battles. Silver-tongued himself, Lloyd George took Haig's notorious inability to articulate his ideas orally as proof of stupidity. The prime minister was vastly more impressed with Joffre's replacement, Nivelle, who was fluently Anglophone, charming, apparently self-assured, and responsible for the successful attacks in the later stages of the 1916 Verdun fighting.[56]

Haig, too, initially related well to Nivelle, sharing the latter's undiminished faith in winning the war by a dramatic breakthrough on the Western Front. Yet there were inevitably some differences. Nivelle concluded that he could achieve decisive success in 1917 only if the BEF came under his command. Lloyd George aligned himself with Nivelle in this matter, but did so without informing Haig, the Chief of the Imperial General Staff (CIGS), Sir William Robertson, or the king. When, on 26 February at a conference at Calais, Nivelle unveiled his proposal to put the BEF under French command, stripping GHQ of all authority on an indefinite basis, Robertson and Haig reacted in consternation, even fury. Facing the possibility of their joint resignation (though this was never explicitly threatened), and knowing that he could not, in such circumstances, rely on the backing of the king or the Conservative MPs on whose support his coalition government depended, Lloyd George backed down. A compromise worked out by the Cabinet secretary, Maurice Hankey, ensured that Nivelle could not communicate with British formations directly, but only through GHQ, and placed Haig under Nivelle's command only for the forthcoming spring offensive.[57]

Nivelle's failed effort to assume formal command of the British army on the Western Front on an indefinite basis might have poisoned Franco-British military relations to a degree that made cooperation between the armies virtually impossible for the rest of 1917. It is a tribute to the better side of Haig's nature that this did not happen. Haig blamed Lloyd George rather than Nivelle for the Calais conference fiasco. While he insisted, against the initial advice and wishes of the French high command, on going ahead with an attack on Vimy Ridge, Haig intended this offensive to be part of a larger British operation in Artois that Nivelle strongly supported.

56 Harris, *Douglas Haig*, pp. 274–86; Grigg, *Lloyd George*, pp. 31–38.
57 Roskill, *Hankey*, I, pp. 361–66; Hankey, *Supreme Command*, pp. 615–21.

The British Artois operation aimed to set the stage for a much larger French offensive later in the spring, an operation that Nivelle intended to decide the outcome of the war. However, a carefully organized German withdrawal, the retreat to the Hindenburg Line, conducted in stages from February to April 1917 undercut the operational rational for Nivelle's offensive plans. This move to a shorter, more easily defensible line caused many senior French generals to have grave doubts about trying to mount a knockout blow on the Western Front that year. At the same time Nivelle's political support in Paris began to unravel. Haig might have exploited Nivelle's difficulties in order to scotch altogether the latter's offensive plans for the spring. This would have allowed him to refocus the British army's resources on a major operation in Flanders, an option he had long preferred. Instead, throughout the spring and into the early summer of 1917, Haig gave Nivelle a degree of loyal, dedicated support that is rather remarkable in the circumstances.[58]

The early stages of the British offensive of 9 April (Easter Monday) in Artois were dramatically successful, the Canadian Corps' seizure of Vimy Ridge being the best-remembered episode. Rather to Lloyd George's embarrassment, Haig's military reputation skyrocketed, at least for a short time. Within a few days, however, British forces fighting the Battle of Arras, as it was later known, became badly bogged down. Ultimately, in terms of attrition, it was the least efficient of all Haig's offensives in 1916 and 1917. But Haig persisted with the battle as long as he did at least in part in a spirit of cooperation with Nivelle and the French army, whose own offensive on the Chemin des Dames was repeatedly delayed.[59]

When finally mounted in mid April, the "Nivelle Offensive," though less bloodily disastrous than many previous French attacks, failed after a few weeks of fighting. Coming on top of the massive losses earlier in the war and a huge psychological disappointment given the promises Nivelle had offered regarding its success, the failed offensive triggered mutinies through much of the French army.[60] Especially after the British successes of 9 April, the French failure left Lloyd George's political face spattered with metaphorical egg. He had been trying to hand over command of the British army to a foreign general whose massive military misjudgments had just caused a collapse of morale in his own. For the next few months Lloyd George was, therefore, in an exceptionally weak position in dealing with the British army and with Haig in particular.[61]

58 Harris, *Douglas Haig*, pp. 291–307.
59 Ibid., pp. 298–327.
60 A. Clayton, "Robert Nivelle and the French Spring Offensive", in Brian Bond (ed.), *Fallen Stars: Eleven Studies of Twentieth Century Military Disasters* (London, 1991), pp. 52–64.
61 Grigg, *Lloyd George*, pp. 93–98, 155–73.

In spring 1917, Haig's loyalty to Nivelle and to his French allies was real enough. But the notion that his offensive operations in Flanders from June to November 1917 were motivated mainly by the need to divert German attention from a demoralized and mutinous French army is a fiction, an *ex post facto* justification for operations that ultimately exhausted and demoralized the British army for limited results. Haig's two-part Flanders offensive – the Battle of Messines in June and the Third Battle of Ypres from late July to November 1917 – was motivated neither by a wish to distract attention from the French army's perilous situation nor by the need to counter the U-boat threat from German bases on the Channel coast, another justification sometimes provided.

Rather, Third Ypres, an operation that Lloyd George thoroughly disliked and about which Robertson, the CIGS, had the gravest doubts, constituted Haig's personal win-the-war scheme for 1917, his equivalent of the Nivelle Offensive. Given the loyal support he had given to Nivelle in the spring, Haig hoped for an equivalent degree of cooperation from the French during the summer. One French army did indeed participate in Third Ypres, but the French had too many of their own problems to offer help on the scale Haig wanted. In any case senior French generals generally had little confidence in offensive operations in Flanders. They considered that area (rightly as it turned out) too low-lying and wet. Allied troops attacking there, they thought, were all too likely to get stuck in the mud.[62]

Under General Philippe Pétain, who succeeded Nivelle on 15 May 1917, the main priority of the French high command was to rebuild the morale of the French army.[63] In 1917 Russia was in a state of internal crisis, revolutions occurring in March and November. The Russian army largely ceased to fight almost a year before a Bolshevik government formally made peace with Germany in March 1918.[64] On the other hand, though lacking an army capable of fighting that of a first-class power, the United States had entered the war on 6 April 1917.[65] In these circumstances, while Pétain was prepared to mount limited attacks to rebuild French confidence and proficiency, his basic strategy was to wait for American help.[66] For France this was undoubtedly the correct course. The British might have been well advised to adopt a similar policy.

62 Harris, *Douglas Haig*, pp. 333–41; Greenhalgh, *Victory Through Coalition*, p. 153.
63 Clayton, *Paths*, pp. 134–36.
64 N. Stone, *The Eastern Front 1914–1917* (New York, 1975), pp. 282–301.
65 E. M. Coffman, *The War to End All Wars: The American Military Experience in World War I* (Madison, WI, 1986), pp. 5–19.
66 Doughty, *Pyrrhic Victory*, pp. 355–404.

But in this matter, as in many others, there was little commonality of Franco-British military understanding or approach.

Ultimately the BEF's operations at Third Ypres (July–November) and Cambrai (November–December) were proportionately more exhausting and demoralizing to it than to the much larger German army. Third Ypres and Cambrai also left British civil–military relations in a dangerous state, which contributed to the government's leaving the BEF unnecessarily weak in the face of the upcoming German offensive the Allies expected in the spring.

With the German war economy struggling under the impact of the Allied blockade and the Americans building a mass army and starting the process of shipping it to France, Germany's sole hope of decisive victory lay in a spring offensive that would compel the French to make peace on German terms before America deployed its full power. The collapse of Russia and the severe defeat inflicted on the Italians by Austro-German forces at Caporetto in late October 1917 enabled the large-scale transfer of German divisions to the Western Front. This transfer – so massive it was impossible for Allied intelligence to miss – seemed, at least to Generals Paul von Hindenburg and Erich Ludendorff, who had assumed joint control of the German war effort upon the fall of Falkenhayn in August 1916, to offer real hope of decisive victory.[67]

Supposedly in an effort better to coordinate Allied strategy and to react flexibly to any German move – but actually to diminish the control of Robertson and Haig over the employment of the British army – in November 1917, at the Rapallo conference, Lloyd George successfully advocated the creation of a Supreme War Council (SWC).[68] He appointed General Sir Henry Wilson, whom both he and the French trusted more than any other British officer, as Britain's military representative, while General Ferdinand Foch, who had commanded French forces on the Somme, became France's military representative.

The SWC, however, would only have real teeth if it controlled a strategic reserve, some divisions being under its control. Lloyd George supported this idea, and the Allies agreed to it in principle in January 1918. This triggered Robertson's resignation as CIGS. Lloyd George, glad to be rid of Robertson, then appointed Wilson in his place. Both Haig and Pétain, however, proved most reluctant to transfer divisions to the control of the SWC and fought a successful rearguard action against the proposal. They argued that any movement of reserves required in the

---

67 Harris, *Douglas Haig*, pp. 381–424; Stevenson, *Backs To The Wall*, pp. 30–53.
68 Greenhalgh, *Victory Through Coalition*, pp. 163–81.

face of the coming German Western Front offensive was best arranged between themselves.[69]

Combined pressure from Lloyd George and the French forced Haig to extend the British sector of the Western Front in early 1918, at a time when the British government was also deliberately restricting the manpower available to the BEF. Lloyd George and some of his colleagues were apparently more worried by the possibility of Haig renewing bloody offensive operations on the Western Front than by the prospect of a German knockout blow there. When the initial German offensive began on 21 March 1918, it did so on the Somme and largely on the British Fifth Army's sector, a poorly fortified area recently taken over from the French. Haig had deliberately left the Fifth Army weak in the belief that its sector was the BEF's least critical. Thus, the defenders found themselves grossly overstretched in relation to the size of the German forces they faced. But Haig was reluctant to reinforce the Fifth Army sufficiently quickly or on a large enough scale, apparently because he believed (at least for a few days) that this German attack was not the main effort and that a heavier blow would shortly follow elsewhere. Though Pétain rushed French divisions to the British Fifth Army sector – a move for which contingency plans had been made – this did not prevent a dangerously deep and rapid retreat that was in danger of becoming a rout.[70]

By 26 March the situation was critical. This is a controversial matter, not entirely agreed upon among historians, but it is at least possible that effective cooperation between Haig and Pétain was on the verge of collapse. Had that happened, the Germans might have captured the city of Amiens, severing a lateral railway critical to British logistical support and driving a physical wedge between the British and the French armies. If the Germans had then concentrated offensive efforts on the BEF, it is not inconceivable that they might have brought about its collapse. It is thus at least arguable that on 26 March 1918 the outcome of the war hung in the balance.

But the highest levels of political leadership in the Allied camp realized the nature and gravity of the emergency. Ministerial intervention took matters out of the hands of Haig and Pétain, both of whom had been under great psychological strain. The most critical Franco-British meetings of the war were held in Doullens on 26 March. Both Lloyd

---

69 D. R. Woodward, *Lloyd George and the Generals* (London, 1983), pp. 253–81; W. Robertson, *Soldiers and Statesmen 1914–1918* (London, 1926), vol. II, pp. 284–92; Griggs, *Lloyd George*, pp. 421–28.

70 Harris, *Douglas Haig*, pp. 432–56; D. French, *The Strategy of the Lloyd George Coalition 1916–1918* (Oxford, 1995), pp. 184–87.

George and Georges Clemenceau, the ruthlessly belligerent French premier, were present. Together they reaffirmed the alliance's solidarity. The French and British armies were to maintain physical contact with each other. Amiens was to be held at all costs. Ferdinand Foch would become an Allied generalissimo, albeit with rather limited and ill-defined powers at this stage, somewhat extended later in 1918. The Doullens conferences of 26 March 1918, three of them altogether, constituted the alliance's finest hour.[71]

Foch could not immediately stop the retreat on the Somme, but it is at least arguable that he reinvigorated Allied resistance there. By 28 March this particular crisis, the worst since 1914, was largely over. Further German offensives continued until mid July, with Foch playing critical roles in coordinating Allied resistance, carefully husbanding reserves and mounting, on 18 July, a mainly French and American counteroffensive, known as the Second Battle of the Marne, which turned the tide of battle irrevocably in the Allies' favor.[72] The French army was, however, on the edge of exhaustion by the end of July. The war could not have been brought to a conclusion in 1918 had not the BEF then taken the lead.

Most of the BEF, too, was exhausted by late summer. Though not primarily responsible for the degree of operational and tactical virtuosity that at least a sizable part of the BEF had acquired by this stage, Haig's determination and force of personality were critical in getting his forces to maintain a virtually continuous series of massive offensive operations, the Hundred Days offensive, that ran from 8 August to 11 November 1918, from the opening of the Battle of Amiens to the Armistice. Almost completely forgotten by the British general public today, these battles are, in terms of sheer scale, the greatest victories in British military history. By 11 November 1918, the BEF was smaller than either the French or the American armies on the Western Front. But during the Allied counteroffensives of 1918 it was the most efficient and the most consistently successful, capturing the most prisoners and guns. Foch's role in coordinating Allied action during the last hundred days of the war was critical even though things did not always go quite as he planned. Foch intended that, from late September, all the armies under his aegis would attack simultaneously until victory was achieved. A "general offensive" of

---

71 Doughty, *Pyrrhic Victory*, pp. 430–40; Harris, *Douglas Haig*, pp. 447–58; Greenhalgh, *Victory Through Coalition*, pp. 12–197.
72 F. Foch, *The Memoirs of Marshal Foch* (London, 1931), pp. 301–425; Greenhalgh, *Foch in Command*, pp. 301–406; M. Neiberg, *The Second Battle of the Marne* (Bloomington, IN, 2008), pp. 98–190.

this nature did indeed occur. At certain critical moments, however, only the BEF was making real headway.[73]

The Western Front was by far the most critical theater of war, but French and British divisions also did important work in the Balkans under the command of Franchet d'Espèrey and on the Italian front, where they had bolstered the Italians after Caporetto. In conjunction with Greek, Serb, and Italian forces, they helped bring about the collapse of Bulgaria and Austria-Hungary.[74] It was apparently news of the Bulgarian armistice in late September, slightly before the BEF's Fourth Army's breaking of the Hindenburg Line, that was the immediate trigger for Ludendorff's partial nervous breakdown. After the British Fourth Army broke the Beaurevoir Line on 5 October, it became apparent that there was no position on the Western Front the German army could hold for any length of time.

In early November the advice of senior German military leaders to their government indicated that the army might soon disintegrate if the Reich failed to achieve a ceasefire quickly. The Armistice of 11 November was, in all but outward form, a German unconditional surrender.[75] In human affairs, however, outward appearances can be extremely important. In retrospect it seems a great mistake to have allowed the German army to salvage any dignity from this debacle. It permitted the generation of a myth that the army had remained undefeated at the front and succumbed only to a "stab in the back" by pacifists, socialists, and Jews, myth-making that began immediately after capitulation.

The Franco-British alliance had held the Germans in check long enough for a large American army to be deployed to Europe, but only just. The French and British could not have achieved decisive victory without American help. It had been necessary to bring in the New World to redress the balance of the Old. The Franco-British alliance of 1914–1918 had been for the most part an awkward, sometimes painful, deeply frustrating business for both parties. Some influential postwar memoirs contained bitter criticisms of the alliance partnership.[76] Though there were people who wanted to preserve or renew a spirit

73 J. P. Harris, *Amiens to the Armistice: The BEF in the Hundred Days Campaign, 8 August–11 November 1918* (London, 1998), pp. 230–32, passim.
74 Stevenson, *Backs To the Wall*, pp. 142–48, 155–61.
75 Harris, *Amiens*, pp. 202–88.
76 V. Huguet, *Britain and the War: A French Indictment* (London, 1928), passim. Huguet served as French military attaché in London before the war and was a liaison officer with Sir John French's headquarters in 1914–1915. During the war some in his own army considered Huget too pro-British, but he had become bitterly critical of his former allies by the time he wrote this account in 1921–1922.

of close military cooperation between the two countries as the threat from Nazi Germany steadily rose, their views did not become dominant before 1939.[77] On the positive side, when the alliance was finally reconstituted, there were indications that prominent people had learned from the previous experience.[78] On this occasion, however, the German Ardennes–Meuse breakthrough largely shattered the alliance before it could develop its considerable latent potential.

The stresses and strains in the Franco-British alliance of 1914–1918 are indicative of the difficulties of hurriedly forging a partnership between two countries with a long history of intense rivalry and intermittent enmity, even when both partners are in acute danger from a third party. It is true that Britain and America were also rivals and had fought each other in a couple of wars before becoming allies during parts of the world wars, the Cold War, and a number of subsequent conflicts. It is also true that the relationship between Britain and America has never been easy. But a somewhat greater cultural affinity and the relative ease of conversing in a (largely) common language allowed the development of a much closer working relationship between these powers in World War II than ever proved possible during the Franco-British alliance in World War I.

---

77 In the United Kingdom two of the most avowedly pro-French figures in the politico-military establishment in the 1930s were Field Marshal Sir Archibald Montgomery-Massingberd, CIGS 1933–1936 and Alfred Duff Cooper, successively Secretary of State for War in 1935–1937 and First Lord of the Admiralty in 1937–1938. On Montgomery-Massingberd's wish for military cooperation with the French see J. P. Harris, "The British General Staff and the Coming of War 1933–1939," in D. French and B. H. Reid (eds.), *The British General Staff: Reform and Innovation, 1890–1939* (London, 2002), pp. 178–87. On Duff Cooper see J. Charmley, *Duff Cooper: The Authorized Biography* (London, 1986), pp. 80–140.

78 For example, Lord Gort, commanding the British Expeditionary Force in 1939, insisted on being placed directly under the French commander in chief to remove all ambiguity about the chain of command. J. R. Colville, *Man of Valour: Field Marshal Lord Gort, V.C.* (London, 1972), p. 125.

6   The Grand Alliance in World War II

Mark A. Stoler

What British Prime Minister Winston S. Churchill labeled in his World War II memoirs 'the Grand Alliance' was one of the most successful wartime coalitions in military history.[1] Despite numerous differences and conflicts among its members, it succeeded in totally defeating the Axis powers and imposing upon them unconditional surrender and military occupation. The Grand Alliance did break apart soon after the war ended as a result of the inability of its members to agree on a desired postwar order. But that fact and the resulting Cold War has tended to blind people to the alliance's enormous success as a military coalition. It should not do so.

The Grand Alliance formed as a result of the failure of the original Anglo-French coalition against Nazi Germany due to the military defeat and surrender of France in 1940, followed by Hitler's 1941 invasion of the Soviet Union and his later declaration of war against the United States a few days after his Axis ally Japan attacked the US fleet at Pearl Harbor. That in effect turned what had been separate regional wars in Asia and Europe into a truly global conflict and led to the official formation of the Grand Alliance on 1 January 1942. But the process of forming the alliance actually began much earlier than that.

With the French defeat and surrender in June of 1940, Churchill turned to the United States for aid. Threatened by the prospect of German control of Europe, US President Franklin D. Roosevelt agreed initially to sell US military equipment to the British, and by March 1941 he had convinced the US Congress to loan such equipment to them via the Lend-Lease program.[2] Simultaneously, US and British military planners meeting secretly in Washington agreed that in the event the United States and Britain found themselves at war with all three Axis Powers, they would assume the strategic defensive against Japan and concentrate in the Atlantic against Germany. Enunciated in the so-called

---

1 Winston S. Churchill, *The Second World War*, III: *The Grand Alliance* (Boston, 1950).
2 See Warren F. Kimball, *The Most Unsordid Act: Lend-Lease* (Baltimore, MD, 1969).

136

ABC-1 agreement nine months before the official formation of the Grand Alliance, this "Germany first" strategy became the cornerstone of the coalition.[3]

Hitler's invasion of the Soviet Union in June 1941 added a third power to this emerging coalition. Despite sharply conflicting ideologies since the 1917 Bolshevik Revolution and extremely poor relations since the 1939 Nazi–Soviet Non-Aggression Pact, both Churchill and Roosevelt welcomed Soviet leader Josef Stalin as an ally and pledged aid to bolster the Soviet Union. Churchill dismissed his previous history as a staunch anti-communist with the comment that if Hitler invaded Hell, the British prime minister "would at least make a favorable reference to the Devil in the House of Commons."[4] Stalin similarly cited a Georgian peasant proverb that when crossing the bridge one was allowed to walk with the Devil until one reached the other side. On 12 July 1941, London and Moscow consequently signed a formal alliance pledging to render each other all possible aid and not to sign a separate peace with Germany. Several weeks later, spurred by the reports of his aide Harry Hopkins, who had met with Stalin in Moscow and had become convinced that Russia would survive the German onslaught, Roosevelt moved to expedite US aid to the Soviet Union. In November the president added Russia to the list of Lend-Lease recipients (at war's end Lend-Lease aid to Allied nations would total more than $50 billion – approximately $650 billion in 2013 dollars). By the time FDR extended Lend-Lease to the USSR, he had also convinced Congress to repeal the Neutrality Acts of the 1930s so that armed US merchant ships could carry Lend-Lease material to its final destination. Moreover, he also ordered the US navy to escort US as well as British ships across the Atlantic.

Three months earlier, in August of 1941, Churchill and Roosevelt had met in person off the coast of Newfoundland. Here they issued the Atlantic Charter, a lofty statement of postwar aims, many taken from Woodrow Wilson's "Fourteen Points" and Roosevelt's more recent "Four Freedoms." The Atlantic Charter became the ideological basis of the American–British alliance, just as Germany-first had become its strategic

---

3 Louis Morton, "Germany First: The Basic Concept of Allied Strategy in World War II," in Kent Roberts Greenfield (ed.), *Command Decisions* (Washington, DC, 1960), pp. 11–47. ABC-1 and the ensuing RAINBOW 5 American war plan are reproduced in Steven T. Ross (ed.), *American War Plans, 1939–1945* (New York, 1992), vol. IV, pp. 3–66, and vol. V, pp. 3–43.

4 Churchill, *The Grand Alliance*, p. 370. See also John Colville, *The Fringes of Power: 10 Downing Street Diaries, 1939–1955* (New York, 1955), p. 404.

basis. By its terms both nations pledged to create a postwar settlement based on a series of fundamental principles: no territorial aggrandizement for themselves; no territorial changes for others without their consent; national self-determination and self-government; equal access for all to trade and raw materials; future economic collaboration; freedom from want and fear; freedom of the seas; disarmament of the aggressor nations; and the establishment of a new League of Nations. Along with this document came the extraordinary symbolism, captured by photographs displayed in the newspapers of both countries, of the two democratic leaders not only meeting with their military chiefs and servicemen, but also attending with them a Sunday morning religious service aboard the British warship *Prince of Wales*.[5]

At the same time Roosevelt was attempting to deter the Japanese, who had been at war with China since 1937 and formally allied with the Germans and Italians in the Tripartite Pact since September of 1940. Throughout 1940 and into 1941 Japan had sought to take advantage of German conquests and the ensuing European inability to defend their Asian colonies by moving into resource-rich Southeast Asia. Roosevelt had responded with a combination of negotiations, economic sanctions, and military moves, including the movement of the US fleet to Hawaii and the imposition of a series of economic sanctions that culminated in the freezing of all Japanese assets in the United States in summer 1941. Japan responded with the surprise attack on Pearl Harbor on 7 December, along with a simultaneous attack on US and British possessions in Southeast Asia and the western Pacific. When Hitler declared war on the United States a few days later, what had been a series of regional conflicts merged into a truly global war.

Fearful that the Pearl Harbor attack might lead the United States to abandon the previously agreed-upon Germany-first global strategy, Churchill traveled by warship to Washington for a second summit meeting with Roosevelt. Code-named ARCADIA, this meeting established both the official alliance and the major structures and decisions by which its key members would fight the war. The two leaders of the great democracies announced the formal alliance on 1 January in the form of the Declaration by the United Nations. By its terms the twenty-six nations then at war with any of the Axis powers pledged to employ their full resources against the nations with whom they were then at war, to

---

5 The Atlantic Charter is in the US Department of State *Bulletin* 5 (Washington, DC, 1942), pp. 125–26. For the conference itself, see Theodore A. Wilson, *The First Summit: Roosevelt and Churchill at Placentia Bay*, 1941, 2nd edn. (Lawrence, KS, 1991). For the religious service, see ibid., pp. 97–100.

cooperate with each other, not to sign a separate peace, and to subscribe to the principles that had been enunciated by Churchill and Roosevelt four months earlier in the Atlantic Charter.[6] The alliance was open to new members who went to war with any of the Axis powers, and it eventually encompassed forty-five nations. It also gave its name to the postwar international organization that its members would create in 1945: the United Nations.

Despite the large number of members, the three most militarily powerful and active nations, Great Britain, the Soviet Union, and the United States, dominated the alliance. It was this triumvirate that Churchill referred to as the Grand Alliance. And within that alliance, the British and the Americans established at ARCADIA and immediately thereafter the basics of what would become, again in Churchill's words, a "special relationship" between the two countries. The military component of this special relationship was the principle of unity of command, whereby all the ground, naval, and air forces of both nations would be under the command of a single officer. Originally this principle was applied to Southeast Asia and the Southwest Pacific via the creation of an American-British-Dutch-Australian (ABDA) command under British Field Marshal Sir Archibald Wavell. Although this particular effort ended in military failure, it established the precedent for unity of command in most of the other theaters around the world that the British and Americans established during the war.

The commanders of those theaters would in turn operate under the direction of a new body created at the ARCADIA Conference, the Anglo-American Combined Chiefs of Staff (CCS), an organization consisting of the army, navy, and air chiefs of each country as well as a personal representative for each of the two heads of government. It received the charge of developing and implementing a global strategy and reported directly to Churchill and Roosevelt.

Roosevelt had originally pressed for a broader body than the CCS, an inter-Allied Supreme War Council based in Washington, while Churchill had proposed a bilateral body based in London. The compromise was the bilateral body that the prime minister desired but located in Washington as Roosevelt desired and meeting in continuous session.[7] Its principal members would meet in person at each of the numerous

---

6 US Department of State, *Foreign Relations of the United States: The Conferences at Washington, 1941–1942, and Casablanca, 1943* (Washington, DC, 1968), p. 375 (hereafter cited as *FRUS* with subtitle of specific volume).

7 Theodore A. Wilson, "Coalition: Structure, Strategy and Statecraft," in David Reynolds, Warren F. Kimball, and A. O. Chubarian (eds.), *Allies at War: The Soviet, American, and British Experience, 1939–1945* (New York, 1994), pp. 86–88.

wartime summit conferences; at all other times the British chiefs would be represented by their joint staff mission in Washington, which would meet with the American chiefs on a weekly basis.

The original British members of the Combined Chiefs of Staff were the members of the British Chiefs of Staff Committee (COS): General Sir Alan Brooke, Admiral Sir Dudley Pound, Air Chief Marshal Sir Charles Portal, and General Sir Hastings Ismay as Churchill's personal representative. Heading the British joint staff mission in Washington would be the army's former chief, Field Marshal Sir John Dill. To parallel the COS organization on the CCS, the Americans established the US Joint Chiefs of Staff (JCS), composed of General George C. Marshall, Admiral Ernest J. King, and General Henry H. Arnold, the last representing the army air forces. In July 1942 former Navy Chief Admiral William D. Leahy joined the JCS as chief of staff to the commander in chief – the predecessor to the current chairman of the joint chiefs of staff. As the war progressed both the JCS and the CCS would add numerous committees (such as the combined planning staff) to advise and make recommendations to them. These committees comprised key ground, naval, and air officers from each service staff.

Overall command would go to the dominant military partner in each theater. The Pacific would thus be under an American commander reporting directly to the JCS, while the Middle East, Indian Ocean, and Southeast Asia would be under British commanders reporting directly to the COS. The European theater would be one of shared responsibility, with the commander reporting to the CCS. Unity of command was not practiced in every theater. The Pacific, for example, was split into two theaters, one under Admiral Chester W. Nimitz (Pacific Ocean Areas or POA) and one under General Douglas MacArthur (Southwest Pacific Area or SWPA) in order to avoid an insoluble inter-service conflict. The Atlantic was likewise split into one British and one American naval theater. In most theaters of war, however, the two powers applied the principle of unity of command successfully.

The decision to establish an Anglo-American rather than a broader Supreme War Council meant that the Soviets would unilaterally determine their own strategy against Germany. Coordination of that strategy with those of the Americans and British would rest in the hands of the three heads of government – Churchill, Roosevelt, and Stalin – who would be in frequent message contact with each other and meet on numerous occasions, either as a twosome or on a few occasions as a threesome. Churchill would meet ten times with Roosevelt and twice with Stalin, while the "Big Three" would meet on three occasions (the last time after Roosevelt's death and replacement by his successor, Harry S. Truman).[8]

China's war against Japan on the Asian mainland would also remain a separate theater not under CCS direction, though here the United States would send General Joseph Stilwell to serve as Lend-Lease coordinator and Chinese leader Chiang Kai-shek's chief of staff in an effort to coordinate Chinese strategy with that of its allies. Chiang would also meet with Churchill and Roosevelt, albeit only once in 1943 at the first Cairo Conference. In effect, however, the four regional conflicts that had now merged into World War II – the Second Sino-Japanese war in China; the Anglo-American war against Japan in the Pacific and Southeast Asia; the Russo-German war in Eastern Europe; and the Anglo-American war against Germany and Italy in the Atlantic, the Mediterranean, and Western Europe – remained separate on an operational level, though linked at the strategic level.

The large number of summit meetings between the Allied leaders and their staffs, and the even larger number of messages they exchanged,

8 The three tripartite summit conferences took place in Teheran on 27 November–1 December 1943 (code-named EUREKA); Yalta on 4–11 February 1945 (code-named ARGONAUT); and Potsdam on 17 July–2 August 1945 (code-named TERMINAL). Churchill was defeated in the 1945 British parliamentary election in the midst of this last meeting and replaced by his successor, Clement Attlee. Both of the Churchill-Stalin meetings took place in Moscow, the first on 12–15 August 1942 (code-named BRACELET) and the second on 9–18 October 1944 (code-named TOLSTOY). The Churchill–Roosevelt meetings took place at Placentia Bay off the coast of Newfoundland on 9–12 August 1941 (code-named RIVIERA); in Washington, DC on 22 December 1941–14 January 1942 (code-named ARCADIA); in Washington again on 19–25 June 1942 (also code-named ARGONAUT); in Casablanca on 14–24 January 1943 (code-named SYMBOL); in Washington for a third time on 12–25 May 1943 (code-named TRIDENT); in Quebec on 14–24 August 1943 (code-named QUADRANT); in Cairo before the Teheran Conference on 22–26 November 1943 and again after Teheran on 4–6 December 1943 (code-named SEXTANT I and SEXTANT II); in Quebec again on 11–16 September 1944 (code-named OCTAGON); and before the Yalta Conference in Malta on 30 January–3 February 1945 (code-named CRICKET). They also met briefly after Yalta on 15 February 1945, aboard the US warship *Quincy* anchored in Great Bitter Lake at the southern end of the Suez Canal, where Roosevelt had previously met with the rulers of Saudi Arabia, Egypt, and Ethiopia. Chinese leader Chiang Kai-shek also attended the first Cairo meeting, and Canadian Prime Minister William Mackenzie King attended the two Quebec meetings. For correspondence between Churchill, Roosevelt, and Stalin, see Warren F. Kimball. (ed.), *Churchill & Roosevelt: The Complete Correspondence*, 3 vols. (Princeton, NJ, 1984); Ministry of Foreign Affairs of the USSR, *Correspondence Between the Chairman of the Council of Ministers of the U.S.S.R. and the Presidents of the U.S.A. and the Prime Ministers of Great Britain during the Great Patriotic War of 1941–1945* (Moscow, 1957); and Susan Butler (ed.), *My Dear Mr. Stalin: The Complete Correspondence of Franklin D. Roosevelt and Joseph W. Stalin* (New Haven, CT, 2005).

were at least partially the result of serious conflicts between them regarding both proper wartime strategy and postwar plans. Although Britain, the United States, and the Soviet Union agreed that their grand strategy should aim at defeating Germany before Japan (the Soviet Union did not even enter the war against Japan until August of 1945), they disagreed sharply as to how that should be accomplished. Similarly they disagreed sharply, despite the Atlantic Charter, as to the desired postwar world that their victory would enable them to create.

As the oldest belligerent, the British had the most clearly articulated military proposals. Strategically they favored a peripheral approach that sought to avoid the frightful casualties they had suffered in the World War I trenches, with an emphasis on a host of alternatives to direct continental confrontation with the *Wehrmacht*. These included naval blockade, military assistance to the Soviets, strategic bombing, commando raids, and support for European resistance movements against the Nazis. Ground campaigns for the coming year were to take place not in Europe but in North Africa and the Mediterranean in order, in Churchill's words, to "close the ring" around Germany and eventually force its collapse. On the long ocean voyage to Washington for the ARCADIA Conference, the British prime minister composed a lengthy strategic memorandum forcefully explaining this approach in detail for the Americans while reasserting the primacy of the European theater over the Pacific. In the process he specifically called for major US forces to undertake numerous peripheral operations in the European theater: occupation of northern Ireland (Operation MAGNET) so as to release British forces for a new offensive that had recently begun against the German *Afrika Korps* and Italian forces in Libya (Operation CRUSADER); a bomber offensive against Germany; and a 1942 invasion of French North Africa (Operation GYMNAST).[9] As for what the world would look like after Axis defeat, Churchill's government essentially desired a return to the *status quo ante bellum*, both in Europe and around the world.

Such British strategic and postwar plans were anathema to the Soviets. Facing over 90 percent of German ground forces and suffering frightful losses of men and territory, Stalin desired, and throughout the second half of 1941 had been demanding, not only military supplies but also the establishment of a major "second front" against Hitler in northern France so as to divert German forces from Russia and force Berlin into fighting a two-front war. As for the postwar era, the old status quo that Britain desired to resurrect had in Stalin's eyes kept the Soviet Union an isolated

9 Kimball, *Churchill & Roosevelt*, I, pp. 294–309.

outcast and allowed German aggression to take place. Consequently, he rejected British policy and instead demanded a postwar framework based upon a wartime agreement both to keep Germany weak and to divide Europe into Soviet and British spheres of influence. Indeed, while Churchill was traveling to Washington, Stalin was laying out for visiting British Foreign Secretary Anthony Eden in Moscow a treaty proposal incorporating these points. By that proposal, Britain would recognize Soviet territorial acquisitions in Eastern Europe that had resulted from the 1939 Nazi–Soviet Pact and agree to a postwar division of Germany, as well as accede to Soviet bases in Eastern Europe, in return for Soviet consent to similar British bases in Western Europe, European confederations that London desired, and a council of victorious powers. Without such wartime agreement regarding war aims in postwar Europe, Stalin warned Eden, "there would be no alliance."[10]

The Americans disagreed vehemently. Even before its official entry into the war, the United States had adamantly opposed such territorial settlements on the grounds that they would violate the Atlantic Charter, reward previous Soviet aggression, and create both diplomatic and public opinion problems similar to those that had been created by the secret Allied territorial treaties during World War I. Pearl Harbor in no way altered this opposition. Churchill was also opposed at this time to the territorial treaty Stalin was proposing, both out of hostility to communism and to sanctioning past Soviet aggression and out of fear of alienating the United States.[11]

US and British postwar goals and policies clashed sharply in other areas, however. Most notable were the conflicts over European colonialism, which the Americans strongly opposed and which Churchill fiercely defended and indeed symbolized, as well as over postwar economic policies, which the Americans wished to be based on free trade as opposed to such protectionist policies as the British Imperial Preference System. Moreover, on strategic issues the American armed forces agreed with the Soviets regarding the need to create a second front in northern France instead of continuing with a peripheral campaign they believed could not lead to German defeat. Only a direct, massive confrontation with the German *Wehrmacht* leading to its destruction, they maintained, could force a German surrender. These fundamental differences in strategic approaches would bedevil both the Grand Alliance and the

10 Anthony Eden, *The Memoirs of Anthony Eden, Earl of Avon: The Reckoning* (Boston, 1965), 334–38. See also Oleg A. Rzheshevsky, *War and Diplomacy: The Making of the Grand Alliance – Documents from Stalin's Archives* (Amsterdam, 1996), pp. 1–62.
11 Churchill, *The Grand Alliance*, p. 630.

Anglo-American "special relationship" throughout the war. Indeed, such differences predated World War II and reflected the different histories, traditions, and experiences as well as the present positions of the United States and Britain.

Britain's precarious position in 1940–1941 had left it with no option save to adopt a peripheral strategy, for under no circumstances immediately after the fall of France could it hope to face Germany successfully in a direct continental confrontation.[12] Throughout much of its history, however, London had often relied upon a similar indirect approach, especially when it found itself lacking a continental ally, so as to make use of its great assets of sea power and geographic separation from the European continent while minimizing the weakness of its relatively small population and army. Such a strategy had in the past enabled it not only to defend itself successfully against more powerful European enemies, but simultaneously to defend and even expand its extensive overseas empire. In World War I, however, Britain had pursued a direct continental strategy in conjunction with France that had resulted in casualties so enormous as to constitute the decimation of an entire generation. Avoiding any repetition of this carnage was a major, if unstated, British goal in World War II.

Furthermore, the British had concluded that their eventual success in World War I had resulted from the collapse of the German economy and will, and that a peripheral strategy could create the conditions for such a collapse to happen again. Air power theories greatly reinforced such beliefs. So did a misreading of the German economic situation (leading to an incorrect belief that the German economy was already stretched to the breaking point),[13] and the need to defend a far-flung overseas empire. Furthermore, Churchill was a strong proponent of the peripheral strategy. Indeed, he had planned the ill-fated Gallipoli expedition in World War I and believed that its failure had been the result of poor implementation rather than a defective strategic approach.

The Americans, on the other hand, had throughout their history seldom put much faith in peripheral strategies aimed at the enemy will. Instead, they had favored a direct approach designed to destroy the enemy *capacity* to resist, most notably during the Civil War of

---

12 Michael Howard in *The Causes of War* (Cambridge, MA, 1983), p. 180, labels Britain's World War II strategy as one "of necessity rather than choice" and "of survival rather than victory."

13 See David Reynolds, "Churchill and the British 'Decision' to Fight on in 1940: Right Policy, Wrong Reasons," in David Reynolds, *From World War to Cold War: Churchill, Roosevelt, and the International History of the 1940s* (Oxford, UK, 2006), pp. 75–98.

1861–1865.[14] Their experiences during World War I had only reinforced this approach, for they had not entered the war until 1917 and had thus seen their first direct offensives in 1918 succeed in obtaining German surrender. In the process they had suffered relatively few casualties compared to their British and French allies. Also unlike the British, the Americans possessed the abundance of manpower and industrial capacity needed for a direct approach, and they had not suffered the humiliating defeats at the hands of the Germans that they claimed made the British overly cautious. As a result of these factors, they believed the British approach to be seriously defective. Continued British adherence to that approach, they argued, was a politically inspired attempt by Churchill to prove his World War I ideas correct and to place US as well as British forces in areas of imperial interest, a political goal antithetical to their own, rather than to win the war as quickly and decisively as possible.

Such military and political differences were nothing new in the history of coalition warfare. Indeed, conflicting strategies and policies had seriously weakened past wartime alliances and had often led to defeat. Napoleon had once quipped that he would never lose if left to fight coalitions, and French Marshal Ferdinand Foch had admitted to having less respect for Napoleon's abilities after having led a coalition command in World War I. But without each other, none of the three major allies could hope to defeat the Axis powers alone. As Benjamin Franklin supposedly said regarding the signing of the Declaration of Independence in 1776, the signatories needed to "all hang together, or most assuredly we shall all hang separately." Churchill said the same thing in different words when he quipped, "There is only one thing worse than fighting with allies, and that is fighting without them!"[15] His trip to Washington was clear recognition of this fact, a recognition shared by his allies but not by his Axis enemies.

Still reeling from the Pearl Harbor attack, the American chiefs of staff did not voice strong objections to Churchill's peripheral ideas during the ARCADIA Conference. By March, however, army planners led by General Dwight D. Eisenhower, the head of Marshall's war plans division (renamed the operations division in March 1942), were preparing alternative plans to cross the English Channel, opening a second front

14 See Russell F. Weigley, *The American Way of War: A History of United States Military Strategy and Policy* (New York, 1973).
15 Carl Van Doren, *Benjamin Franklin* (New York, 1938), pp. 551–52; Alex Danchev and Daniel Todman (eds.), *War Diaries, 1939–1945: Field Marshal Lord Alanbrooke* (London, 2001), p. 680.

that Stalin continued to demand. Unable and unwilling to attempt any such operation in 1942, Churchill in that same month decided instead to agree to Stalin's demand for a treaty that would recognize his 1939–1940 conquests in Eastern Europe.

Strongly opposed to such a treaty, Roosevelt responded with the new plan to concentrate forces in England (Operation BOLERO) for a cross-Channel invasion in either 1942 (Operation SLEDGE-HAMMER) or 1943 (Operation ROUNDUP), an alternative the British agreed to in April primarily because they feared an American turn to the Pacific if they did not. The result would be the visit of Soviet Foreign Minister V. Molotov to both London and Washington in late May and early June 1942, and the public statement that "full understanding" had been reached "with regard to the urgent tasks of creating a Second Front in Europe in 1942."[16]

In reality no such understanding had been reached. The British were convinced that any attempt to cross the Channel in 1942 would end in catastrophe, and Churchill immediately set about convincing Roosevelt, during a second visit to Washington in late June, to return instead to Operation GYMNAST, the invasion of French North Africa. The US Joint Chiefs proposed responding to the British desires with a threat to turn to the Pacific instead, but Roosevelt angrily rejected the proposal as equivalent to "taking up your dishes and going away" as well as "something of a red herring, the purpose for which he thoroughly understood."[17] Instead, he ordered Marshall, King, and his close adviser Harry Hopkins to go to London and reach agreement on an offensive operation of some type in the European theater to begin by the end of 1942. Crossing the Channel remained his preferred option, but if the British refused to agree then his emissaries were ordered to agree to an invasion of French North Africa. With the British remaining adamantly opposed to SLEDGEHAMMER, the American chiefs consequently found themselves forced to agree instead to GYMNAST, now renamed TORCH and placed under the command of Eisenhower, whom Marshall had by then shifted to command of the US European Theater of Operations in England.

Churchill then flew to Moscow to inform Stalin – a mission he compared to "carrying a large lump of ice to the North Pole."[18] He arrived

---

16 *FRUS, 1942*, III, pp. 593–94.
17 Henry L. Stimson Diary, 15 July 1942, Yale University; Larry I. Bland (ed.), *The Papers of George Catlett Marshall*, III: *The Right Man for the Job, December 7, 1941–May 31, 1943* (Baltimore, MD, 1991), p. 276.
18 Churchill, *The Second World War*, IV: *The Hinge of Fate* (Boston, 1950), p. 475.

with the German army approaching Stalingrad and Stalin anything but pleased to hear that no front would be established in France that year and that his allies would instead invade French North Africa, a move Churchill explained as attacking the "soft underbelly" of the Germans. A break between the two was narrowly avoided, but the conference ended with an all-night session at Stalin's apartment with Churchill convinced that he had told Stalin "the worst." What he failed to mention, however, and what he as well as Roosevelt probably refused to believe at this time, was the JCS insistence that launching GYMNAST/TORCH would wreck BOLERO and with it any possibility of launching Operation ROUNDUP across the Channel in 1943. In line with such reasoning, the Americans had insisted during the July meeting in London on a statement that launching TORCH instead of SLEDGEHAMMER rendered a 1943 ROUNDUP "impracticable of successful execution" and meant that with the exception of air operations, the allies had "definitely accepted a defensive, encircling line of action for the Continental European Theater." In line with such reasoning, and as a follow-up to their stunning naval victory at Midway the previous month, the JCS simultaneously sanctioned a counteroffensive in the Solomon Islands in the South Pacific to prevent the advancing Japanese from cutting their supply lines to Australia.[19]

What followed in fall 1942 were a series of epic, lengthy battles: at Stalingrad in Russia; at El Alamein against Field Marshal Erwin Rommel's *Panzerarmee Afrika* in Egypt; Operation TORCH in French North Africa; and at Guadalcanal in the South Pacific – all of which the Allies eventually won and all of which led to profound consequences for the war effort. The Soviet victory at Stalingrad resulted in the encirclement and destruction of the German Sixth Army and the German failure to obtain the Caucasus oil fields. El Alamein similarly resulted in the German failure to capture the Suez Canal. When combined with TORCH, the victory guaranteed Allied control of most of North Africa, but also led to Hitler's takeover of southern France and his decision to hold Tunisia, into which Rommel's forces then escaped. Guadalcanal halted the Japanese effort to isolate Australia and so exhausted their resources that it in effect put them on the defensive from that point on.

---

19 Mark A. Stoler, *Allies and Adversaries: The Joint Chiefs of Staff, The Grand Alliance, and U.S. Strategy in World War II* (Chapel Hill, NC, 2000), pp. 87–91; Maurice Matloff and Edwin M. Snell, *Strategic Planning for Coalition Warfare, 1941–1942* (Washington, DC, 1953), pp. 280–306 (a volume in the US army's multivolume *United States Army in World War II* series).

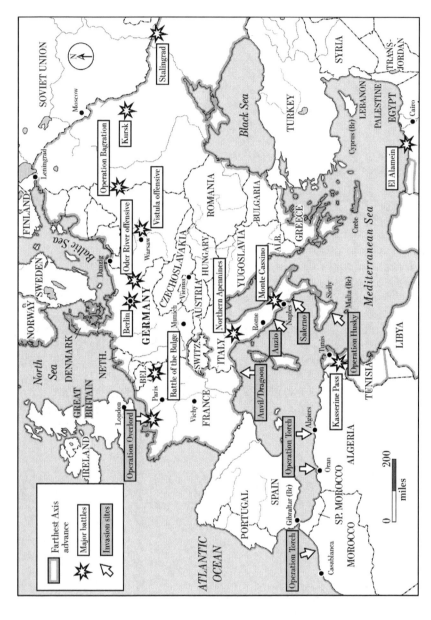

Map 6.1   The War in Europe, 1942–1945

These Allied victories are consequently viewed as the great "turning point" of the war. That judgment is accurate, but only to an extent. After these battles the Axis powers could no longer achieve total victory. But that did not doom them to total defeat. To the contrary, they still controlled enormous empires and were theoretically capable of holding the vast areas under their control by forcing a military stalemate that would lead to a negotiated peace. The Allies would need a coordinated global strategy to avoid this – something quite difficult to accomplish in light of the unconnected nature of their individual victories in late 1942, the fact that there were more US forces deployed against Japan than Germany despite formal adherence to the "Germany-first" strategy,[20] and the continued strategic disagreements among the three great Allied powers.

In January 1943, Churchill, Roosevelt, and the CCS met in the recently captured city of Casablanca in Morocco to plan their next operations. Stalin was invited, but refused to attend on the grounds that he was needed to oversee the final stages of the Stalingrad battle. Without his presence, and with the struggle for Tunisia still in progress, the British succeeded in convincing the Americans to continue operations in the Mediterranean in 1943 via an invasion of Sicily to be launched once the Tunisian campaign ended – albeit in return for additional resources for the Pacific. This decision rendered ROUNDUP all but impossible in 1943, something that Stalin would not be pleased to hear.[21] Reassuring him was one of the reasons Roosevelt at the end of the conference enunciated as the overall Allied goal the "unconditional surrender" of the Axis Powers.[22]

A great deal of mythology arose soon after the war ended regarding this announcement. Contrary to those myths, unconditional surrender was not a new policy in January 1943. Indeed, it had always been the unstated goal of each of the "Big Three" and was in effect the lowest common denominator holding their coalition together. Roosevelt decided to enunciate it publicly at Casablanca to reassure Stalin in the absence of a 1943 invasion of France and Chiang Kai-shek in the absence of greater

---

20 Matloff and Snell, *Strategic Planning for Coalition Warfare, 1941–1942*, pp. 389–95, and Richard M. Leighton and Robert W. Coakley, *Global Logistics and Strategy, 1940–1943* (Washington, 1955), p. 662 (another volume in the US army's multivolume *United States Army in World War II* series).

21 As previously noted, the JCS had predicted this outcome during the 1942 debate over cross-Channel vs North African operations. For an examination of the economic reasons behind the delay of a cross-Channel invasion until 1944, see Jim Lacey, *Keep from All Thoughtful Men: How U.S. Economists Won World War II* (Annapolis, 2011).

22 See *FRUS: Washington and Casablanca*, pp. 487–843.

aid to his beleaguered and isolated armies, as well as the British and American people in the aftermath of the controversial political events that had occurred in French North Africa during the TORCH landings.[23]

With French forces in North Africa fighting against the Anglo-Americans in November of 1942 and unwilling to obey orders not to do so emanating from the British supported French General Charles de Gaulle or the American-supported General Henri Giraud, Eisenhower turned to the French Vichy official Admiral Jean Francois Darlan, who was then in Algiers and who was willing to order his forces to cease fighting in return for administrative control of French North Africa. This so-called "Darlan Affair" angered large segments of the British and American populations, who viewed it as an odious and unacceptable deal with someone who had openly collaborated with the Nazis – one that opened the door to possible future collaboration with German officials and a negotiated peace. Darlan's assassination on Christmas Eve removed him as a specific issue, but it left open the possibility of such agreements being repeated with the Germans. It also created a power conflict between de Gaulle and Giraud for administrative control of French North Africa. Roosevelt "resolved" that conflict by forcing the two to agree to a power-sharing arrangement during a surprise meeting (complete with handshake) just before the press conference that ended the Casablanca Conference. FDR then followed this action with his unconditional surrender announcement to make clear that the Darlan deal would not be repeated with the Germans, or for that matter with the Japanese.[24]

The announcement of unconditional surrender as Allied policy also precluded any possible repetition of the territorial treaty that Stalin and Churchill had attempted to negotiate in spring 1942 despite American opposition. But it did not illustrate, as critics would charge, the lack of any alternative policy by Roosevelt for the postwar world. By this time he had already enunciated in private his idea of a world being run by the World War II allies – which he labeled the "Four Policemen" (Britain, China, the Soviet Union, and the United States) – to preclude any resurgence of German and Japanese military power and with it another world war.[25] It was an idea he would repeat and flesh out during the rest of 1943.

The British and Americans also agreed at Casablanca to wage as their first priority a major battle against German submarines in the Atlantic,

---

23 Raymond G. O'Connor, *Diplomacy for Victory: FDR and Unconditional Surrender* (New York, 1971).
24 Ibid; *FRUS, Washington and Casablanca*, pp. 506, 533–34, 727, 834–37.
25 See, for example, *FRUS, 1942*, III, pp. 572–73.

which at that time threatened the ability of the United States to get Lend-Lease aid to its allies – and indeed the very survival of Britain. They also agreed to launch a combined bombing offensive against Germany (Operation POINTBLANK). Success would not be easy to achieve in either campaign.

The so-called Battle of the Atlantic had been ongoing, with numerous ebbs and flows, since 1940. But by the beginning of 1943 the Germans had reached a high point in their campaign, sinking almost as much tonnage as the Allies could produce, and approaching a monthly figure of 7 million tons that they estimated would force the British to surrender. By May 1943 the Allies were able to halt the German U-boat threat through a number of means: a major intelligence breakthrough that enabled them to decipher German plans and dispositions; the realization that their own naval cipher had been broken and the institution in June 1943 of a new one that would remain secure for the rest of the war; increased American production of merchant ships; the initiation of a highly coordinated anti-submarine campaign that made use of new convoy escort vessels and anti-submarine technology; and the closure of the mid-Atlantic air gap through the use of very long-range, shore-based aircraft and escort aircraft carriers. Between March and May 1943 the allies first halted and then reversed the rate of shipping losses while increasing dramatically the number of submarines they were able to sink. German naval chief Admiral Karl Donitz had to call off his offensive and withdraw his submarines from the North Atlantic in May. He renewed the offensive in September 1943 with little success, and he was forced to halt it again in early 1944.[26] The lifeline to Britain was secure at last.

The Combined Bomber Offensive took substantially more time to achieve success – primarily because the bombers were inaccurate and because, despite claims to the contrary, they could not adequately defend themselves against German fighters and ground defenses. In addition, the British and American air forces adhered to conflicting doctrines, with the British favoring nighttime area bombing to destroy German morale and productive capacity and the Americans favoring daylight "precision" bombing to destroy specific industrial nodes. The two allies resolved this conflict by allowing each air force to pursue its own doctrine, the British bombing at night and the Americans during the day. But in 1943 their losses were prohibitive and the results far below what had been predicted. German morale did not collapse, and German war production

---

26 For a brief summary see Richard Overy, *Why the Allies Won* (New York, 1995), pp. 25–62.

actually rose during the year.[27] By year's end, however, the British and Americans deployed escort fighter aircraft with greater range via the use of detachable fuel tanks and fielded a new long-range fighter, the P-51 Mustang – the best fighter in World War II, superior to German fighters in speed and maneuverability and possessing the range to reach Berlin. Produced in huge numbers and used as long-range escorts, these fighters would in the following year force the German air force into an unwinnable war of attrition.[28]

Meanwhile, in July 1943 the Soviets destroyed the third great German offensive in the east in the battle of Kursk, the largest tank battle in history, and began a series of offensives that would eventually take them to Berlin. Simultaneously, Anglo-American forces successfully invaded Sicily, which in turn led to the overthrow of Mussolini's government, the September allied invasion of the Italian mainland, and the surrender of Italy. Nevertheless, Hitler's decision to hold the peninsula led to near-catastrophe for Anglo-American forces during the Salerno landings and a bloody stalemate for the remainder of the year along the Gustav Line south of Rome.

The British and Americans agreed during their May and August summit conferences in Washington and Quebec to cross the Channel in spring 1944, an operation now renamed OVERLORD. Stalin was infuriated by the additional delay, however, and separate peace rumors filled the air throughout spring and summer of 1943. Secret low-level Russo-German contacts did take place in Sweden, though the extent to which Stalin seriously considered a separate peace at this time remains unclear. What is clear is that the threat reinforced the American insistence that the Channel had to be crossed in 1944 – the earlier the better.[29]

The Allies finally reached agreement on both a coordinated strategy and some postwar policies during a series of pivotal conferences in the last three months of 1943. At an October meeting of the three foreign

---

27 That said, it is worth noting that Bomber Command's massive offensive against the Ruhr in spring 1943 brought the major increases in German war production to a halt. Thereafter only by massive efforts were the Germans able to increase marginally their production of weapons. For a discussion of these issues see Adam Tooze, *The Wages of Destruction: The Making and Breaking of the Nazi Economy* (New York, 2008), pp. 596–98.

28 Williamson Murray, *Luftwaffe* (Baltimore, MD, 1986), ch. 6.

29 See Vojtech Mastny, "Stalin and the Prospects of a Separate Peace in World War II," *American Historical Review*, 77 (December 1972), 1365–88, and *Russia's Road to the Cold War: Diplomacy, Warfare, and the Politics of Communism, 1941–1945* (New York, 1979), pp. 73–85; H. W. Koch, "The Spectre of a Separate Peace in the East: Russo-German 'Peace Feelers,' 1942–1944," *Journal of Contemporary History*, 10 (July 1975), 531–49; Gerhard Weinberg: *A World at Arms: A Global History of World War II* (New York, 1994), pp. 609–11; and Stoler, *Allies and Adversaries*, pp. 135–36.

ministers in Moscow, the British and Americans reaffirmed Operation
OVERLORD for 1944, while the Soviets formally agreed to the unconditional surrender policy and a tripartite military occupation of Germany,
as well as the creation of a new postwar international organization to
replace the League of Nations. Stalin also agreed to a summit conference in Teheran in November and entry into the war against Japan once
Germany had been defeated. On their way to Teheran and again after
the meeting with Stalin, Churchill, and Roosevelt met in Cairo. They
did so the first time with Chiang Kai-shek, who received both strategic and postwar promises. On the strategic level, Roosevelt promised a
1944 amphibious operation in the Bay of Bengal which, in conjunction
with a planned Chinese ground offensive, would reopen a land supply
route to China through Burma. In the postwar realm Chiang received
the so-called Cairo declaration, which promised the return of all territory
Japan had previously conquered.[30]

By this time Churchill was asking for a further delay in OVERLORD
in order to launch amphibious operations in the Aegean to take the
island of Rhodes and to bring Turkey into the war. Roosevelt insisted
that the issue be settled in Teheran in Stalin's presence, with the Soviet
dictator offered either OVERLORD on time or a delayed OVERLORD
along with expanded operations in the Mediterranean. Stalin forcefully
insisted on OVERLORD as scheduled, with a supporting operation from
Italy into southern France (Operation ANVIL), and in return promised
both entry into the war against Japan after Germany's defeat and a major
offensive in the east to coincide with and thereby support OVERLORD.
Roosevelt fully backed him, and in effect the two outvoted Churchill.
After three days of heated arguments, Roosevelt and Stalin forced
Churchill to accede. Upon his return to Cairo, FDR thereupon decided
to appoint Eisenhower rather than Marshall to command OVERLORD
on the grounds that he "could not sleep at night" with the latter, who was
in effect running the global American war effort, out of the country.[31]

Churchill's defeat symbolized Britain's declining power within the alliance and the emergence of what would soon be recognized as the two
superpowers: the United States and the Soviet Union. While Britain had
by 1943 reached its mobilization peak in both economic and manpower

30 See *FRUS, The Conferences at Cairo and Tehran* (1961); and Keith Sainsbury, *The Turning Point: Roosevelt, Stalin, Churchill and Chiang Kai-shek, 1943: The Moscow, Cairo and Teheran Conferences* (New York, 1985).
31 Robert Sherwood, *Roosevelt and Hopkins: An Intimate History* (New York, 1950), p. 803; Larry I. Bland and Mark A. Stoler (eds.), *The Papers of George Catlett Marshall*, VI: *"The Whole World Hangs in the Balance," January 8, 1947–September 30, 1949* (Baltimore, 2013), pp. 52–54.

terms, its two allies had not. Churchill later stated that he first realized at Teheran what a small country Britain actually was. "There I sat with the Great Russian bear on one side of me, with paws outstretched, and on the other side the great American buffalo, and between the two sat the poor little English donkey who was the only one," he nevertheless insisted, "who knew the right way home."[32] The disparity between declining British power on one hand and expanding Soviet and American power on the other would only grow as the war progressed.

The Teheran agreements of late 1943 constituted the great "strategic bargain" of the Grand Alliance: an Anglo-American invasion of both northern and southern France in return for a major and simultaneous Soviet offensive in the east to force Germany into a two-front war it could not win, along with Soviet agreement to enter the war against Japan once Germany was totally defeated. Far from coincidentally, 1944 would be the year of great Allied victories in Europe: the cross-Channel invasion of northern France in June (the first successful opposed crossing of the Channel since 1066), followed by the invasion of southern France in August and the liberation of France and portions of the low countries in the West; the great victories of the Soviets in the East that liberated the rest of the Soviet Union and brought the Red Army into Poland and Romania; the June capture of Rome in the Mediterranean; and finally success for the combined bomber offensive resulting in the destruction of the *Luftwaffe* and most German cities, the ruin of the German oil industry, and the collapse of Germany's transportation network. Provided the coalition remained intact, Germany by year's end was doomed to total defeat.

But 1944 was also the year of stupendous victories in the Pacific, as American industry proved capable of supplying ships and material to launch major successful offensives in that part of the world as well as in Europe, and doing so while continuing to supply its allies with Lend-Lease aid. Indeed, those ships and supplies were even sufficient to allow for simultaneous offensive operations by MacArthur in the Southwest Pacific and Nimitz in the Central Pacific, culminating in the virtual destruction of the Imperial Japanese Navy at the battles of the Philippine Sea in the Mariana Islands and Leyte Gulf in the Philippines, the splitting of the Japanese Empire in half with the invasion of the Philippines, and the ability to bomb the Japanese home islands from bases in the western Pacific. As Churchill aptly stated during another Anglo-American summit conference at Quebec in September, "Everything we had touched had turned to gold."[33]

---

32 David Dilks (ed.), *The Diaries of Sir Alexander Cadogan, O.M., 1939–1945* (New York, 1972), p. 582.
33 *FRUS, The Conference at Quebec, 1944* (1972), p. 313.

Map 6.2   The Pacific War, 1942–1945

The one exception was the China-Burma-India theater, as the Japanese launched major ground offensives in 1944 that threatened India and that captured the airfields from which Chiang Kai-shek and US Army Air Forces under Major General Claire Chennault had hoped to launch massive bombing raids on Japan. Those offensives also came close to knocking the Chinese out of the war completely. Stilwell had long opposed the emphasis of both Chiang and Chennault on air power and had instead argued for the strengthening of the Chinese armies and their use to reopen the supply route through Burma. His warning that the Japanese would overrun the air bases without such strengthening proved accurate. But his numerous, contentious conflicts with Chiang led the Chinese leader to demand Stilwell's recall in October. By that time it was clear that in the future Soviet rather than Chinese forces would have to combat the bulk of the Japanese army on the Asian mainland.[34]

Allied strategic conflicts did not cease to exist with the grand bargain at Teheran and the ensuing military victories. To the contrary, Churchill pressed the Americans throughout the first half of the year for an amphibious landing along the Adriatic coast instead of southern France and an advance through the Ljubljana Gap to Vienna.[35] And in the second half of the year he and his chiefs of staff objected to Eisenhower's "broad front" strategy in Western Europe and his decision to command the ever-expanding ground armies himself rather than leave them in the hands of Montgomery, whose command was now limited to British and Canadian forces (along with the Ninth US Army) in the north and who favored a major thrust in that sector at the expense of the American and French forces to his south. In both cases the British lost the debate, thereby illustrating further their declining power within the alliance.

With the victories in Europe and the Pacific came serious Allied planning in 1944 for the world to be created after the Axis defeat. A conference at Dumbarton Oaks in Washington established the basic structure for the postwar United Nations organization, while another in Bretton Woods, New Hampshire, established the postwar global economic structure with the International Monetary Fund and the World Bank – both largely financed and controlled by the United States, whose economy by this time dwarfed those of all the other world powers and whose leaders forced the British to agree to the abandonment of the Imperial

34 Michael Schaller, *The U.S. Crusade in China, 1938–1945* (New York, 1979), pp. 101–75; Barbara Tuchman, *Stilwell and the American Experience in China, 1911–1945* (New York, 1970), pp. 229–483.
35 Maurice Matloff, "The Anvil Decision: Crossroads of Strategy," in Kent Roberts Greenfield (ed.), *Command Decisions* (Washington, DC, 1960), pp. 383–400.

Preference System.[36] Simultaneously, a European Advisory Commission meeting in London established future military occupation zones for the three allies in Germany.

The American refusal to sanction a shift from southern France to the Ljubljana Gap, combined with the advances of the Red Army into Eastern Europe, led Churchill to travel to Moscow for a second time in October in order to reach agreement regarding Soviet and British interests in Eastern Europe. In effect, the two men agreed to postwar British control of Greece in return for Soviet control of Romania, Hungary, and Bulgaria, with both nations sharing power in Yugoslavia. As Churchill famously explained in his memoirs, on the evening of 9 October he proposed to Stalin that they "settle about our affairs in the Balkans. ... [H]ow would it do for you to have ninety percent predominance in Romania, for us to have ninety percent of the say in Greece, and go fifty-fifty about Yugoslavia?" While this was being translated Churchill wrote it on a piece of paper, added 50-50 in Hungary and 75-25 in favor of Russia in Bulgaria, and pushed it across the table to Stalin, who in turn "took his blue pencil and made a large tick upon it, and passed it back to us. It was all settled in no more time than it takes to set down." A long silence followed. "Might it not be thought rather cynical if it seemed we had disposed of these issues, so fateful to millions of people, in such an offhand manner?" Churchill then said. "Let us burn the paper." "No, you keep it," said Stalin.[37]

Eden and Molotov later altered the percentages to 80–20 in favor of the Soviets for Bulgaria and Hungary, but Churchill's eyes were set on Greece. Indeed, he immediately made use of this agreement to send in a British force to replace the retreating Germans in that country and to install a royalist government. When negotiations with the communist resistance forces broke down and resulted in open revolt in December, Churchill ordered its forceful suppression by British forces. Abiding by his agreement, Stalin said and did nothing.

Churchill and Stalin also attempted in Moscow to reach agreement on what had by that time become the thorniest issue within the Grand

36 See, for example, Robert C. Hilderbrand, *Dumbarton Oaks: The Origins of the United Nations and the Search for Postwar Security* (Chapel Hill, NV, 1990); Armand van Dormeal, *Bretton Woods: Birth of a Monetary System* (New York, 1978); and Georg Schild, *Bretton Woods and Dumbarton Oaks: American Economic and Political Postwar Planning in the Summer of 1944* (New York, 1995).

37 Churchill, *The Second World War*, VI: *Triumph and Tragedy* (Boston, 1953), pp. 227–28. For more recent and accurate accounts of this meeting based on declassified British records, see Albert Resis, "The Churchill-Stalin Secret 'Percentages' Agreement on the Balkans, Moscow, October 1944," *American Historical Review*, 83 (April 1978), 368–87; and Joseph Siracusa, "The Night Stalin and Churchill Divided Europe," *Review of Politics*, 43 (July 1981), 381–409.

Alliance: the future of Poland. Germany and the Soviet Union had carved up that nation in September of 1939, and throughout the war Stalin insisted on retaining the eastern portion that Soviet forces had taken at that time. He also insisted that the postwar Polish government be "friendly" to the Soviet Union. In spring 1943, in response to the Polish government-in-exile's response in London to German revelations regarding the 1940 massacre of thousands of captured Polish officers in the Katyn Forest, he had broken diplomatic relations with the London Poles and established an alternative Polish communist government (the Lublin government). During the Teheran Conference, Churchill and Stalin had resolved the boundary issue in general terms by agreeing that the Soviets would retain eastern Poland and that the Poles would be compensated with German territory on their western border.[38] The issue of the Polish government was a much more difficult matter to resolve – especially in light of the fact that the London Poles were unwilling to accede to the Soviet takeover of eastern Poland.

Furthermore, Anglo-American suspicions of the Soviets had increased during summer 1944 as a result of Stalin's halting of the Red Army on the Vistula River and his refusal to help the Polish underground army in Warsaw that had risen up against the Germans as the Red Army approached – despite Anglo-American entreaties that he do so. Both Warsaw and the Polish underground army were consequently destroyed by a ruthless German counterattack. W. Averell Harriman, the US ambassador to the Soviet Union, aptly summarized the feelings of many when he warned that this refusal to aid the Poles had been based on "ruthless political considerations" and left him "gravely concerned." The Russians were "bloated with power," and relations with them had taken "a startling turn for the worse."[39]

Churchill, of course, discussed Poland with Stalin during the Moscow Conference. But during ensuing negotiations with Polish Prime Minister Stanislaw Mikolajczyk, the Soviet leader in turn refused to compromise on the postwar boundary and demanded Polish agreement to that boundary for any return to normal relations. Mikolajczyk was unable to convince his London colleagues to agree and resigned in late November. On 1 January, Stalin responded by recognizing the Lublin Poles as a provisional government.

The Moscow territorial agreements and ensuing British as well as Soviet behavior directly violated Roosevelt's policy of postponing all

---

38 Churchill, *The Second World War*, V: *Closing the Ring* (Boston, 1951), pp. 361–62, 394–97.
39 *FRUS, 1944*, III, p. 1376; *FRUS, 1944*, IV, pp. 988–98; W. Averell Harriman and Elie Abel, *Special Envoy to Churchill and Stalin, 1941–1946* (New York, 1975), pp. 340–49.

territorial settlements until war's end. They also fulfilled his worst fears by upsetting the American people and led to a frightening resurgence of isolationist sentiments in late 1944, exactly as Roosevelt had anticipated. Clearly, a second Big Three meeting was now necessary to deal with postwar as well as remaining strategic issues.

The future of Poland was the most discussed issue when the Big Three met for a second time, on this occasion at the old tsarist resort of Yalta in the Crimean Peninsula on the Black Sea in February 1945. By the end of the conference they had agreed to the shift in Polish boundaries, with the Soviets obtaining what had been eastern Poland and the Poles being compensated with German territory in the West, and a reorganization of the Lublin Polish government so as to include London Poles, with Western recognition and free elections to follow. But those discussions and agreements took place amid other discussions on how to end the war against Germany and a host of postwar issues – most notably those concerning occupation policies and zones within Germany, postwar governments in the rest of Europe, the future United Nations organization, and Soviet entry into the war against Japan. By the end of the conference the Allies had agreed to combined military operations against Germany and the postwar division of the country into four zones of occupation (one for each of them and one for France, the latter carved out of the US and British zones) as well as a declaration promising democratic elections and institutions in the rest of Europe as promised in the Atlantic Charter. They also resolved previous differences over the postwar United Nations regarding the nature of the veto power in the Security Council and the number of seats the Soviet Union would have in the General Assembly, and they agreed to issue an invitation to other nations to attend an April conference in San Francisco to write a charter for the new international organization. Furthermore, the Soviets pledged to enter the war against Japan within three months of German surrender. In effect, Stalin obtained most of what he wanted on Poland – which his army already occupied – in return for agreeing to a French zone in Germany that did not reduce the size of the Soviet zone, UN veto and voting procedures, and a hard date for entry into war against Japan.[40]

The Big Three and their subordinates left Yalta convinced that they had established the basis for not only final victory in the war, but also for postwar cooperation and world order. As Hopkins later stated, "We really

---

40 *FRUS, The Conferences at Malta and Yalta, 1945* (1955). For the most recent of the many published volumes analyzing the Yalta Conference, see S. M. Plokhy, *Yalta: The Price of Peace* (New York, 2010); and Fraser J. Harbutt, *Yalta 1945: Europe and America at the Crossroads* (New York, 2010).

believed in our hearts that this was the dawn of the new day we had all been praying for and talking about for so many years. We were absolutely certain that we had won the first great victory of the peace – and by 'we' I mean *all* of us, the whole civilized human race. The Russians had proved that they could be reasonable and farseeing and there wasn't any doubt in the minds of the President or any of us that we could live with them and get along with them peacefully for as far into the future as any of us could imagine."[41]

Soon, however, conflict re-emerged – primarily over Soviet installation of communist governments in Poland as well as Romania that Britain and the United States labeled violations of the Yalta agreements. Simultaneously, Stalin accused Roosevelt and Churchill of attempting to negotiate a separate peace in northern Italy, while Churchill pressed Roosevelt and Eisenhower to try to take the German capital of Berlin before the Soviets did.[42] Far from accidentally, these problems and the apparent collapse of trust between the allies coincided with the final military collapse of Nazi Germany. With the defeat of their common enemy on the horizon, the allies no longer needed to compromise their differences as they had successfully done throughout the war.

Amidst these growing controversies, Roosevelt suddenly died of a stroke on 12 April. His successor, Vice President Harry S. Truman, had been in office less than three months and had been told nothing by Roosevelt of his plans for the postwar world. Suddenly faced with momentous decisions, Truman pledged to maintain Roosevelt's policies toward the Soviets, but he did so with a changed tone and manner. While he did not order Eisenhower to alter his plans and try to get to Berlin before the Red Army, he did speak curtly to visiting Soviet Foreign Minister Molotov about Poland. "I have never been talked to like that in my life," Molotov told Truman. "Carry out your agreements and you won't get talked to like that," the new president responded.[43] Simultaneously, the JCS revised and toughened their position on relations with the Soviets, at least partially as a result of warnings and recommendations from General John Deane, the head of their military mission to Moscow, while Ambassador Harriman gave similar warnings and recommendations to Truman.[44] On 29 April, Hitler committed suicide in his Berlin bunker as

41 Sherwood, *Roosevelt and Hopkins*, p. 870.
42 Brewer, *My Dear Mr. Stalin*, pp. 302–20; Stephen E. Ambrose, *Eisenhower and Berlin: The Decision to Halt at the Elbe* (New York, 1967).
43 Harry S Truman, *Memoirs*, I: *Year of Decisions* (Garden City, NY, 1955), p. 82. Molotov's statement was undoubtedly not true given the fact that he worked for Stalin.
44 Diane S. Clemens, "Averell Harriman, John Deane, the Joint Chiefs of Staff, and the Reversal of Co-Operation with the Soviet Union in April 1945," *International History Review*, 14 (May 1992), 277–301; Stoler, *Allies and Adversaries*, pp. 231–36.

the Soviets took the city, suffering over 100,000 casualties in the process. After attempting unsuccessfully to negotiate a separate peace with the British and Americans, Hitler's successor, Admiral Karl Donitz, agreed to surrender unconditionally – first to Eisenhower at his headquarters in Reims on 7 May and then, on Soviet insistence, to Red Army commanders in Berlin on the following day.

Despite growing tensions, the alliance remained intact for now. In June, Truman sent Hopkins to Moscow in an apparently successful effort to repair relations. That meeting resulted in agreement to hold a third Big Three Conference in July, this time in the Berlin suburb of Potsdam. In the middle of that conference, however, Churchill was defeated for re-election and replaced by the new Labor Party prime minister, Clement Attlee. Of the original Big Three, only Stalin now remained.

During the lengthy Potsdam Conference the Allies did manage to agree on some basic policies regarding the four power military occupation of Germany and a temporary German–Polish border at the Oder and Neisse Rivers. They also agreed that Italy would become a member of the UN, and that a Council of Foreign Ministers would be established to continue discussions on the numerous issues left unresolved at the end of the conference. But the very creation of that council illustrated the inability of the Allied leaders to reach agreement on those issues. Despite numerous meetings over the next few years, their foreign ministers would do no better. Indeed, no general peace conference ever took place, and no treaty ending the war with Germany was ever signed.

Of particular importance to the Americans was Soviet entry into the war against Japan. Japan was by this time a beaten foe, its navy, merchant marine, and air force largely destroyed and its home islands under heavy American bombardment as well as a virtual naval blockade. Yet the Japanese continued to fight fiercely and virtually to the last man, inflicting large casualties on the Americans in the Philippines, in the February invasion of Iwo Jima, and in the April invasion of Okinawa. On Iwo Jima the Americans suffered 26,000 casualties. On Okinawa the Japanese killed more than 7,000 and wounded nearly 32,000 US soldiers and marines, while *kamikazes* sank 36 ships and damaged over 360 more, killing in the process 5,000 sailors and wounding another 5,000. Truman and the JCS consequently feared huge casualties in the invasion of the southernmost home island of Kyushu scheduled for November, making Stalin's Yalta pledge to enter the war against Japan within three months of German surrender, and thereby tie down the bulk of the Japanese army in China, more important than ever. Stalin reaffirmed that pledge at Potsdam, promising entry into the war against Japan by 15 August.

In the middle of the conference, however, Truman received word of the successful test of the first atomic bomb at Alamagordo, New Mexico. In the view of some of his advisers, Soviet entry was no longer crucial – or even desirable. Better to try to end the war with the bomb before the Soviets entered the war, they figured, a step that would prevent Stalin from obtaining a Soviet role in the postwar occupation of Japan. Others, however, were not so certain. Even with the successful test at Alamagordo there was no certainty the bomb would detonate when dropped from an airplane, or that if it did it would by itself force the Japanese to surrender. Indeed, even after the atomic bombing of Hiroshima and Nagasaki, Marshall would order his staff to explore the possible tactical use of nuclear weapons to support an invasion of the home islands if such an invasion proved necessary.[45] Consequently, he was quite vague when asked by Stimson at Potsdam if Soviet entry were still necessary, though Stimson inferred from his comments that it was not. Truman was equally vague when he informed Stalin after the Alamagordo test that "we had a new weapon of unusually destructive force," a fact of which Stalin was in any case already aware because of communist spies within the Manhattan Project. The Japanese received even less information, being warned in the Potsdam Declaration to surrender their military forces unconditionally or face "prompt and utter destruction."[46]

On 6 August 1945 an atomic bomb destroyed the city of Hiroshima, killing upwards of 130,000 people. Two days later the Soviet Union declared war on Japan and attacked its army in Manchuria – moves that negated Tokyo's major remaining military asset as well as ending Japanese hopes that Moscow would be willing to mediate a negotiated settlement with the Americans.[47] Then, on 9 August, the Americans dropped a second atomic bomb on Nagasaki. With the intervention of the emperor, military resistance in the Japanese Cabinet to surrender was finally overcome and the Americans were informed that Tokyo's only condition was retention of the emperor. The United States agreed to the condition, with the proviso that the emperor be subject to the supreme commander of Allied occupation forces, General Douglas MacArthur. The emperor again intervened to overcome military opposition and Tokyo accepted these terms on 15 August. Two weeks later, on 2 September, Japan

---

45 Barton J. Bernstein, "Eclipsed by Hiroshima and Nagasaki: Early Thinking about Tactical Nuclear Weapons," *International Security*, 15 (Spring 1991), 149–73; Marc S. Gallicchio, "After Nagasaki: General Marshall's Plan for Tactical Nuclear Weapons in Japan," *Prologue*, 23 (Winter 1991), 396–404.

46 *FRUS, The Conference of Berlin*, I, pp. 378–79 and II, pp. 1324 and 1474–76.

47 For the impact of Soviet entry into the war on the Japanese, see Tsuyoshi Hascegawa, *Racing the Enemy: Stalin, Truman, and the Surrender of Japan* (Cambridge, MA, 2005).

officially surrendered aboard the battleship USS *Missouri* anchored in Tokyo Bay. With the conclusion of the surrender ceremony the deadliest war in human history officially came to an end. Shortly thereafter, the Cold War began. Indeed, many historians date the Cold War back to what happened at Potsdam concerning the bomb, even though the alliance did not completely collapse until 1947.

The breakdown of Allied relations, along with the length and intensity of the ensuing Cold War, has tended to blind many to the great wartime successes of the Grand Alliance. It was an alliance of necessity that brought together three powers of disparate histories, interests, strategies, and ideologies in order to defeat a common enemy that threatened the existence of all. The Grand Alliance succeeded in totally defeating the Axis powers and in forcing both unconditional surrender and military occupation on them. Within that alliance a "special relationship" developed between the two English-speaking powers, one unprecedented in modern military history and which would continue into the postwar era – and indeed down to the present day. Whether it would have continued without the perceived threat posed to both nations by their former Soviet ally is questionable. Certainly that threat played a major role in keeping the United States and Great Britain together and in minimizing the continued military and political differences that had divided them during the war.

The Grand Alliance succeeded for numerous reasons. The first and most important was the fact that military defeat could be avoided and victory achieved only if the coalition remained intact. Of equal importance was the fact that all three leaders realized this and were therefore willing to compromise both their military strategies and to a lesser extent their political aims. Willingness does not always lead to success, however, and in this case primary responsibility for success must rest with Churchill, Roosevelt, and Stalin and the relationships they developed with one another. Churchill and Roosevelt established a deep friendship and, while neither succeeded in establishing a similarly close relationship with Stalin, they did establish personal relationships with the Soviet leader sufficient to enable the three to reach critically important strategic and political agreements throughout the war. In this regard personal relationships at the highest level proved crucial to the success of the alliance.[48]

---

48 For a recent and extensive analysis of the role personal relationships and factors played in both the successes and the eventual breakup of the Grand Alliance, see Frank Costigliola, *Roosevelt's Lost Alliances: How Personal Politics Helped Start the Cold War* (Princeton, 2012).

One might also argue that the decision to postpone discussion of numerous postwar issues, a postponement on which Roosevelt insisted, played a positive and important role in maintaining the alliance by minimizing wartime conflicts. Ironically, that postponement may have also played a major role in hastening the postwar split, for Stalin had told Eden in late 1941 that without postwar territorial agreements there could be no true alliance. But Roosevelt could easily have responded that trying to resolve their postwar disagreements at that time would have weakened if not wrecked the alliance and thus led to disaster.

Of equal importance in maintaining the special Anglo-American relationship within the Grand Alliance were Churchill's and Roosevelt's key civilian and military advisers and their subordinates. Most notable in this regard were the members of the Combined Chiefs of Staff, who consistently overcame disagreements that almost led to blows on more than one occasion and who insisted that cooperation be maintained. Here again personal relationships proved critical, most notably the deep friendship that developed between Field Marshal Sir John Dill and General George C. Marshall.[49] Of perhaps equal importance on the civilian level was the close relationship that developed between Churchill and Hopkins. And on the ground, Eisenhower was an admitted fanatic about Allied unity who made clear that he would treat any quarrel between a British and an American officer as a "cardinal sin which would be mercilessly punished." In North Africa he famously relieved and sent home an American officer not for calling a British officer a "son-of-a-bitch," but for calling him a "British son-of-a-bitch."[50] Furthermore, his "broad front" approach in Europe meant that the armies of the two nations (as well as those of the French and other allies whose forces served under his command) would share battlefield honors and sacrifices; that further bound them together, despite the strong British objections to this strategy. Those personal relationships and memories did not disappear when the war ended. To the contrary, they continued to influence numerous policy makers in both countries and played an important role in maintaining close relations between the two nations.

Successful negotiation of differences between the British and Americans on one hand and the Soviets on the other, however, failed to

49 See Alex Danchev, *Very Special Relationship: Field-Marshal Sir John Dill and the Anglo-American Alliance, 1941–1944* (London, 1986). When Dill died of aplastic anemia in November 1944, Marshall had the British field marshal buried in Arlington National Cemetery, one of only a handful of foreign nationals so honored.

50 Hastings Lionel Ismay, *The Memoirs of General Lord Ismay* (New York, 1960), pp. 262–63; Stephen E. Ambrose, *Eisenhower: Soldier, General of the Army, President-Elect, 1890–1952* (New York, 1983), p. 186.

continue into the postwar era. Interestingly, all three desired a postwar continuation of the alliance, albeit each on its own terms. With the defeat of their enemies, however, there was no longer a pressing need to compromise in order to keep the coalition together. Consequently, the Grand Alliance shared the fate of all other wartime alliances: dissolution. That in no way lessens its extraordinary success in World War II.[51]

---

51 One should not forget, however, that while the Tripartite Grand Alliance dissolved, the Anglo-American "special relationship" did not. Indeed, it became a cornerstone of a new alliance system, NATO, directed against the former Soviet ally.

7 Adapt and survive
NATO in the Cold War

Ingo Trauschweizer

In spring 1985, former West German Chancellor Helmut Schmidt, a frustrated Atlanticist, delivered the Henry L. Stimson Lectures at Yale University.[1] Speaking at a time when the North Atlantic Treaty Organization (NATO) appeared in perpetual crisis, Schmidt concluded that the West lacked a common grand strategy. He outlined four phases of the Western alliance: an attempt at cooperation with the Soviet Union in World War II's immediate aftermath, a Cold War and arms race that began in 1947, a period of détente from the mid 1960s, and, since the beginning of the 1980s, a second Cold War. At no point had NATO integrated its grand strategy, even though one might surmise from Schmidt's comments that he believed the efforts of the allies had been somewhat more successful in the 1950s and 1960s.[2] Here he expanded on an argument he had made the previous year: the United States, Britain, France, and West Germany each had their own grand strategy. Schmidt thought that the Europeans had been more consistent, if rarely ever in full agreement with one another, whereas American leadership had lacked clear direction. As if to illustrate the transatlantic divide, Schmidt's argument drew the ire of former US Defense Secretary James Schlesinger, who accused the Europeans of ungratefulness.[3]

Yet approaching the subject of NATO's grand strategy from a German perspective and at a moment of dissension may unduly emphasize discord. After all, NATO stands out as a unique case among alliances in the modern age. It has far outlived its main rival. What has kept the

1 For Schmidt's frustration with American leadership of the alliance see Matthias Schulz, "The Reluctant European: Helmut Schmidt, the European Community, and Transatlantic Relations," in Matthias Schulz and Thomas A. Schwartz (eds.), *The Strained Alliance: U.S.–European Relations from Nixon to Carter* (Cambridge, 2010), pp. 279–307.
2 Helmut Schmidt, *A Grand Strategy for the West: The Anachronism of National Strategies in an Interdependent World* (New Haven, CT, 1985).
3 Helmut Schmidt, "Leadership in the Alliance," and James R. Schlesinger, "An American Perspective," in Robert E. Hunter (ed.), *Grand Strategy for the Western Alliance* (Boulder, CO, 1984), pp. 27–37, 39–56.

alliance together? A decade after the Cold War's end, the French historian Frédéric Bozo suggested that NATO had always been torn between the specific requirements of defense posture and security in a wider sense.[4] But security was not an end in itself.[5] The Western alliance aimed at stability, which was underwritten both by a desire for prosperity and the need for security. Americans and Europeans did not always agree on whether to emphasize the former or the latter, but compatible political cultures and strategic outlooks offer an explanation for why NATO has endured. It is an alliance of broadly like-minded partners who have learned to weather the storms brought by particular policy crises and by clashes of personalities, by uneven financial and military contributions, and by an often critical public that still looks across the Atlantic – in both directions – with a sense of disapproval.[6] The Western alliance has always rested on national as well as rational interests. The difficulty has been to find sufficient consensus in detail.[7]

But are shared values and political compromise exercised in a committee structure the expression or the foundation of grand strategy? Williamson Murray argues grand strategy is a matter for great powers alone.[8] For the United States throughout the Cold War, different policies of containment fed into a grand strategy of attrition.[9] If the United States could have dictated policy and strategy to its junior partners, NATO's case might readily conform to B. H. Liddell Hart's notion that grand strategy rests on the coordination and direction of "all the resources of a nation, or band of nations, towards the attainment of

4 Frédéric Bozo, "Defense versus Security? Reflections on the Past and Present of the 'Future Tasks' of the Alliance (1949–1999)," in Gustav Schmidt (ed.), *A History of NATO: The First Fifty Years* (Houndmills, 2001), vol. II, pp. 65–80.
5 For an intriguing study of NATO's purpose beyond the focus on security see Mark Smith, *NATO Enlargement during the Cold War: Strategy and System in the Western Alliance* (Houndmills, 2000).
6 See Geir Lundestad, *The United States and Europe since 1945: from "Empire" by Invitation to Transatlantic Drift* (Oxford, 2003) for a historical assessment. For a recent theoretical model see Wallace J. Thies, *Why NATO Endures* (Cambridge, 2009). For shared values see Jeremi Suri, "The Normative Resilience of NATO: A Community of Shared Values amid Public Discord," in Andreas Wenger, Christina Nuenlist, and Anna Locher (eds.), *Transforming NATO in the Cold War: Challenges beyond Deterrence in the 1960s* (London, 2007), pp. 15–31.
7 Harlan Cleveland, *NATO: The Transatlantic Bargain* (New York, 1970); Stanley R. Sloan, *Permanent Alliance? NATO and the Transatlantic Bargain from Truman to Obama* (New York, 2010).
8 Williamson Murray, "Thoughts on Grand Strategy," in Williamson Murray, Richard Hart Sinnreich, and James Lacey (eds.), *The Shaping of Grand Strategy: Policy, Diplomacy, and War* (Cambridge, 2011), pp. 1–33.
9 For the different points of emphasis of US policy between 1945 and the end of the Cold War see John Lewis Gaddis, *Strategies of Containment* (New York, 2005).

the political object of the war."[10] Yet, recent literature reveals that throughout the Cold War neither superpower could order its allies around indefinitely.[11] To meet the requirements of an ideal type of grand strategy and match the perceived military strengths of the Soviet Union and its allies and clients, NATO members faced difficult choices that could have led to the development of full-blown garrison states and the need to substitute alliance integration for national sovereignty. An alliance of sovereign states could hardly fully adjudicate their respective national interests. German reunification, French *grandeur*, Britain's special relationship with the United States, and American superpower status could not always coexist easily even though there was general agreement on the policies of containment and deterrence.

NATO's military strategy for the Cold War era rested on deterrence, which required projecting an image of strength and resolve. In order to succeed, actual military planning, force structure, or logistics did not always have to be fully developed, but the projection had to emerge as sufficiently strong in the eye of the beholder. As long as an element of doubt existed in the minds of Soviet leaders and military commanders that the cost of war would outweigh the benefits derived from victory, deterrence would work. But the foundational Cold War policies of the Western alliance also included a powerful economic track alongside military means: strong transatlantic and intra-European ties through the Marshall Plan and the integration of the Western European Common Market. Western success in the Cold War rested on economic prosperity as much as on military strength. The delicate balance of military requirements and financial and political constraints left NATO with a sufficient deterrent force and it provided Europeans and North Americans a vital stake in the success of their political and ideological system.[12]

Sound foundations? (1947–1957)

Three steps in the late 1940s and early 1950s formed and defined the Western alliance; each one represented a response to real and perceived crises and threats. In the face of severe economic dislocation, leaders

---

10 B. H. Liddell Hart, *Strategy* (London, 1967), p. 322.
11 See, for instance, Mary Ann Heiss and S. Victor Papacosma (eds.), *NATO and the Warsaw Pact: Intrabloc Conflicts* (Kent, OH, 2008).
12 On Europe see Tony Judt, *Postwar: A History of Europe since 1945* (New York, 2005); James J. Sheehan, *Where Have All the Soldiers Gone? The Transformation of Modern Europe* (Boston, 2008). On the United States see, Aaron L. Friedberg, *In the Shadow of the Garrison State: America's Anti-Statism and Its Cold War Grand Strategy* (Princeton, NJ, 2000).

in Western Europe and the United States feared political instability on the continent, particularly because communist election victories in France and Italy seemed possible. The response took shape in June 1947, when Secretary of State George C. Marshall announced that the United States was offering European countries sustained economic assistance. The United States was to invest roughly $13 billion (approximately $95 billion in 2013 dollars) from 1948 to 1952 in Europe's economies, from Scandinavia to the Mediterranean and Britain to West Germany. Unlike the immediate postwar years, when the US had spent over $12 billion in bilateral assistance, the Marshall Plan employed joint decisions on how to distribute US aid money among members of the European Recovery Program. This served as a catalyst for greater integration, rather than mere interdependency of Western Europe's national economies.[13] By the early 1970s the European Economic Community, founded in 1957, had become so successful that it emerged as a competitor to the US economy. Such competition notwithstanding, European economic integration, growth, prosperity, and political stability were vital to the success of the alliance throughout the Cold War.

For most commentators, the Western alliance and NATO are synonymous terms. It thus bears remembering that the economic pillar of the alliance preceded its military structures. Security concerns took center stage in February 1948, when communists seized power in a *coup d'état* in Czechoslovakia. In April of that year, Britain, France, and the Benelux countries (Belgium, the Netherlands, and Luxembourg) formed a defensive alliance, the Brussels Pact, and organized a military command led by Field Marshall Bernard Law Montgomery. The United States was not yet a member, and the Brussels Pact governments still eyed Germany with suspicion, but an anti-Soviet military alliance was beginning to take shape shortly after the wider economic alliance had begun.[14]

NATO itself was formed in April 1949, after considerable discussion about the geographic boundaries for membership in the alliance. Joining the Brussels five were the United States, Canada, Italy, Denmark, Norway, Iceland, and Portugal.[15] These twelve nations, however, did not

13 On the historiography of Marshall Plan and ERP see Robert H. Landrum, "Harry S. Truman and the Marshall Plan," in David S. Margolis (ed.), *A Companion to Harry S. Truman* (Malden, MA, 2012), pp. 347–61.
14 On the linkage of economic and politico-military alliance see Francis H. Heller and John R. Gillingham (eds.), *NATO: The Founding of the Atlantic Alliance and the Integration of Europe* (New York, 1992); and Kenneth Weisbrode, *The Atlantic Century* (Cambridge, MA, 2009), pp. 83–127.
15 On the diplomacy behind NATO's founding see Lawrence S. Kaplan (with the assistance of Morris Honick), *NATO 1948: The Birth of the Transatlantic Alliance* (Lanham, MD, 2007).

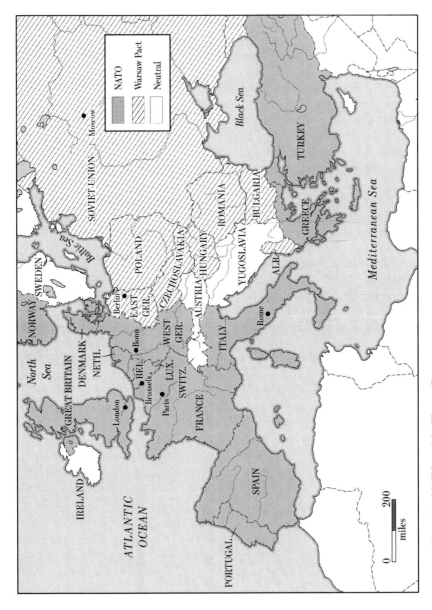

Map 7.1   NATO and the Warsaw Pact

conceive of the North Atlantic Treaty as a full-blown military alliance; while there were consultative committees, there was no military command. Nevertheless, a political pillar had now been added to the transatlantic alliance. The final step was the military structure, addressing immediate fears that came to the fore when North Korean forces invaded South Korea in June 1950. Coming less than a year after the Soviets had tested their atom bomb and China had fallen to communism, the outbreak of the Korean War seemed particularly ominous, and Western European leaders detected the heavy hand of Josef Stalin behind Kim Il-Sung and his army. They feared their countries were to come under attack next.[16] Consequently, NATO installed Dwight D. Eisenhower as Supreme Allied Commander (SACEUR) and four US army divisions followed Eisenhower to Europe to bolster NATO's defenses in the critical Central Region, which included France and the Benelux countries and soon also West Germany.[17]

The Truman administration had already significantly shifted its approach to containment. In the wake of the twin shocks of the Soviet atomic test and the victory of Mao Zedong's communists in the Chinese Civil War, officials in Washington reviewed American strategy and policy. The results were the decision to move ahead with building hydrogen bombs and a far-reaching proposal to triple or even quadruple the defense budget and build up conventional as well as nuclear armed forces to support a heavily militarized strategy of containment. NSC 68, drafted primarily by Paul Nitze, head of the state department's policy planning staff, elevated security above economics. It seems unlikely that Truman would have adopted Nitze's proposal if not for the perception of a worldwide communist military offensive.[18] But if the Korean War persuaded American leaders to rearm, waging the war also required a great deal of manpower and resources otherwise diverted from Europe. In addition, France and Britain found their militaries engaged in protracted wars and counterinsurgencies in Southeast Asia and could not immediately focus on the defense of Western Europe. For France, the war in Indochina

16 For the significance of the Korean War to NATO and to the Cold War in general see William Stueck, *The Korean War: An International History* (Princeton, NJ, 1995).
17 Lawrence S. Kaplan, *The United States and NATO: The Formative Years* (Lexington, KY, 1984) remains the standard account.
18 On the evolving policy and strategy of the Truman administration see Melvyn P. Leffler, *A Preponderance of Power: National Security, the Truman Administration, and the Cold War* (Stanford, CA, 1993).

(1946–1954) was followed by one in Algeria (1956–1962), which kept large parts of France's military preoccupied.[19]

When Eisenhower took command of NATO's armed forces, he had a mere eighteen combat divisions at his disposal. Upon mobilization, he could count on eleven more. But that was only one-third of the ground forces required to implement the alliance's medium-term defense plan for Central Region alone, which called for the employment of fifty-four active combat divisions, and it was a far cry from the 175 active divisions that Western intelligence had estimated the Soviets possessed in the early 1950s.[20] In addition, there was no strategic guidance beyond the medium-term defense plan, operational planning was scant, and infrastructure lacking.[21] Even placing a telephone call from Eisenhower's Supreme Allied Headquarters Europe (SHAPE) at Paris to Oslo, one of the future regional NATO headquarters, took twelve hours and could only be completed with Soviet assistance, as the lines ran through East Germany.[22]

Nevertheless, NATO intended to build ground forces that would serve as a credible deterrent, bolstered by American nuclear potential. At the least, ground forces had to provide the shield behind which the alliance could employ its nuclear forces – NATO's sword for offensive operations into enemy territory. The force goals agreed upon at the NATO summit in Lisbon in February 1952 were an ambitious step toward establishing such a conventional shield. NATO members pledged to increase ground forces to over forty-one active divisions by 1954, with the potential to mobilize forty-nine reserve divisions within one month. Eleven of these ninety divisions were supposed to be American and Canadian.[23] This goal could not be reached without West German armed forces. Although the members of the alliance had not yet agreed on the mechanics

---

19 For a balanced discussion of the demands of small wars, counterinsurgencies, and limited wars on US and European armed forces in the first decades of the Cold War see Jonathan M. House, *A Military History of the Cold War, 1944–1962* (Norman, OK, 2012).

20 DC 13, 28 March 1950, "North Atlantic Treaty Organization Medium Term Plan," in Gregory W. Pedlow (ed.), *NATO Strategy Documents, 1949–1969* (Brussels, 1998), pp. 111–77.

21 For operational planning see Jan Hoffenaar and Dieter Krüger (eds.), *Blueprints for Battle: Planning for War in Central Europe, 1948–1968*, trans. David T. Zabecki (Lexington, KY, 2012).

22 "Statement by Gen. Alfred M. Gruenther, USA, Supreme Allied Commander, Europe, and United States Commander in Chief, Europe," Hearing before the Committee on Foreign Relations, United States Senate, 26 March 1955 (Washington, DC, 1955), p. 2.

23 "Memorandum for the Secretary of the Army, the Secretary of the Navy, the Secretary of the Air Force, and the Joint Chiefs of Staff by the Secretary of Defense," 29 March 1952, "Outline of NATO Force Goals as Accepted at the Lisbon Meeting of the North Atlantic Council," 23 February 1952, Table I: Army Divisions. Office of the Secretary of Defense, Office of the Assistant Secretary (International Security Affairs), Decimal File 1952, CD 092.3 NATO General, RG 330, National Archives, College Park, MD.

of West German rearmament, they expected that the Germans would quickly contribute eight active and four ready-reserve divisions. In reality, the *Bundeswehr* did not reach twelve divisions until well into the 1960s.[24]

The Lisbon force goal projected a formidable fighting force and would have constituted a credible deterrent, but NATO's actual strength never approached this level. The cost of the commitment was prohibitive. Aggregate defense expenditures of European NATO countries stood at $7.4 billion in 1951. To fulfill their commitment, the European allies would have had to quadruple their defense spending.[25] Senior NATO military commanders suspected that Western European leaders never intended to fulfill the Lisbon agreement and that it served primarily as the basis for further negotiations.[26] Moreover, plans to combine the rearmament of West Germany with an integration of European armed forces – the proposed European Defense Community (EDC) – soon stalled and ultimately failed to gain acceptance in the French parliament in 1954. Military officers in the United States and in Europe doubted that the EDC could have worked at the operational level, given the barriers of language, culture, and military traditions, but the EDC had been the most significant proposal to date for closer coordination of military means. As a result, West Germany joined NATO in May 1955 and its national armed forces followed the general strategic guidance defined by NATO's standing group and military committee.[27]

NATO acted and still acts by consensus building in a committee structure. In the first decades of the Cold War, the standing group, comprised

---

24 On German rearmament and the relationship of the US and West German armed forces see A. J. Birtle, *Rearming the Phoenix: U.S. Military Assistance to the Federal Republic of Germany, 1950–1960* (New York, 1991); and Ingo Trauschweizer, "Learning with an Ally: The U.S. Army and the Bundeswehr in the Cold War," *The Journal of Military History*, 72(2) (April 2008), 477–508; and James S. Corum (ed.), *Rearming Germany* (Leiden, 2011).

25 Department of Defense, Office of the Comptroller, 11 April 1952, "Cost of Defense, Defense Expenditures, and External Financing for European NATO Nations and Germany, July 1950–June 1954," Table 1: European NATO & Germany. Office of the Secretary of Defense, Office of the Assistant Secretary (International Security Affairs), Decimal File 1952, CD 092.3 NATO General, RG 330, National Archives, College Park, MD.

26 The incoming SACEUR, Matthew Ridgway, later stated that he was well aware of this. He was convinced that there was no prospect of receiving the divisions that had been promised. Ridgway interview by Maurice Matloff. Matthew B. Ridgway Papers, US Army Military History Institute, Carlisle, PA, pp. 31–32.

27 For a comprehensive introduction to the EDC see Edward Fursdon, *The European Defence Community: A History* (New York, 1980). For more detail and a German and international perspective see also Lutz Köllner *et al.*, *Anfänge westdeutscher Sicherheitspolitik*, II: *Die EVG Phase* (Munich, 1989); and Hans Ehlert *et al.*, *Anfänge westdeutscher Sicherheitspolitik*, III: *Die NATO Option* (Munich, 1993).

of military chiefs of the United States, Britain, and France decided on the fundamental principles and proposed strategy to the military committee, which had a wider membership, but less direct impact. This power structure was altered in 1967, following many years of pressure from smaller alliance partners. In the final decades of the Cold War, the military committee became the crucial decision-making body and the highest military authority of the Western alliance. But even in the smaller standing group, consensus had been difficult to build. The standing group and military committee agreed on adopting massive retaliation as NATO strategy in 1954, but the military make-up and defense plans of SHAPE did not change appreciably.[28] The NATO partners made limited strides in setting up mechanisms for shared logistics in the central region, but fell short of integrating the national resources in that realm.[29] One historian holds that within the committees, political considerations trumped military needs at almost every juncture and that NATO strategy never fully aligned means, ends, and political objectives. Instead, as another NATO historian observes, "even when [the credibility of the deterrent] seemed unlikely in practice, the illusion was maintained."[30]

Eisenhower entered the White House in 1953 with the conviction that American and NATO strategy needed to be reviewed. The alliance required a military build-up in the short term, but the new president doubted the willingness of the Lisbon signatories to deliver on their promise, as active and ready-reserve forces for Central Region were already ten divisions short of the objective.[31] He feared the American contribution to the alliance necessitated unsustainable defense spending. The deterrence of war, the security of the United States, and the defense of America's allies were essential, but in a protracted struggle they could not come at the expense of weakening the American economy. Hence Eisenhower's "New Look" defense policy, introduced after thorough review, attempted

28 MC 48, 18 November 1954, "Report by the Military Committee to the North Atlantic Council on the Most Effective Pattern of NATO Military Strength for the Next Few Years," in Gregory W. Pedlow (ed.), *NATO Strategy Documents, 1949–1969* (Brussels, 1998), pp. 231–50.
29 Herman Roozenbeck, "Waste and Confusion? NATO Logistics from the Dutch Perspective," in Jan Hoffenaar and Dieter Krüger (eds.), *Blueprints for Battle: Planning for War in Central Europe, 1948–1968*, trans. David T. Zabecki (Lexington, KY, 2012), pp. 93–107.
30 Douglas L. Bland, *The Military Committee of the North Atlantic Alliance: A Study of Structure and Strategy* (New York, 1991). The quotation is from the foreword by Robert Jordan, p. xii.
31 Richard M. Leighton, *History of the Office of the Secretary of Defense: Strategy, Money, and the New Look, 1953–1956* (Washington, DC, 2001), pp. 555–58.

to restore the balance of prosperity and security.[32] Nevertheless, military leaders feared that this policy would endanger the credibility of the NATO alliance and weaken the deterrence posture of the United States. The basic premise of the New Look was that the United States had to reduce its overseas deployments if it were to establish a suitable strategic reserve within a sustainable defense budget. Deterrence had to rest on the threat of immediate use of strategic nuclear weapons against the Soviet Union, a concept termed 'massive retaliation' by Secretary of State John Foster Dulles. European alliance members were to provide the bulk of NATO's conventional forces.[33]

With the New Look, US and European strategic priorities came into fairly close proximity, as both the Eisenhower administration and European leaders preferred nuclear deterrence over costlier notions of conventional defense. The exception was West Germany, where the Adenauer administration had not yet come to the realization that any form of defense would turn the country into a smoldering ruin. Only in the course of 1956 did Adenauer and his defense minister Franz-Josef Strauss give up hope of forward defense. Consequently, they, too, now argued that nuclear deterrence had to work at the strategic level.[34] Nevertheless, the availability of tactical nuclear weapons and the slow build-up of German armed forces caused NATO to amend its strategy in 1957 from pure massive retaliation to extended nuclear deterrence. In a masterful display of ambiguity, the military committee confirmed the immediate use of nuclear weapons in a general war, but also allowed for more independent operational use of tactical nuclear weapons in the territorial defense of Western Europe.[35] Nuclear deterrence, some argued, all but assured that the Soviets would not embark on general war, but war by accident or miscalculation remained possible. A short section on limited war suggested that localized conventional attacks should be met initially by conventional forces, but that the Western alliance would employ nuclear weapons as the situation

32 Saki Dockrill, *Eisenhower's New Look National Security Policy, 1953–1961* (Houndmills, 1996) and Robert R. Bowie and Richard H. Immerman. *Waging Peace: How Eisenhower Shaped an Enduring Cold War Strategy* (Oxford, 1998).
33 Robert J. Watson, *History of the Joint Chiefs of Staff*, V: *The Joint Chiefs of Staff and National Policy, 1953–1954* (Washington, DC, 1986), pp. 14–21.
34 Christoph Bluth, *The Two Germanies and Military Security in Europe* (Houndmills, 2002), pp. 43–52.
35 MC 14/2 (revised) (Final Decision), 23 May 1957, "Final Decision on MC 14/2 (Revised): A Report by the Military Committee on Overall Strategic Concept for the Defense of the North Atlantic Treaty Organization Area," in Gregory W. Pedlow (ed.), *NATO Strategy Documents, 1949–1969* (Brussels, 1998), pp. 277–314.

required since "in no case is there a NATO concept of limited war with the Soviets."[36]

In adopting extended nuclear deterrence, the allies widened divisions in the political and economic realms, while the new strategy document did not satisfy those military officers in Europe and the United States who wanted an alternative to the immediate use of nuclear weapons. MC 14/2 served as a milestone in the debate of limited nuclear war, but it did not squash it, as both Eisenhower and Adenauer had hoped. Moreover, American hopes for a more vigorous buildup of conventional forces by their European partners were largely disappointed and Eisenhower's goal of reducing the US troop presence in Europe went unrealized. Moreover, out-of-area deployments continued to serve as a drain on British and French manpower, and crises at Dien Bien Phu in 1954 and Suez in 1956 raised questions about alliance solidarity. More fundamentally, Europeans believed there was a stark choice to be made between butter and guns, and they preferred investing in future prosperity and in the stability offered by the welfare state more than in their immediate security needs.[37]

All of this added up to a strategic framework more than to a common grand strategy at the end of NATO's first decade. The reactive and episodic formative period hardly offered firm ground, and NATO never fully integrated its armed forces and military means. From the outset, politics and economics interfered with a military buildup, as excessive military spending would have interfered with prosperity and political stability. European and American leaders did not agree in detail who should bear how much of the burden of the common defense, but they agreed in principle that everyone's national interest was served by a deterrence strategy. NATO adopted versions of massive retaliation and extended deterrence in 1954 and 1957, respectively. Emergency defense plans appeared more optimistic in the mid 1950s, too. At the beginning of the decade even holding the Rhine River had seemed implausible. By 1957, with West German forces beginning to appear in the order of battle, the main line of defense had moved well into Germany, and by 1963 it had reached the intra-German border.[38] By 1957 NATO's defenses and its deterrent seemed more capable, but national sovereignty impeded fuller integration of resources and politics continued to define strategy and

36 Ibid., p. 291.
37 For an excellent discussion of that dynamic and the rise of the "civilian state" see Sheehan, *Where Have All the Soldiers Gone*, pp. 147–97.
38 For an inside perspective based on access to the classified records of SHAPE see Sean M. Maloney, *War Without Battles: Canada's NATO Brigade in Germany, 1951–1993* (Toronto, 1997).

operational plans. The alliance was about to enter into a trying decade which fully exposed its political divides.

The great debate (1957–1967)

Attempts to build military structures and forces and craft operational plans that promised the defense of West German territory had defined NATO's first decade. Its grand strategy emerged as an unstated system: NATO was part of a wider Western alliance in which its members had to weigh military requirements against political constraints and demands for economic prosperity. Out-of-area crises created tensions between the US and European powers; German rearmament was politically sensitive; and NATO forces never reached manpower levels close to matching those of the Soviets and the Warsaw Pact. But the fundamental interests – stability, prosperity, and security – seemed fairly closely aligned, and American leadership in the alliance appeared the natural result of greater wealth and military capabilities. By the early 1960s, the picture had changed and the cohesion of the alliance had come into doubt. Gaullism, the political and strategic philosophy of French president Charles de Gaulle that offered a challenge to American leadership, gained followers in Germany and elsewhere in Europe; the Berlin crisis shook West German confidence; the nuclear arms race raised grave doubts about deterrence; and the Kennedy administration's proposal for a new military strategy and a grand design for the Western alliance found little agreement from states with rising economies in Western Europe.[39]

With the benefit of hindsight, the mid 1950s appear as the high-water mark of alliance accord, even though the seeds of discord between France and her allies were already sown in the Dien Bien Phu and Suez crises. Perhaps Eisenhower was, as historian John Gaddis suggests, "at once the most subtle and brutal strategist of the nuclear age," because he understood that only the threat of full-blown nuclear warfare rendered war devoid of any political purpose.[40] Western European leaders came to agree with Eisenhower. Winston Churchill, for example, had recognized as early as 1954 that thermonuclear weapons brought "equality in annihilation" that "we may look [to] with hope and even

---

39 For a concise introduction to the confluence of security, economics, and political concerns in the early 1960s see Erin R. Mahan, *Kennedy, de Gaulle and Western Europe* (Houndmills, 2002); and Jeffrey Glenn Giauque, *Grand Designs and Visions of Unity: The Atlantic Powers and the Reorganization of Western Europe, 1955–1963* (Chapel Hill, NC, 2002) explores the grand design of the Kennedy administration.

40 John Lewis Gaddis, *The Cold War: A New History* (New York 2005), p. 66.

confidence."[41] Concerns in France and West Germany by the end of the 1950s revolved around fears of abandonment, not entrapment in a nuclear war that could have only spelled doom for both countries. Yet just as European leaders aligned behind NATO's strategy of extended nuclear deterrence, Eisenhower faced growing opposition at home. Following the launch of *Sputnik* in October 1957, which demonstrated Soviet intercontinental ballistic missile (ICBM) capability, army, navy, and marine corps leaders argued forcefully for the need of preparedness for limited nuclear war and even Dulles, who had once most fervently endorsed massive retaliation, no longer supported a dogmatic interpretation of the New Look.[42]

Three themes fueled the great debate of the late 1950s and 1960s. First, in the military and operational realm, military and political leaders weighed the relative merits of nuclear deterrence, conventional defense, and firebreaks between conventional and nuclear warfare. The question whether future war in Europe could remain in any form limited was central to that discussion. Second, in the political and strategic realm, European and American leaders disagreed on nuclear sharing, expressions of national sovereignty, and the degree of integration of national means for the sake of a stronger defense posture. Finally, in the financial and economic realm, as European economies grew and the United States faced a mounting balance of payments deficit, American politicians raised alarm about the negative fiscal effects of the massive troop deployment in Europe. Consequently, administrations from Eisenhower to Reagan pushed Europeans to contribute more to their common defense. In broad strokes, three positions emerged in the early 1960s: American leadership of the alliance in an age of flexible response, a French challenge directed by President Charles de Gaulle, and forms of Atlanticism in West Germany and Britain that favored strong bilateral relations with the United States. The dividing lines between them were not always clearly defined.

Questions about credibility and applicability of massive retaliation had set in early. In the United States, the army's leaders, who saw their share of the defense budget plummet after the Korean War, opposed the strategic concept from the outset. The argument that emerged from the army staff in the mid 1950s stressed the possibility of limited war, including tactical nuclear warfare in Europe, without immediate resort to strategic

---

41 Jonathan Rosenberg, "Before the Bomb and After: Winston Churchill and the Use of Force," in John Lewis Gaddis *et al.* (eds.), *Cold War Statesmen Confront the Bomb: Nuclear Diplomacy since 1945* (Oxford, 1999), pp. 171–93. The quotation is on p. 191.
42 See, for instance, Trauschweizer, *Cold War U.S. Army*, pp. 58–70.

nuclear weapons. During the second half of the 1950s that argument won greater support from leaders of the marine corps and the navy as well as from some influential Eisenhower administration officials and among members of Congress. Once the launch of *Sputnik* had demonstrated the vulnerability of the United States, nuclear deterrence appeared riskier. European military officers, too, had raised doubts about the operational implications of nuclear strategy, and NATO commanders, with US General Lauris Norstad (SACEUR, 1956–1963) at the forefront, debated notions of firebreaks. It became apparent to critical observers that NATO's war plans could only lead to the destruction of what was to be defended. And political leaders in France and Germany raised doubts about whether the United States would be willing to engage in all-out nuclear war for Western Europe if US territory could now also come under attack.[43]

The strategic shift of the Kennedy administration from massive retaliation to flexible response underscored European fears of abandonment. The European position was somewhat schizophrenic, as nuclear war could have led only to massive destruction if deterrence failed. Yet European leaders generally favored nuclear deterrence because it allowed them to pursue policies of economic growth and social welfare that underwrote the political stability of their countries. If flexible response became NATO strategy, however, a significant buildup of conventional forces would be required at great financial cost. Ominously for the Kennedy administration, both Generals Norstad and Lyman Lemnitzer, the latter the chairman of the joint chiefs of staff, agreed that it was dangerous to raise the nuclear threshold before sufficient conventional forces had been created.[44] Moreover, there was little agreement among Europeans on the threshold. In the mid 1960s, a high-ranking German officer summed up the differences: "It's a question of when [to use theater nuclear weapons] – the Americans say 'as late as possible,' the French say 'as early as possible,' and we say 'as early as necessary.'"[45]

The debate was not exclusively propelled by a disagreement over nuclear strategy. Money, too, was at the heart of transatlantic tensions and so was nuclear sharing. Eisenhower had hoped to entice European cooperation with the New Look by granting access to tactical nuclear

---

43 Ibid., pp. 58–80.
44 Lawrence S. Kaplan, Ronald D. Landa, and Edward J. Drea, *History of the Office of the Secretary of Defense*, V: *The McNamara Ascendancy, 1961–1965* (Washington, DC, 2006), pp. 358–62. For the attitudes of the US service chiefs in the see also Walter S. Poole, *History of the Joint Chiefs of Staff*, VIII: *The Joint Chiefs of Staff and National Policy, 1961–1964* (Washington, DC, 2011), pp. 187–216.
45 Catherine McArdle Kelleher, *Germany and the Politics of Nuclear Weapons* (New York, 1975), p. 217.

weapons, but his policies never evolved beyond preauthorization for NATO commanders to employ low-yield nuclear weapons.[46] Kennedy explicitly linked tariff reductions (open trade) and the multilateral force (nuclear sharing) as the main components of the alliance's grand strategy alongside the political and military structures of NATO.[47]

The problem for Kennedy and for American hegemony in the alliance was that France and Britain, too, had put forward grand designs that were not entirely compatible with one another or with the American model. De Gaulle hoped to establish a directorate of American, British, and French leaders who would coordinate alliance strategy, and he believed that a French-led political confederation of European states would bring the Western alliance into sound balance. Harold Macmillan and the British government found themselves caught between the integrationist path of Washington and de Gaulle's proposal for a more autonomous Atlantic partnership. Macmillan hoped that Britain could enter the Common Market even while retaining its special relationship with the United States.[48]

Western European leaders thus received Kennedy's grand design cautiously. The problem rested on how to balance defense spending, deterrence, and economic growth. The American position was that Europeans in general, and Germans in particular, after a decade of substantial economic growth, should bear a greater share of the burden of the common defense. In speeches at the NATO summit in Athens and in Ann Arbor, Michigan in spring 1962, Secretary of Defense Robert S. McNamara reaffirmed American leadership of the alliance and called on the allies to pay more of NATO's defense expenditures.[49] Germany, empowered by the economic miracle of the 1950s, may have been in the strongest position to do so. Yet its chancellor, the wily octogenarian Konrad Adenauer, questioned the sincerity of the American commitment to Western Europe and specifically wondered if the new president in Washington had the backbone and political experience to stand up to Soviet threats. Adenauer was not pleased by what he saw as a weak American response to Soviet aggression in the Berlin Crisis of 1961.

---

46 William Burr (ed.), "First Declassification of Eisenhower's Instructions to Commanders Predelegating Nuclear Weapons Use, 1959–1960: A National Security Archive Electronic Briefing Book," www.gwu.edu/~nsarchiv/NSAEBB/NSAEBB45/#1. See also Peter J. Roman, "Ike's Hair Trigger: U.S. Nuclear Predelegation, 1953–60," *Security Studies*, 7 (Summer 1998), 121–65.

47 Giauque, *Grand Designs and Visions of Unity*.

48 Klaus Schwabe, "Three Grand Designs: The U.S.A., Great Britain, and the Gaullist Concept of Atlantic Partnership and European Unity," Journal of Transatlantic Studies, 3, Supplement (Spring 2005), 7–30.

49 Simon Duke, *The Burdensharing Debate: A Reassessment* (New York, 1993), pp. 48–49.

From the chancellor's point of view, a wall was not necessarily "a hell of a lot better than a war," as Kennedy famously quipped. Adenauer believed that Soviet leader Nikita Khrushchev had bullied Kennedy.[50] If the Berlin Air Lift of 1948–1949 had shown Germans that the United States could be trusted as an ally, the Berlin Crisis raised new doubts. The resolve shown by Kennedy's emissary to Berlin, retired general Lucius Clay, in the fall came too late to dispel serious concerns among Adenauer's inner circle. In the wake of the Berlin Crisis, Adenauer moved closer to de Gaulle. For the next year and a half, West Germany seemed to favor European integration over transatlantic relations. But the Franco-German treaty of friendship, signed by Adenauer and de Gaulle in January 1963, although surely a foundational document for those erstwhile archenemies, already signified the climax of a potential Paris–Bonn axis within a European third force. Adenauer himself was on his way out and his successors, Ludwig Erhard and Kurt-Georg Kiesinger, returned to Atlanticism as the centerpiece of German foreign policy.[51]

De Gaulle had issued a serious challenge to American leadership. The French president held that Europeans needed their own, reliable nuclear deterrent force. Once France had built its *force de frappe*, he reasoned, it would regain its place among the world's great powers. An innovative study of the Algerian War reminds us that de Gaulle viewed Europe in racial and civilizational terms as set apart from the United States.[52] Just how far de Gaulle, who sketched a utopian vision of a united Europe from Russia to the English Channel, was prepared to go in practical politics remains contested. One historian holds that his challenge was benign and forced the NATO allies to develop sturdier structures and a clearer sense of purpose. Thus, de Gaulle was motivated by concerns about French sovereignty and by a policy of *grandeur*, but he understood that he could only achieve this within the general framework of deterrence and economic growth provided by and fostered in the alliance.[53] Another historian argues in considering the foreign policy of

---

50 Frederick Kempe, *Berlin 1961: Kennedy, Khrushchev, and the Most Dangerous Place on Earth* (New York, 2011). On Adenauer's relationship with Kennedy see Frank A. Mayer, *Adenauer and Kennedy: A Study in German-American Relations, 1961–1963* (New York, 1996).

51 For Adenauer's attitudes toward the alliance see Ronald J. Granieri, *Konrad Adenauer, the CDU/CSU, and the West, 1949–1966* (New York, 2003). For the context of German foreign policy, see Helga Haftendorn, *Coming of Age: German Foreign Policy since 1945* (Lanham, MD, 2006).

52 Matthew Connelly, *A Diplomatic Revolution: Algeria's Fight for Independence and the Origins of the Post-Cold War Era* (Oxford, 2002), pp. 34–38.

53 Frédéric Bozo, *Two Strategies for Europe: De Gaulle, the United States, and the Atlantic Alliance*, trans. Susan Emanuel (Lanham, MD, 2001).

Lyndon B. Johnson that the Gaullist challenge was more serious and could have brought down the alliance system if Johnson had not managed the crisis of the mid 1960s with surprising tact. However, the consensus agrees on the outcome: the Western alliance in general, and NATO in particular, ended the 1960s in a stronger position.[54]

The differences between the United States, France, and Germany extended into the realms of military strategy and operational planning. France insisted on the trip-wire strategy of the early 1950s, the Kennedy administration favored conventional forward defense, Germany provided the battlefield, and the new strategic doctrine could not be spelled out with the same clarity as the old. Unlike massive retaliation, flexible response had to remain an amorphous concept that derived its deterrent value from unpredictability. The Kennedy administration elevated proportionality as a strategic principle without abandoning nuclear deterrence. In practice, it equated the concept with tit-for-tat escalation. For that reason Lemnitzer (SACEUR, 1963–69) banned the term "flexible response" from usage at his headquarters.[55] Many allied officers saw flexible response more as a philosophy than a strategy. As one commentator noted, it "attempts to link an incredible concept of escalation to an inadequate conventional component and an eroded theater nuclear force."[56] Quality of the deterrent varied over time, of course, and NATO forces had grown in strength, but they were still only marginally prepared for the defense of Central Region. In 1962 twenty-five allied divisions faced fifty-nine Warsaw Pact combat divisions that were deployed in East Germany, Poland, Czechoslovakia, and Hungary.[57]

In the process of restructuring alliance relations, the attempt to build an integrated nuclear force had failed. Following years of negotiations, the Johnson administration dropped the proposed multilateral force (MLF) that would have included Britain, France, and West Germany. The initial proposal had come in 1959 from Norstad and US Secretary of State Christian Herter, who hoped that successful implementation would deflect desires for a national nuclear deterrent in France and Germany.

---

54 Thomas Alan Schwartz, *Lyndon Johnson and Europe: In the Shadow of Vietnam* (Cambridge, MA, 2003).
55 Interview with General Lemnitzer, Supreme Allied Command in Europe (1963–1969), 11 February 1970, by Dr. David Nunnerley, pp. 6–7. Oral History Collection, John F. Kennedy Presidential Library. On the persistence of that thinking within NATO see also Remarks by General A. J. Goodpaster, Supreme Allied Commander, Europe, Imperial Defence College, SHAPE Belgium on 17 October 1969. Goodpaster Papers, Box 35, Folder 6, George C. Marshall Library.
56 Bland, *The Military Committee of the North Atlantic Alliance*, p. 1.
57 "Bedingt Abwehrbereit" in the assessment of NATO's 1962 fall exercise by the usually well-informed German news magazine *Der Spiegel*, nr. 41, 10 October 1962.

Some of the more enthusiastic advocates of the MLF proposal at the US State Department hoped that a NATO-wide medium-range ballistic missile force would be a step toward fuller integration of military means in the alliance. Yet the MLF proposal faced opposition in Europe and from defense department officials who did not believe national political, linguistic, and cultural barriers could be overcome to the point of creating fully functional transnational armed forces.[58] By the time Johnson shelved the proposal, France had already developed its own nuclear capability and was building the *force de frappe*. In 1966, West Germany became a permanent member in a new Nuclear Planning Group alongside the United States, Britain, Italy, and three rotating member states.

The breakthrough in resolving the great debate came in 1967. French withdrawal from NATO military commands in 1966 removed political pressure and allowed for the other European states to accept flexible response as strategic guidance. The United States still had to concede two points, however. One is widely recognized: the elevation of détente alongside defense as NATO's fundamental goal. This was formalized in the adoption of the "Report on the Future Tasks of the Alliance" in December 1967 that had resulted from a review of NATO strategy and policy directed by the Belgian Foreign Minister Pierre Harmel.[59] But this solution could not have been achieved without a continued American troop presence, maintained in part by way of Reforger (return of forces to Germany) exercises that allowed for two army divisions stationed in the United States to be counted as forward-deployed because a part of the force and most of the heavy equipment remained in Germany, and by Washington's willingness to invest in NATO more heavily than the Europeans did or could. That sent a strong signal to the European partners and it signaled resolve to the Soviet Union, whose leaders otherwise might have drawn the wrong conclusions from America's concurrent pursuit of a foreign policy of détente amid the mounting frustrations of the Vietnam War.[60]

The burden-sharing debate, which extended from NATO's beginnings to the end of the Cold War, served as a constant reminder of the difficulty of balancing security, stability, and prosperity. Oftentimes it seemed as if Americans were paying a higher price for security, while Europeans emphasized prosperity as the essential goal. Europeans, on the other

---

58 Kaplan, Landa, and Drea, *McNamara Ascendancy*, pp. 385–420.
59 Jane E. Stromseth, *The Origins of Flexible Response: NATO's Strategy Debate in the 1960s* (New York, 1988).
60 For strategy discussions and the application of flexible response after 1967 see Ivo Daalder, *The Nature and Practice of Flexible Response: NATO Strategy and Theater Nuclear Forces since 1967* (New York, 1991).

hand, pointed at less readily quantifiable responsibilities and at their front-line location in a potential nuclear war.[61] Why, then, did American forces remain in Europe in great numbers, despite the great demand of the Vietnam War on American military manpower? Francis Gavin, building on Marc Trachtenberg's revisionist argument for the early Cold War, posits that the German question still posed a greater threat to the international system than did the Soviet Union. That is, integration of German power and containment of German political and economic desires still drove US policy.[62] There may be a simpler explanation in the grand strategy framework of the Western alliance, however: a strong US presence on the ground was a critical ingredient in the complex mix of military might, political stability, and economics that propelled NATO, transatlantic relations, and the European Common Market all at once.

Enduring alliance (1968–1991)

If the Harmel Report and new strategic guidance had put NATO on a more solid footing, these documents did little to resolve the different perspectives on financial burden sharing, disagreements on the utility of tactical and theater nuclear weapons, and the disconnect between strategy and force posture. In addition, the relative weight placed on détente and deterrence arose as a divisive issue. West Europeans in general, and West Germans in particular, saw détente and diplomacy as the critical means to stability of East–West relations in the 1970s and early 1980s, while Americans soured on détente and arms control after the Soviet invasion of Afghanistan in 1979. This divide was a natural extension of the different approaches to stability that had characterized American and European understandings of the alliance. With different degrees of conviction, the European allies strongly favored prosperity as the principal underwriter of stability; fear, which continued to motivate US policy, seemed to them less relevant, and indeed security more assured, in an age of nuclear stalemate. In essence, European leaders, with German chancellor Willy Brandt (1969–1974) at the forefront, saw détente as a means to stability; Americans seemed to treat it is as a function of security.

Détente in the early 1970s was shaped both in Washington and Bonn. German *Ostpolitik* aimed at greater political, cultural, and economic

---

61 Simon Duke, *The Burdensharing Debate: A Reassessment* (New York, 1993), pp. 24–85 on the distinction between burden sharing and responsibility sharing.
62 Francis J. Gavin, *Gold, Dollars, and Power: The Politics of International Monetary Relations, 1958–1971* (Chapel Hill, NC, 2004); Marc Trachtenberg, *A Constructed Peace: The Making of the European Settlement, 1945–1963* (Princeton, NJ, 1999).

engagement of the Soviet Union and its Eastern European clients. It yielded increased trade between the blocs in Europe and helped normalize the relationship between the two German states, as well as between Germany and its neighbors to the east.[63] Détente, on the other hand, had broader aims that ranged from terminating the war in Vietnam to trade and arms control, and included the tenuous relationship of China and the Soviet Union as well as diplomacy between East and West. President Richard Nixon and his secretary of state, Henry Kissinger, preferred to keep the latter on a bilateral basis, and they feared Germany might embark on an overly ambitious foreign policy vis-à-vis the Eastern Europe that could divide the alliance and destabilize the relationships of Eastern European states and the Soviet Union.[64] Bonn and Washington thus did not share an identical conception of the policy.

From an American perspective, détente may be best understood as a conservative response to domestic and international crises of the late 1960s; it represented an attempt to keep the Cold War in a manageable state.[65] Conservatives and liberals in the United States soon criticized the emphasis on arms control and the lack of emphasis on human rights, respectively. Military officers and some political leaders began to wonder if the Strategic Arms Limitation Talks and the agreements of 1972 and 1974 did not give the Soviet Union a critical edge in a theater nuclear war in Europe. Most Europeans saw détente less as a crisis-management mechanism than as a new structure for peaceful coexistence.[66] The continued and indeed heightened state of conflict in the Third World that aggravated the American political class was not as critical to their security concerns or perspectives on the Cold War.

In the wider historical trajectory of the Cold War, Americans appeared to feel less secure over time, propelled by the growing vulnerability of their country to Soviet ICBMs and to the apparent success of

---

63 For a helpful survey see Haftendorn, *Coming of Age*, pp. 157–95.
64 National Security Decision Memorandum 91, 6 November 1970, "United States Policy on Germany and Berlin," p. 2. Richard M. Nixon Presidential Library and Museum, Virtual Library, www.nixonlibrary.gov/virtuallibrary/documents/nsdm/nsdm_091.pdf. For a comparison see Gottfried Niedhart, "U.S. Détente and West German *Ostpolitik*: Parallels and Frictions," in Matthias Schulz and Thomas A. Schwartz (eds.), *The Strained Alliance: U.S.–European Relations from Nixon to Carter* (Cambridge, 2010), pp. 23–44.
65 Jussi M. Hanhimäki, *The Rise and Fall of Détente: American Foreign Policy and the Transformation of the Cold War* (Washington, DC, 2013).
66 For the decline of détente see Raymond L. Garthoff, *Détente and Confrontation: American–Soviet Relations from Nixon to Reagan* (Washington, DC, 1994); and Robert D. Schulzinger, "Détente in the Nixon–Ford Years, 1969–1976," in Melvyn P. Leffler and Odd Arne Westad (eds.), *The Cambridge History of the Cold War*, II: *Crisis and Détente* (Cambridge, 2010), pp. 373–94.

Marxist movements in the Third World. Europeans, who had a much greater familiarity with the realities of living under the guns of historically hostile neighbors, appeared to be more inclined to shrug off the security concerns as long as economic growth promised political stability. For many Europeans the twin crises in Berlin and Cuba in 1961 and 1962 represented the high point of the Cold War. Within the decade, threat perception receded as détente took center stage. Consequently, most Europeans maintained their strong preference for growth and prosperity over defense spending. At the beginning of the 1970s it appeared that Americans and Europeans equally favored détente, but neither Nixon nor Kissinger trusted the motives of West German Social Democrats or de Gaulle's successors in France. The European Common Market had emerged as an economic competitor and Nixon and Kissinger pressed attempts to shift more of the burden of the common defense on wealthier European states. Kissinger also hoped that NATO could refashion a security consensus and that European leaders would stand with him rather than conduct their own diplomacy in attempts to stabilize the Middle East in the midst of the Arab–Israeli conflict and oil crises. Both proved to be unattainable and Kissinger's initiative in declaring 1973 "the year of Europe" was ultimately counterproductive.[67]

Financial burden sharing remained a sore point; it was further exacerbated by the economic crises of the 1970s, by the weakness of the dollar, and by the relative decline of the American economy. The structural problem rested in the balance-of-payment deficit that resulted in part from the US troop presence in Europe in general, and in Germany in particular. Offset agreements in the 1960s between the United States and West Germany, which required Germany to purchase military equipment and Treasury bonds in the United States, did not compensate for the entire deficit and caused resentment and political crisis in Bonn. Moreover, as European economies grew faster than the US economy, the trade balance began to shift toward the former and the dollar came under increasing pressure. Nixon hoped to find alternative ways to structure offset payments, maintain reduced US force levels in Europe, and

67 Daniel Möckli, "Asserting Europe's Distinct Identity: The EC Nine and Kissinger's Year of Europe," in Matthias Schulz and Thomas A. Schwartz (eds.), *The Strained Alliance: U.S.–European Relations from Nixon to Carter* (Cambridge, 2010), pp. 195–220. On Kissinger's thinking about the alliance more generally, see Jeremi Suri, "Henry Kissinger and the Reconceptualization of European Security, 1969–1975," in Andreas Wenger, Vojtech Mastny, and Christian Nuenlist (eds.), *Origins of the European Security System: The Helsinki Process Revisited* (London, 2008), pp. 46–64.

improve US–European relations within NATO.[68] Like those of his pre-decessors, his efforts were to be frustrated.[69] In 1971 Nixon determined to abandon the fixed-rate convertibility of the dollar into gold, a decision that kept the dollar in place as the world's leading currency in a system of flexible exchange. European leaders were not pleased, but one historian concludes that American politicians believed they had to choose between defending Europe and defending the dollar.[70]

Toward the end of the Vietnam War, the United States appeared to be a superpower in decline, both in military and economic terms.[71] By extension, the Nixon Doctrine, issued in 1969 with a specific focus on Southeast Asia, struck observers on both sides of the Atlantic as a por-tent: the US would still honor its alliances, but allies had to provide the bulk of manpower. Nixon himself suggested that Europeans should build up their own conventional forces instead of subsidizing US forces in Europe.[72] Nevertheless, the Nixon administration expressed its com-mitment to help provide the means for NATO's "strategy of initial con-ventional defense for 90 days."[73] The feasibility of sustained conventional defense was not widely accepted and while Western European defense ministers agreed that equal burden sharing was necessary, European leaders hoped that détente would help lower the threat level and render

68 National Security Study Memorandum 6, 21 January 1969, "Review of NATO Policy Alternatives" and National Security Study Memorandum 7, January 21, 1969, "U.S. International Monetary Policy." Richard M. Nixon Presidential Library and Museum, Virtual Library, www.nixonlibrary.gov/virtuallibrary/documents/nssm/nssm_006.pdf and www.nixonlibrary.gov/virtuallibrary/documents/nssm/nssm_007.pdf.

69 Very little seemed to have changed during Nixon's first term in office. National Security Decision Memorandum 214, 3 May 1973, "Balance of Payments Offset and Burden-sharing Negotiations with NATO." Richard M. Nixon Presidential Library and Museum, Virtual Library, www.nixonlibrary.gov/virtuallibrary/documents/nssm/nsdm_214.pdf.

70 Gavin, *Gold, Dollars, and Power*. See also Hubert Zimmermann, *Money and Security: Troops, Monetary Policy and West Germany's Relations with the United States and Britain, 1950–1971* (Cambridge, 2002); and William Glenn Gray, "Floating the System: Germany, the United States, and the Breakdown of Bretton Woods, 1969–1973," *Diplomatic History*, 31(2) (April 2007), 295–323.

71 Dan Caldwell, "The Legitimation of the Nixon–Kissinger Grand Design and Grand Strategy," Diplomatic History, 33(4) (September 2009), 633–52.

72 National Security Decision Memorandum 88, 15 October 1970, "U.S. Force Levels in Europe and 'Burden-sharing'." Richard M. Nixon Presidential Library and Museum, Virtual Library, www.nixonlibrary.gov/virtuallibrary/documents/nsdm/nsdm_088.pdf.

73 National Security Decision Memorandum 95, 25 November 1970, "U.S. Strategy and Forces for NATO," p. 2. Richard M. Nixon Presidential Library and Museum, Virtual Library, www.nixonlibrary.gov/virtuallibrary/documents/nsdm/nsdm_095.pdf.

the cost of defense less prohibitive.[74] Consequently, as the Gerald R. Ford administration drew to a close, NATO's defense posture still did not meet its strategic guidance. The Ford administration concluded, "NATO allies should be encouraged to increase their own sustaining capabilities to 90 days."[75]

While Europeans hoped détente, driven by a multilateral approach, would extend beyond the 1975 Helsinki meeting of the Conference of Security and Cooperation in Europe (CSCE), their outlook on the economic side remained decidedly pessimistic. Slowed down by the shocks of the oil crisis of 1973–1974 and the breakdown of the postwar financial system, Western Europe's national economies faced stagnation. Soviet foreign trade with Western Europe offered an area for growth.[76] The trade volume between the Soviet Union and the European Economic Community had amounted to roughly $1.4 billion in 1967, grew to over $8 billion in 1975, and then expanded to more than $12.5 billion in 1977.[77] West German exports to the Soviet Union quadrupled between 1972 and 1977. In the process, the Soviet Union took on increasing amounts of debt and developed a dependency on West German and Japanese high technology.[78] But the Soviets also offered an alternative option to Europe's energy dependence on Middle Eastern oil. In the second half of the 1970s, West Germany, France, Italy, Belgium, and the Netherlands purchased between 20 and 25 million tons of Soviet crude oil each year, consuming one-quarter to one-third of all Soviet oil exports, and German and French banks were financing a natural gas pipeline from Siberia to Western Europe.[79] There were thus political

---

74 For conventional forces in Central Region and the long-standing debate of reductions of US forces in Europe see Phil Williams, *The Senate and U.S. Troops in Europe* (New York, 1985); and John S. Duffield, *Power Rules: The Evolution of NATO's Conventional Force Posture* (Stanford, CA, 1995), pp. 194–232. For an insightful discussion of the Nixon administration and NATO strategy see Robert Thomas Davis II, "The Dilemma of NATO Strategy, 1949–1968," Ohio University, PhD dissertation, 2008, pp. 293–315.

75 National Security Decision Memorandum 348, January 20, 1977, "U.S. Defense Policy and Military Posture," p. 3. Gerald R. Ford Presidential Digital Library, www.fordlibrarymuseum.gov/library/document/0310/nsdm348.pdf.

76 On the close relationship of East–West trade and *Ostpolitik* see Werner D. Lippert, *The Economic Diplomacy of Ostpolitik: Origins of NATO's Energy Dilemma* (New York, 2011).

77 Angela Stent, *From Embargo to Ostpolitik: The Political Economy of West German–Soviet Relations, 1955–1980* (Cambridge, 1981), p. 244. Note the difference in membership, however: Denmark, Ireland, and Britain joined the EEC in 1973.

78 See Stent, *From Embargo to Ostpolitik*, pp. 209–15 for a breakdown of West German-Soviet trade in the 1970s.

79 Theodore Shabad, "The Soviet Potential in Natural Resources: An Overview," in Robert G. Jensen, Theodore Shabad, and Arthur W. Wright, *Soviet Natural Resources in the World Economy* (Chicago, 1983), pp. 251–74, esp. p. 257.

and economic benefits that emerged from détente. Western European leaders assumed that commerce served as a stabilizing tool and that increasing debt owed to the West placed the Soviet Union in a dependent relationship.

By the mid 1970s, Congressmen in the United States, already disinclined to underwrite further arms control agreements and improved commercial relations that seemed to benefit the Soviets, made any further advancement of détente a difficult struggle. The JCS and secretaries of defense James Schlesinger and Donald Rumsfeld warned of allowing the Soviet military a lead in the nuclear arms race. German Chancellor Helmut Schmidt (1974–1982) and other European leaders, meanwhile, expressed concern that the codification of nuclear stalemate placed even greater emphasis on conventional and tactical-nuclear arms unless ongoing negotiations about mutual and balanced force reductions yielded a positive result. When the Soviets deployed modern SS-20 intermediate-range ballistic missiles that threatened Western Europe, Schmidt reminded the allies in October 1977 that parity at all levels was a necessary precondition for effective deterrence. Schmidt's warning accelerated an ongoing debate that ultimately led to NATO's 1979 dual-track decision to deploy American Pershing-II missiles in Western Europe while continuing to pursue arms control negotiations with the Soviet Union.[80]

Détente in international politics was in remission by the end of the 1970s. In December 1979, NATO's council of ministers determined that the West had to match the buildup of Soviet SS-20 missiles. The Soviet invasion of Afghanistan in the same month further exacerbated the sense of crisis, and the Carter administration returned to a policy of defense through strength. As the missile crisis extended into the first term of Ronald Reagan's presidency it helped give birth to a fast-growing antinuclear movement in Western Europe, and it led to serious disturbances in the transatlantic relationship when Reagan demanded the withdrawal of all SS-20 missiles in return for an American promise not to station its Pershing II missiles in Western Europe. When the Kremlin balked, the United States went ahead with deployment. The protest movement

---

80 Helmut Schmidt, "Political and Economic Aspects of Western Security: The 1977 Alastair Buchan Memorial Lecture, Delivered to the International Institute for Strategic Studies by the Chancellor of the Federal Republic of Germany in London on 28 October 1977," *Survival*, 20(1) (January–February 1978), 2–10. See also Helga Haftendorn, "Das doppelte Mißverständnis: Zur Vorgeschichte des NATO-Doppelbeschlusses von 1979," *Vierteljahrshefte für Zeitgeschichte*, 33(2) (April 1985), 244–87; and Kristina Spohr Readman, "Conflict and Cooperation in Intra-Alliance Nuclear Politics: Western Europe, the United States, and the Genesis of NATO's Dual-Track Decision, 1977–1979," *Journal of Cold War Studies*, 13(2) (Spring 2011), 39–89.

had lost, further illustrated by the return to power of a center-right coalition in Germany. Nevertheless, as tensions in the Cold War mounted the Reagan administration charged ahead with a combination of harsh rhetoric aimed at the "evil empire" and a massive defense buildup.[81] At the same time the deployment of Pershing IIs from 1983 lessened the inherent tension between forward defense and nuclear deterrence. This was a weapons system that could hit airfields and follow-on forces in Eastern Europe that were advancing behind the initial assault formations of Warsaw Pact armies. Pershing IIs could also reach targets in the Soviet Union in about ten minutes from anywhere in West Germany, which reduced the likelihood of a successful Soviet first strike. It was thus possible to match Soviet theater nuclear capability without having to resort to the strategic deterrent force.[82]

Reagan's grand strategy has only begun to draw the attention of scholars and it remains unclear to what extent his administration's more aggressive approach to the Cold War, with its goals of undermining Soviet power and liberating the peoples who were suffering under pro-Soviet regimes, developed along clearly predetermined lines.[83] It is clear, however, that the Reagan administration favored military strength, while Europeans still hoped for more constructive engagement and diplomacy. The defense buildup had already begun in Carter's last year and a half in office. Under Reagan, however, the defense budget grew exponentially – indeed, it doubled in his first term – and the armed services that had been slowly recovering from their own depression following the defeat in the Vietnam War could put money into the mass production of some of their most promising projects. The magnitude of annual increases in the defense budget overwhelmed the Pentagon's capacity to keep spending under control, and Reagan's own infatuation with missile defense deflected some of the money to that endeavor. Nevertheless, the early 1980s saw the emergence of a much more powerful US military in air, sea, and land power.[84]

---

81 Jeffrey Herf, *War By Other Means: Soviet Power, West German Resistance, and the Battle of the Euromissiles* (New York, 1991).
82 For the balance of forces see David M. Walsh, *The Military Balance in the Cold War: US Perceptions and Policy, 1976–1985* (New York, 2008). For the Pershing II see Richard Rhodes, *Arsenals of Folly: The Making of the Nuclear Arms Race* (New York, 2007), pp. 134–67.
83 Francis H. Marlo, *Planning Reagan's War: Conservative Strategists and America's Cold War Victory* (Washington, DC, 2012) offers a basic introduction while James Graham Wilson raises doubts about a coherent grand strategy in *The Triumph of Improvisation: Gorbachev's Adaptability, Reagan's Engagement, and the End of the Cold War* (Ithaca, 2014). See also Alan P. Dobson, "The Reagan Administration, Economic Warfare, and Starting to Close Down the Cold War," *Diplomatic History*, 29(3) (June 2005), 531–56.
84 For a critical assessment see Lawrence J. Korb, "Where Did All the Money Go? The 1980s US Defence Buildup and the End of the Cold War," in Stephen J. Cimbala (ed.), *Mysteries of the Cold War* (Aldershot, 1999), pp. 3–18.

The US army, charged with the defense of West Germany, had already designed tactical and operational doctrine for a fast-paced mobile defense that could now be enhanced by new tanks, infantry fighting vehicles, attack helicopters and fixed-wing aircraft, battlefield missiles, and satellite communications. Reagan intended to exploit new weapons technology in an effort to enhance deterrence and forward defense. He recognized that the United States needed to take the lead, but that it was "NATO's task ... to do a better job of providing the forces and the doctrine to support the strategy."[85] In his first defense budget, Reagan had increased money for tank procurement by 29 percent, for infantry fighting vehicles by 34 percent, and for attack helicopters by 25 percent.[86] If the army's new operational doctrine, Air Land Battle, previously may have seemed far-fetched, weapons and communications technology now gave hope to those who believed that Soviet front-line divisions could be held near the intra-German border, while NATO forces would attack their follow-on echelons deep inside Eastern Europe. The open question remained to what extent – and at what point – nuclear weapons would have to be used. These were the early signs of what soon would come to be called the "revolution in military affairs."[87]

The buildup was underwritten both by government debt and a massive inflow of foreign capital into the American economy. While the budget deficit rose from $78.9 billion in 1981 to $207.8 billion by 1983 and federal debt tripled between 1980 and 1989, the US balance of payments account changed dramatically.[88] In the half decade from 1965 to 1969, it had shown an outflow of some $12 billion. A decade later that had changed to an inflow of $7.4 billion. Astoundingly, that inflow then grew to $146.5 billion in the first half of the 1980s and $660.6 billion in Reagan's second term. The United States particularly gained capital inflow from its major allies: in the 1970s, the other six G-7 countries had taken $46.5 billion from the United States; in the 1980s, the US gained over $374 billion from Japan, France, Britain, Italy, Canada, and

---

85 Ronald Reagan, "Letter to the Speaker of the House and the President of the Senate on NATO Conventional Defense Capabilities," 12 September 1984. *The American Presidency Project*, www.presidency.ucsb.edu/ws/?pid=40367.

86 Daniel Wirls, *Buildup: The Politics of Defense in the Reagan Era* (Ithaca, NY, 1992), pp. 42–43.

87 On technology and the US military in general see Thomas G. Mahnken, *Technology and the American Way of War since 1945* (New York, 2008). On the confluence of new technology, operational art, and the defense of Western Europe see Trauschweizer, *Cold War U.S. Army*, pp. 214–27.

88 Wirls, *Buildup*, p. 54. On the exponential growth of the federal deficit in the 1980s see Dennis S. Ippolito, *Uncertain Legacies: Federal Budget Policy from Roosevelt through Reagan* (Charlottesville, VA, 1990).

West Germany.[89] Reagan's defense buildup, an investment of nearly $3 trillion from 1981 to 1990, may have been debt-financed, but under the economic and financial conditions of this decade, the United States could afford to turn debt into military power.[90] Curiously, deficit-financed defense spending may have come closest to enticing European NATO partners, most notably West Germany, to invest more heavily in the common defense.[91] The Soviet Union, meanwhile, pressured in the global Cold War by the United States as well as by the People's Republic of China, and facing growing debt and increasing strains of the war in Afghanistan, approached collapse.[92]

When the Soviet Union withdrew its support for its erstwhile Eastern European clients in the summer and fall of 1989, the communist empire fell with breathtaking speed. But that raised new concerns in London, Paris, and Washington. Margaret Thatcher had put it bluntly in conversation with Mikhail Gorbachev: neither the West nor the Soviet Union could allow for the redrawing of borders in Europe. The end of the Cold War thus introduced a moment in which instability threatened the postwar order. Ultimately, following the lead of German Chancellor Helmut Kohl, the allies found a solution in the eastward extension of the two institutions that had underwritten stability in Europe throughout much of the Cold War. NATO's and the European Community's (soon to become the European Union) eastward expansion once more revealed the essence of the Western alliance, the linkage of security and prosperity to the overarching objective of maintaining stability.[93]

Conclusion

No common grand strategy in 1985 – but victory at the end of the decade? Had technology and operational art come to stand in for grand strategy in the 1980s? Where a single nation might have pursued a consistent

---

89 Giovanni Arrighi, "The World Economy and the Cold War, 1970–1990," in Leffler and Westad, *The Cold War*, III, pp. 23–44. For the data on balance of payments see pp. 34–35.

90 See Wirls, *Buildup*, p. 207 on the total outlay in 1990 dollars. Defense spending in George H. W. Bush's first year in office was 40 percent larger than it had been in 1980.

91 German critics of US fiscal and trade policies complained that European economies were made to pay for the US deficit by way of inflated interest rates in the United States and an artificially strong dollar. Sloan, *Permanent Alliance?*, p. 67.

92 Vladislav M. Zubok, *A Failed Empire: The Soviet Union in the Cold War from Stalin to Gorbachev* (Chapel Hill, NC, 2007).

93 Smith, *NATO Enlargement during the Cold War*; and Mary E. Sarotte, *1989: The Struggle to Create Post-Cold War Europe* (Princeton, NJ, 2009). For Thatcher's conversation with Gorbachev see Sarotte, *1989*, pp. 27–28.

grand strategy defined by the national interest, the Western alliance flourished by its flexibility and ability to transform itself. At the height of the Cold War, B. H. Liddell Hart concluded that "vitality springs from diversity – which makes for real progress as long as there is mutual toleration, based on the recognition that worse may come from an attempt to suppress differences than from acceptance of them."[94] Put differently, a loosely structured alliance could prove superior in the long term to a more closely integrated coalition that took counsel from its fears. For once such a coalition adopted a dogmatic grand strategy, which required and directed the fullest integration of resources and interests, it was best equipped for present threats or for what was perceived about the recent past and therefore expected for the near future. But such integration could only come at the expense of long-term cohesion. Surely, in dire circumstances such as in 1941–1942, there was little choice. But in 1947, 1957, 1967, or 1977 there were a variety of choices based on a greater degree of flexibility in alliance arrangements.

In a practical sense, the Western alliance helped prevent a third world war. NATO produced strategy documents that committed its members to nuclear deterrence in the 1950s and flexible response after 1967 and developed operational plans for the defense of Western Europe. Yet operational planning and strategic guidance did not always reinforce one another closely and nuclear strategy, force structure and logistics, and financial burden sharing remained centrifugal issues throughout the Cold War. NATO never quite managed to utilize effectively the resources of its member nations. Given the different historical experiences of the major powers, that outcome should not be surprising. For the United States, the world wars had revealed that mobilization for total war could foster economic growth and lay the foundations for lasting prosperity. For Europeans, the world wars had brought massive destruction and grave crisis. Americans could see grand strategy as the pursuit of security through strength and prosperity. Europeans, on the other hand, were more likely to fear an imbalance between defense spending and economic growth. Consequently, the NATO partners held different views on the balance of warfare and welfare.

The dual emphasis on guns and butter led to serious tensions within the alliance. At issue was whether and how to place greater weight on defense and deterrence or on commerce and welfare. Western Europeans generally strongly favored the latter, but they could do so only because

94 Liddell Hart, *Strategy*, p. 354.

American military power helped instill the requisite sense of security.[95] When it appeared that the United States might not be entirely committed to nuclear deterrence and the defense of Western Europe during the great debate over limited war and flexible response, de Gaulle and Adenauer flirted with notions of an autonomous French deterrent and a Franco-German coalition within the alliance. For US administrations from Truman to Reagan, this tension between warfare and welfare and between American and continental European notions of security and prosperity was extremely frustrating. It led to calls for reductions in US forces in Europe and to uncertainty about the balance of nuclear and conventional capabilities. It also led to a general sense of European ungratefulness that was exacerbated in the burden-sharing debates. The underlying tension was never resolved, but it remained manageable even through the great crises within the alliance in the mid 1960s and late 1970s.

What makes the Western alliance – and NATO as an integral part – unique is the ability to balance disagreement and even dissent with a shared worldview based on a common political and intellectual framework. To flesh out that framework with inflexible military strategy, operational plans, and tactical doctrine proved problematic. Perhaps that was a positive feature. Consider: if NATO had completely focused on how to combat Soviet forces in the moment – that is, if military security had trumped economics, finance, and politics – surely the alliance would have been worse off in the long run; it might have found insufficient common ground to persist through the era of détente and almost certainly would have disintegrated at the end of the Cold War. Instead, the Western allies followed a path that resembled the visions of Woodrow Wilson and Alfred Thayer Mahan: world order based on collective security, economic inter-dependency, and free trade underwritten by a military, diplomatic, and political consortium of like-minded nations.[96] That may not be a common grand strategy, but it has ensured peace and stability in the Western world for a length of time unmatched in any other age since the fall of the Roman Empire.

---

95 For a similar argument specific to the United States and West Germany see Thomas Bender and Michael Geyer, "Empires: Might and Myopia," in Christof Mauch and Kiran Klaus Patel (eds.), *The United States and Germany in the Twentieth Century: Competition and Convergence* (Cambridge, 2010), pp. 13–31.

96 On Mahan see Jon T. Sumida, *Inventing Grand Strategy and Teaching Command: The Classic Works of Alfred Thayer Mahan Revisited* (Baltimore, MD, 1997). On Wilson, see, for instance, Thomas J. Knock, *To End All Wars: Woodrow Wilson and the Quest for a New World Order* (Princeton, NJ, 1995).

Part II

The political and military challenges of
coalition warfare

8 The Peloponnesian War and Sparta's strategic alliances

Victor Davis Hanson and David L. Berkey

Paradoxes at Sparta

When the Peloponnesian War broke out in late spring 431,[1] Sparta confronted a variety of strategic dilemmas. It lacked both the population base of Athens and the commercial wealth of the Athenian overseas empire. In addition, the Spartans seemed to be losing cultural influence in Greece at a time when the Athens of Pericles was expanding its soft power. And while Spartan security depended on a loose confederation of freelancing Peloponnesian oligarchies, the Athenian Empire represented a tightly controlled political and economic entity.[2]

---

1 All dates in reference to the events leading up to and during the Peloponnesian War are BC. The following abbreviations will be used throughout this chapter: Hdt. = Herodotus; Thuc. = Thucydides; Xen. = Xenophon, *Hellenica*; Diod. = Diodorus; [Xen.] *Ath. Pol.* = Pseudo-Xenophon, *Athenaion Politeia*.

2 Mogens Herman Hansen, *s.v.* "Attika," in Mogens Herman Hansen and Thomas Heine Nielsen (eds.), *An Inventory of Archaic and Classical Poleis: An Investigation Conducted by the Copenhagen Polis Centre for the Danish National Research Foundation* (Oxford, 2004), p. 627: "In the Classical period, Athens was probably the most populous of all the Hellenic *poleis* ... In 431 Athens had a field army of 15,800 men, of whom 13,000 were citizen hoplites; a defence force of 16,000, of whom 3,000 were metic hoplites, and a navy of 300 triremes (Thuc. 2.13.6–7; Hansen ("The Number of Athenian Hoplites in 431 B.C.," *Symbolae Osloenses* 56 [1981] 19–32)). There were altogether some 50,000– 60,000 adult male citizens (Rhodes (*Thucydides History*, ii [Warminster, 1988]), pp. 271–77; Hansen (*Three Studies in Athenian Demography* [Copenhagen, 1988]) 23–25)." Graham Shipley, *s.v.* "Lakedaimon," in Hansen and Nielsen (eds.), *An Inventory of Archaic and Classical Poleis*, p. 590: "Referring to 480, Hdt. 7.234.2 makes Damaratos say that the *polis* of Sparta contains approximately 8,000 men – possibly the only remotely reliable estimate of total Spartiate numbers. At Plataea in 479 there were 5,000 Spartans (Hdt. 9.28.2), perhaps formally two-thirds of the total levy (Paul Cartledge, *Sparta and Lakonia: A Regional History, 1300 to 362* BC (2nd ed.) [London and New York, 2002] 178–79). Aristotle, *Politics* (hereafter abbreviated as Arist. *Pol.*) 1270a36–38 reports that there were 'once' 10,000 Spartiatai." Sparta certainly suffered a loss to its population in the earthquakes of *c.* 465, but Cartledge rejects Diodorus's statement (11.63.1–2) that they killed more than 20,000 Lakedaimonians (Cartledge, *Sparta and Lakonia*, pp. 190–91). By the time of the Battle of Leuctra in 371, the number of male Spartan citizens had declined precipitously to approximately 1,500 – what Aristotle referred to as *oliganthropia* (*Pol.* 1270a31–34): "History itself has clearly shown the defects of the Spartan methods of dealing with property. Sparta was unable to weather a single defeat

197

To read the Old Oligarch's description (*c.* 440–425) of commercial Athens is to understand that the Aegean's future was to be Ionic, not Doric:[3]

They [*sc.* The Athenians] alone of Greeks and foreigners can be wealthy: where will it dispose of its goods without the agreement of the rulers of the sea? If a city is wealthy in iron, copper or flax, where will it dispose of its goods without the consent of the rulers of the sea? But these are just what I need for ships – wood from one, iron from another, and copper, flax and wax from others. In addition, exports to any city hostile to us will be forbidden on pain of being barred from the sea. Although I do nothing, I have all these products of the land because of the sea, while no other city has two of them; no city has both timber and flax, but where there is an abundance of flax the ground is level and treeless, nor do copper and iron come from the same city, nor any two or three of the other products from one place but one from one city, another from another.

Sparta then understandably favored a preventive war, in fear of the trajectory of Athenian power.[4] Donald Kagan, for example, in this context explains the Spartan decision to go war against Athens:

All three components of Thucydides's explanation justify the Athenians' analysis of the motives at work in the relations between states (1.75.3): fear, honor, and interest. The deepest self-interest of the Spartans required them to maintain the integrity of the Peloponnesian League and their own leadership of it. Their honor, their conception of themselves, depended on the recognition of that leadership and

in the field; and she was ruined by want of men" (trans. Ernest Barker, *The Politics of Aristotle* (Oxford, 1946)). See the differing views also of Charles D. Hamilton, "Sparta," in Lawrence A Trittle (ed.), *The Greek World in the Fourth Century: From the Fall of the Athenian Empire to the Successors of Alexander* (London, 1997), pp. 58 ff.; G. L. Cawkwell, "The Decline of Sparta," *Classical Quarterly*, 33 (1983), 385–400; Cartledge, *Sparta and Lakonia*, pp. 263–72; Paul Cartledge, *Agesilaos and the Crisis of Sparta* (Baltimore, 1987), pp. 37–43.

3   [Xen.], *Ath. Pol.*, 2.11–12, in *Aristotle and Xenophon on Democracy and Oligarchy*, trans. J. M. Moore (Berkeley, CA, 1975), p. 43 and commentary pp. 53–54.

4   All translations of Thucydides are from the revised edition of Richard Crawley in *The Landmark Thucydides: A Comprehensive Guide to the Peloponnesian War*, ed. Robert B. Strassler (New York, 1996). Thuc. 1.23.6: "The real cause, however, I consider to be the one which was formally most kept out of sight. The growth of the power of Athens, and the alarm which this inspired in Sparta, made war inevitable." 1.88: "The Spartans voted that the treaty had been broken, and that war must be declared, not so much because they were persuaded by the arguments of the allies, as because they feared the growth of the power of the Athenians, seeing most of Hellas already subject to them." 1.118.2: "During this interval [*sc.* the Pentecontaetia] the Athenians succeeded in placing their empire on a firmer basis, and themselves advanced their own power to a very great height. The Spartans, though fully aware of it, opposed it only for a little while, but remained inactive during most of the period, being of old slow to go to war except under the pressure of necessity, and in the present instance being hampered at home. Finally, the growth of the Athenian power could no longer be ignored as their own confederacy became the object of its encroachments. Then they felt that they could endure it no longer, but that the time had come for them to throw themselves heart and soul upon the hostile power, and break it, if they could, by commencing the present war."

on maintaining their peculiar polity, whose security, in turn, depended on the same things. In the view of those who voted for war, all this was put at risk by the recent behavior of the Athenians. They feared that its growing power would allow Athens to annoy Sparta's allies still further to the point where the allies would pursue their own interests without regard to Sparta, thereby dissolving the league and Sparta's security with it. The Spartans felt the need to expose themselves to the great dangers of a preventive war to preserve an alliance they had created precisely to save them from danger. They had formed it to serve their own interests but found that to preserve it they had to serve the interests of their allies, even if those threatened their own safety. It was not the last time that the leader of an alliance would find itself led by lesser allies to pursue policies it would not have chosen for itself.[5]

Yet initially Athens had insufficient resources to ensure a winning strategy. Sparta for its part had neither a fleet large enough to stop Athenian maritime commerce and raiding nor a workable method of storming the urban or long walls of Athens and capturing the city. Meanwhile, its own strategic weak spots – mainly the large helot populations of Laconia and Messenia – were vulnerable to enemy sea-borne raiding and amphibious landings along the coast of the Peloponnese. The significance of Spartan paranoia over the possibility of an insurrection by the helots to the formation of Spartan foreign policy is clear in one historian's description:

The major determining factor about Sparta, which in the last analysis affects every other aspect, is the existence of a large subject population of helots and Messenians. Curiously, despite the fact that one clear functional purpose of Thucydides Book I is to introduce us to Sparta and Athens, this factor is far from prominent in that book and is even glossed over when Thucydides describes the slowness of Spartan reaction to Athenian imperialism ... Clear hints about Spartan worries start appearing almost immediately. Before long we learn more explicitly that the Spartans are normally intensely cautious about the helots and that this crisis makes them more willing to get some out of the country with Brasidas and conduct an extensive purge of others. Thucydides eventually asserts that fears about the helots were a determining reason for the Spartans making the Peace of Nikias. How far this was clear from the outside is uncertain; they are at least once said to wish to conceal it from the Athenians. From our point of view, it seems clear, although modern books are shy of saying it, that the Athenians would have no difficulty in winning the Peloponnesian War decisively, had they done a little more to promote helot revolt.[6]

5 Donald Kagan, *On the Origins of War and the Preservation of Peace* (New York, 1995), pp. 57–58.
6 David M. Lewis, *Sparta and Persia: Lectures Delivered at the University of Cincinnati, Autumn 1976, in Memory of Donald W. Bradeen* (Leiden, 1977), pp. 27–28. For another perspective, see Cartledge, *Sparta and Lakonia*, p. 227; Paul Cartledge, "Rebels and *Sambos* in Classical Greece: A Comparative View," in *Spartan Reflections* (Berkeley, CA, 2001), pp. 127–52. See also, G. E. M. de Ste. Croix, *The Origins of the Peloponnesian War* (Ithaca, NY, 1972), pp. 89–93 (also as "The Helot Threat," in Michael Whitby (ed.), *Sparta* (New York, 2002), pp. 190–95).

Sparta was an insular, parochial society without a great deal of experience in the wider Mediterranean. If it needed more than Peloponnesian allies, particularly those with ample naval assets, to win the war, at the outbreak of hostilities it possessed neither the necessary temperament nor experienced diplomats to craft a strategic alliance that went much beyond its Peloponnesian neighbors. In short, Sparta started a conflict against Athens with no more understanding of what such a total war might entail against such a resolute and multifaceted enemy than did Adolf Hitler had when he waged a preemptory strike against the Soviet Union in June 1941.

More importantly, the Spartans recognized a paradox: forging a grand alliance beyond the Peloponnese might be necessary to defeat Athens, but such a transformation in Spartan custom and practice – becoming sailors, stationing bases overseas, sending hoplites abroad for long periods, welcoming foreigners as military equals, monetizing elements of their economy, diverting troops from helot surveillance – might also prove fatal to Spartan traditions. In the classical world, hoplites and triremes were not just investments in particular military assets, but reflected wider social and political preferences – agriculture versus commerce, oligarchy opposed to democracy, conservatism at odds with liberalism. For Sparta to beat Athens, then, it might have to become something other than Sparta.[7]

True, in the so-called first Peloponnesian War of 460–445, Sparta had fought Athens to a standstill – thanks largely to Athenian maritime reverses to the Persian fleet during the Egyptian campaign, and due to the assistance of Thebes in a series of bitter hoplite battles in Boeotia.[8] Those facts, however, reminded the Spartans on the eve of the war in 431 that while their own Peloponnesian League allies could on some occasions ensure a huge expeditionary infantry force of 40,000 to 60,000 hoplites and lightly armed troops, and a sizable allied fleet of mostly

7 Victor Davis Hanson, *The Other Greeks: The Family Farm and the Agrarian Roots of Western Civilization* (New York, 1995), pp. 327–43, esp. pp. 334–36, 339–43.
8 Athens and its naval allies led an expedition to Egypt in 459(?) (Thuc. 1.104.2; Diod. 11.71.4–6), which was defeated in 454(?), resulting in the loss of perhaps as many as 250 triremes (Thuc. 1.109–10; Diod. 11.77.3–5). For a discussion of the divergent accounts of the Egyptian campaign in our sources, see P. J. Rhodes, "The Delian League to 449 B.C.," in *The Cambridge Ancient History* (2nd edn.), vol. V: *The Fifth Century B.C.* (Cambridge, 1992), pp. 50–53 (also as *CAH²* 5.50–53). The events of the First Peloponnesian War are recorded in Thucydides, Diodorus, and also in epigraphical materials. For the Battle of Tanagra (457): Thuc. 1.107.4–108.1; Diod. 11.80, 82. Battle of Oenophyta (457): Thuc. 1.108.2–3; Diod. 11.83.1. For a discussion of Diodorus's account of the Battles of Tanagra and Oenophyta, see A. Andrewes, "Diodoros and Ephoros: One Source of Misunderstanding," in J. W. Eadie and J. Ober (eds.), *The Craft of the Ancient Historian: Essays in Honor of Chester G. Starr* (Lanham, MD, 1985), pp. 189–97. Battle of Coronea (447; for a date of 446, cf. D. M. Lewis, "Chronological Notes," *CAH²* 5.502, n. 9): Thuc. 1.113; cf. also 3.62.5, 67.3, 4.92.6.

Corinthian ships, and while Theban infantry allies were as resolute as ever, such combined forces still might not prove sufficient to defeat an enterprising and innovative Athenian Empire.

After all, Athens itself was largely impregnable to land assault, given its fortifications and the mostly backward status of siegecraft in the Greek world. It was also mostly immune from starvation, in view of the 6-kilometer corridor to the sea provided by the route of the Long Walls to the Piraeus, and the vast numerical superiority of its fleet. Moreover, given the nature of their respective alliances,[9] Athens had a greater ability to mobilize the

---

9 Peter J. Fliess, *Thucydides and the Politics of Bipolarity* (Baton Rouge, 1966), argues that fifth-century Greece was dominated by Athens and Sparta, that smaller poleis eventually had to choose to join in alliance with one of the two powers, that the Peloponnesian War was inevitable, and that the war would end in the subjugation of one of the powers. Malcolm F. McGregor, in his review of Fliess (*Phoenix*, 21 (1967), 306–9), comments that Fleiss's statement (p. viii), "In comparing the international situations then and now, it must be understood that analogous positions were occupied by Sparta and the United States, on the one hand, and by Athens and the Soviet Union, on the other," is "a curious analogy" (McGregor, p. 306). Of this passage, McGregor writes (*ibid.*): "Russia (the modern non-democratic land-power) he likens to Athens (a democratic sea-power); the United States (theoretically at least a democratic sea-power) to Sparta (a non-democratic land-power)... I suspect that Athens is cast as the villain, for Athens was an imperial city and empires are wicked." Fliess, however, is correct to draw this analogy. Donald Kagan, in *On the Origins of War and the Preservation of Peace*, writes (p. 76, n. 10; see also pp. 444–45): "When making this comparison it is important to remember that if the American constitution and way of life are closer to those of the Athenians and the Soviet Union's internal arrangements were closer to those of Sparta, the workings of NATO are more similar to those of the Spartan Alliance and those of the Warsaw Pact more like the Athenian Empire." The rigid control that Athens exerted over its allies is highly reminiscent of the Warsaw Pact. In summarizing the conduct of Athens, Alan Boegehold states in *The Landmark Thucydides*, p. 586 ("Appendix B: The Athenian Empire in Thucydides"): "Athens responded to these uprisings with increasingly firm and harsh measures designed to maintain and even to increase the nature and extent of her rule. Opponents were exiled or executed. Fines were levied, and in some cases land was confiscated and allocated to Athenian citizens. Some states that refused to become members of the alliance were compelled to join it. This odious use of imperial power, perhaps based on the presumption that those who are not with us are against us, was first employed against Carystus in Euboea around 472; it culminated in the brutal conquest of Melos in 415, and collapsed in Athens's total and calamitous failure to subjugate Syracuse two years later." Sparta, on the other hand, was the leader of a hegemonic symmachy. For the Peloponnesian League, see Paul Cartledge, "The Origins and Organisation of the Peloponnesian League," in Michael Whitby (ed.), *Sparta*, pp. 223–30. The same author describes the Spartan alliance in the following way in *The Landmark Thucydides*, p. 595 ("Appendix D: The Peloponnesian League in Thucydides"): "Each of Sparta's allies swore to have the same friends and enemies as their *hegemon* ('leader') and to follow the Spartans wherever they might lead them. In practice, Sparta's leadership was restricted by the obligation to persuade a majority of allied delegates at a duly constituted League congress to follow her in declaring war or in making peace, and to do so on her terms... Allies, moreover, had one important opt-out clause: they were obliged to obey a majority congress decision 'unless the gods or heroes stand in the way' (5.30.3) – unless, that is, they could legitimately invoke a prior and overriding religious obligation." Therefore,

ships of its subject states than Sparta to count on reliable musters of its Peloponnesian League partners.[10]

In view of these obvious facts, it remains a mystery both why in 431 the Spartans believed they could win the Peloponnesian War, and why most of Greece thought so as well. Admittedly on the eve of the war, the maverick Spartan King Archidamus, almost alone of the Peloponnesians, presciently warned the assembly of warriors and his overconfident peers that Athens was a powerful adversary with "many advantages in war," and that Sparta could not harm Athens materially by just devastating farmland – before conceding that under such conditions the war certainly would not be brief.

Nonetheless, Thucydides himself claims that public opinion in Greece was decidedly in favor of Sparta, which appeared to many Greeks as some sort of underdog liberator:

Men's feelings inclined much more to the Spartans, especially as they proclaimed themselves the liberators of Hellas. No private or public effort that could help them in speech or action was omitted; each thinking that the cause suffered wherever he could not himself see to it. So general was the indignation felt against Athens, whether by those who wished to escape from her empire, or were apprehensive of being absorbed by it.[11]

the nature and governance of the Peloponnesian League are more analogous to NATO than to the Warsaw Pact. For the implications of this analogy during the Cold War, see Stephen Hodkinson, "Sparta and the Soviet Union in U.S. Cold War Foreign Policy and Intelligence Analysis," in Stephen Hodkinson and Ian Macgregor Morris (eds.), *Sparta in Modern Thought: Politics, History and Culture* (Swansea, 2012), pp. 343–92.

10 Thucydides, in much the same manner as Homer with the catalog of ships in *Iliad* 2, lists the allies of Sparta and Athens along with their contributions to the war effort. For the Spartan confederacy's naval forces, he writes (2.9.3): "Of these, ships were furnished by the Corinthians, Megarians, Sicyonians, Pellenians, Eleans, Ambraciots, and Leucadians." Chios, Lesbos, and Corcyra furnished ships for the Athenian navy (2.9.5). Pericles enumerated to the Athenian Assembly the polis's financial (2.13.3–5) and military resources (2.13.6–8), and listed 300 triremes as being fit for service. A. W. Gomme, *A Historical Commentary on Thucydides* (Oxford, 1956), vol. II, in a detailed exegesis of these passages comments (*s.v.* 2.13.9): "Similarly with his figures for military strength, apart from his omissions on the Athenian side: he does not give the total of enemy forces, either in hoplites and cavalry, or in ships, with which to compare them; we can only infer from him, from separate figures which he gives elsewhere, that in hoplite strength for the first invasion the enemy must have outnumbered the 10,000 available Athenian hoplites by about three to one (see 10.2 n.); and we have only optimistic hopes about the fleet (7.2)." Regarding Sparta's earlier request of its allies in Italy and Sicily to construct 500 ("an impossible number") vessels, Gomme writes (*s.v.* 2.7.2): "In 432 the Corinthians and their allies, who include nearly every state that could provide ships for the Peloponnesian League, mustered 150, in a great effort. In ii. 66. 1 we hear of a fleet of 100 ships; in iii. 16. 3 of 40; and in viii. 3. 2, from all the cities of the alliance, 100 were ordered."

11 *The Landmark Thucydides*, pp. 93–94.

Map 8.1   The Greek world, 431–404 BC

As a result, the story of the 27-year-long Peloponnesian War is largely the effort of Sparta, haphazardly, and by trial and error, to increase its alliances – from the Peloponnesian League and Thebes, to the Western Greeks on Sicily, and finally the Persian Empire itself – until it could collect sufficient assets simultaneously to attack Attica by land, while sailing into the harbor of the Piraeus itself.

The evolution in Sparta's strategic profile did not come all at once. Only through a long series of reversals, victories, and unforeseen opportunities, a grand Spartan alliance emerged that by the end of the war in 404 bore little resemblance to that of 431. Again, if in 1939 Adolf Hitler had little idea that soon he would be fighting against Britain, the Soviet Union, and the United States, so too Sparta initially had little inkling that nearly three decades later Persia, Syracuse, Thebes, former members of the Athenian Empire, and most of the Peloponnese would finally end up on its side – and all be necessary for ultimate victory over Athens.[12]

Naiveté in the Archidamian War (431–421)

At war's outbreak, the land forces of the Peloponnesian League ensured that Sparta would probably not lose the war, but equally that it lacked sufficient naval resources to defeat Athens. At best, the allied fleet led by Corinth might guarantee that any Athenian naval initiatives against the Peloponnesian coast remained sporadic rather than systematic. There was little likelihood that the ships of Sparta's Peloponnesian allies could achieve naval superiority in the Aegean to break up the Athenian maritime empire, or land troops in Attica.[13]

On the other hand, the key location of Corinth[14] and Megara[15] also made it nearly impossible for an Athenian hoplite force to march southward and cross the Isthmus into the Peloponnese – at least in sufficient numbers to galvanize an anti-Sparta alliance of Argos and Mantinea that might defeat the forces of Sparta, Tegea, and Elis, as the later failure

---

12 On the various suppositions and conventional wisdom before the war, see Thuc. 1.80–81; 2.8–9.
13 See, for example, Thuc. 2.25.1.
14 Thuc. 1.13.5 and n. (s.v. 1.13.5) in Simon Hornblower, *A Commentary on Thucydides* (Oxford, 1991), vol. I, p. 45.
15 Hornblower, *A Commentary on Thucydides*, writes (s.v. 1.67.4): "See Lewis, *CAH* V², ch. 9, for the attractive view that Thucydides had a blind spot about Megara, which was considered at Athens to be of great military importance, as shown both by the twice-yearly invasions of the Megarid in the Archidamian War (ii.31.3; iv.66.1) and by the strenuous efforts against the city in 424 (iv.66ff.). On this view, the Megarian decrees are 'not so much a cause of the war but a first blow in it, designed to force Megara into the empire.'"

at the battle of Mantinea (418) attests. Yet unless Athens committed a number of strategic blunders, or Sparta won some spectacular land victories, it was difficult to see how the remaining major Mediterranean powers, specifically Syracuse and its allies on Sicily and the Persian Empire, might join the Spartan cause.

Consequently Sparta began the Archidamian War with the simple objective of marching into Attica, forcing an evacuation of the rural population, harming the agricultural potential of Athens, and inflicting such psychological damage on the rural population that the Athenians would sue for some sort of concession.[16] That its initial invasion force was huge,[17] and that the stalwart hoplites of Thebes were zealous anti-Athenian allies, with a proven record of infantry supremacy, made such a traditional Hellenic strategy at first appealing.

Sparta and its allies had lots of hoplites. Most of them were qualitatively better than those of Athens. That confidence, however, apparently blinded the Spartans to the larger problem of not only turning likely tactical infantry advantage into strategic victory, but of finding any occasion at all to meet the reluctant Athenian army in battle. At war's end, there had been only two major land battles between hoplites in some twenty-seven years of fighting: at Delium and Mantinea, in addition a few smaller encounters at Solygeia, Amphipolis, and Syracuse.

Yet Spartan allies lacked the unity of Athenian imperial forces, given that the former were more equals and the latter abject subjects. Certainly, there was little allied coordination between Sparta and its key ally, Thebes. Sparta, for instance, had not much of any idea of the planned Theban preemptory attack on the Athenian allied city of Plataea. Indeed, it was eventually forced to help Thebes subdue the small city, a sideshow not critical to defeating Athens itself. At the battle of Delium in 424, Sparta had sent no aid – no doubt in fear of having its own hostages from Sphacteria killed by the Athenians. It was as surprised as anyone that the Thebans alone demolished the invading Athenian army, and ended all dreams of adding Boeotia to Attica.[18]

Far better for Sparta, in the second year of the war, was an unforeseen but devastating plague that peaked in 429. The epidemic killed not only Pericles, the architect of Athenian strategy, but also destroyed perhaps a quarter of the population of Attica:

An aggravation of the existing calamity was the influx from the country into the city, and this was especially felt by the new arrivals. As there were no houses to receive

16 Victor Davis Hanson, *Warfare and Agriculture in Classical Greece* (Berkeley, CA, 1998), pp. 131–53.
17 Plutarch, *Pericles* 33.
18 Thuc. 4.93-4.101.2; 5.14.1; Diod. 12.69–70.

them, they had to be lodged at the hot season of the year in stifling cabins, where the mortality raged without restraint. The bodies of dying men lay one upon another, and half-dead creatures reeled about the streets and gathered round all the fountains in their longing for water. The sacred places also in which they had quartered themselves were full of corpses of persons that had died there, just as they were; for as the disaster passed all bounds, men, not knowing what was to become of them, became utterly careless of everything, whether sacred or profane.[19]

Killing Athenians was not the intent of the Spartan invasion of Attica. Yet the disease did more damage to Athens than all five annual Peloponnesian invasions together, and in fact proved more deleterious than any single military event of the war.[20] The ensuing huge losses ensured that the city for a generation would not have the manpower or wealth to win the war outright and could scarcely ensure the sanctity of its overseas empire in the Aegean and Ionia.

Yet the Spartan land strategy of seasonal devastation soon faltered. It was hard to destroy Attic agriculture in brief annual invasions, or keep the Attic population permanently away from their farms inside the city walls. The allied army stayed home five of the ten years of the war for a variety of reasons: from fear of the plague, to supposed superstitions over earthquakes, to fighting among the allies, to fears that after 425 the Athenians would kill Spartan hostages taken on the island of Sphacteria. In short, apart from the anomaly of the plague, the Spartan strategy of annual devastation proved impotent, neither annual nor particularly devastating.

Again, unless the Peloponnesian fleet could soon match in size and quality the Athenian navy, there was no fallback position for Sparta to capitalize on any defection of subject states of the Athenian Empire, even if some sensed an opportunity after Athens's initial setbacks from the plague and the humiliation of Sparta's invasions. For example, the Athenian navy ensured that the critical subject island of Lesbos – emboldened to revolt after news of the devastating Athenian plague and the city's inability to keep Spartans out of Attica – stayed Athenian in 427.[21] Thucydides notes that budding insurrections elsewhere were likewise quelled:[22]

The cities subject to the Athenians, hearing of the capture of Amphipolis and of the terms accorded to it, and of the gentleness of Brasidas, felt most strongly

19 Thuc. 2.52.1–3.
20 Thuc. 1.23.3; see also 3.87.1–3.
21 Thuc. 3.28; Diod. 12.55.
22 Amphipolis: revolted from Athens in 424 (Thuc. 4.103.4), returned to Athenian control, along with Argilus, Stagirus, Acanthus, Scolus, Olynthus, and Spartolus, in the Peace of Nicias of 422/1 (Thuc. 5.18.5); Torone: political faction invited Spartan general, Brasidas, to take command in 424/3 (Thuc. 4.110–116), captured by Athenian general, Cleon, in 422 (Thuc. 5. 3.1–4); Scione: revolted from Athens in 423 (Thuc. 4.120.1), reduced by Athens in 421 (Thuc. 5.23.1); Mende: revolted from Athens in 423 (Thuc. 4.129.1, 4.130.5–7), captured by Athens in 421 (Thuc. 5.23.1).

encouraged to change their condition, and sent secret messages to him, begging him to come to them; each wishing to be the first to revolt. Indeed, there seemed to be no danger in so doing; their mistake in their estimate of Athenian power was as great as that power afterwards turned out to be, and their judgment was based more on blind wishing than upon any sound prediction; for it is the habit of mankind to entrust to careless hope what they long for, and to use sovereign reason to thrust aside what they do not desire.[23]

Throughout the years of invasion and plague, a weakened Athens somehow managed to harass the Peloponnesian coast,[24] defeat the occasional appearance of the usually smaller Peloponnesian fleet,[25] and finally land forces at Pylos and Sphacteria to stir up some Messenian helots and prompt a Spartan response. That one brilliant strike behind Spartan lines led to the defeat and surrender of several hundred Spartan hoplites, an enormous number given Sparta's small population. The blow would do almost as much damage, in the psychological sense, to Sparta as the plague had to Athens.[26]

Rethinking during peace (421–415)

Sparta's defensive land alliance for the first ten years of the war had scant ability to project power by sea, or even to ensure the sanctity of much of the Peloponnesian coast. The inspired and far-flung expedition of Brasidas to Amphipolis of 422 threatened the rear of Athens's land empire, but ultimately the Peloponnesians lacked the naval resources to consolidate Sparta's gains. Certainly with the death of Brasidas, Sparta had no other leaders of such vision and audacity until the emergence of Gylippus and Lysander. By 421, an exhausted Athens and Sparta returned in large

---

23 Thuc. 4.108.3–4.
24 Thuc. 2.23.2–3, 2.25.1–5, 2.30.1–2, 2.31.1, 2.56.1–5, 2.69.1, 3.7.1–4, 3.16.1.
25 The Athenian fleet (led by Phormio) defeated the Peloponnesian fleet in 429 off Patrae (Thuc. 2.84); off Naupactus (Thuc. 2.90–92); in 425 at the harbor of Pylos (Thuc. 4.13.4–4.14.1–5).
26 Pylos and Sphacteria (425): Thuc. 4.26–4.40; Diod. 12.61–63. Thucydides explains the significance of the Athenian victory at 4.40: "Nothing that happened in the war surprised the Hellenes so much as this. It was the general opinion that no force or famine could make the Spartans give up their arms, but that they would fight on as they could, and die with them in their hands: indeed people could hardly believe those who had surrendered were of the same stuff as the fallen; and an Athenian ally, who some time after insultingly asked one of the prisoners from the island if those that had fallen were noble and good men, received for answer that the *atraktos* – that is, the arrow – would be worth a great deal if it could pick out noble and good men from the rest; in allusion to the fact that the killed were those whom the stones and arrow happened to hit." See also, Donald Kagan, *The Archidamian War* (Ithaca, NY, 1974), p. 248. Simon Hornblower, *A Commentary on Thucydides* (Oxford, 1996), vol. II provides a bibliography of "The Pylos Episode" on pp. 149–150. Thucydides's concludes his history of the Archidamian War (5.24.2) with the announcement of the treaty of alliance between Athens and Sparta, and the Athenians' return of the prisoners to Sparta.

measure to the *status quo ante bellum* under the protocols of the so-called Peace of Nicias.[27] The Peloponnesian land alliance remained what it always had been: a largely reactive infantry force that would protect member states from land invasions of the Peloponnese, and only occasionally march for a few weeks into Attica – and not much of anything else.

Neither side, of course, believed in a perpetual peace to follow the armistice. Each realized that to win the next round of the war, it would be necessary to regroup, rethink, and mirror-image the enemy. In other words, Athens could only prevail when it formed an infantry alliance capable of defeating the vaunted Spartan army in battle, discrediting the reputation of Spartan hoplite invincibility, and thus shattering the unity of the Peloponnesian League, while sowing fears about revolts of the helots. All that would mean an end to Spartan invasions of Attica, and the readiness of some Peloponnesian poleis to join Argos in a permanent anti-Spartan land alliance.

Thus, in 418 the inspired Athenian general Alcibiades intrigued to form a grand coalition of infantry forces with soldiers from the poleis of Argos, Mantinea, and Elis for a quick strike to decapitate the Spartan and Tegean army at the Battle of Mantinea.[28] Yet because Athens, at a time of formal peace, either could not or would not send adequate infantry forces to the alliance, and because the anti-Spartan coalition did not have sufficient numerical superiority to trump the qualitative edge of the Spartan army fighting inside the Peloponnese, the Spartans and their allies defeated the coalition, if only just. Any good will between the two powers accrued during the peace was lost.

We do not know to what degree Alcibiades envisioned a victory at Mantinea as a stepping stone to emasculating Sparta for good, in the way a half-century later the Theban liberator Epaminondas would found the huge fortified cities of Mantinea and Megalopolis to hem Sparta in, while freeing the Messenian helots and building the fortress at Messene to end Sparta's secure source of food and indentured labor. In any case, the victory at Mantinea reminded the Spartans that its present alliance ensured only that it would remain preeminent on land, and yet had little

27 The detailed terms of the Peace of Nicias are found in Thucydides (5.18). In *The Peace of Nicias and the Sicilian Expedition* (Ithaca, NY, 1981), pp. 19–32, 359–360, Donald Kagan discusses the numerous problems and deficiencies of the treaty.
28 Thuc. 5.43.3. Thucydides records the text of the treaty uniting Athens, Argos, Mantinea, and Elis at 5.47. For a discussion of this treaty, see Simon Hornblower, *A Commentary on Thucydides* (Oxford, 2008), vol. III, *s.v.* 5.47 ("The 'Quadruple Alliance' treaty between the Athenians, Argives, Mantineians, and Eleians"), pp. 109–120. The Battle of Mantinea is described by Thucydides at 5.63–74. Again, see Hornblower, *s.v.* 63–75.3 ("The Battle of Mantineia"), pp. 163–94; see also Diod. 12.78–79.

ability either to challenge the recovering Athenian fleet or to project enough infantry forces to occupy Attica permanently. For most of the peace, Sparta waited for an opening against Athens and began approaching Persia to inquire about financial help in building a fleet should war resume.[29]

Opportunities after Sicily (415–413)

The huge Athenian expedition and near total loss of two entire expeditionary forces under Nicias and Demosthenes in Sicily entirely changed the strategic direction of the war. Athens's failure to capture Syracuse and the sinking of much of its deployable imperial fleet suddenly opened all sorts of opportunities for the otherwise notoriously blinkered Spartans. The latter now had both the confidence and the pretext to restart the war directly against Athens. Despite the shaky peace, Sparta wisely had sent opportune aid to the beleaguered Syracusans under the brilliant leadership of Gylippus, a most un-Spartan visionary in the mold of both the late Brasidas and the audacious Lsyander to come. The defeat of Athens on Sicily subtracted well over a hundred imperial warships from the war's calculus, while in theory adding Sicilian triremes to the new Spartan fleet.[30]

---

29 See Barry Strauss, "Sparta's Maritime Moment," in Andrew S. Erickson, Lyle J. Goldstein, and Carnes Lord (eds.), *China Goes to Sea: Maritime Transformation in Comparative Historical Perspective* (Annapolis, MD, 2009), pp. 33–61, esp. pp. 43–48. For an excellent description of Sparta's relations with Persia, see Lewis, *Sparta and Persia*.

30 There are not exact numbers to answer the vexing question of just how many warships never made it back to Athens, versus how many were actually sent to Sicily in the two armadas. The initial expedition set out in 415 with 134 triremes (Thuc. 6.43; see also 6.31), the Athenians sent 10 triremes in the winter of 414/413 (Thuc. 7.16.2), and 73 more in 413 (Thuc. 7.42.1). This amounts to a total of more than 200 triremes. See Hornblower, *A Commentary on Thucydides*, III, "Appendix 2: Athenian troop and fleet numbers and casualties in Sicily, 415–413," pp. 1061–66. The Athenian fleet suffered a severe defeat against the Syracusans in 413 (Thuc. 7.51–54), and was then obliterated when it failed to break out of the harbor of Syracuse later in the failed campaign (7.69–71). Again, see Hornblower, *s.v.* 7.69.3–71, pp. 693–702. After the initial naval defeat, the mood of the Athenians is described by Thucydides (7.55): "The Syracusans had now gained a decisive victory at sea, where until now they had feared the reinforcement brought by Demosthenes, and deep, in consequence, was the despondency of the Athenians, and great their disappointment, and greater still their regret for having come on the expedition. These were the only cities that they had yet encountered, similar to their own in character, under democracies like themselves, which had ships and horses, and were of considerable magnitude. They had been unable to divide and bring them over by holding out the prospect of force, and had failed in most of their attempts, and being already in perplexity, had now been defeated at sea, where defeat could never have been expected, and were thus plunged deeper into bewilderment than ever." While the Athenians loss of ships was certainly a disaster, the loss of their skilled crews was even more devastating.

Far more important than relative gains and losses were the strategic ripples from Athenian miscalculations on Sicily. Sparta was now, in this new third phase of the war, far closer to becoming Athens than Athens was of becoming Sparta: while the Athenians had no chance of recreating an opportunity like Mantinea, the Spartans now saw the outlines of defeating Athens at sea while permanently occupying the Attic countryside. For Sparta, the major Athenian setback at Sicily meant the addition of more allies, internal dissension at Athens, and the garrisoning of a fort at Decelea, a much more imaginative way of harming Attica than the prior sporadic and brief invasions. The key was to match Athens at sea, sow dissension among its allies, cut off its imported food, and ensure rebellious allies of Spartan maritime protection.

The Ionian War and the culmination of the Spartan alliance (413–404)

Almost immediately the renewed war now shifted to the supply lines of the Athenian Empire off the coast of Asia Minor and in the eastern Aegean. Persia, as it envisioned a new sea war in waters off Asia Minor, promised to help build Sparta a fleet and hire crews to ensure that what was absent in quality was more than made up in quantity.[31]

Sparta adroitly used its partners to the best effect in the entire war, despite the vast differences in the make-up of the new alliances and the great distances and expense required to send a fleet to the northern and eastern Aegean. The Thebans and Spartans permanently garrisoned the fort at Decelea in sight of the walls of Athens, creating a clearing-house for booty, runaway slaves, and looting and ravaging parties in the Attic countryside. Athens found itself cut off from its countryside now almost year-round and without access to its overland empire in key places like Euboea. The elements of a winning strategy were at last in play: occupy Attica year-round, wear down the Athenian fleet, encourage rebellion among Athenian allies, and cut off Athenian imports.[32]

---

31 After the Athenian disaster in Sicily, Sparta initiated the construction of a fleet with requests from its allies for ships (Thuc. 8.3.2). Not long afterward, an ambassador from the Persian commander Tissaphernes arrived in Sparta with an offer of financial support should the Spartan army come to the aid of King Darius (II), son of Artaxerxes, against the Athenian forces in Lydia (Thuc. 8.5.4–5). This would be the first such offer of financial assistance from Persia, which would later also include payments for the fleet (for example, Thuc. 8.29, 8.58, Xen. 1.5.1–7).

32 Thuc. 7.27–28.

The fresh Syracusan and Persian alliances, together with newly built Peloponnesian ships, meant that after Sicily, Sparta had a marked advantage in numbers and might lose three ships to Athens's two, and yet still win the sea war. Quickly the allied fleet sought to cut Athens off from its commerce and food imports from the Black Sea and coast of Asia Minor. A long series of sea battles off the coast of Asia Minor followed in which Athenian seamanship so trumped Peloponnesian numbers that, by 406, after the incredible victories of Cynossema, Cyzicus, and Arginusae, Sparta was willing to negotiate a peace that would return to the general outlines of the Peace of Nicias fifteen years prior.[33]

Although Sparta had finally crafted the necessary alliance for victory – Persian money to build a huge fleet, coordination with Thebes to occupy Decelea, and active participation of the Syracuse and Corinth fleets – it had underestimated the resilience of the Athenian Empire, especially the Athenian ability to feed the city by sea and draw resources from throughout the Aegean to build new triremes and train competent crews. It had also discovered that what its supposedly supportive allies promised in ships, they often did not deliver. And finally one cannot calibrate naval superiority in terms of mere ships and manpower, but more often than not it rests on the skill and stamina of the crews, and the insight and experience of admirals. Even after Sicily, in both areas Athens maintained unquestioned preeminence, and Sparta learned that naval parity was not so easily purchased with Persian gold.

But with the second exile of Alcibiades, the architect of the Athenian naval renaissance, and domestic turmoil at home, arising over the trial of the victorious generals of Arginusae, Athens missed the opportunity for a draw, and so lost the strategic momentum. It soon suffered a crushing naval defeat inflicted by Lysander at Aegospotami in 405.[34] Unlike prior battle defeats, this time the Athenian fleet was all but destroyed; the

---

33 Syme 412/1, Thuc. 8.42; Cynossema 411, Thuc. 8.104–107, Diod. 13.39–40; Cyzicus 411, Thuc. 8.107, Xen. 1.1.11–22, Diod. 13.49.2–52.1; Notion 406, Xen. 1.5.10–14, Diod. 13.70–71.4, *Hellenica Oxyrhynchia* Fr. 8; Arginusae 406, Xen. 1.6.24–38, Diod. 13.97–100.

34 Cf. Xen. 2.1.17–32; Diod. 13.104.8–106.8. At the Battle of Aegospotami, the victorious Spartans, under the leadership of Lysander and Eteonikos, had destroyed or captured 170 of the 180 Athenian triremes and executed perhaps as many as 3,500 Athenian prisoners. See Barry S. Strauss, "Aegospotami Reexamined," *American Journal of Philology*, 104 (1983), 24–35, esp. pp. 32–34; and "A Note on the Tactics and Topography of Aegospotami," *American Journal of Philology*, 108 (1987), 741–45. Donald Kagan, *The Fall of the Athenian Empire* (Ithaca, NY, 1987), describes the plight of the Athenians at p. 393: "The Athenians' resources were exhausted; they could not again build a fleet to replace the one lost at Aegospotami. Athens had lost the war; the only questions that remained were how long it would hold out before surrendering and what terms the Athenians could obtain."

resources of the empire were exhausted; and there was now no way to feed the city either by land or sea. Lysander soon sailed into the Piraeus, while King Agis approached Athens with a huge allied force from Decelea. The Athenians went into weeks of frenzied panic, and ultimately revolution, before finally surrendering in 404.

Strategic lessons

After the war began, Sparta followed the paradigm of the prior Peloponnesian War and thus thought concessions might follow from invading Attica. But it lacked any serious plan to occupy Attica permanently, to coordinate strategy closely with its ally Thebes, or to defeat the Athenian navy. And because it had no such vision of a war to unfold like none other in Greek experience, it never forged the necessary initial alliances, so much so that even the opportune Athenian plague did not bring victory. In short, Sparta began the war wishing to fight only the war it was best at, without appreciation that it was impossible to defeat Athens without more allies and a vastly different strategy.

By 424 with the capture of Spartan hostages on Sphacteria and existential fears of a wider helot revolt, Sparta had jettisoned its initial strategy and of necessity outsourced the war to Brasidas to disrupt the Athenian empire in the north by land in a way that it could not by sea. Yet the northern adventure was a stopgap measure that could harm but not defeat Athens. The subsequent stalemate after the death of Brasidas and the Peace of Nicias gave Sparta an opportunity for reflection and review. Both the near-run victory at Mantinea and Athens's disaster on Sicily galvanized the Spartans to appreciate that only the creation of a huge fleet, a transfer of the war to a new theater off the coast of Asia, the breakup of the Athenian Empire in the Aegean and Asia Minor, and a permanent occupation of the Attic countryside could defeat Athens. All were necessary measures and all required far more assets than Sparta possessed. Athens's bold move into Sicily was the catalyst that reignited the war on terms very different from the first decade-and-a-half.

The result by 415 was a grand alliance of Thebes, Syracuse, Persia, Sparta, and the Peloponnesian League that coordinated strategy and resources in a way unthinkable at the war's outset sixteen years earlier. Despite petty rivalries and jealousies and broken promises over contributions, the alliance held together well enough to destroy the Athenian fleet at Aegospotami, garrison the fort at Decelea, and soon end the war on its terms. Athens suffered the fate of Napoleon, the Kaiser, and Hitler: uniting its enemies into unlikely but effective temporary alliances to destroy the common and hated enemy.

Two ironies characterize the Spartan victory. First, the more imaginative Athenians had likewise attempted to widen their coalition by persuasion to include key infantry powers of the Peloponnese, and by coercion to incorporate the western Greeks to hem Sparta in. Yet it was the supposedly dense and awkward Spartans who crafted the more effective alliance, not the cosmopolitan Athenians, who failed at Mantinea as they did on Sicily.

Second, grand strategies and innovative alliances are rarely fully preconceived before war, but more likely grow *ad hoc* from the course of defeat and victory.[35] Although some in Sparta at the war's beginning may have talked about building a fleet and breaking up the Athenian maritime empire, it was only the victory at Mantinea and the Athenian disaster on Sicily that gave Sparta the insight and opportunity to fight the war in a far different manner. Defeating hoplites at Mantinea did not offer a glimpse of strategic victory, while the weakening of the Athenian fleet by far distant allies most certainly did. Those two successive events might have taught Sparta that Athens could be defeated – but not just by Sparta and not by the Spartan way of war.

In conclusion, if we were to draw universal lessons from the Spartan experience in the Peloponnesian War, then the following seem most compelling:[36]

(a)   Wars are won by *ad hoc*, rather than preconceived, grand strategies and by a greater willingness to adapt and innovate; what seems viable at war's outbreak will seem fossilized by war's end. Invading Attica for a few weeks by 404 was as nonsensical as it had appeared vital in 431.

(b)   Tactical victories do not necessarily translate into strategic advantages. Dramatic allied wins over the Athenians at Mantinea or Delium did not presage the end of Athens, whose ultimate power did not rest on its hoplites.

(c)   The best opportunities often appear from unexpected enemy lapses. The unforeseen capture of Spartan hoplites on Sphacteria ended the annual Peloponnesian invasions of Attica. Sicily gave Sparta a glimpse of victory, and so it seized the moment by sending out

---

35 For a discussion of grand strategy during the Peloponnesian War, see Athanassios G. Platias and Constantinos Koliopoulos, *Thucydides on Strategy: Grand Strategies in the Peloponnesian War and their Relevance Today* (New York, 2010), *passim*, but esp. ch. 4 ("Spartan Grand Strategy"), pp. 61–80. See also the review of this work by Paul A. Rahe, *Journal of World History*, 23 (2012), 155–59.

36 See also Harold T. Parker, "Reflections on Thucydides and Some Aspects of Modern Coalition War," *The South Atlantic Quarterly*, 78 (1979), 73–83. The authors are grateful to Andrew Roberts for calling this work to their attention.

Gylippus while approaching Persia for help rather than idly abiding by the peace.

(d)   Wartime coalitions are often of convenience, need not outlast the war, and can unite unlikely and disparate powers that otherwise have no shared interests other than defeating the common enemy. Sparta hated Persia as much as did Athens and would fight it immediately following the war, a fact of no importance in soliciting its help. The Theban and Spartan wartime alliance was as steady as their postwar hatred and fighting were predictable. Balances of power often trump ideological affinities.

(e)   Victors embrace assets, allies, and strategies that are in theory antithetical to those they began the war with; the side that makes the most unlikely adjustments usually wins. Sparta built a fleet to enter Piraeus before Athens assembled an army to storm Sparta and free the helots. The final defeat to Napoleon came not just through the superb British fleet, but was delivered by a British general in charge of tens of thousands of allied troops in a frontal infantry confrontation on French-speaking soil.

(f)   Decisive victory comes only by ending the enemy's ability to conduct war. Once Sparta saw that only permanent occupation of Attica, combined with the physical destruction of the Athenian fleet and the cutting off of Athenian imports could ensure Athenian defeat, then it put all of its resources to those ends. Athens never developed a sophisticated strategy to defeat the Spartan army in battle, occupy the Peloponnese, turn Sparta's neighbors against it, and free the helots, all of which would have been necessary to defeat the Spartan state, as Epaminondas understood later between 371–362.

(g)   Mavericks are vital for victory; usually the most effective thinkers come to leadership positions only after the beginning of the war, and under circumstances that demand radical changes. The blinkered Spartans gave full support to their three most innovative, but untraditional generals, Brasidas, Gylippus, and Lysander, only after annual devastations of Attica had failed to check Athenian power. The liberal and open-minded Athenians let their emotions run wild and serially shunned and ostracized the erratically brilliant Alcibiades, butchered or exiled the victorious generals after Arginusae, and turned the fleet over to mediocrities at Aegospotami. Athens was supposedly an enlightened city, but in the battles for Syracuse, Gylippus, not Nicias, proved the visionary. And in the Ionian War, Lysander was more adroit than any of the Athenian admirals.

In conclusion, the course of the Peloponnesian War hinged on which side best fathomed how to destroy utterly its adversary's sources of power; and, given that the task was beyond the resources of even Greece's two most powerful city states, how to craft the necessary alliances to achieve that aim. Sparta won the war by more effectively identifying its ends and then acquiring the means to obtain them.

9 The Anglo-Burgundian alliance and grand strategy in the Hundred Years War

Clifford J. Rogers

The formation and significance of the Anglo-Burgundian alliance

From 1419 to 1435, the alliance between England and the nascent state of Burgundy, an agglomeration of territories spanning the border between France and the Holy Roman Empire, deeply influenced the course of the great war between France and England known as the Hundred Years War (1337–1453).[*] The alliance with Burgundy fundamentally changed the English approach to the war. Before 1419 King Henry V of England broadly adhered to the diplomatic position staked out by his great-grand-father Edward III during the first phase of the war: although the crown of France belonged to him by hereditary right, in the interest of peace he would be willing to compromise and accept sovereign rule over just a half or a third of the kingdom, with the rest (and the title king of France) passing to his opponent, the Valois King Charles VI.[1]

Even though England had at best a third of the population and wealth of France, the two kingdoms were fairly well matched in military strength, as demonstrated by the inability of either side to end the conflict in victory from 1337 to 1419. The French always had the advantage in number of soldiers, but the disparity was not as great as the difference between the national populations. The English royal government was more efficient than the French bureaucracy, and Parliament, as a mechanism for enlisting national consensus behind the war effort, provided the kings of England a substantial edge in the mobilization of resources. Moreover, English qualitative military superiority usually

---

[*] My thanks to Professor Craig Taylor for assistance with this study. Considering its intended audience, I have where possible cited translations rather than texts in Latin or French.

[1] For Edward III, see Clifford J. Rogers, "The Anglo-French Peace Negotiations of 1354–1360 Reconsidered," in James Bothwell (ed.), *The Age of Edward III* (York, 2001), pp. 193–213. For Henry, see Christopher Allmand, *Henry V* (Berkeley, CA, 1992), pp. 68–74; and Anne Curry, *Agincourt: A New History* (Stroud, 2005), pp. 40–49.

offset, sometimes dramatically, French advantages in quantity. That qualitative advantage had enabled them to win every full-scale battle of the war up to the formation of the Anglo-Burgundian alliance – including the famous victories of Crécy (1346), Poitiers (1356), and Agincourt (1415) – and most of the lesser fights as well.

Three qualitative factors are most important for explaining these tactical successes. First, the English archers, whose extraordinarily powerful longbows could drive 4-ounce arrows with enough accuracy to hit an individual target at 220 yards and enough kinetic energy to penetrate most armor, were by far the best infantry of their day.[2] Second, the whole English army, from foot-archers to army commanders, was deeply imbued with what Clausewitz calls "the military spirit."[3] Third, in most periods of the war the top English commanders demonstrated far greater tactical and strategic competence than their French adversaries. When the French found good generals such as the Constable Bertrand DuGuesclin and "Le bon duc" Louis of Bourbon, resources tipped the balance marginally in their favor, but the advantage of the defensive in the siege-based campaigns that constituted the period's predominant form of warfare prevented them from driving the English off the continent and ending the conflict.[4] The strength of the defensive also, however, meant that even when they enjoyed a large advantage in political and military leadership, as they often did, the English simply did not have the manpower to conquer all of France, or even to defend, in the long run, any substantial gains they might temporarily make.

So long as English qualitative advantages balanced French quantitative ones, there was little prospect of either side bringing an end to the conflict by achieving complete military victory. There were times when political leaders on both sides appreciated this and worked to resolve the conflict through diplomacy and negotiations. Time and again, these

2 The ability of longbow arrows to penetrate armor remains controversial. The statement above is not meant to imply that armor was of no use against arrows; arrows often glanced off plate surfaces, and even when an arrow did penetrate, armor could still mean the difference between a grave wound and a relative pinprick. See Clifford J. Rogers, "The Battle of Agincourt," in L. J. Andrew Villalon and Donald J. Kagay (eds.), *The Hundred Years War (Part II): Different Vistas* (Leiden, 2008), pp. 109–13; for the best statement of a more conservative view of the longbow's efficacy, see Matthew Strickland and Robert Hardy, *The Great Warbow: A History of the Military Archer* (New York, 2005), ch. 15.

3 Carl von Clausewitz, *On War*, ed. and trans. Michael Howard and Peter Paret (Princeton, NJ, 1984), pp. 187–89.

4 See Clifford J. Rogers, "The Medieval Legacy," in Geoff Mortimer (ed.), *Early Modern Military History* (London, 2004), pp. 6–24, and "The Artillery and Artillery Fortress Revolutions Revisited," in Nicolas Prouteau, Emmanuel de Crouy-Chanel and Nicolas Faucherre (eds.), *Artillerie et Fortification, 1200–1600* (Rennes, 2011), pp. 75–80.

efforts foundered on the fact that the minimum acceptable terms of the two sides were fundamentally incompatible. The essential issue of the war was not how much land within France the English should rule – on that there could have been compromise – but rather the question of whether the English territories in France should be sovereign possessions of the kings of England, or should remain legally and politically subordinated to the crown of France. The political theories of the earlier Middle Ages had been able to accommodate divided jurisdictions and shared suzerainties comfortably, but the conception of sovereignty that had developed over the course of the thirteenth and early fourteenth centuries, under the influence of the revival of Roman law, insisted on the absolute and ultimately inalienable power of the state. There was therefore no middle ground on which the English or French could construct a durable peace.[5]

The impossibility of finding a diplomatic compromise derived in part from the dynastic aspect of the struggle – the fact that the kings of England, as heirs of Edward III, claimed to be the rightful kings of France. If an English king accepted anything less than sovereignty over a share of France, he would in effect be dishonoring himself and his ancestors, and admitting that they had for generations waged an unjust war, at the cost of countless lives, immense treasure, and terrible devastation. If a French king surrendered sovereignty over any portion of France, he would be doing the same.

So long as compromise was impossible and the military balance between England and France was too even to allow either side to overcome the strategic inertia imposed by the superiority of the defense to achieve complete victory, there was no way to bring the war to an end. But in the early fifteenth century, the intermittent madness of King Charles VI of France led first to intense factionalism in the court and then to outright civil war as two parties struggled to gain control over the royal government and revenues. One of these factions was led successively by the king's brother, the duke of Orléans, then that duke's son and successor, then by Bernard d'Armagnac, constable of France (after whom this party is often referred to as "the Armagnacs"), and finally by the dauphin Charles, the future Charles VII. The other party was headed by King Charles VI's cousin, John the Fearless, duke of Burgundy, then by John's widow, Margaret of Bavaria, and his son and successor, Philip the Good of Burgundy.

5 For the negotiations after 1360, see J. J. N. Palmer, "The War Aims of the Protagonists and the Negotiations for Peace," in Kenneth Fowler (ed.), *The Hundred Years War* (London, 1971).

The dukes of Burgundy were direct rulers of two large, wealthy, and compact territorial blocs. One, southeast of Paris, comprised the duchy of Burgundy, the county of Charolais, and the county of Burgundy (the Franche-comté). The other bloc, northeast of the capital, included Flanders and Artois, among the most urbanized and wealthiest areas of France outside of Paris. In addition, the comparably rich and populous Imperial duchies of Brabant and Namur and counties of Hainault, Holland, and Zeeland were bound firmly to Burgundy throughout this period, and eventually acquired by Philip himself. The duke's chief adviser reckoned in 1431 that the Burgundian territories, including the lands listed above as well as the counties of Auxerre and Mâcon and the castellany of Bar-sur-Seine (acquired in 1424), collectively contained from a third to a half as many parishes as the entire kingdom of France.[6] The whole area between these two blocs was throughout the period one in which the duke of Burgundy had great influence. He also had many supporters in Paris and the surrounding towns.

Until 1417, the Orléanist or Armagnac faction generally controlled all of France west and southwest of Paris, except for the English duchy of Guienne or Aquitaine (centered on Bordeaux), and Brittany, which followed an independent policy. Starting with the capture of Harfleur in 1415 and continuing until 1422, but mainly between 1417 and 1419, Henry V of England reduced the dominions of the Orléanist or Armagnac faction by the military conquest of Lower Normandy and various adjacent areas.

In the fourteenth century, the English had taken advantage of local civil wars within Flanders and Brittany to gain temporary dominance in those provinces, and the conflicts among Charles of Navarre (a member of the French royal house with extensive possessions in the north of the realm as well as king of his own small Pyrenean kingdom), the bourgeoisie of Paris, and the house of Valois had contributed substantially to the collapse of French resistance that led to the Treaty of Brétigny in 1360.[7] But the civil war between Orléans and Burgundy was different: the two contenders were sufficiently balanced with each other and with England that what had been a game of two main players (the kings of England and the kings of France) and a variety of pawns became a three-way

---

6 The memorandum actually favors the figure of one-half, but takes one-third to be conservative. *Oeuvres de Ghillebert de Lannoy, voyageur, diplomate et moraliste*, ed. Ch. Potvin and J.-C. Houzeau (Louvain, 1878), p. 488; Richard Vaughan, *Philip the Good: The Apogee of Burgundy* (Woodbridge, 2002), p. 260.

7 Jonathan Sumption, *The Hundred Years War*, vols. I–II (London, 1990–1999); or more concisely, Clifford J. Rogers, *War Cruel and Sharp: English Strategy under Edward III, 1327–1360* (Woodbridge, 2000).

contest for dominance. Partly because of this change in dynamics, the stakes changed too.

As late as the spring of 1419, the two main questions were: first, what portion of France, if any, would be detached from the kingdom and transferred *de facto* or *de jure* to English sovereignty; and second, which French faction would dominate the remainder of the kingdom? That changed in September 1419, when, despite the recent reconciliation between the two French factions, Duke John the Fearless was murdered while meeting with the dauphin.[8] This naturally drove his son and successor, Duke Philip the Good, into the arms of the English. Since Philip's faction controlled Paris and mad King Charles VI, he was able to offer a great deal in exchange for English help in securing himself against his enemies and in gaining vengeance for his father's murder. The result was the Treaty of Troyes (1420), by which Charles VI and his queen disinherited their only surviving son (the dauphin), provided for the marriage of their daughter Katherine to Henry V, and made their new son-in-law the regent of France and heir to the French throne. Henry was to rule France along with a council of French nobles of the Burgundian party.[9]

As the terms of the treaty indicate, Henry no longer had any interest in pursuing a partition of France along the lines of the Treaty of Brétigny. The combination of recent English military successes and the alliance of England and Burgundy created prospects that Henry V might make good the long-standing English claim to the French throne and end the war in complete victory rather than merely a favorable compromise. From that point onward, for the first time since 1337, none of the main protagonists was pursuing the strategic goal of dividing France. The prize at which all aimed was not the largest share of French territory, but to maximize their power within a united France. This fundamental change in the nature of the war resulted directly from the creation and cementing of the Anglo-Burgundian alliance.

---

8 Allmand, *Henry V*, 132–35, offers a good summary of these events; for a fuller treatment, see Richard Vaughan, *John the Fearless: The Growth of Burgundian Power*, 2nd edn. (Woodbridge, 2002), ch. 10.

9 The Treaty of Troyes is in E. Cosneau, *Les Grands Traités de la Guerre de Cent Ans* (Paris, 1889), pp. 102–15; for the council, see clauses 7, 27. Armstrong's conclusion that clause 27 "reserved to the duke of Burgundy the second place [after Henry V] in the government of the realm of France" rests on a misquotation of the text; to be precise, clause 27 only gave Burgundy that role in governing the arrangements for Charles VI personally. Nonetheless, there is no doubt that the overall spirit of the treaty did imply that Philip, as the head of the Burgundian faction, would have a leading role in guiding royal policy. C. A. J. Armstrong, "La Double Monarchie France-Angleterre et la maison de Bourgogne (1420–1435). Le déclin d'un alliance," in *England, France and Burgundy in the Fifteenth Century* (London: 1983), p. 343.

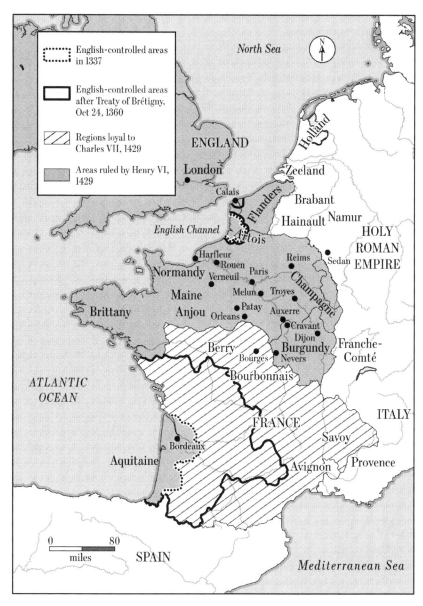

Map 9.1   The Hundred Years War, 1337–1429

The maintenance of the alliance

To achieve their new strategic goal, the English had to do two things. First, they had to retain the support of Burgundy. Second, they had to continue to capture the fortified towns and castles that brought with them domin-ion over the surrounding agricultural countryside, one after another, until the balance of resources tipped so far that a complete Lancastrian vic-tory seemed inevitable. At that point the Armagnac leaders would have to submit to Henry's authority and the war would end. From 1415 to 1419 English armies had made fairly rapid progress towards that goal, despite having to keep a wary eye towards Burgundian territory. The crushing English victory at Agincourt had left the dukes of Orléans and Bourbon prisoners in England, Brittany intimidated into English-leaning neutrality, and a whole generation of French men-at-arms worse than decimated.[10] John the Fearless, meanwhile, had also gained substantial ground (includ-ing control of Paris, and of Charles VI himself) despite needing to defend the line of the Seine against the English.[11] Under these circumstances, the complete military defeat of the dauphin's party was not an unrealistic goal, even if the English and Burgundians cooperated only in the loosest fashion: each sparing the other the need to guard their mutual frontier, and both pressing the war wherever it suited their interests.[12]

On the other side of the equation, it was practically impossible for the Armagnacs to win the war outright so long as the alliance between Burgundy and England held.[13] Their priorities, therefore, had to be to

10 The number of noble families in France at this time can be estimated at around 30,000; the number of adult males of fighting age (which was a wide range at that time) can be roughly approximated at around 35–40,000: Philippe Contamine, "The French Nobility and the War," in Kenneth Fowler (ed.), *The Hundred Years War* (London, 1971), pp. 136–39. The number of nobles killed at Agincourt was probably at least 5,000–6,000: Rogers, "Agincourt," pp. 104–5 n. 234. In World War I, French military dead amounted to roughly 10 percent of the adult male population of 1914. Among the nobility, therefore, the single day of Agincourt was a greater demographic catastrophe than World War I was for France as a whole.

11 Vaughan, *John the Fearless*, pp. 216–27, 263.

12 I am thus in agreement with Mark Warner, "The Anglo-French Dual Monarchy and the House of Burgundy, 1420–1435: The Survival of an Alliance," *French History*, 11 (1997), 103–7, rather than Allmand, *Henry V*, pp. 439–42, 146, who sees the Treaty of Troyes and Henry's commitment to insist on the throne of France as a "serious error of judgment," and seems to think the "rapidly growing sense of national spirit" in France made the prospect of a Lancastrian dynasty ruling France chimerical. See also two articles from La *'France Anglaise' au moyen âge. Actes du 111e congrès national des sociétés savantes (Poitiers 1986)* (Paris, 1988): Philippe Contamine, "La 'France Anglaise' au XVe siècle. Mythe ou réalité?," pp. 24–29 and A. Leguai, "La 'France bourguignonne' dans le conflit entre la 'France française' et la 'France anglaise' (1420–35)," pp. 41–52.

13 John de Waurin, *A Collection of the Chronicles and Ancient Histories of Great Britain, Now Called England (1422–31)*, trans. Edward L. C. P. Hardy (London, 1891), p. 202.

stave off Anglo-Burgundian conquests and buy time, hoping for the rescue of their cause by extraneous factors – probably a break between England and Burgundy, or perhaps a civil war within England. The latter seemed like a possibility, considering that Henry V was the son of a usurper and not, from a genealogical perspective, the rightful heir of Richard II, who had been deposed in 1399 and murdered in 1400.[14] The French also clearly had to do whatever they could to lure Philip the Good to reconcile with the dauphin, or at least to minimize his support to the English war effort.[15] Despite the murder of John the Fearless, this was not out of the question. More than once before over the course of the Hundred Years War, the bitterest enemies within France had patched up their differences to check English advances.

Once the three-way game was rolling and the English had, in effect, committed to pursuing the rule of all France rather than the acquisition of a part of it, all three players needed a partner to succeed, but only two pairings were possible, since the ambitions of the dauphin and Henry V were polar opposites and irreconcilable. It would either be Charles and Philip against Henry, or Philip and Henry against Charles. In other words, both Henry and Charles had only one choice of partner, but Philip had two, and the ultimate possessor of the crown of France was therefore likely to depend on which side he supported.[16] Both English and French strategy for the war, therefore, needed to aim at retaining or gaining his support. That required some understanding of his objectives.

What did Philip the Good want? One can summarize his goals under five headings.[17] First, and most important, came security. His father had effectively built Burgundy into an independent polity; Philip wanted, above all other priorities, to retain his *de facto* sovereignty over his own lands. That meant defending their territorial integrity and also protecting his own person, his family, and his supporters against his enemies in the civil war, the partisans of Orléans and Armagnac and (though less

14 The seriousness of this possibility was underlined just before Henry V sailed to reopen the war in 1415; a plot headed by the earl of Cambridge aimed at murdering Henry and replacing him on the throne with Edmund Mortimer, earl of March, who was descended from Edward III's second son rather than (as Henry was) from his third son. Allmand, *Henry V*, pp. 74–77.

15 There is a significant distortion involved in referring to the dauphinist party as "the French," since many Frenchmen, including the duke of Burgundy and most of the citizens of Paris, were on the side of Henry V and Henry VI for most of the period under discussion. However, historians often do so in order to keep their prose readable, and I have sometimes done the same in this chapter.

16 Waurin summarizes the whole period 1420–1431 by saying Henry V "reigned mightily in his own name in the kingdom of France, and that principally through the favour and alliance of the noble duke Philip of Burgundy." Waurin, *Chronicles*, p. 244.

17 In this paragraph I largely follow the analysis of Vaughan in *Philip the Good*.

inexorably) the dauphin.[18] Second, he sought to expand his territorial holdings, meaning not so much increasing the area he controlled *de facto*, but rather adding new hereditary lands to his own and his family members' patrimonies. Third – partly as a means to the first end, but partly as another goal in itself – he wanted power and influence within the kingdom of France.[19] Fourth, he demanded vengeance for his murdered father. And fifth, he wanted to be respected as a knight and a military leader.[20] A *sine qua non* constraining his pursuit of these five objectives was to "guard his honor, against which he would not take any action, regardless of any consequences."[21]

---

18 On the primacy of this consideration, note that the point that declining to ally with England would mean allowing Philip's mortal enemy to come to the throne of France was used as the clinching final argument by the counselors arguing in favor of an alliance with Henry V. See the summary of the debate in Allmand, *Henry V*, p. 140.

19 In 1418 John the Fearless had controlled Paris and Charles VI, and with the support of Queen Isabeau had therefore controlled the royal government of France itself, though due to the civil war his power did not in practice make itself felt in all parts of the realm. Philip clearly had less interest in being the power behind the French throne than his father had demonstrated, and ultimately he put much less effort into this goal than into the expansion and consolidation of his own territories, but that seems to have been a contingent rather than a predetermined development. Chance developments gave him a series of favorable opportunities to gain hereditary territories; had he not put so much energy into pursuing those opportunities, he might have made more effort to dominate the Parisian government instead. It should be noted that before the Treaty of Troyes Philip sought appointment as lieutenant-general of the realm from Charles VI and Queen Isabeau, and in the Treaty of Troyes itself Philip ensured a by-name place for himself in overseeing the "government" of Charles VI's person and household, and that the government of the realm would be undertaken "with the counsel of nobles and wise men" who were "obedient" to Charles V – that is, Frenchmen of the Burgundian party. Leguai, "La 'France bourguignonne,'" p. 44; Cosneau, *Grands traités*, pp. 105, 112–13.

20 Two key pieces of evidence reveal how important this was to him; it was not merely a matter of conventional rhetoric. First, when he accepted and went into intense training in preparation for a duel with Humphrey of Gloucester, his actions backed up his professed willingness to defend his knightly honor at the risk of his own life. Second, a memorandum of Philip's counselor Hughes de Lannoy, who knew him well, shows that Lannoy felt there was a risk that the duke would act contrary to his own interests if he felt that "his honor ha[d] been tarnished" by his failed siege of Calais. Vaughan, *Philip the Good*, 38–39, 105–6. (It is indicative of the one major weakness of Vaughan's otherwise excellent work that he found it "bizarre" that "Philip really was naïve or impetuous enough to entertain serious dueling intentions.") Also, Waurin, a Burgundian soldier who was present at the time, described Philip in 1423, when he arrayed with the English to resist an expected French relief army outside Mâcon, as "considered the most chivalrous prince in the world" and affirms that "the thing that duke Philip most desired was to find himself in arms." Waurin, *Chronicles*, 48.

21 Those familiar with the literature on Philip, which tends to depict him as a rather shifty or duplicitous figure, may be surprised to see this assertion, but the words are from private Burgundian diplomatic documents. They are from a point in 1423 when Philip first opened negotiations with the court of the dauphin over a possible reconciliation between him and Charles. Vaughan, typically, saw these negotiations as a sign that Philip, "far from

The creation, maintenance, and disruption of the Anglo-Burgundian alliance was, therefore, the business of rulers, their councils, and their diplomats. Modern historians – unlike contemporary observers – have usually treated it from the perspective of diplomacy and high politics, sometimes adding in biographical and interpersonal considerations, but often largely divorcing the subject from military events and actions. To be more precise, scholars have examined how changes in the alliance affected the war, but have said relatively little about how the war affected the alliance. This perspective is well summarized in the remarks of the leading Anglophone historian of Valois Burgundy, Richard Vaughan, about the period when the Anglo-Burgundian alliance was being forged:

> For the Burgundian chroniclers, and perhaps for the participants, Philip the Good's French campaigns in the years after 1420 seemed of paramount interest. But for us, viewing the whole long reign in the perspective of history, these military activities assume a secondary importance. It was the diplomatic system [developed by Philip] which ensured the peace and security of Philip's lands in these years, not the battles and sieges.[22]

appearing as an outright English partisan ... now emerged as a sort of *tertius gaudiens*, prepared to negotiate seriously with either side, and intent on extracting material advantages for himself by playing one off against the other" (*Philip the Good*, 8). But in fact in these documents Philip does show himself a continued partisan of Henry VI (referring to Charles as the dauphin rather than the king, and calling the dauphinists "la partie adverse"), and insistent on sustaining the alliance he had committed to with the Treaty of Troyes. At his instructions, Philip's ambassadors emphasized to the duke of Savoy, who was acting as a mediator, that Philip expected him to "guard his honor, against which he would not take any action, regardless of any consequences" ("contre lequel il ne vouldroit rien faire pour chose qu'il lui pust avenir"), and provided Savoy with copies of his treaties, promises and oaths towards the king of England so that Savoy could know what would be necessary to keep his honor safe. Then Burgundy's chancellor, Nicolas Rolin, told the dauphin's representatives directly that Philip would not "break his oath and promises" for any reason, and that he was only willing to proceed with negotiations insofar as they did not violate his treaty with the English. Rolin did suggest terms on which reconciliation between Charles and Philip might be possible – but only, as he explicitly said, as part of a three-way peace with England as well. Arsène Perier, *Nicolas Rolin, 1380–1461* (Paris, 1904), pp. 98–107. Even when in 1435 Philip had become inclined to break the treaty with England, the strongest argument that his pro-English counselor Hughes de Lannoy mustered to dissuade him from doing so was that breaking the treaty of Troyes would stain the duke's honor, "which honor is something that all princes and knights should have their principal regard for, above all wordly things." The pro-French party had to counter this argument by agreeing that the duke "should desire to seek good renown, founded on virtue," above all else, then turning the argument on its head with the threat that if he did *not* break the Treaty of Troyes (which, they argued, was illegal anyway), the cardinals overseeing the negotiations would report him as being false to his promise to seek peace. Joycelyne Gledhill Dickinson, *The Congress of Arras, 1435: A Study in Medieval Diplomacy* (New York, 1972), pp. 70, 74, and 77. See also n. 41 below.

22 Vaughan, *Philip the Good*, p. 10.

And yet, of the five goals adumbrated above, the *results* of military operations had large and direct influences on the first (Burgundian security), the second (Burgundian expansion), and the fourth (vengeance), while Burgundian *participation* in active warfare was absolutely essential to the fifth (martial honor). As to the third, Burgundy's power in the France depended in the first instance on the power of his Lancastrian ally in the game of thrones, which in turn depended on military success. Moreover, the strength of the Anglo-Burgundian alliance was to a substantial degree shaped not just by the outcomes of various military operations, but also by what happened in the *process* of conducting coalition warfare.

Another major factor that has not received quite the attention it deserves (though it has been given more notice than the military dimensions of the alliance) is how the chances of births, deaths, and marriages and their implications for family politics affected the rise and fall of the alliance, and thereby the fate of the Lancastrian kingdom of France. Historians have long recognized that the 1423 marriage of Philip the Good's sister Anne to John, duke of Bedford, Henry VI's uncle and his regent in France, was an important factor in binding England and Burgundy together, at least until her death in 1432.[23] (The infant Henry VI succeeded to the dual monarchy of England and Lancastrian France after Henry V's and Charles VI's deaths in 1422.) What has not received adequate emphasis is that a key strategic weakness of England in the 1420s was Henry VI's lack of marriageable relatives. Philip the Good's first wife was the daughter of Charles VI and the sister of both the French dauphin and Henry V's queen, Katherine of Valois; in 1421 this meant Philip was uncle by marriage, but not by blood, to the future Henry VI, and brother-in-law to the Lancastrian queen of France, Katherine.[24] Thus, it was through his wife that Philip had two fairly strong family ties to the Lancastrian dynasty, but she died in 1422, the same year as Henry V, leaving Philip both without an heir and without close family ties to the infant Henry VI. Duke Philip remarried in 1425, and then again in 1430. Had a suitable English bride been available to tie Burgundian and Lancastrian family interests together, and had Henry VI's counselors made wise arrangements, the collapse of the alliance in 1435 might perhaps have been avoided, with incalculable consequences for the war and the subsequent history of Europe. On the other hand, the marriage of Jacqueline of Hainault

---

23 For example, E. Carleton Williams, *My Lord of Bedford* (London, 1963), pp. 100–105, 125, 174, 222; B.-A. Pocquet du Haut-Jusse, "Anne de Bourgogne et le testament de Bedford (1429)," *Bibliothèque de l'école des chartes*, 95 (1934), pp. 284–326.

24 He was also brother-in-law to the dauphin, but the latter's role in the murder of John the Fearless made that connection moot.

with Henry V's brother Humphrey of Gloucester, and the events that followed from it – including Philip's challenging Humphrey to a duel, and Humphrey's acceptance of the challenge – probably did more than any other single factor to harm Anglo-Burgundian relations. Moreover, Bedford's hasty and probably ill-advised choice of a second wife, after the death of Philip's sister, was another significant factor in undermining the alliance.[25] This should remind us of the power of personality, chance, and contingency in the realm of grand strategy and alliance politics as well as in other areas. It should also remind us that culturally determined values, in this case the high priority placed by fifteenth-century rulers on family ties, dynastic inheritances, and martial honor, vary across time and place. Analysts who ignore them in favor of supposedly invariable geostrategic principles and *raison d'état* are likely to misunderstand the motivations that can sustain or break alliances.

The first crisis: transition of leadership

If it were possible to quantify the strength of the Anglo-Burgundian alliance and to graph it over time, one peak of cohesion would be in late 1421 or early 1422. In December 1421 the future Henry VI was born; this seemed practically to ensure a long-term set of close dynastic ties between the Lancastrian monarchy and Burgundy, since this made Philip, already the brother-in-law of the current king and queen of England, also uncle-by-marriage of the heir apparent. Thus, the expected future "king of England and France" would be first-cousin to any children born to Philip and his wife, Queen Katherine's sister.[26] Moreover, Henry V and Duke Philip, working together, had recently advanced a whole series of steps towards the ultimate defeat of the dauphin and the solidification of Henry V's status as regent and future king of France: the Treaty of Troyes, the occupation of Paris and the creation of an effective Anglo-Burgundian government based there, and the elimination of most dauphinist strongholds in northern France. Henry seemed invincible in battle or in siege, was respected and feared by all and loved by many. It seemed clear that by supporting him Philip would be backing

---

25 These are all discussed below.
26 He would also, admittedly, be first cousin to any son of the dauphin. But the dauphin as yet had no children, and the degree of hostility between the houses of Valois and Burgundy was still so high that the familial bonds could not weigh against it. The degree of dynastic linkage between Burgundy and Lancaster, in other words, was a question of absolutes rather than of comparatives.

the winning horse.[27] Henry had an extremely strong reputation as a strict upholder of justice and law, and he clearly appreciated the importance of the Burgundian alliance and in almost all ways did everything in his power to strengthen it.[28] So Philip could feel confident of the security of his long-term relationship with the comrade-in-arms beside whom he had conducted the sieges of Sens, Montereau, and Melun in summer 1420 (to the benefit of his own martial reputation).

But in the middle of 1422 the alliance hit its first period of crisis, triggered by the early death of Henry V and compounded by the passing of both Charles VI and his daughter Michelle (Philip the Good's wife and Queen Katherine's sister), at about the same time. These developments posed three basic problems for the Anglo-Burgundian coalition. First, the trio of deaths almost entirely dissolved the structure of family ties binding together the dynasties of Lancaster and Burgundy. In a matter of months, Philip went from being the son-in-law of the (Lancastrian-controlled) King Charles VI, the brother-in-law of the king's regent and heir to the crown (Henry V), and the uncle-by-marriage of the expected future king (Henry VI), to being nothing but the uncle-by-a-previous-marriage of the infant king, with no particular connection to the regent and heir apparent (Bedford).[29] Second, especially in combination with the death of Charles VI, Henry's death called into question the

27 The chronicler of St. Denis, for example, described him as throughout his reign "worthy in arms, prudent, [and] wise," adding "No prince of his time appeared to surpass him in capability to subdue and conquer a country," by reason of his prudence and other good qualities. *Chronique du religieux de Saint-Denys: contenant le règne de Charles VI, de 1380 à 1422*, vol VI, ed. and trans. L. Bellaguet (Paris, 1840), p. 480.

28 The one major exception being his reception of Jacqueline of Bavaria, heiress of Hainault, who was Burgundy's vassal, first cousin, and first cousin's wife, who had fled from her husband to England, contrary to Burgundy's wishes and interests. But, despite this, Henry *did* appreciate the importance of the Burgundian alliance; on his death-bed (according to Monstrelet, and this has been accepted by most historians) he enjoined the guardians of his legacy to offer the regency of France to Burgundy and emphasized as strongly as he could the need to protect the Anglo-Burgundian alliance, "for should any there be any ill-will between you, which God forbid, the affairs of this realm, which are now in a very promising state for our side, could go very much worse." Enguerrand de Monstrelet, *Chroniques*, ed. L. Douët d'Arcq, 6 vols. (Paris, 1857–1862), vol. IV, p. 110; Enguerrand de Monstrelet *Chronicles*, trans. Thomas Johnes (London, 1840), vol. I, p. 483; Jenny Stratford, *The Bedford Inventories* (London, 1993), p. 6.

29 Though I should acknowledge here that the status of "uncle" by way of marriage to a maternal aunt who died before the nephew was old enough to have known her may have meant more to the parties involved that it likely would under similar circumstances to a modern person. In diplomatic correspondence Henry VI and Philip always referred to each other as "most dear uncle" and "most dear nephew," and they may have felt that way. We know Philip was close to his blood nephew, John of Cleves: see his letters in Vaughan, *Philip the Good*, p. 131; he was also close to his sister Anne (Pocquet du Haut-Jusse, "Anne de Bourgogne," pp. 318 et passim), who was Henry VI's aunt by marriage to Bedford, which may have enhanced his avuncular feelings towards Henry.

Burgundians' calculation that they had joined the winning side in the war between Lancaster and Valois.[30] Third, the loss of Henry's firm hand released his younger brother Humphrey of Gloucester to take actions that seriously threatened the alliance. Humphrey soon married Jacqueline of Bavaria and moved to occupy her inheritance of Hainault, steps that put Gloucester (and so England) directly at odds with the policies of Duke Philip, who expected to inherit that valuable province himself.

Under these circumstances there was perhaps some small chance that, despite his personal hatred for the dauphin, whom he blamed for his father's death, Philip might switch sides. A much more likely risk was that he might simply pull back from the war effort to formal or *de facto* neutrality and let the contenders for the rule of France fight it out, weakening each other, while he benefitted from peace to build up his resources and focus on his policy of territorial acquisition in the Low Countries. The first sign of the seriousness of the danger to the Anglo-Burgundian alliance came when Philip declined the efforts of the new leader of the house of Lancaster, the duke of Bedford, to bring him back to a leading position in the Parisian court, which probably included an offer to make Philip the regent of France.[31] The second was when Philip declined membership in the prestigious Order of the Garter, on the grounds that he could not commit himself (as the statutes required) to refrain from fighting other members of the order, suggesting he was getting ready to fight Humphrey of Gloucester, who after Henry V's death headed the regency council in England.[32] By the end of the year, he had even opened negotiations with the court of the dauphin, including seeking a partial truce on his borders.[33]

Yet within a year of Charles VI's death, the health of the Anglo-Burgundian alliance had been fully restored and England seemed back

30 Leguai, "La 'France bourguignonne,'" p. 45.
31 Armstrong, "La Double Monarchie," p. 344; but cf. Leguai, "La 'France bour-guignonne,'" pp. 46–47. Henry V himself seems to have worried that his premature death would doom the Treaty of Troyes, since on his deathbed he urged his followers to continue to fight for it, but in effect authorized them to accept, if necessary, a settlement by which the English would give up the crown in exchange for retaining Normandy (and presumably Guienne) as sovereign possessions: Monstrelet, *Chroniques*, VI, p. 110. Since the single most important reason for Burgundy's backing of Henry had been to ensure that the dauphin, the murderer of John the Fearless, did not become king of France (Vaughan, *Philip the Good*, p. 4), this provision may have been worrisome to the Burgundians, and may be one reason that by the end of the year Philip was looking towards a three-way peace. (See above, note 19.)
32 He had temporized on this subject since before Henry V's death, but finally gave this answer between 22 April 1423 and 6 May 1424. George Beltz, *Memorials of the Order of the Garter* (London, 1841), pp. lxii–lxiii.
33 Perier, *Nicolas Rolin*, p. 99.

on the path to winning the war. This change was due almost entirely to the efforts of the man who succeeded Henry V as regent of France: his brother John, duke of Bedford. Fully aware of the importance of the Burgundian alliance, Bedford immediately set about doing all he could to strengthen it. In pursuit of this objective he had two major cards to play, one military and one dynastic. Although the chronology of the steps Bedford took to resolve the crisis is complicated, and each strand of policy interacted with the other two, one can best understand his actions by looking at them in terms of the three basic problems he had to address.

The first was the restoration of family ties between the two dynasties. The obvious way to address that problem was with a new marriage, but here Bedford faced a difficulty that would continue to plague English diplomacy for the rest of the war: a distinct scarcity of marriageable men and women close enough to the royal family to serve as significant bonds between the two dynasties. In 1423, King Henry VI had no siblings, no offspring, no nieces or nephews, and not even a single first cousin of Lancastrian blood. The young king, thus, had only two close, dynastically relevant, unmarried relatives: his widowed mother and his uncle, Bedford.[34] To appreciate the significance and unusualness of this fact it is necessary to contrast it with the situation of earlier English kings at key diplomatic moments of the Hundred Years War. In 1337, when the war began, Edward III's unmarried close relatives included his mother, his eldest son and heir, another son, two daughters, two blood nephews, twelve other nephews and nieces, a sister-in-law, and nine first cousins of Plantagenet descent (of whom five were English), a total of twenty-nine individuals. In 1420, before the Treaty of Troyes, Henry V's unmarried close relatives included three brothers, a half-uncle, and nineteen Lancastrian first cousins (fourteen of them English) – a total of twenty-three individuals.[35]

Since he could not realistically have offered the marriage of Henry VI or the remarriage of the Queen Mother (neither of which would have

34 His one maternal uncle was Charles VII; his one maternal aunt and three maternal first cousins were Valois rather than Lancastrian, so of little use to bind Burgundy to Lancaster over Valois.

35 These numbers are based on various genealogical references and may not be exactly accurate since, for example, we do not know the marriage year of some of the cousins. I have included as "unmarried" those few who were betrothed or in holy orders, since it was not unknown to cancel a betrothal or to pull someone out of a convent in order to make a dynastic marriage alliance, and because it seemed best to make no exceptions rather than to decide what factors should remove an individual from the count. I have also counted many individuals too young to consummate a marriage, as such were often used for dynastic marital alliances. Note that sharing a common grandfather makes two individuals first cousins even if they have a different grandmother, hence Henry's Beaufort cousins (descended from John of Gaunt, duke of Lancaster) are not distinguished from his cousins via Philippa and Elizabeth of Lancaster.

been allowed by Gloucester and the council in England) Bedford had only one dynastic card to play: himself. But it was a powerful card. As a man in his prime, regent of Lancastrian France, one of the greater territorial magnates of Europe, and heir presumptive to the dual Lancastrian crowns, Bedford may have been the single most dynastically desirable bachelor in Christendom. Since Henry VI was an infant and many children died before producing heirs,[36] there was more than a small chance that Bedford, and ultimately his son, would be king of England and France. Even if that did not transpire, Bedford in his own right not only held extensive lands in England,[37] but also could be expected to carve a substantial apanage within France out of lands confiscated from Henry VI's enemies, as he indeed did in mid 1424, when he took the titles of duke of Anjou and count of Maine.[38]

So, in order to restore the family linkages between England and Burgundy, Bedford took the strongest possible step by marrying Philip's sister Anne. This boosted the alliance in a fourfold way. First, it turned Bedford and Philip into brothers-in-law and made Anne, who was dear to Philip and became so to Bedford, a permanent force for harmony between them. Second, it amounted to giving a great gift to Philip, the hand of one of most eligible bachelors of Christendom, which could be expected to inspire some gratitude (especially since Bedford not only married Anne, but made her a happy bride).[39] Third, the gift was valuable not just for its own sake, but also because the decision to give it to Philip showed clearly how extremely highly the regent valued Burgundy's friendship, and thus gave Philip something else he wanted, which was public and irrevocable affirmation of his importance as a partner in the alliance. And fourth, it created the prospect of tight bonds between Lancaster and Burgundy into the next generation. The two men would

---

36 For example, Duke Philip at this point had had only one child, who had died in infancy; later he would have three more legitimate children, of whom only the third (Charles the Rash) survived to adulthood; of Henry IV's sons, his first died in infancy, his second (Henry V) barely lived long enough to produce one child, his third (Clarence) died young before producing legitimate offspring, and his fourth and fifth (Bedford and Gloucester) also died without legitimate progeny.

37 As duke of Bedford, earl of Richmond, and earl of Kendal, his income in 1418 had been estimated as on the order of £5,000 (making him one of the two or three richest magnates in England), and since then he had acquired other valuable offices and estates. Jenny Stratford, *The Bedford Inventories*, p. 4; *Proceedings and Ordinances of the Privy Council of England*, ed. N. H. Nicolas, 7 vols. (London, 1834–1837), vol. II, p. 243.

38 Stratford, *Bedford Inventories*, p. 9.

39 Williams, *My Lord of Bedford*, pp. 103–4. Philip had been angling for a marriage between one of his sisters and one of Henry V's brothers since before the Treaty of Troyes, and indeed that prospect had been emphasized by his counselors in making the case for the creation of the Anglo-Burgundian alliance in the first place. Allmand, *Henry V*, p. 140.

be uncles to each others' children (assuming they had children in the future); those children would be each others' first cousins. Moreover, the marriage of Bedford and Anne created a possibility of an actual unification of the dynasties of Lancaster and Burgundy. Philip's thirteen-year marriage to Michelle of Valois had not produced any surviving children, he had no legitimate brothers, and he had not yet remarried. His heirs were therefore his sisters and their progeny; if Anne and Bedford had a son, that son would stand to inherit the Burgundian county of Artois, and possibly other shares of the principality of Burgundy after the death of his aunts (Philip's other sisters, of whom only one as yet had children), as well as standing to inherit England and Lancastrian France, if Henry VI had no children.[40]

The same round of marital diplomacy that led to the rebuilding of familial ties between Lancaster and Burgundy also helped address Bedford's second problem: to re-establish the credibility of his side as a potential winner in the civil war within France. The succession of a helpless infant in place of a seemingly unstoppable warrior-king, combined with the loss of the legitimizing force of control over the mad King Charles VI (which had made it easy for those ready to accept defeat or contemplating switching sides to do so), seemed to leave the English in a much weaker position in 1423 than they had been in at the start of 1422. But Bedford undertook a series of mutually reinforcing military and diplomatic efforts that both benefitted from, and in turn added strength to, the Burgundian alliance. One reason Duke Philip was willing to renew and strengthen his bonds with England through the marriage of his sister to Bedford was that he and the regent had significantly improved England's chances for ultimate victory by turning one more major player in the game from enemy to ally: the duke of Brittany had agreed to switch sides and join Burgundy and England in a triple alliance, fortified by the marriage of Philip's only other unmarried sister, Margaret, to the Breton duke's brother, Arthur de Richemont.[41]

---

40 The prospects of this dynastic extension into the next generation were enhanced by the fact that both Bedford and Burgundy already had illegitimate children and so were known to be fertile. On the planned division of Burgundian territories among Philip's sisters if he died without heir of his body, see Pocquet de Haut-Jusse, "Anne de Bourgogne," p. 307.

41 At the same time, two of the principal barons of the Gascon frontier, the counts of Foix and Comminges, also switched to the English side. Foix had been the leading figure in dauphinist Languedoc. G. du Fresne de Beaucourt, *Histoire de Charles VII* (Paris, 1882), vol. II, p. 12; Vaughan, *John the Fearless*, p. 265. Mark Warner sees the triple alliance among Brittany, Burgundy, and Lancaster as "the opening of an elaborate double game on the part of the duke of Burgundy" because "the day after the main treaty, the dukes of Burgundy and Brittany met without their ally and brother of

The successes of Bedford's marital diplomacy were due in part to the successes of his simultaneous martial endeavors. In the aftermath of Henry V's death, the dauphin's captains had undertaken several minor operations in hopes of benefitting from English disarray, but in most cases the gains they made were quickly undone by Anglo-Burgundian responses. Most significantly, the French captured the strategic bridge-town of Meulan, on the Seine between Rouen and Paris. Bedford (with some Burgundian as well as English and Anglo-French troops) went in person to take it back, and conducted the siege so adroitly that he not only impressed the chronicler Jean de Waurin (a veteran soldier) and recaptured the place but also compelled the French lords inside to surrender other fortresses they held, as part of their capitulation. As a result, Montl'héry and Étampes, among other places, fell under English control. In the same spring and into the summer, other English and Burgundian detachments also captured Montaiguillon, Noyelles-sur-Mer, Rue, Le Crotoy, Ivry, La-Charité-sur-Loire, Compiègne, Sedan, and other places. Thus the regent demonstrated that the military tide was still flowing in favor of the English, despite Henry V's death.

Bedford to conclude a 'secret' treaty whereby it was agreed that their alliance would remain in force in the event that either party should decide to commence negotiations with Charles VII." This would seem to be a prime piece of evidence for the argument that the Anglo-Burgundian alliance was never strong; that the traditional view of Philip as a duplicitous politician is correct; and that an eventual reconciliation between Burgundy and the dauphin was nearly inevitable. But, first, we do not actually know that this was a "secret" treaty. Suggesting the contrary, it opens with the standard diplomatic language of an open treaty or letter patent: "Philip duke of Burgundy and John duke of Brittany, to all those who may see and hear the present letters: Greetings. We inform you that…" (Dom U. Plancher et al., *Histoire générale et particuliere de Bourgogne, avec les preuves justificatives* (Dijon, 1781), vol. IV, pièce justificative no. XXIII, p. xxvij.) Second, more importantly, Warner mistakes the terms of the document. In it the two dukes promise each other that if one makes peace or agrees to a truce with the dauphin, he will nonetheless continue to support the other *against the dauphin* (or anyone else who attacks him). It was a version of the standard diplomatic clause prohibiting the parties in an alliance from making a separate peace and hanging their partners out to dry. In the text Burgundy actually refers to the *triple* alliance ("of which alliance the tenor is as follows: 'John [duke of Bedford], regent of the realm of France, &c …'") and promises to adhere to that alliance, vis-à-vis Brittany, regardless of any treaty or accord made with the dauphin. There is no indication that the document was looking towards a peace that would violate Burgundy's treaty with Bedford; rather, it probably was envisioning the possibility of a three-way Anglo-French-Burgundian peace (See above, n. 22.) Burgundy's dealings with the dauphinists appear much less "two-faced" (cf. du Fresne de Beaucourt, *Histoire de Charles VII*, pp. 413–14; Warner, "The Anglo-French Dual Monarchy," p. 122) if one refrains from presuming that Philip knew that no Anglo-French compromise peace was possible. In fact, as late as 1432 and 1433, despite military setbacks and the failure of the English to provide him with the support he expected (as discussed below), he refused to accept any separate peace treaty with Charles that did not include the English. Du Fresne de Beaucourt, *Histoire de Charles VII*, pp. 450–1, 456–57.

The strongest proof of that fact came in the summer of 1423. The dauphin's party made its largest military effort of the year in an attempt to capture Cravant. The town was in an important strategic location, and was made more important because a group of prominent Burgundian captains had hastily entered the town in order to cast out a French force that had seized it by a ruse. Capturing these Burgundian nobles along with the town, argued one French captain, would mean the capture of Auxerre and control of that whole region, and would "give the Burgundians so much to do, that they will not know on which foot to dance."[42] Because Cravant was badly provisioned, it had to be rescued rapidly, but the French had sent a full-scale army against it at a time when the English and Burgundians had many troops occupied in other operations. In this emergency, Bedford managed to collect some 2,500 troops to join a Burgundian force of similar size in crushing a much larger Franco-Scottish army at the battle of Cravant. The defeated dauphinists lost some 5,000 men killed or captured, including both of the army's commanders. This was a major setback for the French, who were already losing ground. It practically ended the threat to Philip's southern domains and provided Philip with a potent reminder of the military value of English military assistance. After the battle, English and Burgundian soldiers worked together to clear several more dauphinist strongholds from the borders of Philip's territories. At one point the duke of Burgundy himself formed up in battle array alongside the English captain Sir William Glasdale, ready to fight a force that Charles of Bourbon was expected to bring to raise the siege of the castle of La Roche outside Mâcon.[43] The Burgundian chronicler Jean de Waurin, who was in the army as a man-at-arms, remarks that there had been much brotherly affection between the English and Burgundians even before they fought and won the battle of Cravant together.[44] The strength of comradely feeling by the end of the successful joint campaign is easy to imagine.

It is a good example of the interrelationships of diplomatic and military developments that the Anglo-Burgundian victory at Cravant seems to have been a crucial factor in another diplomatic coup that added

---

42 Waurin, *Chronicles*, p. 40. The besieged, in pleading for help from the dowager duchess of Burgundy (who was in charge of the region while her son was in the north) wrote that if they were not supported, "the country of Burgundy would be destroyed." *Livre des trahisons de France envers la maison de Bourgogne*, in Kervyn de Lettenhove (ed.), *Chroniques relatives à l'histoire de la Belgique sous la dominations des ducs de Bourgogne* (Brussels, 1873), vol. II, p. 169.

43 Waurin, *Chronicles*, pp. 47–48.

44 Jean de Wavrin [Waurin], *Recueil des croniques et anchiennes istoires de la Grant Bretaigne, à present nommé Engleterre (1422–1431)*, ed. William Hardy (London, 1879), p. 66: "se misrent auz champz en grant fraternite."

significantly to the probability of the English outright winning the Hundred Years War. Since the death of Henry V, his son's regency council in England had been working to settle the century-old conflict with Scotland. King James I was more than amenable to peace. Although he had been a prisoner of the English since 1406, by 1419 James had effectively been co-opted by Henry V, to the point of serving as one of Henry's senior captains in the war against France.[45] Again matrimonial and personal considerations were important here: as James's famous poem *The Kingis Quair* reveals, he was deeply in love with Henry's first cousin, Joan Beaufort, daughter of the earl of Somerset.[46] But although diplomacy working towards a "final peace" between England and Scotland had been initiated as early as February 1423, it was not until 19 August – probably within days of receiving word of the outcome of Cravant (fought on 1 August) – that Murdoch Stewart, the regent of Scotland, authorized the Scottish chancellor to begin the formal negotiations that produced the Treaty of York, agreed on 10 September.[47] Although it was not immediately effective, this agreement represented the prospect of removing the dauphin's most significant foreign ally from the playing board.

Through these actions and his general conduct, Bedford had proven himself a man of stature and a worthy successor to Henry V as co-leader of the Anglo-Burgundian war effort. He "was a man of energy and worth," remarked a contemporary Frenchman, "humane and just, who greatly loved those French noblemen who adhered to him, virtuously striving to raise them to honor. So for his whole life he was greatly admired and cherished by the Normans and French of his party."[48]

Thus, by the end of the summer of 1423, Bedford had done an extraordinary job of restoring English prestige and solidifying the Anglo-Burgundian alliance. But he still faced a third danger to the strength of the coalition: the reckless actions of his younger brother, Duke Humphrey of Gloucester, Protector of England and head of Henry VI's

45 At the siege of Dreux in 1421. Michael Brown, *James I* (East Linton, 2000), p. 23.
46 Skeptics inclined to presume that this was actually a simple marriage of state romanticized by poets and chroniclers, and that *The Kingis Quair* is merely a conventional work of literature which reveals little about the poet's actual romantic feelings, should note that while James and Joan had eight children, James had no known bastards. By contrast, his royal father and grandfather had at least two and nine illegitimate children, respectively.
47 *Foedera, Conventiones, Litterae etc.*, ed. Thomas Rymer (The Hague, 1739–1745), 4:4:97–98; note also 4:4:85–86; 4:4:93 (March; Scots to Pontefract); 4:4:97 (English ambassadors and James to Pontefract; Douglas "for a final peace with Scotland"); 4:4:111 (truce for seven years starting 28 March 1424, neither to assist enemies of the other).
48 Thomas Basin, quoted Williams, *My Lord of Bedford*, p. 108.

regency council in England. In January 1423, Humphrey had married Jacqueline of Bavaria, heiress of Hainault (and, disputably, of Holland and Zeeland), who had earlier fled to England to escape ill-treatment by her first husband, John, duke of Brabant. This marriage, and Gloucester's consequent claim to lordship over those three provinces, was an intolerable affront to Philip of Burgundy. Both Jacqueline and John of Brabant were Philip's first cousins, and the Burgundian duke had arranged to inherit the couple's lands if they had no children, which he had probably also arranged with Brabant to ensure would be the case. Thus, Gloucester was both sticking his nose into Burgundian family business and setting himself directly in opposition to Philip's most important policy agenda, his pursuit of territorial expansion into the Low Countries.[49] The duke of Burgundy clearly felt that Bedford's failure to prevent Gloucester's action was something of a stab in the back, one that called into question the regent's commitment to the alliance, and hence its value.

This challenge too was met by Bedford's diplomacy, at least for the time being. He and Philip had both recently been reminded by the scholars of the University of Paris that if war broke out between Burgundy and Gloucester, it would likely lead to the rupture of the Troyes settlement, the devastation of France, and the prompt victory of the dauphin, who had been responsible for the murder of Philip's father. To avert this disaster, Bedford and Burgundy leaned hard on Gloucester and Brabant, respectively, to accept their joint mediation in their dispute, and to refrain from resorting to force in the interim. This did not resolve the issue, but for the time being it was satisfactory to Burgundy, since his protégé was left in possession of the disputed lands.[50]

With this crisis averted, or at least deferred, Bedford had successfully responded to all three of the dangers to the Anglo-Burgundian alliance resulting from Henry V's death: he had re-established family ties between the two houses, demonstrated clearly that England and Lancastrian France were still allies with good prospects for ultimate victory, and had prevented his brother from causing a rupture between England and Burgundy. He had moreover made positive steps to strengthen the alliance even further, most significantly by providing substantial

---

49 There has been no full study of Humphrey since K. H. Vickers, *Humphrey Duke of Gloucester: A Biography* (London, 1907), which remains useful.

50 For Bedford and Burgundy's judgment essentially passing the matter on to the pope, dated 19 June 1424, see *Cartulaire des comtes de Hainault*, ed. Léopold Devillers (Brussels, 1889), vol. IV, p. 391; note also Joseph Stevenson (ed.), *Letters and Papers Illustrative of the Wars of the English in France during the Reign of Henry the Sixth, King of England*, 2 vols. (London: Rolls Series, 1861–1864), vol. II, pt. 2, pp. 388–89. For the eventual result (on 27 February 1426) see *Cartulaire des comtes de Hainault*, pp. 539–41.

military forces to aid Burgundy against the dauphin.[51] The joint Anglo-Burgundian military operations not only contributed to the solidity of the alliance by their successful results, but they also built up ties of affection between leading men on both sides in the process of achieving those results, as Waurin testifies.[52]

The second crisis

In May and June of 1424, Bedford took further steps to strengthen the alliance. First, he secured from both Jacqueline and Humphrey an extension of the period for arbitration of their dispute with Brabant, until the end of June. Then, over three days, Duke John and Duke Philip agreed on a general settlement of various matters. First, on 19 June, they jointly issued their conclusion on the dispute over Jacqueline's lands. In essence, they agreed that the matter should be decided, if the two sides could not come to a mutual agreement, by a papal decision on the validity of Jacqueline's marriage to Brabant.[53] This was not an ideal outcome from Burgundy's perspective, but it was good enough, since it left his cousin and ally in possession, and since Philip probably expected the pope's decision to go in his favor, which is what eventually happened. Second, Bedford accepted from Henry VI's regency council the titles of duke of Anjou and count of Maine. Although these areas were not yet under English control, they were next on the agenda for conquest. This grant, provided it could be made a reality, stood to make Bedford (and thus eventually, it could be hoped, his heir, Philip's blood nephew) roughly on a par with the duke of Brittany and the duke of Burgundy as one of the three great magnates of northern France.[54] Third, Bedford essentially handed over the principal spoils of the recent Anglo-Burgundian military operations by signing over to Philip the counties of Auxerre and Mâcon and the castellany of Bar-sur-Seine, together a considerable addition to Burgundy's domains.[55]

---

51 For another example of Bedford's conciliatory diplomacy (which left the valuable castellanies of Peronne, Roye, and Montdidier in Burgundy's hands) see Plancher et al., *Histoire générale et particuliere de Bourgogne*, pièce justificative no. XXV, pp. xxviij–ix (8 September 1423).

52 Waurin, *Chronicles*, p. XX

53 *Cartulaire*, pp. 391–92.

54 According to William of Worcester, well informed on such matters, Maine alone, after its conquest, produced an annual revenue of £10,000 in support of the war effort. William of Worcester, *The Boke of Noblesse. Addressed to King Edward the Fourth on His Invasion of France in 1475*, ed. John Gough Nichols (Edinburgh, 1860), p. 19.

55 These were officially granted for a limited term only, to be restored to the royal domain if Philip failed to demonstrate that they were compensation due him for debts owed to

Events demonstrated the excellent health of the alliance shortly there-after. The dauphin, despite the defeat at Cravant, managed to assemble the largest French army collected since Agincourt, perhaps 14,000 men, to attack Lancastrian Normandy. Returning in full measure the aid he had received at Cravant, the duke of Burgundy rushed his best commander, the sire de l'Isle Adam, to Bedford's assistance with a force estimated at 3,000 men, including 1,000 men-at-arms[56] – a very large contingent for a Burgundian army, considering that the duke himself had mustered only about 1,500 soldiers for the battle of Mons-en-Vimeu two years earlier, where he had fought in person, and that Henry V had only had 1,000 men-at-arms at Agincourt.[57] Bedford himself took the field at the head of about 9,800 soldiers,[58] so that with the Burgundians, the opposing armies were nearly equal. The French seemed ready to fight a general engagement, even without a large numerical superiority, something unusual for them, and perhaps a sign of their strategic desperation. Shortly before a battle was expected, Bedford paid honor to this Burgundian contribution by delivering the royal banner of France to be carried by its leader, the sire de l'Isle Adam.[59]

Yet within seven weeks of the day the Burgundians joined Bedford's army, the situation had changed radically. From an active cooperation of two powers against one, the alliance between England and Burgundy had become little more than a non-aggression pact; Philip had signed a truce with Charles and was effectively leaving the English to fight the French by themselves.[60]

The reasons for this shift are complex. One major factor was the intervention of Humphrey of Gloucester in Hainault, against Philip's wishes and interests, which is further discussed below. But historians have largely ignored another important cause. When the vanguard of the Anglo-Burgundian army was just 12 miles distant from the French and battle seemed imminent, Bedford took an astounding step: he detached the entire Burgundian element of his army, nearly a quarter of his strength, and sent the troops marching for Picardy, reportedly saying that he had

his house by the Lancastrian government. Plancher et al., *Histoire générale et particuliere de Bourgogne*, pièces justificatives nos. XXXIV–XXXV.

56 F. W. Brie (ed.), *The Brut or the Chronicle of England* (Oxford, 1908), vol. II, p. 564.
57 Mons-en-Vimeu: Vaughan, *Philip the Good*, p. 14 (figuring one *gros valet* per man-at-arms); Juliet Barker, *Conquest: The English Kingdom of France in the Hundred Years War* (London, 2010), p. 78. Burgundy would later again have about 4,000 at Brouwershaven, where he fought in person. Vaughan, *Philip the Good*, p. 43.
58 Waurin, *Chronicles*, p. 67.
59 Ibid., p. 69.
60 Plancher et al., *Histoire générale et particuliere de Bourgogne*, pièce justificative no. XXXVII.

enough men to defeat the French without them. Two days later, now facing odds of almost 3:2 instead of roughly 1:1, Bedford commanded during a hard-fought battle at Verneuil. The combat was much tougher than Agincourt, according to a soldier who served in both engagements, and Bedford came near disaster when well-armored Lombard cavalry broke one of his wings of archers, but the English eventually won the battle quite decisively.[61]

The whole episode of Bedford's dismissing l'Isle-Adam's contingent before the battle is not even mentioned by Philip the Bold's biographer, nor in Juliet Barker's recent history of this phase of the war.[62] No surviving evidence offers much insight into the cause of Bedford's surprising action, and the regent's biographer, E. Carleton Williams, devotes just two unenlightening sentences to it: "In view of the disparity existing between the two armies his action is difficult to understand. Perhaps the duke was emulating Henry V's defiant exhortation before the battle of Agincourt, or it might be for the graver reason that he felt the Burgundians were untrustworthy."[63] Given Bedford's reputation for prudence, and the fact that since Agincourt he had witnessed the example of his brother Clarence, who underestimated the French and in consequence was killed at Baugé in 1421, the former hypothesis seems highly improbable. Even if Bedford was so confident in divine providence, English prowess, or both, that he sincerely believed he had no *need* of the Burgundians, he also would not have given up much of the glory of a potential victory by allowing them to participate, since (without Burgundy himself being present) he, Bedford, would unambiguously have been the commander of the army. It is also unlikely that he dismissed the Burgundians because he thought they were "untrustworthy" in the sense of being less reliable troops than his Englishmen. They had already shown at Cravant that they could be good battlefield comrades, and even if he did doubt their

---

61 Waurin, *Chronicles*, pp. 72–79; for the departure of the Burgundian troops (not identified as such), note also *The Brut or the Chronicle of England*, II, p. 564.

62 Vaughan, *Philip the Good*, p. 11; Barker, *Conquest*, p. 78. (Barker notes l'Isle Adam's arrival but not his departure.)

63 Williams, *My Lord of Bedford*, 133. The chronicler Waurin, who was in the army, puts the best face on the matter by saying Bedford commanded the Burgundians to return to their siege of Nêle, as "he was well able to spare them" and "they had great need and very legitimate cause for returning to their said siege of Nelle." Yet, he notes that the Burgundian leaders "would have liked better to remain with him to accompany him to the battle" and "left with great regret," and in fact there is no credible way to argue that the siege of Nêle was anywhere near as important as increasing the odds of victory at Verneuil. Moreover, Waurin states earlier in his narrative that l'Isle Adam had left the force maintaining the siege "well provided for." Waurin, *Chronicles*, pp. 67–72. Realistically, the only thing that would have prevented its fall would have been an English defeat at Verneuil.

steadiness or effectiveness, and feared that they might make a weak spot in his battle line, he could have avoided that by using them as a reserve or enveloping force. Sending them away was a clear statement that he actively did not want them to participate. Williams's second guess thus seems the only credible explanation, but if it is the correct one, it means Bedford was gravely mistaken, since there is no indication in Burgundian archives that the Burgundians were plotting a betrayal, despite the high level of tension over Gloucester's intervention in Hainault.[64]

If we, with access to English archives, can only guess at Bedford's reasoning, the same must have been true of the scorned duke of Burgundy and his council.[65] It seems that the Lancastrian regent's action must have sent three basic messages to Burgundy, all of which ran directly counter to the diplomatic message Bedford had sent earlier by marrying Anne. First, and most explicit: we don't need you. Second, we don't trust you: either we don't trust you to fight courageously and well, or, more likely, we don't trust you not to stab us in the back.[66] Third, we don't want to be in your debt.

An alliance of convenience with the English still had clear advantages for the Burgundians in 1424 (they had profited greatly from English aid in 1423), but by definition could only be expected to remain in force so long as it remained advantageous for them. Only a stronger alliance, fortified by sentiment and mutual investment, could be expected to weather hard times for the English, when it would be needed most, and which (given the history of the war thus far and of human affairs generally) could be expected before the conflict was finally resolved. But the value of a long-term, solid alliance rested, for Philip, on his ability to be confident that his views and interests would receive due weight in the counsels of the Lancastrian governments of France and England. That confidence in turn rested on the knowledge that the English needed and valued his assistance, and that Henry VI's government trusted him. Trust is not always rewarded, but distrust almost always undermines relationships. National alliances, like marriages, may survive on the basis of mutual need even when mutual respect and affection are absent, but in such

---

64 Vaughan, *Philip the Good*. However, in Bedford's defense, it is worth noting that the night before the battle a number of Frenchmen in his army deserted and went over to the dauphin's side; it was the morning after that event that Bedford sent the Burgundians away. Waurin, *Chronicles*, pp. 72, 80–81.

65 Even if Bedford gave some now-lost explanation or excuse to them, they would have had no way to be certain of its sincerity.

66 "More likely" because, as noted already, if Bedford had only been worried about Burgundian competence rather than Burgundian intentions, he could have employed the Burgundian force as a reserve or an enveloping detachment.

cases fidelity is too much to expect. Alliances of this sort are rarely sound bases for the inherently *long-term* considerations of grand strategy.

The shared victory of Cravant had built up a reservoir of good will in Burgundy towards the English; the slap in the face Bedford delivered to the Burgundians on the eve of Verneuil must have significantly drained that reserve. It probably also led Philip to reassess his situation vis-à-vis the other bone of contention between him and Bedford: the ambitions of the duke of Gloucester in the Low Countries. As already noted, as part of his effort to resolve the first crisis of the alliance, Bedford had gotten Gloucester and his duchess to accept himself and Burgundy as mediators in the dispute over Hainault, Holland, and Zeeland. But the truce included in that agreement expired in June, and the mediators had not been able to agree on anything beyond referring the matter to the pope. Immediately on receiving word of this non-resolution of the dispute, Humphrey set in motion plans to "pass over the sea with God's might in our own person for to receive and take into our hands our lands and lordships there with due obeisance of our subjects," borrowing whatever funds he could to that end.[67] His preparations, which also included collecting ships and soldiers, can hardly have remained unknown to the duke of Burgundy, who had already promised to back John of Brabant with military force if necessary. Philip thus confronted the possibility of a two-front war, against Humphrey and against the dauphin. Since Bedford seemed unable to leash the former, while Charles was eager for a truce with Burgundy (as a first step towards rupturing the Anglo-Burgundian alliance so that he could concentrate on fighting the English), Philip proceeded to negotiate a truce on his southern borders, the "truce of Chambéry," with the dauphinists. Significantly, and doubtless as part of the price of getting the truce he wanted, in the document the Burgundian duke referred to Charles as "the king," a step away from the previously invariable Anglo-Burgundian diplomatic practice of completely denying Charles's right to that title.[68]

67 *Historical Manuscripts Commission, Twelfth Report, Appendix, Part IX. The Manuscripts of the Duke of Beaufort, the Earl of Donoughmore, and Others* (London 1891), p. 395: a letter dated in London on 28 June, to the Prior of Ely requesting a loan of £200. Remarkably, in a sign of either gross dishonesty or complete self-deception, Gloucester asked for the help "considering that ye know of ... this our voyage as likely to turn to right great ease and welfare of this realm." (Quotation modernized.) It is hard to imagine how he could have persuaded even himself of that likelihood.

68 Printed Plancher et al., *Histoire générale et particuliere de Bourgogne*, pièce justificative no. XXXVII. It is not quite right, however, to say (as is said in various books) that Burgundy in this document called Charles "King of France." It is doubtless an intentional diplomatic nuance that Charles is simply called "le Roy" rather than "le Roy de

The two brothers-in-law were each disappointed and angry with the other: Bedford was furious about the Franco-Burgundian truce; Philip was outraged by Bedford's failure to keep his younger brother in check, as Gloucester prepared to use force against Burgundian interests rather than submitting to papal judgment of the matter, the only option that could prevent fighting between English and Burgundian troops without shaming one duke or the other. There was a shouting match between them in Paris in October. But although bruised, the alliance did not break. John and Philip continued to like and respect each other,[69] and to be bound together by their mutual love for Anne of Burgundy, ever the peace-maker between them, and by their mutual enmity towards Charles VII. Their argument may have been heated, but came in the midst of many consultations as they tried to find a way to peaceably settle the Hainault affair.[70]

The main causes of their mutual discontent, the truce of Chambéry and Gloucester's intervention in the Low Countries, looked like they might blow over. The truce was only valid until the start of the next campaigning season (1 May 1425), and Gloucester lacked the strength to sustain a position on the continent against Burgundy's power unless he got backing from Bedford or from the royal government in England, neither of which had any intention of offering him support. If a Burgundian army deterred him from actually moving into Hainault from Calais (where he had just landed on 17 October), or persuaded him to accept the arrangement which Bedford and Burgundy had agreed on (letting the pope resolve the matter), the problem would be much ameliorated. If neither the regent nor Philip had gotten quite the full level of backing they would have liked from the other, they could each appreciate the other's situation: Philip could hardly expect Bedford to go so far as to send troops against his own brother, and Bedford could not blame Philip too much for seeking a truce in the south when he, Bedford, had failed to protect his ally from a threat in the north. And while each may have

---

France." In a later truce document (from 1431) Philip refers to Charles as "calling himself king of France." Ibid., pièce justificative no. CX, p. ciij.

69 This can be seen clearly in Burgundy's willingness to accept Bedford – Gloucester's own brother – as the judge of the duel he wanted to fight with Gloucester in 1425 (for reasons explained below), "for he [Bedford] is a prince of such character that I know and truly recognize that to you, to me, and to all others he would wish to be a righteous judge." Waurin, *Chronicles*, p. 99. I think Armstrong, "La Double Monarchie," p. 373, and Leguai, "La 'France bourguignonne,'" p. 49, underestimate the "amical" element of the Anglo-Burgundian alliance – or rather, the Bedford–Burgundy alliance – for most of its duration.

70 They continued to dine and socialize together, and even both participated in the jousting that accompanied the wedding of Burgundy's *maître d'hôtel*.

wanted more from the other, each also preferred the other's neutrality to the other's active opposition. Philip needed Bedford to continue to refrain from assisting his brother militarily, and Bedford needed Philip to stay bound to England and not switch to supporting France. Moreover, if Bedford's conduct during the Verneuil campaign had been an insult to Burgundy, it was an insult that could be diplomatically papered over, and the crushing nature of the regent's victory, the second destruction of a French army in two years and the third in a decade, left the dauphin (as the English and Burgundians generally continued to call Charles VII) militarily weak. The Lancastrian dynasty still looked like the winning horse.

So the English still seemed to have a good chance of restoring their alliance with Burgundy to a full, active partnership working towards the defeat of the dauphin and his party. But neither marital nor martial circumstances offered strong opportunities for strengthening the alliance. Philip was at this time a widower, but already seeking papal dispensation for a marriage to Bonne of Artois, dowager countess of Nevers, a woman with dauphinist ties. The Lancastrians would doubtless have been happy to offer a "higher bid" and to reinforce their ties with Burgundy by supplying Philip with an English bride, but there simply was no suitable Englishwoman available.[71] Nor was there a suitable male relation of the king who could marry Burgundy's one remaining unwed sister, Agnes. She instead married the heir of the duke of Bourbon, a leading supporter of the dauphin.[72] In the short term, joint Anglo-Burgundian military operations that would benefit Burgundy were also impracticable, first because Philip was readying for the possibility of war with Bedford's brother Humphrey of Gloucester in Hainault, and secondly because of the truces between Burgundy and the French territories on his borders.

Although Duke Humphrey occupied Hainault with an army in late 1424, Bedford had a brief window to tamp down the resulting

71 A letter of 1425, written shortly after Bonne's death, noted five possible brides for Philip; four were specific individuals, one was generically "une grant dame en Angleterre." Louis Stouff, *Catherine de Bourgogne et la féodalité de l'Alsace Autrichienne* (Paris, 1913), pt. 2, p. 181; Vaughan, *Philip the Good*, p. 55. The usual interpretation is that Burgundy prudently chose not to strengthen his alliance with England through marriage (Armstrong, "La Double Monarchie," p. 369), or brushed aside advice to do so (Warner, "The Anglo-French Dual Monarchy," p. 113 [misdated]). But it is more likely that the reason the letter does not identify the great English lady is because there was no one suitable to name, since the marriage of Joan Beaufort (Henry V's first cousin) to the king of Scots in February 1424.

72 John Beaufort, duke of Somerset, first cousin of Henry V, would have been suitable but was not available because he was a French prisoner from 1421–38.

Anglo-Burgundian rift before it did much damage. Duke John did prevent the disaster of major fighting between Gloucester and Burgundy, by the simple expedient of refusing to back his brother against his ally. Without Bedford's support, Gloucester lacked the strength for a war with Burgundy over Hainault. However, Humphrey's diplomatic efforts to avoid that outcome took an unexpected turn when, in an exchange of letters, Gloucester and Burgundy accused each other of lying; Burgundy challenged Gloucester to a duel, and the latter accepted. This whole affair cannot be explained simply in terms of the political: it was also personal, and must be understood in terms of Philip's lifelong concern with avoiding any blemish on his knightly honor.[73]

Bedford succeeded in preventing the duel from taking place and also helped ensure that Gloucester withdrew, with his forces, from Hainault.[74] But he had not done so fast enough. At the end of January 1425, just after Philip had issued his challenge to Humphrey and while there was still an English army in Hainault, Philip agreed to prolong his truce with the dauphin until 25 December.[75] Then in February he arranged a new, open-ended truce with the duchess of Bourbon, tied to the forthcoming marriage of Agnes of Burgundy with Charles of Bourbon. Because of the geography, this practically ensured there would be no fighting between Burgundians and dauphinists for the foreseeable future.[76] In effect the duke of Burgundy withdrew, for five years, from active participation in the Hundred Years War, and turned his attention almost entirely to expanding his territorial control in the Low Countries.[77] The game of two against one was back to one against one.

During those years English arms continued to be successful, though only moderately so, against the concentrated efforts of Charles VII's

---

73 See Vickers, *Humphrey Duke of Gloucester*, ch. 4, and Vaughan, *Philip the Good*, ch. 2.

74 Bedford was deeply involved in preventing the duel; how much he had to do with causing Gloucester's withdrawal from Hainault is unclear, but at a minimum it included the important fact that he refused to support his brother's ambitions.

75 Then on 2 December the truce was further extended into the following year; further extensions followed later. Plancher et al., *Histoire générale et particuliere de Bourgogne*, pièce justificative no. XLVII, p. liij.

76 The area north of the Loire had been practically cleared of dauphinist territories; the Loire separated Burgundian Nevers from dauphinist Berry; all territories of Burgundy's southern border were fully shielded by the truce, which included Forez and Beaujolais. Very unusually, the proclamation of this truce did not include an end-date. Ibid., pièce justificative no. XL, pp. xlviii–xlix.

77 I.e., from fall 1424 to late summer 1429. For practically this whole period Philip was occupied in a "long, hard, costly war" to gain control of Hainault, Holland, and Zeeland; Gloucester effectively abandoned Jacqueline, but she and her partisans nonetheless did not surrender her independence or her heritage without a fight. Vaughan, *Philip the Good*, pp. 40–50.

France. In 1428, English forces began the siege of Orléans, the main dauphinist city north of the Loire. Even without active Burgundian assistance to the English[78] it seemed to many that a Lancastrian victory in the war had become imminent. As Marguerite la Touroulde recalled some years later:

At that time there was such misery and such shortage of money in this kingdom ... that things were in a pitiable state. And even those who were loyal to the King [Charles VII] were all nearly in despair. I know this because my husband was at the time the Receiver General, and he had not four crowns all told, of the King's money or his own ... At that moment there was no hope except in God.[79]

Subsequent events, including the chance death of the best English military commander (the Earl of Salisbury) and the arrival on the scene of Joan of Arc, turned the tide against the English, though not decisively so until Burgundy went from passive support to active opposition in 1436. Still, it seems fair to say that, considering how close to complete defeat the French came, it is likely that the dauphin's position would have collapsed before 1428 if in 1424–1427 he had been forced to meet active pressure from Burgundy at the same time as he faced the still-flowing tide of English conquests.[80] If one accepts this logic, it makes the Franco-Burgundian

---

78 Williams, *My Lord of Bedford*, pp. 165–67, does say that Burgundy initially contributed a contingent to the siege of Orléans, then withdrew it in fury when Bedford refused a French proposal to turn the city over to Philip to hold on behalf of its duke, who had been a prisoner of the English since Agincourt. The offer and Bedford's refusal are in Monstrelet, *Chronicles*, vol. I, pp. 551–52, and Waurin, *Chronicles*, p. 169 but neither Monstrelet nor Waurin makes any mention of Burgundians either participating in or withdrawing from the siege, which they almost certainly would have if there had been any. In fact, Waurin reports that Bedford's council objected to the idea of Burgundy gaining the city "without striking blow," implying his men had not participated in the siege. Williams's source is not clear, and I find the episode doubtful.

79 Marguerite la Touroulde, in Régine Pernoud, *The Retrial of Joan of Arc: The Evidence at the Trial for Her Rehabilitation, 1450–1456*, trans. J. M. Cohen (London, 1955), p. 94, translation slightly modified; for the Latin (which reports the testimony in third person form), see Pierre Duparc (ed.), *Procès en nullité de la condamnation de Jeanne d'Arc* (Paris, 1977), vol. I, pp. 376–77. Similarly Monstrelet, *Chronicles*, vol. I, pp. 548, 545–46: "king Charles was in very great distress; for the major part of his princes and nobles, perceiving that his affairs were miserably bad, and everything going wrong, had quite abandoned him"; he believed "should [Orléans] be conquered, it would be the finishing stroke to himself and his kingdom." Jacques Gélu, archbishop of Embrun, wrote in 1429 of how "it was hard to find anyone who was obedient to their lord the king ... [who] was so weakened that he had just barely enough [funds] to live, not even for his household, just for his own person and that of the queen. Things had reached such a point that there did not seem to be any way the lord king could recover his domains by any human agency..." Quoted Contamine, "La 'France Anglaise'," pp. 18–19.

80 Even after the arrival of Joan of Arc and the victory at Patay, Charles, according to Waurin, knew "it would be impossible for him to resist the forces of the king of England and the duke of Burgundy joined together." Waurin, *Chronicles*, p. 202.

truce of September 1424 (the treaty of Chambéry) as much of a turning point in the history of the Anglo-Burgundian alliance, and in the course of the war, as the much more famous treaty of Arras in 1435, by which Philip formally renounced his bond with the English and re-entered the war on the side of Charles VII.

The third crisis

Before that final collapse of the Anglo-Burgundian alliance, there was a third brief period when the coalition seemed as tight as ever. The advent of Joan of Arc and the failure of the high-stakes English siege of Orléans in 1429, followed by the English battlefield defeat in a meeting engagement at Patay, then the dauphin's successful drive on Reims and his coronation there as Charles VII, posed an existential threat to Lancastrian France. The dauphinists' capture of a string of towns on the way to Reims also gave the French bases for operations against Burgundy's own lands, in an area not covered by Philip's southern truces.

Philip could have responded by switching sides at this point, and almost certainly could have gotten from Charles, as the price of his transfer of loyalties, significant territorial contributions, public repentance for the murder of John the Fearless, and a voice in the French council.[81] The fact that a few years later he not only considered but actually did take that course indicates that such a decision was not out of the realm of possibility in 1430. But instead he shifted away from his position of *de facto* near-neutrality to resume active military cooperation with the English. As the government in London readied a royal expedition to carry Henry VI to France for his own coronation there, Burgundy even accepted the position of royal lieutenant for his English nephew.[82]

Some of his motives for staying true to the English alliance were the same as they had been since 1423. He was still bound to Bedford by friendship, by mutual investment, and by his sister Anne. Charles's role in the murder of Philip's father, and most importantly[83] the potential stain on his honor that breaking his alliance with the Lancastrians might bring, still militated against switching sides. Moreover, during the years of the Truce of Chambéry the main bone of contention between the two dukes had lost its significance. Bedford had declined to support

81 Plancher et al., *Histoire générale et particuliere de Bourgogne*, pièce justificative no. LXX.
82 Vaughan, *Philip the Good*, pp. 22–26; Monstrelet, *Chronicles*, I, p. 566 says the two dukes agreed "that each would exert his whole powers to resist their adversary Charles de Valois, and then solemnly renewed the alliances that existed between them."
83 See above, n. 22.

his brother's ambitions in the Low Countries, in effect allowing Philip to drive Gloucester out of Hainault (which he did April 1424) then to defeat and force the surrender of Jacqueline herself (finally in 1428). This, in combination with the pope's declaration that Jacqueline was legally married to Brabant rather than Gloucester, and various other developments, had made Burgundy's acquisition of Hainault, Holland, Zeeland, Friesland, Brabant, and Namur quite secure. And although recent events had weakened the English position in France, Henry VI's position was far from desperate. On the other hand, recent Lancastrian setbacks could be expected to raise English appreciation for Burgundian contributions, and prevent any future snubs à la Verneuil.

Indeed, already within days of the capture of the earl of Suffolk at Jargeau in June 1429, Bedford had again stepped up to make the strongest diplomatic step within his power to signal how much he valued the alliance and to increase the strength of Burgundy's commitment to Henry VI's position as king of France. As noted above, in 1424 the Lancastrian government of France had granted to Bedford a large apanage, including the rich county of Maine. Since Bedford and Anne remained childless, the prospect of his territories passing to a half-Burgundian heir were fading. But on 14 June 1429, Bedford sealed a new will which made Anne his heir to his French lands (now including the counties of Maine and Dreux, the viscounty of Beaumont, and title to the duchy of Anjou)[84] not just with a life tenancy, but as recipient to full title over them.[85] That made it likely that the lands would ultimately go either to half-Burgundian heirs (Anne's children by Bedford or a later husband) or else, quite possibly, *actually become part of Burgundian territory*, since if Anne never had children, her heir would be her older brother, Philip, or Philip's heirs. Assuming Henry VI's government honored the terms of Bedford's will,[86]

84 Stratford, *Bedford Inventories*, p. 12. Bedford also held a number of lesser but significant lordships, and the county of Harcourt, but most of these were actually part of Anne's dower-lands already and held by Bedford in her right.

85 Pocquet de Haut-Jusse, "Anne de Bourgogne," pp. 311–12, 324–25.

86 This was not a given, since most of Bedford's French lands were technically held from Henry VI in tail male, which did not allow him to bequeath them to his wife, or for her to pass them on to Philip. Ibid. Note also that I have followed all the historians who have written on this subject in taking the will as meaning to transfer to Anne all Bedford's French lands, but it should be noted that it actually refers to his "conquestz immeubles," which could be taken to mean that the lands he had purchased (such as Dreux) would not be included. Still, the will itself indicates Bedford thought such an arrangement would stand, and it would have been hard for Henry VI's government to refuse to honor the will, since that would alienate Philip, whose support would be all the more needed after Bedford's death. This could have been done legally by declaring that the lands had reverted to the crown on Bedford's death, then making a new grant of them to Philip or someone of Philip's choosing.

there seemed to be only two likely ways that duke's extensive French lands might *not* come into the Burgundian family. The first would be if Bedford outlived Anne, but she was fourteen years younger than her husband and in good health, so this did not seem likely.[87] The second would be if Charles VII defeated the English and restored his power north of the Loire. Thus, Bedford's new will gave Burgundy a powerful incentive to ensure the survival of the Lancastrian domination of northern France. It was a clever move, and one that has not received the recognition it deserves from historians. (Operating on the same principle, in March of 1432 Bedford would arrange for the grant of the valuable county of Champagne, part of the royal domain, to Philip. Since it had at that time recently been largely overrun by the French, Philip would have to fight actively to gain the benefit of the grant, and he could not well expect to keep it if the Valois knocked the English out of France.)[88]

Five days after sealing his new will, Bedford urgently requested that Philip come to Paris for consultation. The Burgundian duke promptly did so. Bedford promised him financial recompense for the costs he incurred in resuming active campaigning against France. This packet of incentives aligned Burgundy's long-term and immediate interests with his inclinations. After several days of conferences the two dukes "promised one another ... that each of them with all his power would employ himself in resisting against the enterprises of King Charles."[89] Philip then threw himself vigorously into the war against Charles VII, immediately providing troops to garrison Meaux-en-Brie, the expected target of the anticipated French offensive. Bedford, in Rouen, set about collecting a field force, including reinforcements from England. Once Bedford's army had assembled, he pursued the army Charles VII had led into Champagne and challenged the French to battle. When combat seemed imminent, 700–800 Burgundian soldiers formed up with English and Lancastrian-French men-at-arms in the main battle line, and the banner of Lancastrian France was again carried by the Burgundian captain the sire de l'Isle-Adam.[90] This time he was not sent away. No battle ensued, but a little later, other Burgundian men-at-arms played a key role in repulsing the French attack on Paris. Then Duke Philip brought the largest force he could muster, 4,000 combatants, to the capital. At Bedford's urging, he undertook to defend Paris over the winter (1429–1430), pending a joint spring offensive to recover the towns recently taken by

---

87 This is nevertheless what did happen, as it turned out.
88 The grant is noted by Armstrong, "La Double Monarchie," p. 353.
89 Stevenson, *Letters and Papers*, II, pt. 1, pp. 101–6; Waurin, *Chronicles*, p. 190.
90 Waurin, *Chronicles*, p. 200.

Charles's army.[91] Despite French efforts to break him away from the English alliance, the widespread belief among his own people (including the large majority of his councilors) that it was time to make a separate peace with Charles, and his own preference for a campaign in a different direction, Philip, at Bedford's direction, led his men to Compiègne to try to recover it from the French.[92] When these troops captured Joan of Arc in a skirmish, Philip promptly delivered her to Bedford.

The degree of Philip's active support for English efforts in this period is all the more noteworthy because at the same time he was facing several other problems which made demands on his attention and his resources. Throughout 1430 he faced a rebellion in a substantial part of Flanders. In the summer and fall of 1430 he also had to deal with a separate war between the principality of Liège and his recently acquired duchy of Namur. In June 1430 one of his principal vassals suffered defeat at the hands of the French in a disastrous ambush in the Dauphiné; in December, another substantial Burgundian force was defeated in a battle at near Bar-sur-Seine. In July 1431 Frederick, duke of Austria (induced by Charles VII) added to Philip's difficulties with a declaration of war against Burgundy. Practically no military action followed from this development, but it did add to the overall pressure on Philip to make terms with the French.[93]

Looking back from 1435, when Philip sealed the Treaty of Arras with Charles VII and switched sides, historians have tended to see the Anglo-Burgundian alliance as on a declining course from 1429, or even from 1423, and to depict its ultimate failure practically inevitable.[94] Yet, the truth is that Philip's actions in this crisis for the Lancastrian government show he still had a strong preference for Bedford and Henry VI over Charles VII.[95] His resumption of active participation in the Hundred Years War was admittedly quite short-lived, since he signed a new and indeed more-extensive truce with Charles in late 1431. But he did so

---

91 Ibid., pp. 210–11.
92 Ibid., 206; Stevenson, *Letters and Papers*, II, pt. 1, pp. 166–67; note also Armstrong, "La Double Monarchie," p. 372.
93 Vaughan, *Philip the Good*, pp. 57–67.
94 E.g., ibid., 20; 27: "As early as 1423 the peace of Arras was in sight; ten years later, it was imminent." Historians almost inevitably seem to treat the negotiations between Philip and partisans of the dauphin as steps towards Philip's switching sides, never considering that they could have led instead to him bringing more partisans to the Lancastrian side – as he did with the duke of Lorraine in 1422. Plancher et al., *Histoire générale et particuliere de Bourgogne*, pièce justificative no. XVII, p. xx.
95 Cf. the contrasting opinion of Warner, "The Anglo-French Dual Monarchy," p. 123, who thinks Burgundy stayed with the English alliance in 1424–1427 only "because if he had not his discarded allies would have exploited the situation in Hainault and Holland to destroy him."

because he was constrained to, not because he wanted to. The main reason was the failure of Henry VI's governments to provide him with adequate support, financial or military. During the siege of Compiègne the money that was to come from Henry to help pay for Philip's soldiers fell two months in arrears. The English contingent of his forces, under the earl of Huntingdon, also failed to receive its wages and had to retire from the operation for lack of funds. Philip thus found himself compelled to rely on his own resources to protect his lands. This he was not strong enough to do effectively against the resurgent forces of Charles VII, so that his territories were being ravaged and his revenues, in consequence, were drying up.[96]

He nonetheless expressed willingness to stay in the fight, provided that help from Henry would be forthcoming. When that aid proved not to be available, he made a truce with the French.[97] Even then, however, it is remarkable that he managed to get the French to allow a proviso in the agreement that would allow him to send 500 men-at-arms to Bedford's support without it counting as a violation of the truce.[98] This cannot have been something to which the French were happy to agree, so he must have insisted on it, which shows he was by no means endeavoring to minimize his ties to Henry VI in preparation for turning his coat. Essentially the same offers he ultimately did accept in 1435 were already on the table as far back as August 1429,[99] but Philip did not accept them then. Instead, he actually stepped up his commitment to the Anglo-Burgundian alliance until he could no longer do so without disastrous consequences for his own interests, and even then continued at least passive adherence to the Treaty of Troyes.

96 Plancher et al., *Histoire générale et particuliere de Bourgogne*, pièce justificative no. LCCV, pp. lcxxxv–lcxxxvi; Stevenson, *Letters and Papers*, II, pt. 1, pp. 156–81. His ambassadors made this point to Henry VI's council in November 1430 and April 1431, but it was not mere "flights of diplomatic hyperbole"; the same logic was reflected in an internal memorandum to Philip by one of his principal counselors in 1436, noting that in war many garrisons were needed, that maintaining them required great expenses, that "wherever war is waged and the countryside is destroyed and plundered by friend and foe alike and the populace is restless, little or no money can be raised," and that the ducal domains "which are mortgaged, sold or saddled with debts," could not raise the needed funds. Vaughan, *Philip the Good*, pp. 102–3.
97 It was such a truce, not (as Vaughan, *Philip the Good*, p. 26, suggests) a separate peace, that the Burgundian ambassadors to England hinted at as the result if the promised English financial support was not delivered. See Plancher et al., *Histoire générale et particuliere de Bourgogne*, pièce justificative no. LXXV, p. lxxxvj. For the truce and its revision, ibid., pièce justificative nos. LXXIX and CX.
98 Plancher et al., *Histoire générale et particuliere de Bourgogne*, pièce justificative no. XCI, p. cviij.
99 Ibid., pièce justificative no. LXX.

The end of the alliance

Since Burgundy had a broad truce with Charles between 1431 and 1435, the French were not really in a position to push him out of alliance with the English in that period. They also did not make any major new offers to lure him over to their side in those years. This is perhaps why historians have tended to think he was already ready or nearly ready to switch sides well before he did. But that leaves unanswered the question of why he did not indeed make a separate peace in 1431, instead of a truce which specifically allowed him to provide 500 men-at-arms to assist Bedford. What was different in 1435?

The main answer seems to be the breakdown of the personal relationship between the two dukes, beginning with the death of Anne of Burgundy, duchess of Bedford, in November 1432.[100] Philip, before 1432, was already being pressed by his subjects and counselors to reconcile with Charles VII. But his personal and familial bonds with Anne and Bedford worked against that, especially after Bedford made Anne (and through Anne, Philip) the heir of his extensive French lands in 1429. Anne's death took both of those bonding factors out of the equation.[101] It also had an important indirect effect on the undermining of the alliance. Quite soon after Anne's passing, Bedford married Jacquetta of Luxembourg, daughter of the count of St. Pol. Bedford's reasons were probably more personal than political,[102] but Philip took the marriage as a slap in the face. It was a matter on which he should have been consulted for two reasons, even aside from being the brother of Bedford's late wife: first, because he was the leading peer of Lancastrian France, and Bedford's marriage had major political and diplomatic implications; and second, because Jacquetta was the daughter of one of Philip's vassals and should not have been allowed to marry anyone without his consent. If he

---

100 Doubtless the turn of the military tide against England also contributed to his decision, but it cannot have been a large factor, since that tide was flowing more against the Lancastrians in 1429–1430, when he *increased* his commitment to them, than between 1432 and the final Anglo-Burgundian breach in 1435.

101 I agree with Armstrong, "La Double Monarchie," p. 369, that "the alliance would perhaps have survived" had Anne not died young.

102 Williams thinks that Bedford's "main motive for remarrying was the belief that union with the House of Luxembourg would be the best means of strengthening the English position in France" at a time when "it was painfully clear to Bedford that the Anglo-Burgundian alliance was in the process of dissolution." *My Lord of Bedford*, p. 223. But the House of Luxembourg, of whom Louis was by far the most important member at this stage, was already firmly bound to the success of the Lancastrian dynasty, on which his own position depended, and while there were certainly signs of stress in the Anglo-Burgundian alliance, it was at this stage far from obvious that it was doomed, and if acting for reasons of state, Bedford would have sought a marriage that would help rebuild the bond with Burgundy, not one that would threaten to break it.

had been asked permission, moreover, he probably would not have given it. Jacquetta's uncle Louis of Luxembourg, the bishop of Thérouanne and chancellor of Lancastrian France, had been a thorn in Philip's side at least since 1427. Under Luxembourg's chancellorship, Philip had faced increasing difficulties with the *Parlement* (the high court) in Paris, which repeatedly interfered with his control over his French territories.[103] After Anne's death, Bedford's health went downhill, and he relied increasingly on the chancellor. Following his marriage to Jacquetta, the regent seemed to a contemporary Parisian to be leaving the governance of the realm to Louis.[104] One major reason for Philip to maintain the alliance was to retain a strong voice and privileged position in the political matters decided in Paris. If the man who undermined him there was not only to be given increasing authority, but even to be brought into Bedford's close family by marriage, what did that say about the future of Burgundy's relations with the Lancastrian crown?

Just weeks after Bedford's second wedding, his uncle, Cardinal Beaufort, made a strong effort to soothe Burgundy's hurt feelings and restore his relationship with Bedford. The two dukes came to St. Omer for a conference, but their relationship had so soured that a point of diplomatic etiquette that would surely have been resolved or at least side-stepped if Anne had still been alive was allowed to prevent any progress towards reconciliation. Bedford, as regent of France, thought that Duke Philip should recognize his superiority by coming to see him; Philip, who viewed himself as the regent's peer within his own territories (including St. Omer) thought both should meet at the appointed place. Neither budged; there was no meeting. Before this, Bedford had always stepped up to repair the Anglo-Burgundian alliance when it frayed, but not this time.[105]

Nonetheless, Philip still felt that he needed English support against the dauphinists, because he could not trust the latter to be faithful to their

---

103 Armstrong, "La Double Monarchie," pp. 359–62, 370–71 (quotation 362). Already in 1430–1431 Philip had also begun to meet rebuffs in his economic diplomacy with England; the matters under discussion were not under Bedford's control, but Philip seems also to have felt that the Anglo-Burgundian alliance was not helping him as it should on that front either. John H. Munro, "An Economic Aspect of the Collapse of the Anglo-Burgundian Alliance, 1428–1442," *The English Historical Review*, 85 (1970), pp. 232, 237–38.

104 Williams, *My Lord of Bedford*, p. 223; Bourgeois de Paris, *Journal* , ed. A. Tuetey (Paris, 1881), pp. 295, 296 ("laissoit du tout regenter"). By early 1434, in Paris "there was no news of the regent, and no one ruled but the bishop of Thérouanne, chancellor of France," who was hated by the people because of his opposition to peace. Ibid., p. 298.

105 Williams, *My Lord of Bedford*, p. 224.

promises.[106] Then in late June 1433, just a month after the non-meeting at St. Omer, a palace coup eliminated Charles VII's chief minister, Philip's enemy George de la Trémoille. Among those most influential with the king thereafter were Philip's brothers-in-law Arthur de Richemont and Charles of Bourbon.[107] With this change, but not before, the transfer of allegiance of Duke Philip from the Lancastrian to the Valois dynasty, and the complete rupture of the Anglo-Burgundian alliance, became close to inevitable. The Treaty of Arras, negotiated while Bedford lay dying in Rouen, followed in 1435.[108]

Conclusion

What, then, are the lessons for modern strategists in the variable success and the ultimate failure of the Anglo-Burgudian alliance during the Hundred Years War? Based on the analysis above, one can highlight three. First, it is crucial to appreciate the motivations of allies, which is the first step towards ensuring that the coalition's grand strategy can meet their needs sufficiently to maintain the alignment of interests of the partners. Allies' concerns must be appreciated in culturally sensitive ways, and with due regard to personal relationships, rather than being reduced to general considerations of *Realpolitik*. What matters most to them might not be what we would expect, or what would be our main interest if we were in their shoes. Second, that mutual action can strengthen the bonds between allies, and that this binding together is as much about being willing to trust a partner and to *receive* aid gracefully as it is about being willing to *give* aid. Third, that since the strength of an alliance will inevitably, during extended wars, have its ups and downs, and since shared success can strengthen alliances both by its own effects and by promising ultimate victory and its rewards, when a favorable military situation coincides with a period of strong attachment between allies, that is the time to vigorously press combined operations.

---

106 Du Fresne de Beaucourt, *Histoire*, pp. 415–16, 456–57; Warner, "The Anglo-French Dual Monarchy," pp. 112–14.
107 Mark Warner considers that "it was this change of regime which would be the principal factor in the reconciliation between Charles VII and Duke Philip." "The Anglo-French Dual Monarchy," p. 114; see also M. G. A. Vale, *Charles VII* (Berkeley, CA, 1974), p. 72.
108 On the negotiations leading to the treaty, see Dickinson, *Congress of Arras*.

10 The Franco-American alliance during the War for Independence

Mark Grimsley

When British Lieutenant General Charles Cornwallis surrendered his army at Yorktown, Virginia, on 19 October 1781, he feigned illness and instructed his second-in-command, Brigadier General Charles O'Hara, to represent him at the humiliating surrender ceremony. O'Hara initially intended to offer his sword, not to General George Washington, commanding the American forces, but rather to Lieutenant General Jean-Baptiste Donatien de Vimeur, Comte de Rochambeau, who led the smaller French contingent. A French staff officer had to intervene and point O'Hara toward Washington, identifying him as "the commander-in-chief of our army."[1] Although the British general could well have intended his gesture as a deliberate snub to Washington, it also accurately reflected British perceptions about who had really beaten them: not the rag tag American rebels, but rather the French monarchy, which had for years sustained those rebels through lavish financial, naval, and military support. And indeed, the 1778 alliance between the powerful kingdom of France and the infant American republic had played an important, perhaps even decisive, role in Great Britain's defeat and the securing of American independence.

In some respects, it had been an unlikely partnership. The American colonists had, after all, engaged in no fewer than four major wars against the French during the century preceding the American Revolution. Although drawn into these conflicts by the foreign policy of their mother country, from an American point of view the goal increasingly became the elimination of French power from North America, particularly the Ohio Country. The outcome of the French and Indian War (Seven Years War) in 1763 achieved this outcome.[2]

---

1 Richard M. Ketchum, *Victory at Yorktown: The Campaign That Won the Revolution* (New York, 2004), p. 251.
2 The best overview of these conflicts remains Howard H. Peckham, *The Colonial Wars, 1689–1762* (Chicago, 1965). On the climactic French and Indian War, the standard account is Fred Anderson, *Crucible of War: The Seven Years' War and the Fate of Empire in British North America, 1754–1766* (New York, 2000).

A deep antagonism between the overwhelmingly Protestant American colonists and the overwhelmingly Catholic French had also characterized the wars with France in North America. The conflicts were tinged with the air of religious crusades, with the American clergy frequently exhorting their congregations (and the members of the provincial armies) to take up the task of ejecting the "Papists" from North America.[3] Then too, the irony of a republic that had declared independence from, and denounced the inherent tyranny of, a constitutional monarchy forming an alliance with the most powerful absolute monarchy on the European continent was almost too obvious to require mention. The alliance therefore represented the triumph of *realpolitik* over historical, religious, and ideological considerations.

From an American perspective, the guiding force behind their interest in French assistance was obvious. The colonists needed all the help they could get in fending off the efforts of the British, one of the most powerful nations in the world, to crush their rebellion. French motives for assisting the Americans were more complex. Some historians have put forth a "revenge theory," under the supposition that the French essentially wanted payback for their humiliating loss of Canada in the Seven Years War. But French thinking was in fact based not on anger but upon a careful, cold-blooded analysis of balance of power politics on the European continent. The key analyst was the French foreign minister, Charles Gravier, the Comte de Vergennes, a canny student of balance-of-power politics. Vergennes had in fact foreseen the probability of an American revolution as early as the 1750s, while still an ambassador to the Ottoman Empire. Typically, he had based his assessment on purely geopolitical considerations. If France lost Canada, he predicted, "England will soon repent of having removed the only check that could keep her colonies in awe. They will stand no longer in need of her protection. She will call on them to contribute towards supporting the burdens they have helped bring on her, and they will answer by striking off all dependence."[4] A man of strong views who could express them with equal strength, Vergennes wielded great influence on King Louis XVI, a

---

3 According to Francis G. Cogliano, New Englanders considered the French and Indian War to be an "anti-papal crusade." See his *No King, No Popery: Anti-Catholicism in Revolutionary New England* (Westport, CT, 1995), p. 15. But although the antipathy of Protestant America toward Catholic France undoubtedly existed, it can be exaggerated. Alan Heimert thinks anti-Catholic sentiment was knee-jerk and shallow rather than deep and thus never posed a significant impediment to a Franco-American alliance. See his *Religion and the American Mind: From the Great Awakening to the Revolution* (Cambridge, MA, 1966).

4 Quoted in Ketchum, *Victory at Yorktown*, p. 15.

youthful and inexperienced monarch, just 21 at the war's outbreak, who had sat on the throne for barely a year.

Geopolitical considerations also animated Vergennes's interest in supporting the American revolutionaries. Diplomatic historian Jonathan Dull offers a good summary of his probable line of thought. In 1772 Austria, Prussia, and Russia had between them partitioned much of Poland, a development that alarmed Vergennes because it indicated a *de facto* concert of these great Central and Eastern European powers. This, in turn, meant that France could no longer secure any of them as an ally, which effectively left the country alone on the continent. However, only Britain and France had the financial resources to make the other powers truly dangerous. In Vergennes's mind, therefore, the French had to humble the British enough to prevent British financial aid to Austria, Prussia and Russia. Perhaps France might even get British cooperation to restrain or even discourage any future aggressiveness on their part. As Dull observes:

The question was how to obtain it. The British looked on France with contempt; it seemed that only through a reduction of their power could they be brought to deal with France as an equal. The American rebellion presented France with just that opportunity to weaken the power of Britain ... The American war was not for Vergennes a war of revenge; it was a preventative war fought to avert future catastrophe by rearranging the balance of power.[5]

In effect, what Vergennes had in mind was the geopolitical equivalent of a bank shot in billiards, with intervention in North America intended primarily to influence the strategic situation in Europe.[6]

France undertook to supply this support rather early in the conflict. This runs counter to a still common belief, found in many American history textbooks, that one can trace the origins of the alliance to the US victory by General Horatio Gates over General John Burgoyne's army at Saratoga in October 1777. This triumph resulted in the wholesale capitulation of one of Britain's field armies and the capture of some 6,000 British and Hessian prisoners.[7] The argument runs that a victory of such magnitude convinced

---

5 Jonathan Dull, "France and the American Revolution Seen as Tragedy," in Ronald Hoffman and Peter J. Albert (eds.), *Diplomacy and Revolution: The Franco-American Alliance of 1778* (Charlottesville, VA, 1981), p. 84.

6 For a somewhat contrasting interpretation, see Orville T. Murphy, *Charles Gravier, Comte de Vergennes: French Diplomacy in the Age of Revolution, 1719–1787* (Albany, NY, 1982). Murphy argues that "Vergennes deliberately provoked a war with England... to recover for Louis XVI a role in European affairs which the French king had presumably lost in 1763... [H]e saw England as a formidable obstacle to Louis XVI's becoming the arbiter of Europe." (p. 257) Thus, according to Murphy, Vergennes was principally concerned with Britain itself, not the great powers of Central and Eastern Europe.

7 Richard M. Ketchum, *Saratoga: Turning Point of America's Revolutionary War* (New York, 1997), p. 437.

the Court of Louis XVI that the American cause stood a good chance of success and only at this point did the French leap into the conflict.[8]

In fact, the French government had involved itself in the American cause well before the battle of Saratoga, albeit covertly. Its intervention initially took the form of a project to funnel arms, ammunition, and other military equipment to American rebels. The impetus of the project came from an unlikely source. In large measure it stemmed from the fertile imagination of French playwright Pierre-Augustin Caron de Beaumarchais, who in 1775 had proposed to the Court of Versailles that a mechanism should be put in place to secretly aid the rebels. Insisting that the Americans had 78,000 men under arms (a wild exaggeration but one he evidently believed), Beaumarchais assured Vergennes "that such a nation must be invincible."[9] Vergennes was initially cautious. But when news of the March 1776 British evacuation of Boston reached Europe, Vergennes decided to pledge a million *livres* (about $4 million in current dollars) to the project, and on 1 May, the king signed a check for that amount. The Spanish government, whose ruling house, like that of France, was Bourbon and which also viewed Britain as a long-standing rival, matched the sum with an equivalent contribution.

Although enthusiastic about aid to the American rebels, Vergennes prudently insisted that it must be clandestine in nature. "In the eyes of the English and American governments, the operation must assume the aspect of a speculation by an individual," he instructed Beaumarchais. The playwright activist would operate "at his own risk." He would not "demand money by the Americans because they have none, but you will demand payment from the produce of their soil."[10] An energetic man, Beaumarchais soon collected 3 million *livres* from all sources, including private investors, and embarked on this undertaking.

Beaumarchais funneled the funds through Roderigue Hortalez and Company, a supposedly private Portuguese trading company established and administered by Beaumarchais, which in turn purchased military equipment at heavily discounted prices and shipped it to the rebels in North America. Although mostly obsolescent (some of the artillery dated from the seventeenth century), the weaponry was a welcome addition to the American arsenal.[11] Indeed, by one estimate, when the

8 This claim is also made in the best account of the Saratoga campaign. See ibid., p. xi.
9 Quoted in Murphy, *Charles Gravier, Comte de Vergennes*, p. 233.
10 Quoted in Harlow Giles Unger, *Improbable Patriot: The Secret History of Monsieur de Beaumarchais, the French Playwright Who Saved the American Revolution* (Lebanon, NH, 2011), p. 112.
11 Brian N. Morton, *Beaumarchais and the American Revolution* (Lanham, MD, 2003), pp. 17–52; Unger, *Improbable Patriot*, pp. 97–117.

Americans fought the Saratoga campaign, fully 90 percent of its arms and ammunitions came from French sources.[12] The magnitude of this pre-Saratoga clandestine aid has convinced many diplomatic historians of the American Revolution that by 1778 a military alliance was almost inevitable, even in the absence of a major American victory over the British. French and American interests had converged so greatly that the seeds of an alliance were already firmly sown.[13]

The Americans, of course, had taken active steps of their own to secure European financial and military aid. In November 1775 the Second Continental Congress created a Committee of Secret Correspondence, a sort of informal foreign office. In March 1776 it tasked Connecticut businessman Silas Deane with instructions to go to Paris and make efforts not only to secure arms but also to explore the possibility of an alliance. At that time the colonists were officially fighting to obtain con-cessions from the British government, not to achieve outright independ-ence. But a movement toward independence was well underway, and one argument used by its advocates was an insistence that such a decla-ration was necessary to secure financial and military support from for-eign powers. Richard Henry Lee, an influential Virginia delegate to the Continental Congress and a major voice for independence, argued, "It is not choice then, but necessity, that calls for Independence, as the only means by which [a] foreign Alliance can be obtained."[14] And indeed, soon after Lee presented Congress with Virginia's resolution on inde-pendence, Congress established not only a committee to draw up the famous Declaration of Independence but also one to prepare treaties to be proposed to foreign powers.

Deane, meanwhile, was already in transit to Europe. Arriving in Paris in early July, he presented himself to the court of Louis XVI and quickly won a sympathetic hearing from Vergennes, who in turn introduced him to Beaumarchais. Nothing if not ambitious, Deane not only solicited French aid and broached the subject of an anti-British alliance; he also suggested a French invasion of two British allies, the kingdom of Portugal

---

12 Claude Van Tyne, "French Aid before the Alliance of 1778," *American Historical Review*, 31(1) (October 1925), pp. 37–40.

13 For a recent argument that discounts the importance of Saratoga in the creation of the Franco-American alliance, see Chris Tudda, "'A Messiah that Will Never Come': A New Look at Saratoga, Independence, and Revolutionary War Diplomacy," *Diplomatic History*, 32(5) (November 2008), pp. 779–810. The diplomatic historians who have endorsed or rejected the significance of Saratoga are conveniently summarized on p. 780, n. 3.

14 Quoted in Alexander DeConde, "The French Alliance in Historical Speculation," in Ronald Hoffman and Peter J. Albert (eds.), *Diplomacy and Revolution: The Franco-American Alliance of 1778* (Charlottesville, VA, 1981), p. 3.

and the principality of Hanover. Vergennes brushed off this rather fantastic proposal. Still, although Deane did not succeed in achieving a French alliance – Vergennes was not yet ready to take this irretrievable step – it was through Deane's influence that a further clandestine flow of French aid, in addition to that supplied by Beaumarchais, began to make its way to the United States. Deane also gained the services of a number of European soldiers of fortune, including Marie-Joseph Paul Yves Roch Gilbert du Motier de La Fayette, the Marquis de Lafayette. Lafayette would arrive in the United States in June 1777, fight under Washington's command, and become a significant advocate of French aid for the American cause.[15]

In September 1776, Congress dispatched Arthur Lee and Benjamin Franklin to join Deane as co-commissioners. Deane served with them only briefly: alleged financial indiscretions, coupled with his profligate recruitment of numerous foreign officers, most of them mediocrities, excited the indignation of Congress, which soon recalled him and replaced him with John Adams. Adams initially undertook to negotiate only a non-military treaty with France, based on a "Model Treaty" devised by a Congressional committee (and officially accepted by Congress on 24 September 1776) as a template for all foreign relations. The treaty had three main components: free access to ports, the freedom of neutrals to trade non-contraband goods with the United States, and agreement upon a list of items to be deemed contraband.[16]

This was as far as Adams wanted to go. Earlier he had written, "I am not for soliciting any political connection, or military assistance, or indeed naval, from France. I want nothing but commerce, a mere marine treaty with them."[17] Adams deprecated a special relationship with one country in favor of the establishment of commercial ties with several nations, on the theory that economic interdependence would best serve American interests. Adams was not alone in wanting to keep the United States from becoming too interlocked in French affairs. Other influential Americans shared his view that a military alliance would, in the phrase of diplomatic historian Alexander DeConde, "tie the United States to French policy like a tail to a kite," with potentially mischievous results.[18] And indeed, Congress initially instructed the commission *not* to seek a military alliance with France, but rather to solicit additional military aid,

15 Jonathan R. Dull, *A Diplomatic History of the American Revolution* (New Haven, CT, 1985), pp. 51–52, 63–64.
16 Howard Jones, *Crucible of Power: A History of American Foreign Relations to 1913* (Wilmington, DE, 2002), pp. 7–8.
17 Quoted in DeConde, "The French Alliance in Historical Speculation," p. 5.
18 Ibid., p. 13.

secure most favored nation trade status with France, and reassure any Spanish delegates to the French court that the United States harbored no designs upon Spanish holdings in North America.

From Vergennes's perspective, however, a merely commercial treaty was never in the cards. The British government would surely reject the validity of *any* treaty with the United States, since this would entail recognizing the independence of the United States, something the British absolutely could not accept. Thus, any power that signed an agreement based upon the "Model Treaty" would automatically place itself on a collision course with Britain. Vergennes understood this even if the American commissioners did not. However, Vergennes did not immediately press for a military alliance. Instead he maintained a somewhat tentative posture, partly because news from America indicated that Washington's Continental Army had suffered several reversals at the hands of the British, but primarily because a major French naval build-up was underway. He did not want to act against the British until it had reached fruition. Nonetheless, he fully endorsed clandestine military aid and looked favorably upon a trade treaty with the United States. With those measures, Vergennes placed France on the road to an alliance even before he was willing to explore that possibility openly.

News of the Saratoga victory, which reached Paris in early December 1777, placed negotiations on a fast track. The result was the signing of two treaties between France and the United States: a Treaty of Amity and Commerce based upon the Model Treaty; and a defensive Treaty of Alliance, both of them signed at the palace of Versailles on 6 February, 1778.[19] The two treaties were in effect like the blades of a pair of scissors. The Treaty of Amity and Commerce would effectively challenge the British to dispute its provisions for free trade between the United States and France. British action would then trigger the military alliance. As the treaty's preamble made clear, it would come into effect whenever "Great Britain in Resentment of that connection and of the good correspondence which is the object of the said Treaty [of Amity and Commerce], should break the Peace with France, either by direct

19 "Treaty of Alliance between the United States of America and His Most Christian Majesty," in Richard Peters (ed.), *Treaties between the United States and Foreign Nations, from the Declaration of the Independence of the United States to 1845* (Boston, 1867), pp. 6–11; and "Treaty of Amity and Commerce between the United States of America and His Most Christian Majesty," ibid., pp. 7–31. Cited hereafter as "Treaty of Alliance" and "Treaty of Amity and Commerce," respectively. (In both cases, the text is printed in both English and French.) The text of both treaties is also available at numerous sites on the Internet. All citations, however, are to the Peters edition. The text of the military alliance, though not that of the Treaty of Amity and Commerce, may also be found in Dull, *A Diplomatic History of the American Revolution*, appendix 1, pp. 165–69.

hostilities, or by hindring her commerce and navigation, in a manner contrary to the Rights of Nations, and the Peace subsisting between the two Crowns."[20]

The Treaty of Alliance had thirteen articles. The first four stipulated the fundamental terms of the alliance: if war broke out between France and Britain, the United States and France would make common cause with one another; that the "essential and direct End of the present defensive alliance is to maintain effectually the liberty, Sovereignty, and independance absolute and unlimited of the said united States, as well in Matters of Gouvernement as of commerce;" that each party would exert itself to the fullest; and that if either party planned an operation requiring the concurrence of the other, it would first seek and obtain that concurrence before embarking upon the operation.

Articles 5 through 9 addressed the terms and conditions of the eventual peace treaties with England. An important feature was the repudiation by France of any intention to expand its position in North America coupled with agreement that France could seize and hold any British possessions in the Gulf of Mexico. The other was that there would be no separate peace between the United States and Britain or between France and Britain. In Article 10, the United States and France agreed "to invite or admit other Powers who may have received injuries from England to make common cause with them, and to accede to the present alliance." This ostensibly general invitation was directed primarily toward the kingdom of Spain, which entered the war in April 1779, but in December 1780 the Dutch accepted it as well. Article 11 involved a pledge to honor the land claims of both nations forever in the future, with the King of France in particular making "guarantees on his part to the united states, their liberty, Sovereignty, and Independence absolute, and unlimited, as well in Matters of Government as commerce and also their Possessions, and the additions or conquests that their Confederation may obtain during the war, from any of the Dominions now or heretofore possessed by Great Britain in North America." Article 12 underscored that the provisions of the treaty would be triggered by British hostilities, while Article 13 exhorted both sides to achieve the ratification of the treaty within six months.[21]

It did not take long for the British to bring the alliance into effect. On 13 March the French ambassador informed the British government that France had officially recognized the United States as an independent nation. Four days later, the British government declared war on France. However, both powers initially refrained from actually coming to blows,

20 "Treaty of Alliance," p. 6.
21 Ibid., pp. 6–11.

for each hoped to place upon the other the burden of firing first, which would attract an unfavorable reaction from the other great powers of Europe and, in the case of Britain, allow its ally, the Netherlands, to remain out of the conflict, since the alliance required Dutch intervention only in case Britain were actually attacked. Hostilities did not finally commence until 17 June, when British warships fired upon two French frigates in the Channel.

The resulting contest took place in three primary cockpits: European waters, especially the Channel and the western Mediterranean Sea; the Caribbean Basin; and North America. Throughout the conflict, French naval strength comprised a constant latent threat to Britain itself. Several naval engagements occurred in waters around Britain and France, and although the British won their share of these encounters, they achieved nothing like a decisive victory. In cooperation with Spain, France persistently, though unsuccessfully, besieged Gibraltar from 1779 to 1783. It did, however, capture Minorca from its British defenders in February 1782. British and French forces also clashed in faraway India, although in this subsidiary theater the British nearly always retained the upper hand.

Most extensive were the battles in the Caribbean Basin. It is common for Americans to suppose that the American colonies were, from a British perspective, the most important prize, but in fact the British regarded their wealth-generating possessions in the West Indies as of greater importance. It was in this theater that the French, in combination with the Spanish, posed the most serious threat. France's navy predominated in the West Indies, capturing Dominica, Grenada, Saint Vincent, Montserrat, Tobago, St. Kitts, and the Turks and Caicos (although France lost St. Lucia at the war's outset). Jamaica dodged a bullet when a projected Franco-Spanish invasion was aborted after the Battle of the Saintes in April 1782.[22]

Initial French strategy, however, was for a strike directly at New York City, the center of British military power in North America. A dozen ships of the line, under Charles Hector, Comte d'Estaing, were to sail from Toulon to North America. D'Estaing had instructions to attack the British fleet under Admiral Lord Richard Howe, which, though based in New York, was actually dispersed along the American coast. The hope was that d'Estaing could defeat Howe's scattered ships in detail and then blockade New York into capitulation.[23] Meanwhile, the main French fleet at Brest would deter Britain from sending reinforcements to American

22 Jonathan Dull, *The French Navy and American Independence: A Study of Arms and Diplomacy, 1774–1787* (Princeton, NJ, 1975), pp. 123–24, 160–61, 238, 283.
23 Ibid., pp. 109–12.

waters, while French ground units would move toward the English Channel coast, so as to give the impression of a possible invasion.

D'Estaing managed to get safely across the Atlantic, but once in American waters he proved singularly ineffective. First, he failed to locate, much less annihilate, Howe's fleet. Second, in early July he discovered that his deep draft ships of the line drew too much water to pass Sandy Hook at the entrance to New York's Lower Bay, thus rendering operations against New York impossible. This bitterly disappointed the Americans, who urgently desired d'Estaing to blockade New York harbor and seemed not quite to grasp the practical obstacle to achieving this. The first inter-action between French and Americans thus proved a disappointment.[24]

So did the second. After his failure at New York, d'Estaing next sailed to Newport, Rhode Island, the deep-water port nearest New York. Newport was then held by a British garrison estimated at 4,000–6,000 men. American and French planners organized a joint attempt to seize the town, an initiative that held great symbolic importance, since it would be the first test of Franco-American military cooperation. D'Estaing had 4,000 troops aboard his transports. General John Sullivan led the American por-tion of the effort and worked diligently to assemble the needed American troops. With only a few continental troops at his disposal, Sullivan found himself forced to gather militia in order to create a viable strike force. That effort took longer than expected and d'Estaing grew restive, fearing that a British naval force would materialize to relieve the Newport garrison.

He proved correct. On 10 August, the eve of the planned assault on Newport, d'Estaing put to sea to confront Howe's fleet. The battle that ensued was inconclusive, but a hurricane separated the fleets and heav-ily damaged the French fleet. When on 20 August d'Estaing returned to Point Judith, near Newport, he told Sullivan, who at last was poised to attack, that five out of his eleven ships of the line needed repairs and consequently he would sail to Boston. The Americans, supported by Lafayette, urged that the assault proceed as planned, arguing that d'Estaing could refit at Newport after its capture. D'Estaing refused, a prudent decision but one that infuriated the Americans. It particularly galled Sullivan that d'Estaing's abandonment of the attack led 5,000 of his militia to abandon the field and go home. Sullivan's remaining force had to abandon the siege and retreat to Providence.[25]

Having repaired his warships, d'Estaing abandoned North America altogether and set sail for the West Indies. The following year, however, he

24 Ibid., p. 123; Christopher Ward, *The War of the Revolution*, ed. by John Alden, 2 vols. (New York, 1952), vol. II, p. 588.
25 Ward, *The War of the Revolution*, II, pp. 587–93.

essayed a second joint operation, this time sailing to Savannah, Georgia, which British forces had captured in December 1778. In response to American requests for assistance, d'Estaing had discontinued operations in the Caribbean and sailed northward. A few vessels preceded him, arriving in Charleston, South Carolina, on 3 September 1779. French emissaries began discussions with American General Benjamin Lincoln concerning how to recapture Savannah, and Lincoln soon marched upon the town with 2,000 men.

A week later, d'Estaing arrived off Savannah. On 12 September the French began landing some 3,600 troops near the city, investing it four days later. Lincoln arrived soon thereafter. Initially d'Estaing insisted upon a bombardment of the town, hoping that this would suffice to compel a British surrender, and off-loaded enough naval cannon to serve the purpose. This effort failed, however, and d'Estaing, against the advice of most of his subordinates, decided on an infantry assault. Launched on 9 October, the brief but fierce attack ended in a complete, costly defeat. D'Estaing and Lincoln abandoned the siege on 17 October, and the French admiral returned to the Caribbean. For yet a third time he had disappointed his American allies.[26]

Thus ended French efforts in North America for the time being, though scarcely French efforts overall. In April 1779 Spain entered the war, a happy development for France but at the same time somewhat problematic. On the one hand, the entry of the second Bourbon monarchy added 58 ships of the line to the allied fleet, for a combined total of 121 ships of the line. This armada vastly overmatched the ninety ships of the line in the Royal Navy, placing Britain at a naval disadvantage from which it never recovered.[27] On the other hand, the price of the alliance with Spain not only obliged France to assist in achieving Spain's objectives (mainly the recovery of Gibraltar and Minorca), but also to plan a joint invasion of England, which Spain hoped would end the war before Britain could attack Spain's vulnerable colonial empire in the New World. This, of course, undercut Vergennes's objective of a limited war designed to trim but not eliminate Britain's great power status. "Even if I could destroy England," he had declared, "I would abstain from doing so, as

---

26 Franklin Benjamin Hough, *The Siege of Savannah: By the Combined American and French Forces, Under the Command of Gen. Lincoln and the Count D'Estaing, in the Autumn of 1779* (Albany, NY, 1866); John S. Pancake, *The Destructive War: The British Campaign in the Carolinas, 1780–1782* (Tuscaloosa, AL, 1985), pp. 34–35; Dan Morrill, *Southern Campaigns of the American Revolution* (Baltimore: Nautical & Aviation Press, 1993), pp. 60–64; Dull, *The French Navy and American Independence*, pp. 161–62.

27 Dull, *A Diplomatic History of the Revolution*, p. 110, has a useful table that tracks the shifts in the naval balance of power between 1778 and 1782.

from the wildest folly."[28] But Vergennes had little choice but to go along with Spanish plans. In summer 1779 the Bourbon monarchies organized an armada of one hundred warships to sail to England, accompanied by 30,000 troops, to invade the Isle of Wight and possibly seize Portsmouth on the mainland. On 15 August 1779, the fleet made landfall at Lizard Point, then turned east into the Channel. Outnumbered, the British lost control of the Channel. Fortunately for them, a storm blew up, scattering the Franco-Spanish fleet. The expedition came to nothing.[29]

As much as anything else, this setback made Vergennes turn his gaze more firmly toward North America and begin the planning that led to the creation of an expeditionary force code-named the Expédition Particulière. On 2 February 1780, the King's Council formally approved the plan for the Expédition, placing the land force under Lieutenant General Jean-Baptiste Donatien de Vimeur, Comte de Rochambeau, and the naval support under Admiral Charles-Henri-Louis d'Arsac, Chevalier de Ternay. The Council's basic thinking was to mount a military effort large enough to do some good, but not so big as to risk American paranoia concerning France's ultimate intentions. Given that knowledge of the military situation in North America was at best imperfect and quite probably out of date, the Council ventured no definite objective for the expedition. Conceivably it might land anywhere between Newport and Savannah, although within a few days the Council expressed a slight preference in favor of Newport. Ternay was immediately ordered to Brest, there to assemble a convoy sufficient to transport 4,000 troops.[30]

The expedition made its way across the Atlantic in a flotilla consisting of forty-six transports and their escorting warships. On 4 July 1780, the flotilla made landfall off Cape Henry, a blunt bend of land delineating the southern side of the entrance to the Chesapeake Bay. Six thousand seamen manned the vessels. On board the transports were the 4,000 infantry under the command of the 55-year-old Rochambeau. A veteran of the two major conflicts that had wracked Europe in the mid-eighteenth century – the bloody War of the Austrian Succession (1740–48) and the even bloodier Seven Years War (1756–1763) – Rochambeau was a reliable soldier, solid if not gifted.[31]

28 Quoted in Piers Mackesy, *The War for America, 1775–1783* (Cambridge, MA, 1964), p. 190.
29 Dull, *The French Navy and American Independence*, pp. 150–59.
30 Lee Kennett, *The French Forces in America, 1780–1783* (Westport, CT, 1977), p. 12.
31 The beginning of the Seven Years War is sometimes dated 1754 because of the battles between the French and British in North America that preceded hostilities in Europe. The best biography of Rochambeau in English is Arnold Whitridge, *Rochambeau* (New York, 1965).

The flotilla had sailed to Cape Henry not because of its intrinsic importance but because Ternay and Rochambeau had only a vague idea of what the military situation would be when they reached American shores. This was scarcely surprising. Three thousand miles of ocean separated the continent from North America. The time of transit – the flotilla's voyage from Brest had taken sixty-three days (in those days a fairly rapid crossing) – underscored the utter hopelessness of any European power having up-to-date intelligence about the situation in North America. Consequently, awaiting them by prearrangement was one Major Galvan, a French officer serving as liaison with General George Washington, commander of the Continental Army.

Galvan informed Ternay and Rochambeau that Washington desired them to continue up the Atlantic coast to Sandy Hook, New Jersey, at the entrance to Lower New York Bay. Ternay replied that he would do no such thing. Intuiting that his flotilla was being pursued by British warships, the admiral refused to sail to a place with no safe harbor, for the British held New York City strongly. Rochambeau nonetheless preferred to comply with Washington's wishes. Plainly New York was the place where his expedition could do the most good. But Ternay insisted, and Rochambeau had to accept, that the flotilla would make instead for Newport, Rhode Island, which, as d'Estaing had already discovered, was the port closest to New York that offered a safe anchorage. According to last reports, Newport was held by American forces (the British having voluntarily abandoned it).[32]

The transit to Newport required six days. The French, as they neared the objective, turned their spyglasses toward the town. To universal relief, they discerned the white-and-gold banner of their native land, a prearranged signal that the Americans indeed controlled the town. The following day, Tuesday, 11 July Rochambeau disembarked his 4,000 infantry, fanning out through the town into the surrounding countryside, where they could begin the work of constructing a fortified camp. This seemingly modest development, the addition of a mere 4,000 men to a conflict that involved much larger forces, actually had enormous political, strategic, and symbolic implications. It meant that the government of Louis XVI had for the first time committed a significant force to the contest on land in North America. It meant that the British now had to include this new force in their calculations. It meant that the beleaguered Americans had tangible proof that the French would support their struggle for independence directly, which aside from d'Estaing's abortive

---

32 Kennett, *The French Forces in America, 1780–1783*, p. 32.

stabs had previously focused on the West Indies. None of this was lost on General Sir Henry Clinton, commander in chief of all British forces in North America. The French occupation of Newport, he fumed, "has revived a dying cause. Washington has raised an army, and the whole continent seems alive upon it."[33]

Clinton's bitter outburst underscored the psychological importance of the alliance. But the alliance dynamics can be teased out of the flotilla's operations once it reached American shores, for these operations highlight its loose-jointed nature. From first to last there was never any unified command, even among the French forces, to say nothing of the French and American forces combined. Thus, Ternay could sail to Newport with both warships and transports despite the fact that Rochambeau, the landing of whose Expédition Particulière was the entire point of the mission, preferred a different destination. Once ashore and entrenched, however, the Expédition was inert for months, as it was too weak to mount independent operations. The best that could be said of it was that, as a force in being, it became a factor the British had to take into account in devising their next moves.

Plainly the Expédition could achieve significant results only in combination with the American army under Washington, then hovering outside New York. But nearly two months passed before Washington, Rochambeau, and Ternay met to discuss future operations. The conference, which took place at Hartford, Connecticut from 20 to 22 September, gave the three senior commanders their first chance to size one another up. By all accounts, each liked what he saw. The French were particularly impressed. Typical was the comment of an officer in attendance who wrote that Washington's "dignified address, his simplicity of manners, and mild gravity surpassed our expectation and won every heart."[34] Admiration for Washington, however, did not translate into support for his obvious desire that action be taken in the near future. The trio discussed and discarded a number of possible ventures, ultimately rejecting any immediate offensive. Rochambeau in particular felt that the campaign season for the year was over.

Hoping to accomplish at least something before winter, Washington then proposed that the French fleet might sail to Boston while Rochambeau's force joined his own army outside New York. Rochambeau parried with a number of objections. Washington quietly but persistently pursued the

---

33 Sir Henry Clinton, *The American Rebellion; Sir Henry Clinton's Narrative of his Campaigns, 1775–1782, with an Appendix of Original Documents* (New Haven, CT, 1954), p. 208.
34 Quoted in James Thomas Flexner, *George Washington in the American Revolution* (Boston, 1967), p. 371.

matter. Finally Rochambeau flatly informed Washington that he had instructions of which the American commander was unaware. In order to prevent potential friction between French and American troops, and to provide maximum insurance against desertion, Rochambeau's orders required him, until a battle actually loomed, to keep his army united and on an island.[35]

For Washington this news was obviously a disappointment. Still, the conference did at least yield a joint memorandum indicating agreement on four points. First, New York should be the chief object of operations. Its capture would deal the British a blow from which they likely would not recover. Second, this objective would require more troops: at least 24,000 and possibly as many as 30,000, most of which would have to be assembled by the Americans. Given Washington's chronic difficulty in raising troops, coupled with the certainty that many men would leave the army when their enlistments expired at the end of the year, this represented a very tall order.[36] But third, *both* parties would seek reinforcements. Ternay would try to secure more ships. Rochambeau would request 10,000 additional infantry, and he had hopes of the arrival of a "second division" to augment the force already at Newport. Finally, unless reinforced, the Expédition would stay on the defensive.[37]

For eight months the French and American forces in Newport and around New York remained quiescent. In the interim, however, operations in the southern theater, to which the British had transferred most of their offensive efforts, became increasingly serious. On 12 May 1780, a British army under General Charles Cornwallis captured the important port of Charleston, South Carolina. On 16 August Cornwallis routed an American force at the battle of Camden and by year's end had overrun the entire state. The American army in South Carolina, however, was at least strong enough to stand a reasonable chance of preventing further British successes. This status did not obtain in Virginia, where British forces under the turncoat General Benedict Arnold were ravaging that state almost with impunity.

---

35 Flexner, *George Washington in the American Revolution*, pp. 371–73. A somewhat more up-tempo account of the Hartford Conference is in Douglas Southall Freeman, *George Washington: A Biography*, 7 vols. (New York, 1948–1957), V: *Victory with the Help of France*, pp. 192–95. The same is true of Whitfield, *Rochambeau*, pp. 100–103.

36 Washington's difficulties in recruiting and retaining an adequate force can scarcely be overestimated. See Don Higginbotham, *Military Attitudes, Policies, and Practices, 1763–1789* (New York, 1971), pp. 389–419; James Kirby Martin and Mark Edward Lender, *A Respectable Army: The Military Origins of the Republic, 1763–1789* (Arlington, IL, 1982), pp. 87–93, 158–64; Charles Patrick Neimeyer, *America Goes to War: A Social History of the Continental Army* (New York, 1996), pp. 130–65.

37 Kennett, *The French Forces in America, 1780–1783*, pp. 59–60.

To retrieve the situation, Washington and his French counterparts organized a two-pronged expedition. Washington would send 1,200 troops to Virginia. Meanwhile a French squadron under Rear Admiral Charles René Dominique Sochet, Chevalier Destouches would ferry another 1,200 French infantry to the beleaguered state. Destouches sailed from Newport on 8 March with eight ships of the line and three frigates carrying the troops. However, Admiral Mariot Arbuthnot, who commanded the Royal Navy's North American station, pursued Destouches and overtook him off the entrance to the Chesapeake on 16 March. Although both sides suffered significant damage, the British defeated Destouches and forced him to return to Newport.[38] Lafayette thus faced a larger force under Arnold, now reinforced by 2,600 British troops under Major General William Phillips, who arrived at Portsmouth on 26 March. Even when reinforced by Steuben with recently recruited Continentals and untrained militia, Lafayette could do little against these superior forces. The British continued to ravage Virginia practically at will. Affairs became even worse when Cornwallis transferred his own army to Virginia, arriving in Petersburg on 20 May.[39]

Such was the situation that faced the allies in the spring of 1781. In Newport the main development during the interim was Ternay's sudden death from typhus in December 1780.[40] His replacement, Commodore Jacques-Melchior Saint-Laurent, Comte de Barras, did not arrive from France until 10 May 1781. When he did, he came with orders not to assist Washington, but rather to operate in the waters off Newfoundland. Accompanying Barras was the son of Rochambeau, who informed his father that the King's Council had decided that in the 1781 campaign the main French effort would be made in the West Indies. Six hundred replacements for the Expédition were en route, but beyond that Rochambeau would receive no reinforcements. The only bright note in this dismal picture was a letter from the French minister of the navy, Charles Eugène Gabriel de La Croix de Castries, Marquis de Castries, informing Rochambeau that a fleet under Admiral François Joseph Paul de Grasse, then sailing for the West Indies, would be available for operations in North American waters beginning in July or August, "to act with you in any enterprise you may wish to undertake."[41]

38 David Russell, *The American Revolution in the Southern Colonies* (Jefferson, NC, 2000), p. 254; Whitfield, *Rochambeau*, pp. 117–22.
39 Ward, *The War of the Revolution*, II, pp. 870–75.
40 "Arsac de Ternay, Charles-Henri-Louis D'," *Dictionary of Canadian Biography Online* (www.biographi.ca/en/bio.php?id_nbr=1737).
41 Quoted in Whitfield, *Rochambeau*, p. 133. See also Kennett, *The French Forces in America, 1780–1783*, pp. 104–5.

De Grasse's availability was actually a sort of consolation prize for the Council's refusal to reinforce Rochambeau. The Council based its reasoning not only upon the cost of sending reinforcements but also doubts as to their utility: they still might still be insufficient to enhance the limited strategic options available to Rochambeau. Most interestingly, the Council withheld the reinforcements for the same reason it had kept the original Expédition of modest size: concern over the risk of American paranoia if a large French force were to land on American soil. But although troops might be resented, the Council confidently assumed that financial aid would not. It therefore offered 6 million *livres'* worth of military supplies and credit to subsidize Washington's army. The Council also instructed Rochambeau that henceforth he would operate under Washington's direct command.[42]

After digesting this news, Rochambeau requested a conference with Washington. Washington agreed, and on 21–23 May, the two commanders met at Wethersfield, Connecticut, just south of Hartford. Accompanying Washington were his chief of artillery Henry Knox and Frenchman Louis Lebègue Duportail, the chief engineer in the Continental Army, who served as interpreter. Rochambeau brought with him Major General François Jean de Beauvoir, Marquis de Chastellux, who had for some time been serving as the principal liaison officer between the French commander in chief and Washington. Barras could not come. For one thing, he anticipated the arrival of a French convoy of fifteen ships conveying military supplies and the promised 600 infantry replacements. The frigate *Concorde* had already brought almost a million *livres* in specie. The convoy was bringing still more. In addition, Barras had to worry about a flotilla under Arbuthnot, which had appeared off Block Island about 10 miles south of Newport.

Neither commander spoke frankly. Since the *Concorde* had accompanied de Grasse's convoy partway, Rochambeau knew its size, twenty-six ships of the line, and the approximate time it would reach the West Indies. He also knew that de Grasse was authorized to operate in North American waters. But instructions from the French minister of war, Philippe Henri, Marquis de Ségur, forbade him to give the Americans any details for fear that the secret would get out. Rochambeau therefore spoke of naval reinforcements from the West Indies as a "speculation,"

42 Dull, *The French Navy and American Independence*, p. 239. It is worth noting that Rochambeau's instructions placed him under Washington's *personal* command. They did not contemplate a situation in which Washington might leave the main body of the Continental Army and place another general in temporary command. This had the practical effect of preventing Washington from undertaking any independent operations with a portion of his force.

though of course he knew it to be a certainty.[43] Washington was himself less than candid about the numbers he would have for a summer campaign – understandably since he didn't know himself. (At the moment, he had barely 3,500 troops on hand.)[44] And although Chastellux had in fact given him the specifics regarding de Grasse's instructions – he was a great admirer of Washington and had written to Washington twice on the subject, in confidence – Washington had to pretend that the prospect of de Grasse's assistance was merely speculative, too.[45]

Although Washington and Rochambeau discussed a southern campaign, each feared that a march south in summer would decimate both armies, either through heat (most of Washington's troops were New Englanders) or desertion. Therefore they selected New York as their objective. Washington particularly favored this option. An American privateer had intercepted a dispatch to Clinton from Lord George Germain, Secretary of State for America, directing him to intensify operations in the South. Washington thus reasoned that New York's garrison must either be sufficiently reduced that it would fall outright, or else that Clinton would have to recall troops from Virginia, "the doing which will enfeeble their Southern operations, and in either case be productive of capital advantages." Moreover, a shift to New York would actually bring the allied forces closer "to the Southward as circumstances and a Naval superiority might render more necessary & eligable [sic]."[46]

Rochambeau was skeptical of the New York scheme. For one thing, he doubted that allied forces were strong enough to capture the city. For another, he knew that naval support would be unavailable, since d'Estaing's misfortune had already demonstrated that French ships of the line drew too much water to get over the Sandy Hook bar. But the fact that he could contribute to the campaign no more than the four regiments already at Newport sharply reduced his negotiating power. In the end he bowed to Washington's wishes.[47] Or at least he seemed to do so. In fact, scarcely had the conference ended than Rochambeau sent two letters via frigate to de Grasse in Saint Domingue, outlining the bleak military situation, particularly in Virginia, and intimating that de Grasse ought to make the Chesapeake his objective should he exercise his option to leave the West Indies for American waters. Rochambeau

---

43 Kennett, *The French Forces in America*, p. 105.
44 Ward, *The War of the Revolution*, II, p. 879.
45 Kennett, *The French Forces in America*, p. 105.
46 Entry for 22 May 1781, *George Washington's Diaries: An Abridgment*, ed. Dorothy Twohig (Charlottesville, VA, 1999), pp. 207–8.
47 Whitfield, *Rochambeau*, pp. 137–38.

made this recommendation explicit in a subsequent letter to Anne-César, Chevalier de la Luzerne, *de facto* French ambassador to the Continental Congress.[48]

In the meantime, however, his Expédition marched to link up with Washington's army. By 8 July it had arrived at Philipsburg, New York, a small hamlet on the shore of the Hudson River about 30 miles north of Manhattan. Washington had concentrated his army a few miles away at White Plains. For the next six weeks, Rochambeau and Washington studied their options for an attack on New York, briefly considering a *coup de main* to storm the upper part of Manhattan Island and conducting a reconnaissance in force to determine whether the British garrison could in fact be overrun. Presently they discovered, just as Rochambeau had foreseen, that nothing short of a major siege could compel the fall of New York, and without major naval support this was simply impossible.[49]

On 20 June the frigate *Concorde* sailed for Saint Domingue carrying reports from Barras, Rochambeau, and Luzerne regarding the situation in the Colonies. The reports recapped the situation in Virginia and the operations near New York City, but Luzerne laid emphasis on the crisis in Virginia, writing to de Grasse: "It is you alone who can deliver the invaded states from the crisis which is so alarming that it appears to me there is no time to lose and that for their existence it is necessary to do all you can by your instructions."[50] Rochambeau concurred on the advisability of sailing to the Chesapeake. This is what de Grasse decided to do. He conveyed his intention to Barras and Rochambeau on 28 July; the *Concorde* sailed back to Newport, arriving on 11 August.

Crucial to de Grasse's decision was the cooperative spirit of the Spanish governor of Louisiana and Cuba, Bernardo de Gálvez y Madrid, and his key administrator, Francisco de Saavedra de Sangronis. Rather than balking at a movement that could expose Spanish colonies to British attack, Gálvez endorsed the venture. He concurred with Saavedra's assessment of Cornwallis's vulnerability: "[We] could not waste the most decisive opportunity of the whole war."[51] Saavedra himself did de Grasse an astonishing service upon learning that de Grasse urgently required 1.2 million *livres* in order to pay Rochambeau's troops. With insufficient government funds on hand, Saavedra turned to the citizens of Havana,

48 Ibid., p. 138, 140.
49 Ibid., pp. 154–58; Kennett, The *French Forces in America*, pp. 117, 119–20; Ketcham, *Yorktown*, pp. 146–48.
50 Quoted in Dull, *The French Navy and American Independence*, p. 243.
51 Quoted in Thomas E. Chávez, *Spain and the Independence of the United States: An Intrinsic Gift* (Albuquerque, NM, 2002), p. 198.

who in a single day collected the equivalent of 5 million *livres*, which more than covered the French admiral's need.[52]

Word of de Grasse's chosen destination reached Rochambeau and Washington on 14 August. Washington probably had somewhat mixed feelings about the news. On the one hand, the prospect of at last receiving major naval assistance must surely have been exciting. On the other, he still regarded New York as the true center of British military power in North America. But the French had, in effect, forced his hand, and Washington immediately gave instructions that set in motion 2,500 Continentals and Rochambeau's 4,000 troops toward Yorktown, Virginia, where Cornwallis had encamped his army while awaiting naval resupply.

The march southward began on 19 August. Washington executed an effective deception plan that blinded Clinton to the allies' real intention until the armies reached Philadelphia on 2 September, by which time Clinton could do nothing by land. But Barras's departure from Newport on 27 August with his full force (eight ships of the line, four frigates, and eighteen transports carrying the priceless siege train) had already convinced British admirals Sir Thomas Graves and Sir Samuel Hood that Barras must be sailing to join de Grasse, whom they deduced must himself be making for the Chesapeake. Thus they crowded sail for the Chesapeake with their entire fleet, nineteen ships of the line. Unfortunately for the British, when they reached the Virginia capes on 5 September, they found de Grasse already there.

Sailing from Cuba, de Grasse had reached the Chesapeake on 30 August, and his ships immediately captured two British frigates on patrol there. With 29 ships of the line, the French flotilla easily outgunned the British fleet. Although the ensuing Battle of the Capes was in purely tactical terms only a marginal French victory, strategically it was a triumph. Cornwallis now found himself cut off from the sea. Barras slipped into the bay with his own force, left his ships of the line to buttress de Grasse's fleet, and sailed with his lighter vessels (plus the two captured British frigates) to Head of Elk, Maryland, where his ships took aboard a portion of the French contingent, and thence to Baltimore and Annapolis, where most of the allied ground troops embarked. The Franco-American army arrived at Williamsburg, Virginia, on 14 September. Augmented by forces already in the area, especially those under Lafayette, Washington had 11,000 troops at his disposal. De Grasse had brought 3,000 troops from the West Indies. These gave Rochambeau a total of 7,000 troops, for an allied total of 18,000, augmented by the siege train brought by Barras. A

---

52 Ibid., pp. 200–203.

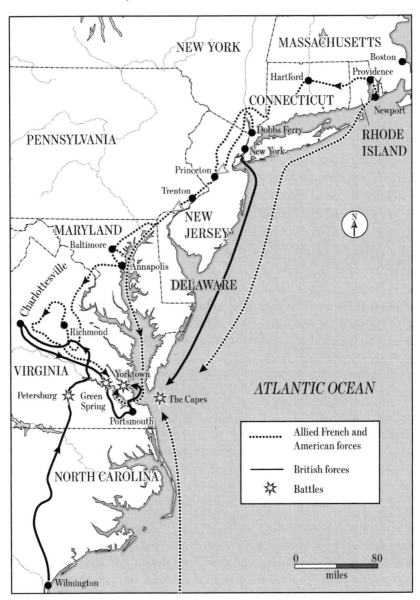

Map 10.1   The Yorktown campaign, 1781

formal siege of Yorktown soon began. With only 9,750 troops, Cornwallis faced certain doom and surrendered his forces on 19 October.[53]

Ironically, although Cornwallis had too few troops to stave off defeat, he had far too many for that defeat to be perceived as anything short of total disaster. When news of Yorktown reached Britain on 25 November, Lord North, the prime minister, exclaimed, "Oh God! It is all over."[54] And yet it was not over. For although the British government promptly decided to suspend offensive operations in North America, it continued to wage full-scale war against France, Spain, and the Netherlands. A major naval victory in the West Indies on 9–12 April 1782 (the Battle of the Saintes) further emboldened the British. The United States, obligated by treaty to remain at war as long as France remained at war, regarded the situation with increasing dismay. The French discovered that American gratitude was short-lived. The French financial, military, and naval support which had sustained the cause for most of the conflict, and had been absolutely indispensable to the triumph at Yorktown, soon counted for less in the minds of many Americans than the fact that the continued war between France and Britain now comprised the main obstacle between British recognition of their independence and a final peace settlement.

Slowly but surely, and perhaps inevitably, the four American peace commissioners in Paris began quiet negotiations with their British counterparts. This was a violation not only of the treaty of alliance with France, which forbade a separate peace, but also the commissioners' express instructions from Congress, which required them to consult with Vergennes on all matters and even to defer to his recommendations. But the British offered terms that were so generous as to be nearly irresistible. These included not only recognition of American independence but also American land claims from the Appalachians to the Mississippi River; navigation rights on the Mississippi; and even fishing rights off Newfoundland. In turn, the British required only the vaguest assurances (virtually ignored, as it turned out) that the Loyalist population in the United States would be treated well. "[T]he English buy peace more than they make it," noted a bemused Vergennes. "Their concessions, in fact as much as to the boundaries as to the fisheries and loyalists, exceed all that I should have thought possible."[55] By the end of 1782, the Americans had concluded a preliminary peace treaty with Britain and, of course,

53 The troop estimates are drawn from Mark M. Boatner III, *Encyclopedia of the American Revolution* (New York, 1966), p. 1248.
54 Quoted in Mackesy, *The War for America*, p. 435.
55 Quoted in William C. Stinchcombe, *The American Revolution and the French Alliance* (Syracuse, NY, 1969), pp. 196.

had long since become useless as allies to the French. Not only had they no desire to continue to fight an adversary who had lost all desire to fight them, but they had no capacity, even had they possessed the will, to assist France in its ongoing operations in the West Indies. A consummate realist in diplomatic affairs, Vergennes wasted no energy lamenting this fact. By early 1783, for reasons largely unrelated to the American posture, the French had decided it was time for peace. In March France and Britain terminated hostilities. On 3 September 1783 the British signed peace treaties with France and Spain at Versailles. That same day, in Paris, they concluded a formal treaty of peace with the United States.[56]

Although highly dramatic, the Franco-American triumph at Yorktown paints a misleading picture of how the Franco-American alliance operated. Plainly, direct cooperation between French and American forces was much the exception, not the rule. As we have seen, such cooperation as did exist was limited to the abortive stabs at Newport (1778) and Savannah (1779). Not until the summer of 1781, more than three years after signing the Treaty of Alliance, did the French really undertake major offensive operations in North America. For the most part, they conducted operations elsewhere.

Indeed, the victory at Yorktown was almost in the nature of a happy accident. Leaving aside the folly of Cornwallis in placing himself in such a vulnerable position, or the fact that de Grasse reached the Virginia capes ahead of the British fleet and managed to block it from entering the Chesapeake Bay, the vital cooperation of the allies was itself highly contingent. If de Grasse had not received instructions that gave him permission to operate temporarily in American waters; if he had chosen to remain in the West Indies; if Luzerne had not urged him so forcefully to proceed to the Chesapeake rather than New York; if Spanish governor Gálvez had protested rather than endorsed the departure of de Grasse from Caribbean waters; if Barras had not ignored his instructions to operate off Newfoundland in favor of lending support to the effort against Cornwallis; in short, if any of these contingencies had not occurred, the Yorktown victory would not have occurred.

The very terms of the alliance made a victory such as Yorktown unlikely, for they plainly contemplated the waging of a parallel war: the Americans fighting the British in North America while the French fought them in Europe, the West Indies and (to a lesser extent) India. Article 4 of the treaty made clear that cooperation would be the exception, not the norm. It laid out the procedure that would obtain "*in case* either of the [allies]

---

56 Hostilities between Britain and the Netherlands did not formally end until 20 May 1784.

should form any particular Enterprise in which the concurrence of the other may be desired"[57] (emphasis supplied).

Predictably, the parallel war model created conditions in which coordination between the French and Americans was a rather loose-jointed, ramshackle affair. At the political level such coordination as did exist took the form of consultations between the Continental Congress and the two French ministers plenipotentiary to the United States, Conrad Alexandre Gérard de Rayneval, who served from May 1778 through September 1779, and his successor, Anne-César, Chevalier de la Luzerne, who served from then until 1784. Both Gérard and Luzerne quickly discerned that the Americans were less than candid about both their military strength and their will to continue the struggle.

Gérard, for instance, initially believed Vergennes's impression that the United States possessed 50,000 first-line troops, an impression created largely by the Americans themselves.

But as Gérard researched US capability intensely he came to a different conclusion, estimating the Americans in fact had no more than 15,000 troops.[58] In September 1778 he gave an equally bleak assessment of American will, warning that an evident "general cooling of all martial ardor among the people, the nonchalance with which some states furnish their military contingents, the miserly spirit could lead to the Americans seeking a separate peace without considering the dangers involved nor of the long-term advantages to be drawn from a more enlightened policy."[59] When Luzerne replaced Gérard his reports to Vergennes were in much the same vein.

In response, Vergennes issued express instructions to Luzerne that he must advise Congress that Britain was making preparations to continue the war "with vigor;" and that while France and Spain would do their part to maintain control of seas and create a diversion in Europe and the West Indies, it was "absolutely necessary, that the United States, on their part, should make efforts proportionable to the greatness of the object for which they are contending."[60]

Congress, however, continued its dissembling. When Luzerne asked what force the United States could field in 1780, Congress replied that it could field 25,000 effectives (exclusive of commissioned officers),

57 "Treaty of Alliance," p. 8.
58 Orville T. Murphy, "The View from Versailles: Charles Gravier Comte de Vergennes' Perceptions of the American Revolution," in Hoffman and Albert (eds.), *Diplomacy and Revolution*, pp. 134–35.
59 Quoted ibid., p. 136.
60 Quoted ibid., p. 141.

adding that with militia reinforcements and naval support, the United States could carry on an offensive war.[61] This turned out to be complete nonsense, as Luzerne discovered when Washington candidly informed him that his army, already much reduced by the expiration of terms of service, "will be so much more diminished in the course of a month or two from the same cause, as scarcely to suffice for the exigence of the service, and to afford just cause for uneasiness should the enemy by actuated by a spirit of enterprise before we receive the reinforcements intended for the next campaign."[62]

This briefly led Luzerne to the opposite conclusion: that rather than exaggerating their strength the Americans were deliberately poor-mouthing in order to secure an even higher level of French support. Luzerne learned differently, however, when he actually visited Washington's winter encampments at Morristown, New Jersey: "I was afraid that there was a concerted plan to exaggerate the suffering of the army, but on my way through camp I myself saw the constant recurrence of its necessities, the Generals being often unable to show themselves to the men without demands made upon them for bread and clothes."[63]

Congress, for its part, harbored elements that remained as wary of French assurances as the French became of American assurances, albeit with far less reason. Much of this tracked back simply to a residual antipathy left over from the decades of colonial wars between the English colonies and France. Indeed, this may actually have delayed the advent of major French intervention on land, because when French agents first proposed it they discovered that "the most enlightened members of Congress, though convinced of the necessity of the aid, have dared not propose it for fear of alarming the people by the introduction of a foreign army."[64] When, in May 1780, Congress informed the states of the imminent arrival of French troops, it was therefore careful to point out that the French "would be directed by American counsels and rendered subservient to their interest."[65]

Coordination of operations was almost as loose-jointed as coordination of strategy. This was true even of French coordination between the King's Council and its military subordinates, partly because the vast expanse of the Atlantic rendered futile any attempt to give more than general guidelines and partly because the Council never appointed a commander in

---

61 Quoted ibid.
62 Quoted ibid., pp. 141–42.
63 Quoted ibid., p. 144.
64 Quoted in Kennett, *The French Forces in America, 1780–1783*, p. 39.
65 Quoted ibid., p. 40.

chief with full charge of French operations in the Western Hemisphere. During the early phase of the alliance, d'Estaing functioned essentially in that role, since initially his was the only fleet in the Western Hemisphere, and it carried a contingent of ground troops under his direct command. But as we have seen, the Expédition Particulière had no commander with authority over both military and naval elements. Instead the norm was for commanders to "cooperate" with one another. Rochambeau cooperated with Ternay and subsequently Barras; both cooperated with de Grasse. Initially Rochambeau had instructions to cooperate with Washington; only in 1781 were these altered to place him under Washington's direct command. The drawbacks of this arrangement puts one in mind of a pungent comment made by one Union general to another during the American Civil War: "General Meade, I'll be God d – d if I'll cooperate with Sedgwick or anybody else. You are the commander of this army and can give your orders and I will obey them; or you can put Sedgwick in command and he can give the orders and I will obey them; or you can put me in command and I will give the orders and Sedgwick will obey them; but I'll be God d – d if I'll *cooperate* with General Sedgwick or anybody else."[66]

In the absence of clear chains of command, personal relationships, always important among senior leadership, were absolutely critical. The bureaucratic trait that sociologist Max Weber would eventually dub "routinization" did not yet exist in the eighteenth century. Consequently, the military alliance depended to an outsized degree upon the personal character of the French and American flag rank officers and the strength of the relationships they forged with one another. At sea the key figures included d'Estaing, Ternay, Barras, and de Grasse. On land they included Washington and Rochambeau. Chance and probability thus played a greater than usual role in the mechanics of the military alliance. The fact that, by and large, the senior leadership committed itself to harmony in the face of numerous potential pitfalls was absolutely crucial to the success of the alliance.

Still, there were sticky moments. When in 1778 d'Estaing abandoned the effort to capture Newport and instead sailed for Boston, Sullivan's officers roundly lambasted the French. The extent of their outrage filled Lafayette with a rage of his own. Although like the Americans he had urged d'Estaing to follow through with the Newport operation, he was galled to hear "the name of France spoken without respect, and perhaps

---

66 Quoted in Mark Grimsley, *And Keep Moving On: The Virginia Campaign, May–June 1864* (Lincoln, NE, 2002), pp. 230–31.

with disdain, by a herd of Yankees from New England."[67] Learning that one of Sullivan's generals reportedly had extended his view of d'Estaing's timidity to apply to the French nation at large, Lafayette briefly considered fighting a duel with him. Sullivan, for his part, added fuel to the fire when, with breathtaking stupidity, he wrote and disseminated a daily order that charged France with abandoning the United States. Thinking better of this tirade, Sullivan soon tried to walk back the statement but could not. A rift between the allies loomed. But both Washington and, to his great credit, the maligned d'Estaing worked to repair relations. The crisis passed.[68]

Washington himself inadvertently generated potential friction when in March 1781 he penned a private letter expressing his displeasure with Destouches and his abortive expedition to Chesapeake Bay, attributing its failure to inexcusable delays on the part of Destouches. The letter was captured by Loyalists, who passed it along to Sir Henry Clinton, who made sure that it was published in Rivington's *Gazette*, the best-known Loyalist newspaper in New York. He made equally sure that a copy of the issue reached Rochambeau. Upon seeing the letter, Rochambeau was "deeply hurt," according to his biographer, and curtly asked Washington if it were genuine.[69] Washington conceded that it was, but somewhat abashed, said that he had written it on the basis of incomplete information and might have been mistaken in his assessment. Rochambeau could well have taken umbrage. This was, in effect, a gaffe not much different from Sullivan's earlier salvo against d'Estaing in particular and France in general. Instead Rochambeau, who understood the need to preserve a spirit of cooperation, dismissed it. His forbearance came a bit more easily because he was himself annoyed by Destouches' ineffectual efforts.

The parallel war paradigm carried risks that went beyond the distended system of coordination between French and Americans. It created conditions in which a triumph like that of Yorktown was never a concerted aim of the allies but rather a happy accident. Thus, if operational *success* in North America, not merely a Fabian survival, proved critical to American victory, the Franco-American alliance could well have been of limited utility. It may not have been possible for the American commissioners to have secured a French commitment to direct concerted military action in North America, but it would certainly have been advisable to try.

Still, even a completely parallel war would have been of enormous benefit to the American cause. It would not have altered the extent of

67 Quoted in Kennett, *The French Forces in America, 1780–1783*, p. 51.
68 Ibid., pp. 52–53.
69 Whitfield, *Rochambeau*, p. 123.

French financial and military aid to the United States. The former has been reckoned at about 1.3 billion livres ($13 billion in 2011 dollars). This was not only a substantial amount of money in itself, but it largely took the form of specie, which helped to shore up a Continental fiscal policy hampered by an inability to collect taxes directly – the Continental Congress depended instead upon irregular voluntary contributions from member states – and by an overreliance upon paper money that lost value practically the instant it emerged from the printing press. The steady flow of French arms, ammunition, and supplies to the United States also did much to sustain American troops in the field.

Simply by entering the war, the French indirectly made probable an American victory by convincing the British, even in the absence of a second disaster to rival Saratoga, that it was nearly impossible to devise a strategy that could force the revolutionaries to succumb. The British simply never had enough forces to occupy the colonies. With the exception of a few strongholds like New York, they passed through territory or occupied it temporarily, creating the expectation among the American population that, whether they liked the revolutionaries or not, sooner or later the revolutionaries would return to exact vengeance on citizens who had cooperated with the British.[70] (The failure of the British southern campaign strategy is a particularly salient case in point.) In this scenario, the French contribution consisted mainly of enabling the revolutionary cause to survive long enough for the British to alter their policy. And French operations in other theaters, particularly the Caribbean, played a significant role in forcing the British to re-evaluate their entire strategic position and weaken their efforts in North America to the point where victory was no longer attainable.

From an American perspective, the military alliance with France was clearly a worthwhile endeavor. No other assessment is even possible. Whether the alliance was worthwhile from a French perspective is much more debatable. In the view of diplomatic historian Jonathan Dull, the strategic calculations that led France to ally with the United States was underlain by three fallacies. First, the driving force behind the alliance, foreign minister Vergennes, underestimated the fragility of French government finances, although other counselors, most notably minister of the navy and controller-general Anne-Robert-Jacques Turgot, Baron de Laune, did not. Second, Vergennes assumed that the British government would weigh balance of power considerations as dispassionately as

---

70 John Shy, "The Military Conflict Considered as a Revolutionary War," in *A People Numerous and Armed: Reflections on the Military Struggle for American Independence* (Ann Arbor, MI, 1990), pp. 213–44.

he did, failing to recognize that, in a parliamentary system like Britain, public opinion mattered, that British opinion would not forgive France for its interference in the American revolt, and that in consequence the British government would have to take this opinion into account. Thus, if Vergennes thought he could eventually obtain British support as a counterweight for adventurism on the part of any of the eastern powers, he was very much mistaken. Third, Vergennes assumed that the loss of its North American colonies would weaken the British Empire. Although, to be sure, many Britons also thought this, it was in fact a dubious and ultimately mistaken assumption, since political independence did not mean that the United States would abandon Britain as a major trading partner.[71] However, all of these fallacies became evident only after the fact. At the time, support for the Americans seemed one of the most effective means by which France could protect its status in Europe.

Of these fallacies, the most fateful proved to be Vergennes's underestimation of the financial burden of a Franco-American alliance. Ultimately this burden proved dangerously expensive, both in terms of aid to the United States and in terms of the cost of military operations themselves. France's director-general of finance, Jacques Necker, understood as well as Turgot how tenuous was France's fiscal system and was therefore quite cautious about the advisability of engaging in an avoidable war with Britain. It is no accident that within six years of the treaty ending the War for Independence, Louis XVI found himself confronted with a fiscal crisis so serious that in order to confront it, he had to summon the Estates General, a move that directly triggered the French Revolution.

Even leaving aside its inadvertent contribution to the French Revolution, the Franco-American Alliance produced little tangible advantage for the French. It may have compelled Britain to relinquish the thirteen colonies, but it did not significantly disrupt Britain's military, maritime, or economic power. Indeed the chief trading partner of the British remained the United States. As for the eventual peace treaties, collectively known as the Peace of Paris (September 1783), wherein the United States achieved not only independence but also territories extending westward to the Mississippi River, France accepted an arrangement consisting of small mutual accommodations here and there which amounted to the *status quo antebellum*. France did not even acquire a geopolitical ally in the United States. The Americans may have

71 Dull, "France and the American Revolution Seen as Tragedy," pp. 85–89.

appreciated the help of France, but this did not translate into a warm relationship with the absolutist French monarchy.[72]

Thus, from a French perspective the alliance may have seemed like a rational calculation, and indeed it may have been *except* for the tenuous, and as events proved, fatal French fiscal position. But in fact, if the objective was the erosion of British power, courting a direct military confrontation with Britain was a problematic way to go about it. The Americans could contribute next to nothing to augmenting French power and eroding British hegemony, and as events would demonstrate, even the loss of its American colonies did not erode that hegemony. It would have been wiser to have continued to funnel money and supplies to the Americans clandestinely, by methods that may have irritated the British but stopped short of inaugurating war. If these efforts produced American independence, well and good. But if not, continued British control of the colonies would not have harmed the French geopolitical posture. From the French perspective, then, the Franco-American military alliance may well have been exactly what historian Jonathan Dull has maintained: "a tragedy."[73]

72 The advent of the French Revolution, surprisingly, made things even worse. Americans initially welcomed the revolution in its first, moderate phase. But as it became more radical, Americans became highly divided in their view of it. Adherents of the political philosophy of Thomas Jefferson tended to retain their sympathy with the revolution. Federalists, adherents of the philosophy of Alexander Hamilton, became alarmed by its seeming excesses, particularly the execution of Louis XVI and the Reign of Terror. This bred significant domestic divisions. More importantly, when Revolutionary France went to war with Britain (among other nations) it began to seize American merchant vessels on the high seas, leading to an undeclared naval war with the United States in 1794. At that point the alliance was, *de facto*, extinct. It was formally dissolved in 1800. And the alliance did nothing at all to convert Washington from the view that the correct foreign policy for the United States was to avoid entanglements with Europe.
73 Dull, "France and the American Revolution Seen as Tragedy," pp. 73–106.

11 The alliance that wasn't
Germany and Austria-Hungary in World War I

Marcus Jones

> One country may support another's cause, but will never take it so seriously as it takes its own. A moderately-sized force will be sent to its help; but if things go wrong the operation is pretty well written off, and one tries to withdraw at the smallest possible cost ... But even when both states are in earnest about making war upon the third, they do not always say, "we must treat this country as our common enemy and destroy it, or we shall be destroyed ourselves." Far from it: the affair is more often like a business deal.[1]

As a noted historian has pointed out, alliances result from "motives of self-interest, usually that of self-protection," however much their members may appeal to emotional, national, racial, or other bonds.[2] States enter into military alliances in order to pursue critical objectives and safeguard critical interests. Alliances may serve the defensive purpose of protecting the joint or individual interests of allied states against the encroachments of others, or the offensive purpose of directing the power of each member against a third or another coalition. The stipulations that bind allied states together may be either clear or vague depending on the degree of discretion each demands; at the very least, meaningful alliances elaborate the terms by which each is bound to fight on behalf of the other, in the sense of fulfilling the *casus foederis* and *casus belli* alike.

The ability of a country to work smoothly with alliance partners is basic to strategic effectiveness and yet another benchmark by which one can judge the competence of military organizations.[3] Ideally, alliances

---

1 Carl von Clausewitz, *On War*, ed. and trans. Michael Howard and Peter Paret (Princeton, NJ, 1976), ch. 6, p. 728.
2 Paul M. Kennedy, "Military Coalitions and Coalition Warfare over the Past Century," in Keith Neilson and Roy A. Prete (eds.), *Coalition Warfare: An Uneasy Accord* (Waterloo, 1983), p. 3.
3 The literature on the history and dynamic of alliances is extensive. See Glenn H. Snyder, *Alliance Politics* (Ithaca, 1997); a good short discussion of the logic of alliance politics is Glenn H. Snyder, "The Security Dilemma in Alliance Politics," *World Politics*, 4 (1984): 461–95; another, comparative perspective is offered in James D. Morrow, "Arms Versus Allies: Trade-Offs in the Search for Security," *International Organization*, 47 (1993): 207–33.

284

provide a framework for working through the practical problem of utilizing combined military power efficiently and effectively, a process that depends on a great deal more than mere formal alliance agreements. States must forge relationships between individuals and institutions based on realistic and shared assumptions about one another and the circumstances they face, particularly as those circumstances shift and evolve through time. It is in those latter terms above all that successful alliances in history are to be judged, and not simply whether the outcomes realized were consistent with the original intent of the alliance.

By this standard, historians have long judged the Dual Alliance – the defensively oriented alliance of 7 October 1879 between the newly formed German Empire and the multinational dual monarchy of Austria-Hungary – as an almost complete failure.[4] Yet, they have devoted much less attention to the Dual Alliance than its importance for the history of World War I would suggest is necessary. This is especially surprising in light of the unmanageably vast literature on the diplomatic and strategic events leading to the outbreak of the war itself, and the sensitivity of those events in most narratives to the strange internal history of the relationship between Germany and Austria-Hungary. To address that gap at least in part, this chapter will consider the grounds on which Germany and Austria-Hungary came together as allies and how the military aspects of the relationship changed between 1879 and 1914, leading to the decidedly dysfunctional relationship evident during World War I. As General August Cramon, who served as the German wartime representative to the Austro-Hungarian command from January 1915 to war's end, later recounted in two books and several articles, the German army was surprised at the poor performance of its ally because the German general staff knew little about the Austro-Hungarian army, or even much about Austria itself. Only during the war, he wrote, did the fundamental weaknesses of almost every aspect of the Austro-Hungarian military establishment become painfully obvious.[5] Why was this so? To what extent did the

---

4 The treaty of 7 October 1879 is reproduced in Ernst Rudolf Huber (ed.), *Dokumente zur deutschen Verfassungsgeschichte*, II: *Deutsche Verfassungsdokumente 1851–1900*, Document 309, 3rd rev. edn. (Stuttgart, 1986), pp. 494–95; although initially secret, Emperor Wilhelm I revealed its existence a month later to Tsar Alexander II. All iterations of the treaty before 1914 are found in Alfred Franzis Pribram, *The Secret Treaties of Austria-Hungary, 1879–1914*, English ed. Archibald Cary Coolidge, 2 vols. (Cambridge, 1920–1921).

5 A. von Cramon, *Unser österreich-ungarischer Bundesgenosse im Weltkrieg* (Berlin, 1920); A. von Cramon and P. Fleck, *Deutschlands Schicksalsbund mit Österreich-Ungarn* (Berlin, 1932); August von Cramon, "Von unseren Bundesgenossen," in W. Jost and F. Felger (eds.), *Was wir vom Weltkrieg nicht wissen* (Leipzig, 1929), pp. 428–39; August von Cramon, "Feldmarschall Graf Conrad von Hötzendorf und seine Stellung zu

military leaders of Germany and Austria-Hungary cooperate to frame a common approach to the problem of combined warfare? What prevented them from working together more successfully when World War I broke out? And how should historians judge the efficacy of their efforts for the outcome of the war?

More than any other factor, the Dual Alliance resulted from Otto von Bismarck's anticipation of the need for a closer German association with Austria-Hungary in the late 1860s.[6] Against the shortsightedness of the Prussian officer elite and the concerns of his monarch, in the wake of the victory at Königgrätz in 1866 he had argued strongly for the preservation of the Habsburg monarchy, which he viewed as indispensable to the stability of Central Europe and hence the security of the nascent German nation. Based on his experiences as a diplomat during the German Confederation of 1815–1866, Bismarck balanced carefully between cultivating a critical ally and tying Germany to Austro-Hungarian interests in Southeastern Europe, which he viewed as an enormous liability in relations with Russia.

In negotiations in the late 1870s with Julius Andrassy, the Austro-Hungarian foreign minister, Bismarck leaned heavily on a stated prejudice against involvement in the internal affairs of other states and specifically discounted German interests in the Balkans. His real motive was to leave

---

Deutschland," *Deutscher Offizier-Bund*, 15 (Berlin, 25 May 1927): 636–37; see also the outstanding article by Tim Hadley, "Military Diplomacy in the Dual Alliance: German Military Attaché Reporting from Vienna, 1906–1914," *War in History*, 17 (2010): 296 and n. 6. Hadley argues tantalizingly that the depth of German knowledge of its ally was actually considerable. When it appears, Hadley's dissertation on the full history of the military relationship between the allies promises to overturn the broad historiographical consensus represented here.

6 At present the most essential background study of the Dual Alliance is Jürgen Angelow, *Kalkül und Prestige: der Zweibund am Vorabend des Ersten Weltkrieges* (Cologne, 2000); others of note include Helmut Rumpler and Jan Paul Niederkorn (eds.), *Der 'Zweibund' 1879: das deutsch-österreichisch-ungarische Bündnis und die europäische Diplomatie: Historikergespräch, Österreich-Bundesrepublik Deutschland 1994* (Vienna, 1996); Lothar Höbelt, "Österreich-Ungarn und das Deutsche Reich als Zweibundpartner," in Heinrich Lutz and Helmut Rumpler (eds.), *Österreich und die deutsche Frage im 19. Und 20. Jahrhundert* (Vienna, 1982), pp. 256–81; Nicholas der Bagdasarian, *The Austro-German Rapprochement, 1870–1879: From the Battle of Sedan to the Dual Alliance* (Rutherford, 1976); F. R. Bridge, *From Sadowa to Sarajevo: The Foreign Policy of Austria-Hungary, 1866–1914* (London, 1972); and István Diószegi, *Die Aussenpolitik der Österreichisch-Ungarischen Monarchie, 1871–1877* (Budapest, 1985); not to be overlooked are the collected essays in Michael Gehler (ed.), *Ungleiche Partner? Österreich und Deutschland in ihrer gegenseitigen Wahrnehmung: Historische Analysen und Vergleiche aus dem 19. Und 20. Jahrhundert*, part IV, *Vom Zweibund zur Partnerschaft im Zeichen von Mitteleuropa: Österreich und Deutsches Reich 1879–1918* (Stuttgart, 1996), pp. 271–398; among the earliest treatments is Eduard Heller, *Das deutsch-österreichisch-ungarische Bündnis in Bismarcks Aussenpolitik* (Berlin, 1925).

himself as much discretion as possible to keep Austria-Hungary at arm's length should tempers with Russia flare. He was especially careful not to encourage Austrian policy in the Balkans with promises of military support, and worked initially to prevent meaningful contact between the countries' military establishments, which could not but constrain him and limit his options in future crises. As Bernhard von Bülow put it in his memoirs:

Bismarck always wants a free hand. He says himself that states and their leaders can only bind themselves, even by the most solemn agreement, for so long as the effects and repercussions of such an agreement do not conflict with the interests of their own country. Certainly, of all other alliances, Bismarck would prefer under terms of a mutual guarantee the status quo of both countries.[7]

As Bismarck saw it, an alliance with his southern neighbor served to uphold the strategic balance in a Europe with a strong Germany at its center. It would cement the "partially hegemonic" position of Germany on the continent – won through the annexation of Alsace-Lorraine in 1871 – and provide a hedge against the eternal hostility of the French. It would also redirect Austro-Hungarian influence from away from Western Europe, leaving Bismarck a freer hand to represent Central European interests as a block.[8] Finally and perhaps most importantly, an alliance allowed Germany to soothe Russian concerns about Austro-Hungarian threats to its interests in Southeastern Europe, removing any pretext for the Russians to seek support from the French and encircle the German Empire. One historian has described the strategy as "neutralizing the conflicting interests of the other great powers and redirecting the tensions on the whole from the core of Europe to the periphery."[9]

In those early days, Bismarck could count on a loose affiliation of the conservative European monarchies – Russia, Austria-Hungary, and Germany – to soothe tensions. To his own monarch, Bismarck was not above tugging at German heartstrings:

With Austria we have more in common than we have with Russia. Common German origins, historical memory, the German language, our interest in Hungary, contribute to making an alliance with Austria more popular and perhaps more enduring than an alliance with Russia. Only dynastic relations and especially the personal friendship of Emperor Alexander speak persuasively for a Russian

---

7 Bernhard von Bülow, *Memoirs of Prince von Bülow: Early Years and Diplomatic Service 1849–1897* (Boston, 1932), p. 393.
8 Konrad Canis, "Der Zweibund in der Bismarckschen Außenpolitik," in Helmut Rumpler und Jan Paul Niederkorn (eds.), *Der "Zweibund" 1879: das deutsch-österreichisch-ungarische Buündnis und die europäische Diplomatie* (1996), pp. 41–67.
9 Andreas Hillgruber, *Bismarcks Aussenpolitik* (Freiburg im Breisgau, 1972), p. 137.

alliance. It behooves us as an irrefutable requirement of Your Majesty's policy to tend more carefully than heretofore to our relations with Austria as this advantage of the Russian alliance becomes uncertain, let alone fades.[10]

Ultimately, one cannot discount the undeniable geographical facts that compelled Germany and Austria either to be allies or enemies after 1871. The countries shared the longest and least defensible frontier in Europe. Bismarck could afford to discount somewhat the strategic relationship with Austria-Hungary for the first decade of Germany's existence, but only because Germany faced no serious prospect at that time of a conflict with Russia. Should tensions with Russia arise, however, and with the growing threat in the 1880s of a Russian–French alliance, no German statesman could afford to leave Austria unattached and free to choose sides, potentially leaving the southern German frontier uncovered.[11] Likewise, Austro-Hungarian statesmen and officers recognized in the 1870s how difficult meeting any contingency would be without a German ally along the country's northwestern border.

During a meeting with Andrassy and Franz Joseph, Bismarck wrote Wilhelm from Vienna on 24 September 1879 emphasizing the Dual Alliance's usefulness in restraining the French and preventing a war between Germany and Russia.[12] He even suggested that Austria-Hungary was more reliably conservative than Russia, where he had come to fear the rise of an expansionist pan-Slavic ideology and an unstable social landscape. The ideological climate inside Russia had taken a turn for the worse after the Crimean War, which had revealed the erosion of its military power, and Bismarck grew increasingly skeptical over time of the radical revolutionary potential of the population.[13]

In its original formulation the Dual Alliance addressed two potential contingencies. The first was an attack on either Germany or Austria-Hungary by Russia or by a power supported by Russia. The second was a war in which Russia was not involved, in which case each party pledged benevolent neutrality. Initially, the uneven division of military labor between the two allies reflected their disparity of power.[14] At no point

---

10 Bismarck to Wilhelm I, Bad Gastein, 24 August 1879, in Johannes Lepsius et al., *Die Große Politik der Europäischen Kabinette 1871–1914. Sammlung der Diplomatischen Akten des Auswärtigen Amtes*, III: *Das Bismarckische Bündnissystem* (Berlin, 1922), pp. 16–20.
11 Eduard Heller, "Bismarcks Stellung zur Führung des Zweifronten-Kriegs," Archiv für Politik und Geschichte, 7 (1926): 677 ff.
12 Lepsius et al., *Die Große Politik*, III, pp. 39–43, 52–58, 76, 79–83, 93–94.
13 See the remarks of Bismarck to Wilhelm I, Bad Gastein, 5 and 7 September 1879, Lepsius et al., *Die Große Politik*, III, pp. 39–59.
14 On the specifically military aspects of the alliance, see Helmut Otto, "Zum strategisch-operativen Zusammenwirken des deutschen und österreich-ungarischen Generalstabes bei der Vorbereitung des ersten Weltkrieges," *Zeitschrift für Militärgeschichte*, 2 (1963);

was Austria-Hungary in a position to make demands of Germany, a fact that the Austrian military plenipotentiary in Berlin, Prince Liechtenstein, foreshadowed as early as 1880, arguing that the price of German military support against Russia must eventually result in "the loss of political autonomy for the imperial monarchy," and that Austria-Hungary would "be compelled to enter into [a] dependent relationship with Germany."[15]

To be sure, as long as Bismarck understood the alliance as serving the existing power balance in Europe, its military implications were secondary and the staff chiefs did little to explore them. Tragically for Germany, the structure of civil–military relations in the state did not encourage German officers to think about broader strategic issues, at least as long as Bismarck was in charge. What passed for strategic policy in Germany formally lay within the purview of the kaiser and was often handled by his federal chancellor, namely Bismarck. No institution bore formal responsibility for the ultimate role of military power in the pursuit of the national interest, to say nothing of the other instruments of national power. Indeed, no civilian or military agency, least of all the Reichstag, had any power to oversee or review strategic policy.

The Prussian general staff, which lacked authority over the German navy and had limited influence even over the rest of the Prussian army, was the only body able to plan for waging war with an ally. The military implications of the alliance, therefore, depended heavily on the personal relationship between the respective chiefs of staff, on military attachés, and on the visitations and interactions that occurred on maneuver.[16] Contact between the general staffs was often divorced from political considerations. In the German Empire, the chief of the general staff enjoyed the *Immediatrecht*, or direct access to the monarch, a privilege

see also his seminal synthesis of the problem of joint operational planning: Helmut Otto, *Schlieffen und der Generalstab: der preussisch-deutsche Generalstab unter der Leitung des Generals von Schlieffen 1891 bis 1905* (Berlin, 1966); more dated is Gerhard Seyfert, "Die militärischen Beziehungen und Vereinbarungen zwischen dem deutschen und dem österreichischen Generalstab vor und bei Beginn des Weltkrieges," PhD dissertation, Leipzig, 1934.

15 Bericht Obst Prinz Liechtenstein, 15 January 1880, Militärkanzlei Seiner Majestät, SR K. 60, Fasz.72, Nr.74 a; from Günther Kronenbitter, *"Krieg im Frieden:" die Führung der k.uk Armee und die Großmachtpolitik Österreich-Ungarns 1906–1914* (Munich, 2003), pp. 285–86.

16 Holger H. Herwig, "Asymmetrical Alliance: Austria-Hungary and Germany, 1891–1918," in Peter Dennis and Jeffrey Grey (eds.), *Entangling Alliances: Coalition Warfare in the Twentieth Century* (Canberra, 2005), p. 57; also Georg Graf Waldersee, "Über die Beziehungen des deutschen zum österreichisch-ungarischen Generalstabes vor dem Weltkrieg," *Berliner Monatshefte*, 8 (1930); and Johann Christoph Allmeyer-Beck, "Die Archive der k.u.k. Militärbevollmächtigten und Militär-Adjutants im Kriegsarchiv Wien. Ein Beitrag zur militärgeschichtlichen Quellenkunde," *Österreich und Europa. Festgabe für Hugo Hantsch zum 70. Geburtstag* (Graz, 1965).

enjoyed by few other officials and advisors, the great majority of whom were senior military officers.[17] Senior civilian political officials were in no position to reconcile military priorities with broader strategic or political concerns.

In the political house that Bismarck built, only the kaiser had that authority, and Wilhelm II, the Hohenzollern king of Prussia and emperor of the German Empire after 1890, showed himself temperamentally and intellectually incapable of fulfilling this crucial constitutional function.[18] Discussions and debates over important foreign policy issues – as during the Bosnian Crisis or the lead-up to war after 1912 – took place without practical regard for the operational capacities and limitations of the German military. By contrast, access to the monarch in Austria-Hungary was strongly constrained by civilian political influence. Diplomatic and political considerations weighed heavily on official thinking, as in 1911, when the chief of staff, Franz Conrad von Hötzendorf, was sidelined for a year after clashing with the foreign minister over policy toward Italy. But in Austria-Hungary – as in Germany – there was little civilian understanding of the operational details of military policy, which dangerously constrained the effectiveness of decision-making and made almost any proactive diplomacy risky. It was not merely the case that the process of strategic and military policy in both countries lacked democratic or popular legitimacy; rather, military policy was crafted in almost wholesale isolation from the strategic and diplomatic context that renders it a useful instrument of state.

Early discussions between the military staffs began in 1882, when disagreements between Germany and Russia over customs policies effectively ended hopes for strategic coordination among the three conservative monarchies.[19] The then-chief of the Austro-Hungarian general staff, Friedrich von Beck-Rzikowsky, met in August 1882 with the quartermaster-general of the Prussian army, Alfred von Waldersee, in Strobl and a month later in Breslau with Helmuth von Moltke the Elder, chief of the German general staff. Thereafter, staff chiefs often attended each other's annual maneuvers and formally exchanged representatives after 1890–1891.

---

17 On the conceptual background, see Carl Schmitt, "Der Zugang zum Machthaber. Ein zentrales Verfassungsrechtliches Problem," in Carl Schmitt, *Verfassungrechtliche Aufsätze aus den Jahren 1924–1954* (Berlin, 1958), pp. 430–39.

18 See Geoff Eley, "The View from the Throne: The Personal Rule of Kaiser Wilhelm II," *Historical Journal*, 28 (1985): 469–85.

19 Harald Müller, "Zu den Anfängen der militärischen Absprachungen zwischen Deutschland und Österreich-Ungarn im Jahre 1882," *Zeitschrift für Militärgeschichte*, 7 (1968): 206–15; and Ernst R. von Rutkowski, "General Skobelev, die Krise des Jahres 1882 und die Anfänge der militärischen Vereinbarungen zwischen Österreich-Ungarn und Deutschland," *Ostdeutsche Wissenschaft*, 10 (1963): 81–151.

Austria-Hungary had maintained permanent military attachés at Berlin since 1860 and in 1872 added a flag-rank officer responsible for keeping the chief of the general staff informed of Prussian-German military and political developments. Germany likewise maintained a military plenipotentiary in Vienna and a naval attaché after 1911.[20] In the earliest days of the alliance, Bismarck ensured that the military staffs had little to think about. In 1887 the German military attaché at Vienna raised the question of Germany's role in an Austro-Russian war, whereupon Bismarck curtly informed him that his policy was "at all costs to avoid this war" and that the "foreign policy of His Majesty the Emperor is advised not by the general staff but exclusively by me."[21]

Thus, the staffs framed the mobilization programs of their militaries in isolation from one another and indeed from their own political authorities. In fact, the revised Austro-Hungarian mobilization plan of August 1880 stipulated that the participation of Germany in military operations could not be assumed.[22] They need not have been concerned. With the deterioration after 1879 of German relations with Russia, Moltke had decided on his own to fight a holding action against France while throwing the bulk of his forces against Russia. The plan shared with the Austrians in 1882 foresaw some 400,000 men deployed offensively in the east; Moltke, with some concern for his sudden dependence on an ally that he already suspected was militarily questionable, sought from the Austro-Hungarian staff clear assurances that it intended to attack Russian forces in Poland at the same time. Moltke remained acutely sensitive to that dependence as military competition with France heated up in the 1880s.[23] Fortunately, the Austro-Hungarians had similar ideas about the best way to handle an eastern campaign. Beck envisioned a two- or even three-front campaign against Russia, Italy, and Serbia and anticipated a rapid succession of stunning offensive blows to end the war quickly and decisively. It was essential,

---

20 Holger H. Herwig, "Disjointed Allies: Coalition Warfare in Berlin and Vienna, 1914," *Journal of Military History*, 54 (1990), 268; on staff interaction, see Günther Kronenbitter, *"Krieg im Frieden:" die Führung der k.u.k. Armee und die Grossmachtpolitik Österreich-Ungarns 1906–1914* (Munich, 2003), pp. 248–314; and Georg Graf Waldersee, "Über die Beziehungen des deutschen zum österreich-ungarischen Generalstabe vor dem Weltkriege," *Berliner Monatshefte*, 8 (1930): 103–42.

21 Gesandschaft Wien. Dienst Instruction und Stellung des Militär-Attaches 1875–1911, vol. la, Auswärtiges Amt, Politisches Archiv; from Herwig, "Disjointed Allies," pp. 270–71, n. 8.

22 Lothar Höbelt, "Schlieffen, Beck, Potiorek und das Ende der gemeinsamen deutsch-österreichisch-ungarischen Aufmarschpläne im Osten," *Militärgeschichtliche Mitteilungen*, 36 (1984), 8; for background, see Scott W. Lackey, *The Rebirth of the Habsburg Army: Friedrich Beck and the Rise of the General Staff* (Westport, 1995).

23 Angelow, "Der Zweibund zwischen politischer Aufwertung und militärischer Abwertung," pp. 48–49.

he said, that he be able to depend on German support and recognition of Austria-Hungary as a coequal partner. Both parties expressed satisfaction, perhaps surprisingly, with their earliest interactions. As Albrecht, duke of Teschen wrote to Franz Joseph, "I can report with considerable satisfaction that, even without prior consultation between Vienna and Berlin, Field-Marshal von Moltke and General Count Waldersee expressed exactly the same views of our eventual joint operations against Russia as have been held here for years."[24]

Tilting toward disaster

No formal change in the military relationship between Germany and Austria-Hungary arose from its inception to the Bosnian Crisis of 1908–1909. But two events – the dismissal of Bismarck from the chancellorship of the German Reich in 1890 and appointment of Alfred von Schlieffen as the chief of the German general staff in 1891 – marked a critical transition. The decision of Wilhelm II to dismiss Bismarck elicited howls of elation from senior Austrian military officers, who had begun to favor a more aggressive policy in Southeastern Europe and who were convinced that Bismarck was their chief obstacle. It was of a piece with the monumental transformation then underway, as the Metternichian order of the nineteenth century fell apart under Kaiser Wilhelm II.

The foreign policy milestones of Wilhelm's reign – the failure to renew the Reinsurance Treaty with the Russians; a program of fleet building against Britain; the advent of *Weltpolitik* and ill-conceived colonialism in Africa, Asia, the Middle East, and South America – all served to heighten the significance of the Berlin–Vienna tie.[25] In an early sign of his proclivities, Wilhelm II told Emperor Franz Joseph on 13 August 1889 that "the day of Austrian mobilization, for whatever cause, will also be the day of mobilization for my army, whatever the chancellors may say."[26] His utterance, made without consultation with his political and military advisors, amounted to a substantial concession to Austro-Hungarian interests with no corresponding advantage to Germany. It was certainly contrary to Bismarck's intentions. For

24 H. Schäfer, "Die militärischen Abmachungen des Dreibundes vor dem Weltkrieg," *Militärwissenschaftliche Mitteilungen*, Heft 9 (1922); from Norman Stone, "Moltke and Conrad: Relations between the Austro-Hungarian and German General Staffs, 1909–1914," in Paul M. Kennedy (ed.), *The War Plans of the Great Powers, 1880–1914* (London, 1979), p. 224.
25 Herwig, "Asymmetrical Alliance," p. 56.
26 Abstracted from from Edmund Glaise von Horstenau, *Franz Josephs Weggefährte. Das Leben des Generalstabschefs, Grafen Beck, nach seinen Aufzeichnungen und hinterlassenen Dokumenten* (Zürich and Vienna, 1930), p. 338.

the Iron Chancellor, the Dual Alliance had been as much about reassuring Russia as it had been about binding the two German powers.

As Bülow put it, "Bismarck never ceased to be concerned with the relations between ourselves and Russia ... Without the benevolent neutrality of Russia Bismarck could not have carried out his policy, either in 1866 or in 1870 and 1871."[27] At no time was Bismarck, given any other option, predisposed to renounce Russia entirely for Austria-Hungary. "Neither to sacrifice Austria-Hungary nor let ourselves be entangled by her in war with Russia seemed to Bismarck by no means an easy task," Bülow recounted, "but possible of achievement by quiet and skillful German policy, especially if we were clever enough not to oppose Russia in the Dardanelles, but to leave that to others."[28] The point was captured even more poignantly by Friedrich von Holstein, a senior official in the Foreign Office, when he suggested that it was Germany's secret to determine when "the psychological moment has come" to rush to Austria's aid.[29] The kaiser's declaration of support, however little it meant for the practical military relationship, committed Germany to more than was prudent, and was all the more arresting for the absence of reciprocity on the Austro-Hungarian side.

Even as Germany's strategic dependency on Austria-Hungary deepened, the military relationship between the two countries deteriorated. By 1890–1891, the Russians had succeeded in significantly shortening the length of time required to mobilize their army and had fortified defenses along the Narew river, a tributary to the east of the Vistula. Their work called into question German plans for quick victory in the east through a vast pincer operation against Russian forces in Poland.[30] Convinced that Germany's only hope for success in a major war lay in winning quickly, Schlieffen, the new chief of the general staff, undertook in 1892–1893 to revise the overall German plan and shift the initial strategic emphasis to the west, leaving it to Austria-Hungary to stabilize the Eastern Front and risking large parts of East Prussia with a perilous flanking march to the south.

As his plans for a joint breakthrough in central Poland did not broadly contradict those of the Austro-Hungarians, they met with general agreement in Vienna. Beck – along with his operations chief, Oskar von Potiorek – was cautiously amenable to a smaller German involvement in

27 Bülow, *Memoirs*, p. 308.
28 Ibid., pp. 308, 394.
29 Holstein to Eulenburg, 9 February 1896, in Norman Rich and M. H. Fisher (eds.), *The Holstein Papers* (Cambridge, 1963), vol. III, pp. 592–94.
30 Dennis E. Showalter, "The Eastern Front and German Military Planning, 1871–1914: Some Observations," East European Quarterly, 15 (1981): 163–80.

the east at the beginning of a war with Russia if it meant a decisive commitment later. In May 1895, however, Schlieffen revised his plans yet again to include a modified encirclement offensive based on a division of Austrian forces, the most important feature of which was a point of decision west of the Vistula River.[31] In the interim he had come to doubt the effectiveness and reliability of the Austro-Hungarian army and preferred to plan operations in the east against more limited and attainable objectives. The paradoxical effect was to place the ultimate burden for victory there on the Austro-Hungarians, a shift which Beck stridently rejected. In exchanges marked by increasing tension and mistrust, the Austrian chief of staff argued for a return to the earlier plan from the 1880s out of a desire to uphold even the distant fiction of unified combined offensive.[32] If Schlieffen outwardly yielded, it was with sour reluctance, and he abandoned meaningful efforts at allied planning after January 1896.[33] Subsequent discussions in 1897 and 1899 avoided issues of operational substance, and such matters featured only at the margins in senior staff contacts through the remainder of Schlieffen's tenure as chief of the general staff.[34]

One must acknowledge that larger factors also contributed to the loosening of ties between Germany and Austria-Hungary. Relations between Vienna and St. Petersburg improved considerably after 1897, which lessened the urgency in Austria-Hungary to plan for a major war against the Russians and reduced the sense of dependency on Germany.[35] But the decisive factor in the diminishing military relationship was undoubtedly Schlieffen's declining faith in Germany's ally, which had never been great. Beck had encountered the German chief of staff for the first time at the funeral of the elder Moltke in 1891 and found him aloof and unforthcoming, hardly an auspicious start to the

---

31 Gerhard Ritter, "Die Zusammenarbeit der Generalstäbe Deutschlands und Österreich-Ungarns vor dem ersten Weltkrieg," in Wilhelm Berges (ed.), *Zur Geschichte und Problematik der Demokratie: Festgabe für Hans Herzfeld anlässlich seines fünfundsechzigsten Geburtstages am 22. Juni 1957* (Berlin, 1958), pp. 532–33.
32 Höbelt, "Schlieffen, Beck, Potiorek und das End der gemeinsamen Aufmarschplanung," p. 23.
33 Ibid., pp. 21–23.
34 Jürgen Angelow, "Der Zweibund zwischen politischer Aufwertung und militärischer Abwertung (1909–1914): Zum Konflikt von Ziel, Mittel und Struktur in Militärbundnissen," *Mitteilungen des österreichischen Staatsarchivs*, 44 (1996): 51–53; Wilhelm Deist describes high-level staff exchanges dealing with matters of irrelevant political, instead of urgent operational import in *Militär, Staat und Gesellschaft: Studien zur preussisch-deutschen Militärgeschichte* (Munich, 1992), pp. 19–41.
35 On the broad trend, see Walter Rauscher, *Zwischen Berlin und St. Petersburg: die österreichisch-ungarische Aussenpolitik unter Gustav Graf Kálnoky, 1881–1895* (Vienna, 1993).

relationship on which so much would depend.[36] Beck spoke resentfully to his military attaché in Berlin of his counterpart's "sensitivity," "mistrust" of Austria, and his taciturn behavior.[37]

The Austrian's impressions were not incorrect. In a private letter to the Reich's military attaché at Vienna, Schlieffen wrote that he expected little from an Austrian offensive in the east, that he was no longer interested in the details of the Austrian operations plan, that he regretted past promises of aid to the Austrians and would make no further commitments, and that all depended on German success in the west regardless.[38] Later he wrote that "the war on two fronts need not be taken into consideration at all. The war against France alone is quite enough to strain every nerve. Counting on the intervention of our allies!! What an illusion!"[39]

Looming in Schlieffen's view was an increasingly threatening French military capability. As far back as 1885, when the focus of French strategic policy had shifted from colonial pursuits to retrenchment in Europe, War Minister Boulanger initiated a sweeping reform of the French army structure, citing the Prussian army conscription laws of 1 April 1888 and the need to keep pace. Thereafter, German military planners locked themselves into a tit-for-tat military race with the French which, when seen together with the Franco-Russian alliance of August 1892, continually escalated the perceived threat to Germany until the outbreak of war in 1914. The stark impossibility of permanently governing Alsace and Lorraine, the French territories annexed as protectorates in 1871, and the unswerving commitment of the French to restore those territories – even through war if necessary – dictated the broad priorities of German planning until World War I. By responding to this growing threat and reorienting the emphasis of initial German operations to the west, Schlieffen addressed concrete needs in concrete ways. But by giving lip service at the same time to the Austro-Hungarians for a spoiling offensive against the Russians, Schlieffen began a process that refused to account realistically for the limited military capabilities of the alliance after the 1890s and led directly to the difficulties

36 Glaise-Horstenau, *Franz Josephs Weggefährte*, p. 344; Seyfert, "Die militärische Beziehungen," p. 37.
37 Letter of 5 February 1894, Operations Büro Generalstab, F59, Österreichisches Staatsarchiv-Kriegsarchiv; from Holger H. Herwig, "Disjointed Allies: Coalition Warfare in Berlin and Vienna, 1914," in Gary Sheffield (ed.), *War Studies Reader: From the Seventeenth Century to the Present Day and Beyond* (London and New York, 2010), p. 93, n. 12.
38 Herwig, "Disjointed Allies," pp. 272–73; citing Gerhard Ritter, *Der Schlieffenplan. Kritik eines Mythos* (Munich, 1956), pp. 28–29.
39 Reichstag, Untersuchungsausschuss über die Weltkriegsverantwortlichkeit. *Zur Vorgeschichte des Weltkrieges*, Heft 2: *Militärische Rüstungen und Mobilmachung* (Berlin, 1921), pp. 73–76; from Ritter, *Der Schlieffenplan*, n.33.

in the east in the first months of World War I. From the 1890s on, German planning for a two-front war expressed an assumption that the Austro-Hungarian leadership could never easily endorse – namely, that the fate of their two countries would be decided not along the tributaries of the Vistula, but by German forces on the Seine. Only decisive victory over France would permit the transfer of strong German forces to the east, which for understandable reasons was of greatest concern to the Austro-Hungarians. The latter continued to hope for an initial commitment of German forces strong enough to reinforce their own limited operations against the Russian army.

In contrast, the German general staff sought first to crush France in an encirclement of massive proportions, involving a sweep through Holland, Belgium, and Luxembourg (a violation of those countries' neutrality) and a crossing of the Meuse north of Liege. After traversing the Dutch province of Limburg, German forces would reach Dunkirk, dig in around Antwerp, and launch an assault along the Verdun–Dunkirk line with thirty-five army corps. A mere five corps around Metz would pin down the French in Lorraine. Fundamental was a powerful right wing to break the French left and force a retreat along the rivers Meuse, Aisne, Somme, Oise, Marne, and Seine. Schlieffen outlined the basic parameters in a famous memorandum of 31 December 1905, which he intended as a legacy to his successor in February 1906.[40] It has become commonplace among modern historians to criticize the technical rigidity of Schlieffen's operational scheme, which would seem to distinguish his thinking from the more adaptable and accommodating planning of the elder Moltke. Quite apart from that, Schlieffen badly underestimated the defensive and offensive capabilities of the French, and despite grave doubts about the German ability to prevail so quickly, was willing to run enormous political and strategic risks against the likelihood of failure. Aspects of his scheme were straightforwardly fanciful, such as the presence of

---

40 See Ritter, *Der Schlieffenplan*, pp. 44–99 *passim*, who argues that the memorandum was understood to have been a theoretical exercise; on the larger historiographical question, see Annika Mombauer, *Helmuth von Moltke and the Origins of the First World War* (Cambridge, 2001), pp. 73–78; see also Terence Zuber, *Inventing the Schlieffen Plan: German War Planning, 1871–1914* (Oxford, 2002), who argues that the Schlieffen Plan was a post-World War I fabrication concocted by postwar officers to blame the younger Moltke for failing to execute the master plan correctly. However, historians of the *Militärgeschichtliches Forschungsamt* turned up a long-misfiled copy of the plan and critically undermined Zuber's arguments in 2006: Hans Ehlert, Michael Epkenhans und Gerhard P. Gross (eds.), *Der Schlieffenplan: Analysen und Dokumente* (Paderborn, 2006); more accessible is Gerhard P. Gross, "There Was a Schlieffen Plan: New Sources on the History of German Military Planning," *War in History*, 15 (2008): 389–431.

eight army corps which at the time were nonexistent.[41] Historians have inveighed against the incalculable political risk of violating the neutrality of the Low Countries, an intention of which all German chancellors were made aware after 1900 and which none opposed, including Bernhard von Bülow, who hotly denied it later.[42]

One must assume that no chancellor contested the political consequences of Schlieffen's plan because all were quite convinced that Germany would prevail. Of course, it will never be clear whether alternative operational schemes offered more favorable prospects for success, or if success was achievable at all. The historian can reasonably question what measure of responsibility for the outcome of events after 1914 Schlieffen and the rest of Germany's military leadership should bear. What none seemed willing to admit was that, with or without the Austro-Hungarian alliance, the prospects of the German Reich in a major European war had been untenable since 1892–1893 and perhaps earlier, when Bismarck's precarious balancing act among the European powers no longer insured the Reich against French revanchism and a Franco-Russian accommodation. One can argue that no plausible operational plan – least of all one based on a risky offensive involving phantom units and audaciously optimistic assumptions – could accomplish what an honest and realistic reconsideration of the country's place among the major powers might have otherwise achieved. After a long tenure, Schlieffen retired as chief of the general staff on 31 December 1905, having arguably failed at what amounted to an impossible task. He compounded Germany's poor strategic position with an adventurous plan that far exceeded the resources and strategic potential of the Reich, made worse by the authoritarian culture of the general staff which made self-criticism or recognizing – let alone coming to terms with – the bankruptcy of the country's predicament impossible.[43] Moreover, his grossly dysfunctional relationship with the Austro-Hungarians compromised the only strategic relationship on which Germany could depend.[44]

Schlieffen's perspective on Germany's military prospects clearly influenced his successor, Helmuth von Moltke the Younger, whose own assessments and planning displayed a bizarre mix of cultural arrogance

41 Ritter, *Der Schlieffenplan*, pp. 143, 152.
42 Hermann Graml, *Bernhard von Bülow und die deutsche Außenpolitik: Hybris und Augenmaß im Auswärtigen Amt* (Munich, 2012), p. 19.
43 See Isabel V. Hull, *Absolute Destruction: Military Culture and the Practices of War in Imperial Germany* (Ithaca, 2005), for a penetrating analysis of the broader cultural problem.
44 See Glaise-Horstenau, *Franz Josephs Weggefährte*, p. 348, on Schlieffen's unwillingness to discuss strategic matters with his Austrian counterpart.

and pessimistic fatalism.[45] He had the benefit of German military intelligence assessments in the years before the war that accurately summarized the liabilities of the German plan against France. The French army had achieved effective parity in size with the German army and attained a level of technical proficiency in some weapons systems that exceeded it. Having perceived the basic outlines of the planned German offensive, the French had arrayed their defenses to hinder it.[46] In his assessment of the military situation for the Reich leadership in December 1911, Moltke cast serious doubts on the ability of the German army to realize a quick victory in the west. Since 1905 the French had introduced large numbers of new artillery batteries – effectively threatening the German advantage in heavy guns – and completed an imposing chain of modern, technically well-equipped border fortresses across key avenues of the German advance.[47]

These dark assessments saturated his remarks at the last prewar conference between the German and Austro-Hungarian staff chiefs at Karlsbad in May 1914. To his counterpart's anxious question about his plans if victory over the French could not be won quickly, Moltke replied, "Yes, I'll do what I can. We are not superior to the French."[48] Moltke's fatalism laid bare the fact that the military challenges facing the Central Powers were no longer amenable to rational solution, and its generals were no longer capable of crafting an approach to major European war with a reasonable chance of success.

The unfavorable position of the Reich relative to France forced Moltke to be much less concerned about the Eastern Front than the Austro-Hungarians. By his calculations, the initial German push in the west required no less than eight-ninths of the German army, and his planning flowed from that imperative. Given increasingly long odds and an urgent need to destroy the French army quickly, it remains puzzling why Moltke continued to nurture the impression that Germany would be in

45 See the excellent study by Mombauer, *Helmuth von Moltke*; among the earliest concise considerations of the staff chief is Konrad Leppa, *Moltke und Conrad: die Heerführung des Generalobersten von Moltke und des Generals der Infanterie Freiherr von Conrad im Sommer 1914* (Stuttgart, 1935).
46 On German assessments, see Robert T. Foley, "Easy Target or Invincible Enemy? German Military Intelligence Assessments of France before the Great War," *Journal of Intelligence History*, 5 (2005): 1–24.
47 Denkschrift Helmuth von Moltke d.J. an Theobald von Bethmann-Hollweg, 21 Dezember 1912, BA-MZA Potsdam, W-10, 50199, 360 and 71–72; from Angelow, "Der Zweibund zwischen politische Aufwertung und militärischer Abwertung," pp. 59, nn. 118–20.
48 Conrad Graf von Hötzendorf, *Aus meiner Dienstzeit 1906–1918* (Vienna, 1921–1925), vol. III, pp. 669ff.

a position to move units to the Eastern Front after only forty days. After all, much depended on the determination of his ally and the compliance of his enemies, French and Russian alike, and he did little to reinforce Austria-Hungary's determination. Only fourteen German divisions defended East Prussia from the Russians, along with a *Landwehr* corps attached to the left wing of the Austro-Hungarian army.

For much his tenure as chief of staff, Moltke airily promised the Austro-Hungarians a joint offensive against Russian forces in Poland with these minimal forces in the first days of the war. He also entertained another plan, parallel to a major offensive in the west and intended to provide strategic flexibility in unforeseeable circumstances, involving the immediate deployment of thirty-nine infantry and six cavalry divisions against Russia. It was to have been based on the unlikely possibility of diplomatically isolating Russia from other potential entanglements.[49] German planners had not envisaged an alternative disposition as late as 1913, when Moltke, without apprising the civilian Reich leadership, suddenly dropped even the pretense of an early offensive in the east and focused exclusively on the west. When Wilhelm II asked him on 1 August 1914 about English neutrality and the possibility of localizing a conflict with Russia, Moltke made clear that with the outbreak of hostilities, German options were strictly limited. "Your uncle would have given me a different answer," was Wilhelm's scathing reply.[50]

Austro-Hungarian strategic priorities could be reconciled only with difficulty to the western focus of German planning. From the earliest joint talks in 1882, Austrian plans called for a significant German offensive to relieve overwhelming Russian superiority in the east, an assumption that the Germans never categorically denied.[51] The Germans had originally promised a push to Grodno within ten days of hostilities, even as the bulk of their forces remained along the right bank of the Vistula toward Novogeorgievsk. The Austro-Hungarian staff reasoned that German forces would cross the Narew and Bug rivers by the thirtieth

---

49 Seyfert, "Die militärische Beziehungen und Vereinbarungen," pp. 33–46; from Angelow, "Der Zweibund zwischen politischer Aufwertung und militärischer Abwertung," p. 62, n. 128.

50 Generaloberst Helmuth von Moltke, *Erinnerungen, Briefe, Dokumente 1877–1916: Ein Bild vom Kriegsausbruch, erster Kriegsführung und Persönlichkeit des ersten militärischen Führers des Krieges*, ed. Eliza von Moltke. (Stuttgart, 1922), p. 20; for context, see Ritter, *Staatskunst*, II, p. 336.

51 Hubert Zeinar, *Geschichte des österreichischen Generalstabes* (Vienna, 2006), pp. 413–43; also Heinrich Lutz, "Politik und militärische Planung in Österreich-Ungarn zu Begin der Ära Andrássy," Protokoll der Wiener Geheimkonferenzen vom 17. bis 19. Februar 1872, in Gerhard Botz, Hans Hauptmann und Helmut Konrad (eds.), *Geschichte und Gesellschaft – Festschrift für Karl R. Stadler* (Vienna, 1974), pp. 23–44.

day of mobilization and that they would take Warsaw and invest Brest about ten days later.

Driving early staff concerns was the sluggish pace of Austro-Hungarian mobilization, which meant that their forces in any conceivable scheme would amount to little more than a reserve army in early German encirclement operations in Poland. The Austro-Hungarian army required some thirty-three days to assemble in Galicia from its jumping off points, and another ten to twelve beyond that to organize and achieve concentration. No operations of significance against the Russian border were possible in fewer than forty-five days. By November 1883 an extended and rationalized railway system and more refined mobilization techniques shortened the assembly period to twenty days, and Austro-Hungarian staff officers felt that they had the flexibility to plan for limited operations against Lublin in the initial phases of war. By the late 1880s, they could finally plan to participate in offensive operations designed to envelop the mass of Russian forces in the earliest phases of a war, a possibility beyond their means only ten years earlier.

The problem was that Russian efforts to shorten mobilization timetables by the late 1880s were no less successful, a fact which placed yet more pressure on the Austro-Hungarian timetable for deployment and concentration.[52] Moreover, the gradual reduction of German forces in the east and steady expansion of Russian forces in the western military districts in the 1880s and 1890s meant that Austria-Hungary could no longer take for granted a force structure adequate to its offensive intentions. By 1897, Schlieffen's relegation of the Eastern Front to a theater of secondary importance should have forced Austro-Hungarian planners to flirt again with the need to operate initially against the Russians without German support. Instead, the assumption of a considerable German eastern offensive continued to lurk behind all Austro-Hungarian mobilization and operational planning down to 1914, even as the Germans implied otherwise on several occasions. But the lack of firm evidence to support their planning assumptions, which Schlieffen's aloofness did nothing to reinforce, could not dampen Austro-Hungarian optimism. By the first few years of the new century, the plainly wishful objective of the Austro-Hungarian army in Galicia became the encirclement and destruction of the Russian southwestern army, coincident with an operation against Serbia.

---

52 Jacob W. Kipp, "Strategic Railroads and the Dilemmas of Modernization," in David Schimmelpenninck van der Oye and Bruce W. Menning (eds.), *Reforming the Tsar's Army: Military Innovation in Imperial Russia from Peter the Great to the Revolution* (Cambridge, 2004), pp. 82–105.

Franz Conrad von Hötzendorf, who succeeded Beck as chief of the Austro-Hungarian staff in 1906, planned to drive Russian forces between the Bug and Vistula rivers southwards to protect Berlin, Vienna, and Budapest from invasion, a plan which retained the virtue, it must be admitted, of ensuring continued contact with German forces in the event of failure.[53] Fundamental to his planning through the summer of 1908 was the notion that German forces would first throw their weight against Russia and only then turn to deal with France. As much as anything else, that aspect of Conrad's thinking reveals the almost complete failure of the allies to collaborate meaningfully during Schlieffen's tenure.[54]

Not content to craft implausible plans against only one opponent, Conrad also devoted a great deal of time to planning an offensive against Italy, a junior alliance partner of Germany and Austro-Hungary.[55] He was convinced, as were many leading Austro-Hungarian officials, that Italy would flout its treaty obligations and take advantage of a war elsewhere to annex Italian-speaking parts of the Habsburg monarchy. He therefore included a preventive war against Italy – and, after the Bosnian Crisis of 1908–1909, against Serbia as well – as part of any war plan to relieve Austria-Hungary's larger strategic dilemma of comparative decline, a clear sign of which were the continual budgetary challenges that the Austro-Hungarian army faced. Funding necessary to maintain a reasonable state of readiness was entirely lacking, and worsened in the years prior to the outbreak of war as the navy claimed an increasing share of the military budget, so much so that in early 1914 Conrad sarcastically

---

53 For background, see the excellent biography by Lawrence Sondhaus, *Franz Conrad von Hötzendorf: Architect of the Apocalypse* (Boston, 2000); and Oskar Regele, *Feldmarshall Conrad* (Vienna, 1955); the institutional context is surveyed ably in Oskar Regele, *Generalstabschefs aus vier Jahrhunderten: Das Amt des Chefs des Generalstabes in der Donaumonarchie: seine Träger und Organe von 1529 bis 1918* (Vienna, 1966).

54 Conrad's plans are elaborated in "Grundzüge für den Kriegsfall gegen Russland. Vorraussetzungen. Deutschland von Haus aus als Verbündeter der Monarchie. Deutschland mit bedeutender Kräften (Hauptmacht) vorerst gegen Russland – erst hierauf gegen Russland," in Österreichisches Staatsarchiv, Kriegsarchiv, Generalstab, Operationsbüro, Faszikel 737 (Grundzüge für den Kriegsfall gegen Russland 1908); from Jürgen Angelow, "Vom 'Bündnis' zum 'Block.' Struktur, Forschungsstand und Problemlage einer Geschichte des Zweibundes 1879–1914," *Militärgeschichtliche Mitteilungen*, 54 (1995), 154, n. 99.

55 Conrad defended these controversial plans even after the war: Conrad von Hötzendorf, *Private Aufzeichnungen. Erste Veröffentlichungen aus den Papieren des k.u.k. Generalstabs-Chef*, ed. Kurt Peball (Vienna, 1977), pp. 65, 210; also Diether Degreif, *Operative Planungen des k.u.k. Generalstabes für einen Krieg in der Zeit vor 1914, 1880–1914* (Wiesbaden, 1987); also Hans Jürgen Pantenius, *Der Angriffsgedanke gegen Italien bei Conrad von Hötzendorf: ein Beitrag zur Koalitionskriegsführung im Ersten Weltkrieg* (Cologne, 1984).

predicted that the time would come when a victorious Austrian navy would steam home to find the country in enemy hands.[56]

Conrad nevertheless spent what he could on mountain troops, heavy guns, and fortresses along the south-western border of the empire, none of which wound up being of use against Russia. Even so, he expected the Russians to seize upon an Austro-Hungarian war with Serbia and Italy, and so struggled to remain flexible against possible Russian intervention in the early stages of an Austro-Italian or Austro-Serbian war. The division of Austro-Hungarian forces against so many enemies made impossible any effective action against the strongest of them, particularly in the early months of a general European war and even in light of the false hopes about German intentions which Conrad nurtured. For their part, the Germans were aware of Conrad's wayward planning against the lesser European powers and allowed themselves to be soothed by wishful thinking, reckoning on a rapid Austrian victory over Serbia and the neutrality of Italy.

The optimism of the German and Austro-Hungarian military leadership could not overcome the fact that they almost certainly lacked the military resources necessary to overcome the challenges that their countries' misguided strategic policies had created over a generation, and that neither wishful assumptions nor faith in willpower could carry them successfully through a campaign that lasted more than a few weeks. In the final plan, the Germans planned to transfer forces to the east only after a breathtaking offensive victory over the numerically superior French army; in the meantime, a token German force would screen East Prussia and a reserve element would support the Austro-Hungarian army. Until 1914 Conrad (whose tenure was interrupted briefly by General Blasius Schemua in 1911–1912) based his operational planning on perfunctory German pledges in 1909 – abandoned when hostilities commenced – to strike against Russian defensive fortifications along the Narew line and to transfer forces to the east within four weeks of the war's onset.[57] The Germans supported Austro-Hungarian plans for a rapid initial offensive against Serbia despite the fatal consequences this presented for effective action against Russia.[58] Neither side displayed any inclination to ask

---

56 Hadley, "Military Diplomacy in the Dual Alliance," p. 302.
57 Perspective is provided in Theobald von Schäfer, "Deutsche Offensive aus Ostpreußen über den Narew auf Siedlic," in *Österreich-Ungarns letzter Krieg 1914 – 1918*, Ergänzungsheft 1 (Vienna, 1930), pp. 1–16.
58 The details of German and Austro-Hungarian planning in the period after the Bosnian Crisis are covered ably by Norman Stone, "Moltke and Conrad: Relations between the Austro-Hungarian and German General Staffs, 1909–1914," in Paul M. Kennedy (ed.), *The War Plans of the Great Powers, 1880–1914* (London, 1979), pp. 222–51; and Norman Stone Norman Stone, "Moltke – Conrad: Relations between the Austro-Hungarian and German General Staffs, 1909–1914," *The Historical Journal*, 9 (1966): 201–28.

hard questions, to reconcile its strategic intentions to those of the other, or to plan joint operations; rather, both sides remained content simply to inform the other of its plans, ignore the obvious inconsistencies, and count on the most favorable possible outcome to see them through.

Reaching out to one another was hard, in any case. Substantive interaction between the military staffs tailed off almost entirely by the end of the Schlieffen era, although both sides observed social conventions and pleasantries.[59] The Bosnian Crisis of 1908 stimulated a partial renewal of high-level joint talks on operational matters between the staff chiefs, and Germany vowed unconditional support to Austria in the event of a Russian attack, even one provoked by an Austrian offensive against Serbia. Moltke's assurances, anecdotally referred to as the General Staff Treaty, fundamentally transformed the defensive alliance into an offensive one, a measure which Schlieffen would have undoubtedly thought abhorrent given his low opinion of the Austro-Hungarians and which one historian has described as overpromising "to the point of irresponsibility."[60] Even so, the agreement of 1909 was informal at best and knowledge of it remained confined to a small circle of associates by virtue of its offensive orientation.

Discussions between German and Austro-Hungarian staff officers therefore assumed an almost conspiratorial character. On the few occasions when meetings between them occurred, operational plans were communicated only in cursory and superficial form. In contrast to the communications between the elder Moltke and Beck in the early phase of the alliance, neither the Germans nor the Austro-Hungarians were disposed to subject the plans of the other to critical debate or reflection, which would have led inevitably to the conclusion that the Dual Alliance had scant hope of realizing its objectives in the event of major conflict. Confronting in an open manner the lack of persuasive solutions to their military problems would have provoked consideration of strategic policies to lessen the likelihood of major conflict at all costs. Particularly after the Bosnian Crisis, both countries would have had no choice but to re-evaluate the strategic value of the Dual Alliance as well. But the political and military leadership in both countries crafted policy without such constraints, and so could justify almost any assumption, no matter how unrealistically optimistic, in terms of power and prestige.

---

59 The relationship is best glimpsed through Conrad, *Aus meiner Dienstzeit*, pp. 46–75.
60 Jürgen Angelow, *Kalkül und Prestige: der Zweibund am Vorabend des Ersten Weltkrieges* (Cologne, 2000), pp. 151–74; also Stephan Verosta, *Theorie und Realität von Bündnissen: Heinrich Lammasch, Karl Renner und der Zweibund 1897–1914* (Vienna, 1971); the historian is Gerhard Ritter, *The Sword and the Scepter: The Problem of Militarism in Germany* (Coral Gables, 1970), vol. II, p. 239.

The result of the Bosnian Crisis was impulsive resignation by both staff chiefs to accept the intentions of the other, however incompatible they were.[61] The Austro-Hungarian leadership tacitly accepted the need for Germany to defeat France first in the west, while the Germans agreed to the Austro-Hungarian plan to crush Serbia before facing the Russians in Poland. But Moltke the Younger, who promised Conrad on 19 March 1909 outright to collaborate in a major offensive against Russian forces with the limited German forces in the east, was especially irresponsible. Conrad based his subsequent planning entirely on this pledge, which Moltke reinforced on multiple occasions (only to renounce it in 1914). Accordingly, Conrad thought himself to have a free hand against Serbia and Italy, even as he understood that Moltke would turn to the Russians in force only after defeating France. Offensive operations against the Russians would then commence regardless of whether Austria-Hungary was still engaged against Serbia. This sequence was fundamental for the Germans, as a defensive posture in the east left Berlin almost entirely unprotected.

But Conrad's promise of early and effective action against the Russians was a false hope, which even a cursory review of Austro-Hungarian plans in 1914 could have dispelled. The Austro-Hungarians and Germans alike made promises they could not and would not keep after August 1914. The official Austrian history later pointed out that both sides "beat around the bush," while a German historian argued that "neither [side] laid their cards on the table ... Neither Moltke nor Conrad always spoke their innermost thoughts."[62] Coordination on the deeper level of joint planning was completely inadequate. Neither side paid much attention to the details of military capabilities or the operational potential of the other. The Germans, in particular, had almost no conception of the organization, command system, or national composition of the Austro-Hungarian army, and even less of its technical features, such as its tactical doctrine, logistics, or rail support.[63] Without question, the most serious shortcoming in the military relationship was the lack of a combined operational command for the east, which was essential if their plans against Russia were to be effective.[64]

---

61 On the prewar phase of planning, see Hans-Meier Welcker, "Strategische Planungen und Vereinbarungen der Mittelmächte für den Mehrfrontenkrieg," *Österreichische Militärische Zeitschrift*, 2 (1964), 15–22.

62 Edmund Glaise von Horstenau and Rudolf Kiszling (eds.), *Österreich-Ungarns Letzter Krieg 1914–1918* (Vienna, 1931), vol. I, p. 333.

63 Gordon A. Craig, "The World War I Alliance of the Central Powers in Retrospect: The Military Cohesion of the Alliance," *The Journal of Modern History*, 37 (1965): 339.

64 Angelow, "Der Zweibund zwischen politischer Aufwertung und militärischer Abwertung," pp. 72–73.

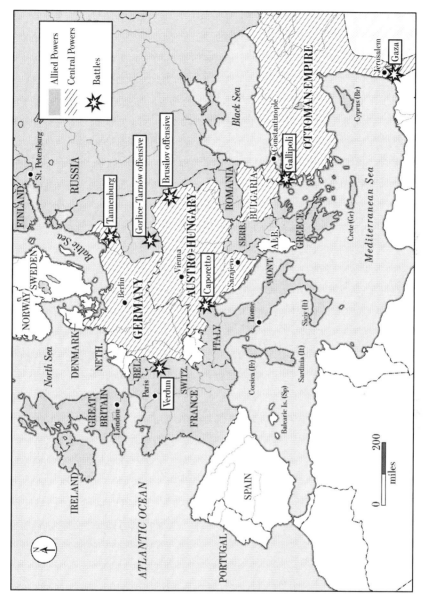

Map 11.1   The Central Powers in World War I

War and the alliance

As a result, when war came, the Central Powers lacked a "systematically developed war plan," and their operations failed to unfold as anticipated, particularly in the east.[65] The Germans did not attack the Russians from their jumping off points in East Prussia and were plainly shocked by the speed of Russia's mobilization and the rapidity with which the Russian Northwest Front's First and Second armies advanced into East Prussia, although they rallied to produce an inspired defensive victory at Tannenberg. The Austro-Hungarians intended to reckon first with Serbia, but changed their minds at the last minute and shifted the weight of their forces to screen Berlin, albeit too late to prevent their rout in Galicia and the Russian occupation of Lemberg.[66]

The confusion reflected especially poorly on the failure of the senior member of the alliance to think through the strategic implications of their entanglement, despite the admonitions of Karl von Kageneck, the German military attaché in Vienna, who urged Moltke's deputy to "play with absolutely open cards in order that we follow the lessons of all coalition wars."[67] Realizing too late that his ally had scant prospect of screening the Prussian frontier and tying down the Russians long enough for him to finish off the French and turn east, Moltke gloomily confided to his diary on 2 September 1914 that "[i]n Austria it's going badly. The army is not moving forward. I see it coming, they will be defeated."[68] In response to feverish questions about why the Austro-Hungarians had such difficulty against Russian forces that were thought to have been little better than a militia, a senior German military representative in Vienna pointed out that the Austro-Hungarians were themselves little better than a militia, and there were far fewer of them. He went on to describe in detail the poor state of affairs in the high command, the officer corps, among the troops, and the shortages

---

65 Ludwig Beck, *Studien*, ed. Hans Speidel (Stuttgart, 1955), p. 110.
66 The best treatment of the early combined campaigns is Günther Kronenbitter, "Von 'Schweinehunden' und 'Waffenbrüdern:' Der Koalitionskrieg der Mittelmächte 1914/15 zwischen Sachzwang und Ressentiment," in Gerhard P. Groß (ed.), *Die vergessene Front–der Osten 1914/15: Ereignis, Wirkung, Nachwirkung* (Paderborn, 2006), pp. 121–46; also Rudolf Kiszling, "Bündniskrieg und Koalitionskriegführung am Beispiel der Mittelmächte im Ersten Weltkrieg," *Wehrwissenschaftliche Rundschau* 10 (1960): 633–41; on the general course of military events, see Michael S. Neiberg and David Jordan, *The Eastern Front 1914–1920: From Tannenberg to the Russo-Polish War* (London, 2012), esp. chs. 1 and 2.
67 Karl von Kageneck, Diary, 4 August 1914, BA-MA MSg 1/1914; from Richard L. DiNardo, *Breakthrough: The Gorlice-Tarnów Campaign, 1915* (Santa Barbara, CA, 2010), p. 7.
68 von Moltke, *Erinnerungen, Briefe, Dokumente, 1877–1916*, p. 383.

of ammunition, weapons, reserves – in short, a litany of the information that a well-conducted and honest prewar alliance policy should have made clear.[69]

As a prominent German historian has pointed out:

[i]t is difficult to study the campaigns of 1914 without being impressed by the incompleteness of Austro-German planning for their joint military venture and the dearth of their knowledge about each other, and without being convinced that the major share of the responsibility for this must be assigned to the stronger of the allies.[70]

Having endured heavy losses and anxious that Russian troops would cross the Carpathians and seize core territories of the Habsburg Empire, the Austro-Hungarians requested the very reinforcements that Moltke had regularly promised since 1909. However, the Germans informed them curtly that they should expect no relief until mid September at the earliest. On 18 September Ludendorff met Conrad – whom he described as "an educated officer, but no great man"[71] – to discuss the strategic situation and to be subjected to a harangue about Germany's failure to live up to its obligations. Ludendorff, after conceding that German support to that point may not have been wholly adequate but no less aghast at the Austrian situation, told him that relief was imminent.[72]

Conrad was forced to face the fact that some 1 million Austrian casualties in the first months of the war effectively relegated him to a subordinate role in the alliance, and he fulminated about German arrogance and perfidy. When the Germans proposed in the fall of 1914 to form a headquarters under a German field marshal for the overall coordination of the Eastern Front, Conrad – clearly a man born in his mind to command an organization other than the one fate left him – vowed hotly not to permit Austro-Hungarian forces to serve under a foreign power, even if allied.[73] The exigencies of the increasingly dire war effort were undeniable, however, and the German proposal finally culminated in November 1914 with the establishment of the *Ober-Ost*, or supreme command of German forces in the east.

---

69 Exchange between General Hugo von Freytag-Loringhoven and General Hermann von Stein, 2 September 1914 and 11 September 1914, BA-MA, PH3/328; from Hadley, "Military Diplomacy in the Dual Alliance," p. 295.
70 Craig, "The World War I Alliance of the Central Powers in Retrospect," p. 339.
71 Erich Ludendorff to Helmuth von Moltke, 2 January 1915, Nachlass Ludendorff, BA-MA N 77/2; from DiNardo, *Breakthrough*, p. 16.
72 Graydon A. Tunstall, Jr., *Planning for War against Russia and Serbia: Austro-Hungarian and German Military Strategies 1871–1914* (Boulder, CO, 1993), pp. 255–56.
73 Conrad, *Aus meiner Dienstzeit*, V, pp. 301, 377; from Herwig, "Asymmetrical Alliance," p. 64.

As German prospects for quick victory in the west evaporated in late fall 1914, the chief Austro-Hungarian concern was the Galician fortress of Przemysl, where the Russians besieged more than 100,000 Austro-Hungarian troops under desperate conditions. Without consulting his ally, Conrad embarked upon one the greatest blunders in the history of Habsburg arms, a major offensive that resulted in the ruinous collapse of his forces and surrender of the fortress. His folly placed the Germans at a strategic crossroads. The Battle of the Marne, which they had lost by the thinnest margin, left the new chief of the general staff, Erich von Falkenhayn, with the option of seeking a decision in the west or fighting a holding action there and seizing the offensive in the east to knock Russia out of the war.

Most senior German officers were convinced, as they had been for a generation, that only decisive victory against France would persuade the Western allies to settle on favorable terms; in other words, no degree of success in the east could win for Germany the only outcome that ultimately mattered.[74] "In my opinion," Moltke put it shortly before the war, "the whole European war depends on the outcome of the struggle between Germany and France, and so the fate of Austria will not be decided on the Bug, but ultimately on the Seine."[75] It seemed incontestable that Britain and France would continue to fight even if opposition to the Central Powers collapsed elsewhere. Moreover, to place the strategic emphasis of German efforts on the east would tie the fate of the German army closely to that of Austria-Hungary, a decidedly dubious proposition.

Torn by these considerations, the German military leadership fell back into its cultural habit of denying the choice to be made and effectively prevaricated until the withdrawal of Russia from the war in 1918. Throughout the crucial middle years of the war, it shifted forces across Germany's internal lines of communication to deal with one opportunity or threat after another on both fronts. If this had the effect of supporting Germany's wheezing ally and leading opportunistically to the collapse of the tsarist regime in Russia, it was not for a surplus of purposeful intent. To be fair, the German high command displayed remarkable efficiency and a deft skill in forming fresh units and positioning them to maximum effect between 1915 and 1918, all the while keeping the

74 On the place of the Eastern Front in the thinking of senior German officers, see Terence Zuber, "Strategische Überlegungen in Deutschland zu Kriegsbeginn," in P. Groß (ed.), *Die vergessene Front–der Osten 1914/15: Ereignis, Wirkung, Nachwirkung* (Paderborn, 2006), pp. 35–48.

75 Conrad, *Aus meiner Dienstzeit*, III, p. 145; from DiNardo, *Breakthrough: the Gorlice-Tarnów Campaign*, p. 4.

Austro-Hungarians on strategic life-support and lending a hand when absolutely necessary. But just getting by is far different from winning.

More than any other single factor, German operational initiative lengthened the conflict and consistently renewed the alliance's lease on life, a circumstance that weighed early on. Success against the Austro-Hungarians in the first months of the war had extended Russian forces deep into western areas and exposed them to counterattack; the German eastern command, headed by Paul von Hindenburg and Erich Ludendorff, glimpsed a chance in 1915 to strike a blow of immense proportions against an overstretched and precarious Russian position in Poland. They secured Falkenhayn's reluctant assent for an offensive in the region around Gorlice-Tarnów, which resulted in an almost complete rout of the tsar's armies in Poland and became perhaps the foremost example of successful coalition operations between Germany and Austria-Hungary.[76]

German forces used artillery to stunning effect in the operation, smashing Russian defensive positions, making possible an infantry breakthrough and encirclement, and thereby restoring to the Eastern Front a degree of mobility and offensive initiative unknown in the west until the final stages of the war. The field commanders of the Gorlice-Tarnów offensive, most notably Hans von Seeckt and August von Mackensen, became luminaries in the pantheon of German military leaders. However, success in narrow operational terms had the paradoxical effect of blinding German and Austro-Hungarian leaders to the bankruptcy of their overall position, as developments on peripheral fronts underscored. The Italian government had long sought territorial gains at the expense of Austria-Hungary, and in the interest of persuading Italy to remain neutral or join the Central Powers, Germany pressured its ally to give up those parts of its empire.

The Austro-Hungarian leadership – including Emperor Franz Joseph and his foreign minister – rejected all suggestions of truncating the empire for the sake of the strategic effectiveness. Conrad, better aware than any other Austro-Hungarian leader of the alliance's diminishing prospects, seemed more willing to countenance measures to consolidate the Austro-Hungarian position and make its strategic dilemmas more manageable. He tipped his hand by doing almost nothing to counter an Italian offensive simultaneous to his Galician campaign, a gamble that paid off only because the Italians failed to exploit the diversion. From

---

76 DiNardo, *Breakthrough*, esp. pp. 116–44; a ground-level perspective is afforded by Heinrich Kraft, *Der Anteil der 11. Bayerische Infanterie Division an der Durchbruchsschlacht von Gorlice-Tarnow und an den anschliessenden Verfolgungskämpfen bis zum Übergang der Division über den San* (Munich, 1934).

that point on, Germany and Austria-Hungary waged most subsequent major operations independent of the constraints of combined planning. Even when arguably successful – as with the South Tyrolean offensive of May 1916 and the Verdun offensive of February 1916 – their individual campaigns served to aggravate the strategic situation of the alliance as a whole. After the Russian Brusilov offensive of June 1916 nearly wiped out the remaining operational capacity of Austro-Hungarian army, there was no question but that Germany would determine the military fate of the coalition, thereby realizing the worst prewar apprehensions of the Austro-Hungarians.[77]

As one historian has argued, "The failure of Berlin and Vienna to devise a coherent and coordinated strategy before 1914 lay primarily in the fact that both pursued national strategies that were not mutually beneficial," an outcome abetted by the fact that "neither side was blessed with soldier-statesmen able to conduct joint strategic planning."[78] Neither Germany nor Austria-Hungary conceived of the Dual Alliance as having an explicitly shared strategic focus at any point in its history. From the 1890s on, the German military leadership saw scant value in the Austro-Hungarian connection, discounting the quality of its potential contribution to a major war and sharing as little information as possible about plans and intentions. In the end, the Germans expected their ally only to provide the rearguard against the Russians for their primary push into France, a task to which the Austro-Hungarians were plainly not equal, especially in light of their interests on other fronts. For their part, the Austro-Hungarians expected considerably more German support against the Russians than Schlieffen or the younger Moltke ever honestly contemplated, freeing them to settle accounts elsewhere. Each ally had its own, quite divergent reasons for seeking the collaboration of the other, conceived primarily in narrow operational terms when articulated at all.

Presumably, a combined command structure established at the outset of the relationship and nurtured over time to share information and plans would have enabled the coalition to face these bitters truths, and perhaps to become more efficient and focused. However, neither ally could see its way to the concessions that genuine collaboration invariably involves – in this instance, a willingness by the Germans to concede the importance

---

77 Timothy C. Dowling, *The Brusilov Offensive* (Bloomington, 2008); the campaign is ably surveyed by John Schindler, "Steamrollered in Galicia: The Austro-Hungarian Army and the Brusilov Offensive, 1916," *War in History*, 10 (2003): 27–59; see Erich Köhn, *Österreichisch-ungarische Politik der Jahre 1916–1918* (Vienna, 1936) on the broader implications of the campaign for the Habsburg empire.
78 Herwig, "Disjointed Allies," p. 278.

of the Eastern Front in a balanced war effort, and a willingness by the Austro-Hungarians to forego peripheral theaters for the sake of a coherent strategy and overall success. Of course, collaboration based on genuinely open communication and frank appreciation of their capacities may well have led to recognition that victory in a war against the combined power of the other European empires lay well beyond the limited capacities of the Central European coalition.

To be sure, one may reasonably suggest that the coalition of Germany and Austria-Hungary proved as successful in realizing its admittedly narrow operational aims, which in the end amounted to no more than repulsing the Russian army from Eastern Europe, as the coalition of the Entente powers, which faced its own considerable problems of coordination and especially harmonization of command structures. The major operational successes that Germany and Austria-Hungary, either singly or together, achieved on the Eastern Front, especially the successful offensives against Serbia in 1915 and Romania a year later, is surprising given the gross dysfunction of their alliance relationship. Moreover, in 1917 the Austro-Hungarian army, supported by sizable German units and copious amounts of poison gas, routed Italian forces at Caporetto and drove as far as the Piave River. But neither Germany nor Austria-Hungary proved willing before or during the war to confront the cold fact that they lacked the strategic depth and wherewithal to prevail against all of the enemies they faced.

Their operational triumphs amounted to fingers in the dike: they could alleviate short-term strategic crises by military means, but could not relieve the immense wartime demands on their limited resources to bring about a durable settlement in their interests. The important question that remains is whether the outcome of the war would have been different had the Central Powers coordinated strategically and operationally and cultivated a seamless relationship based on combined planning. The answer is almost certainly not. The war was lost because Germany and Austria-Hungary were outclassed by decisive Western advantages in geography, economic and financial resources, and manpower, and the failure of German and Austria-Hungarian leaders to realize the hopeless position into which their strategic bungling placed them by the outbreak of hostilities in 1914.

Above all else, the case of Germany and Austria-Hungary before and during World War I underscores the primary importance of compatible strategic objectives at the highest levels between powers who seek to reinforce their security through an alliance. At least since the 1890s – and arguably earlier – Germany and Austria-Hungary weighed the significance of operations against Russian forces in different terms, and further understood the potential success of such operations to factor differently into their respective hopes of a victorious war. Civilian officials and military officers on each side basked in comfortable illusions about the intentions and capabilities of the other, doing little to substantiate or dispel them through hard discussions. Matters were not helped, to be sure, by the distinct distrust that poisoned professional relations between the German and Austro-Hungarian staffs, but even a healthier personal rapport between officers would not have clarified the planning and execution of joint operations. Only firm agreement about the ultimate ways and means of realizing victory would have provided the basis for effective planning, and such agreement lay well beyond the conceits of the alliance's leaders.

12   The Axis

Williamson Murray

In recent decades, several books dealing with the history of World War II have emphasized the squabbling that marked the conduct of the war by the Allied powers both at the strategic level and in the conduct of military operations.[1] No one looking at the war against Nazi Germany could reach any other conclusion but that the Soviet Union was a recalcitrant, secretive ally that contributed immensely to the destruction of the Third Reich, but at the same time cooperated to the minimum extent possible with its British and American allies. Nor were Charles de Gaulle and his Free French government in exile much more cooperative.[2] And even the British and Americans proved to be at loggerheads for much of the war, particularly in coordinating their combined strategic approach to the problems raised by a global conflict.[3] Yet, in the end whatever difficulties the Anglo-American alliance encountered, it proved an effective and crucial determinant in the war's course and eventual outcome.[4] Although there were differences between the British and the Americans, the result of their arguments was a series of decisions that shortened the conflict's length and reduced its cost.

What many of the discussions of inter-Allied arguments miss is that to work well, an alliance must inevitably involve a contentious dialogue. It is never the case that allied powers merely agree in principal to a number of grand aims. At a minimum a successful alliance demands a degree of common understanding of the other members, recognition of where their aims might differ, and a willingness at times to sacrifice narrow,

---

1 See among others in this genre, David Irving, *The War between the Generals: Inside the Allied High Command* (London, 1982).
2 Churchill once described his experiences in dealing with de Gaulle as the equivalent to bearing the "Cross of Lorraine."
3 Gerhard Weinberg's *A World at Arms: A Global History of World War II* (Cambridge, 1994) is particularly good on the politics of grand strategy between the Anglo-American powers.
4 For an excellent discussion of these differences and how in the end they contributed to the successes of Anglo-American military power in achieving the coalition goals, see Peter Mansoor's outstanding essay on the subject in Williamson Murray and Richard Hart Sinnreich (eds.), *Successful Strategies* (Cambridge, 2014).

national interests for the general good.[5] It also demands a certain openness and transparency as to one's own aims, objectives, and approach to war in dealing with allies. Certainly, the fact that the British in their first major dealings with the Americans opened up not only their intelligence sources but shared their technological advances as well played a major role in the success of the Anglo-American alliance.

It is difficult in those terms to regard the Axis powers, in particular Nazi Germany, Imperial Japan, and Fascist Italy as forming a real alliance. Their so-called alliance represented little more than the most basic agreement to cooperate in attempting to steal as much of the world as possible.[6] The result was a general inability to create an alliance strategy that made any sense and in a number of cases resulted in counterproductive approaches to the war that further contributed to their defeat. There was certainly no transparency among the three powers, but rather great secrecy in the strategic, military, and operational realms. Nor did they understand "the other." Perhaps the only thing that held them together was the fact each power possessed quite different aims that, when the alliance was formed, seemingly would not come into conflict.[7]

In particular, these three regimes were deeply motivated by an ideological view of the world and their desire to remake it along racial lines.[8] The most extreme of these *Weltanschauungen* was Adolf Hitler's, which aimed at no less than (1) the destruction of the European state system created by the peace of Westphalia that had guided Europe since 1648; (2) the establishment of a Germano-Arayan Empire in its place that would dominate Europe from the North Cape to the Alps and from the Atlantic to the Urals; (3) the elimination of Jews within the new German 'living space,' either by emigration or murder if necessary; and (4) the destruction and enslavement of the Slavic peoples of Eastern Europe,

---

5 Here one might add to Sun Tzu's adage that to be successful in war, one needs to understand not only oneself and one's opponent, but one's allies as well: their aims, their goals, their history, and their *Weltanschauungen* (world views).

6 There were a number of other smaller powers that attached themselves to the Axis, but in effect they were nothing more than satellites, largely forced to do the bidding of their masters. Among these states were Hungary, Romania, Slovakia, Finland, Bulgaria, and Thailand. Weinberg's *A World at War* is particularly good at pointing out the narrow uncooperative relations among the various Axis powers in pursuing the larger strategic aims of the coalition.

7 The only place where there were conflicting aims was in the Balkans. Germany's interest in the Balkans largely focused on the raw materials of the area, particularly Romanian oil, while Mussolini viewed Greece and Albania as part of Italy's quest for a reconstitution of the Roman Empire in the Mediterranean area. These aims came into conflict when Italian commanders botched the invasion of Greece, thus dragging Germany into Italy's "Parallel War" in Southeast Europe.

8 Substituting class for race, this was also the case with the Soviet Union.

including Poland, the Ukraine, and virtually all of European Russia.[9] Monstrous though this program was, it was popular with the great majority of Germans – a terrible comment on human nature.

Mussolini's aims were less megalomaniacal than those of his partner in crime across the Alps, but given Italy's relative weaknesses, particularly in the military sphere, and its lack of resources, they were, nevertheless, grandiose. Fascist Italy aimed at no less than a return to ancient Rome's control of the entire Mediterranean basin, or the creation, in Roman terms, of a *mare nostrum* (our sea). And as Mussolini was to display throughout his twenty-one-year rule, especially in Libya and Ethiopia, he was more than willing to use the most ruthless and murderous means to achieve his ends.[10]

And finally, there were the Japanese on the other side of the world. It is difficult to pin down any sort of attempt by the Japanese leadership to develop a coherent strategy. The greatest difficulty lay in the fact that the Japanese army and navy held diametrically opposed views as to the most advantageous strategic direction for the their nation to pursue: the army looked toward the Asian mainland, while the navy looked toward the European colonial empires of Southeast Asia. Moreover, in terms of the strategic balance in the Pacific, the navy fretted about the latent threat that American industrial and military power represented, while United States does not appear to have existed in the army's calculations, which were more focused on the Red Army in Mongolia and Siberia.

In effect, the Axis powers sought no less than the conquest of much of the world. What made the alliance possible was that their aims rarely conflicted, but at the same time that disparity made the development of a coherent strategy virtually impossible. At the same time, the leaders of all three powers proved to be profoundly contemptuous of the fighting power and capabilities of their opponents. In the German case, the nature of Nazi ideology, with its emphasis on the innate superiority of the Aryan races, made it impossible not just for Hitler, but his senior military officers to judge with any degree of sophistication the capabilities and staying power of their opponents or for that matter their allies.[11]

---

9 The most thorough discussion of Hitler's W*eltanschauung* and ideology remains Eberhard Jackel, *Hitler's Worldview* (Cambridge, MA, 1981).

10 For the most scholarly examination of Italian strategic aims as well as Mussolini's ruthlessness in attempting to realize them, see MacGregor Knox, *Hitler's Italian Allies: Royal Armed Forces, Fascist Regime, and the War of 1940–1943* (Cambridge, 2009).

11 Nothing makes this clearer than the fact that the Soviets were able to deceive German intelligence as to the location of every single major offensive they were to launch from Stalingrad through to the end of the war. For the groundbreaking analysis of this major factor in Soviet operational art see the works by Colonel David Glantz.

This was true from the Battle of Britain through to the end of the war. It proved to be equally true of the Japanese, who believed that the warrior ethos of *Bushido* provided their soldiers with an unbeatable superiority over the soft, degenerate soldiers of their opponents.[12] The Italians held less of a racist attitude; nevertheless, their behavior in Abyssinia suggests they were not far behind the Germans in their contempt for others, including, perhaps with reason, their attitudes toward the political leaders of the democratic nations, at least in the prewar period.

The result of such ideological views on the articulation and development of an alliance strategy was profound. In the first years of the war, it led Germany's leaders (and not just Hitler), as well as Japan's leaders to make disastrous choices, the result of a general inability to see the world through anything but ideological tinted glasses. This proved to be the case not only in terms of military capabilities, but crucially in terms of the economic strength of their opponents, particularly the United States. With some reason, Winston Churchill was to judge the war as strategically won by December 1941 with the attack on Pearl Harbor and Hitler's subsequent declaration of war on the United States.

The diplomatic and prewar background

The disaster of World War II resulted largely from the catastrophic smash up of World War I, combined with the impact that the Great Depression exercised on the world's economic and political stability. Too often historians have credited the Treaty of Versailles as being responsible for the next terrible conflict. In fact, that treaty only reflected the strategic realities that had emerged from the incomplete Allied victories in the fall of 1918.[13] Significantly, Allied military forces had yet to reach the Reich's territory when revolution broke out and discipline in a defeated German army collapsed. Even as the representatives of the major powers were signing the treaty, a number of the major pieces that would lead to the next war were already in place. Russia, still in the thrall of its civil war, was heading toward the Bolshevik tyranny that would reject the entire settlement, while at the same time attempting to regain the territories lost from the domains of tsarist Russia in the war's strategic and diplomatic aftermath. The Germans were already arguing, and perhaps more importantly believing, that their army

---

12 There were of course exceptions, Admiral Yamamoto of Japan being a particularly good example.
13 For a discussion of the real causes behind Versailles's failure see Williamson Murray, "Versailles: The Peace Without a Chance," in Williamson Murray and James Lacey (eds.), *The Making of Peace: Rulers, States, and the Aftermath of War* (Cambridge, 2009).

had remained unbroken and unbeaten in the field in the fall of 1918, only to be stabbed in the back by the socialists, communists, and Jews at home. Even in the Allied camp there was profound disillusionment. The Italians, having suffered over 600,000 dead in the endless fighting along the Isonzo River, believed they deserved far more than the slivers of territory they had gained at the peace table. The United States, of course, rejected the Versailles Treaty and retreated into isolationism.

It was the Italians who first broke with the postwar political settlement. In 1922 Benito Mussolini, still a youthful street agitator and combat veteran, seized power with the clear aim of breaking out from the limits of Italian power to reestablish ancient Rome's domination of the Mediterranean. Nevertheless, as long as Mussolini remained relatively contained, as the Corfu incident of 1923 indicated, there were considerable limits on how far *il Duce* would be willing to go to achieve this aim.[14] Simply put, Italy's economic and military strength was insufficient to overturn the European balance of power without considerable outside help.[15]

But matters altered with the arrival of Adolf Hitler in power in Nazi Germany in January 1933.[16] Four days after assuming the chancellorship, Hitler met with the Reich's senior military leaders to lay out his future aims. He immediately made clear that he had no intention of minor adjustments to the Treaty of Versailles and Germany's frontiers.[17] As he had underlined in *Mein Kampf*, Hitler declared for the generals' and admirals' benefit that Germany would have to expand its territory massively or die. The military leaders may not have really believed Hitler's megalomaniacal goals, but they were certainly delighted to receive a blank check with which to begin a massive program of rearmament.[18]

---

14 The Italians, outraged by the murder of one of their generals and his accompanying officers in Albania, an act for which they blamed the Greeks, bombarded and occupied Corfu. British and French pressure then made them withdraw.

15 For German–Italian relations in the late 1930s, see also D. C. Watt, "The Rome-Berlin Axis, 1936–1940: Myth and Reality," *The Review of Politics*, 22 (1960).

16 For the most complete examination of the roots and intellectual factors that determined how Mussolini and Hitler came to power see MacGregor Knox, *To the Threshold of Power, 1922/33: Origins and Dynamics of the Fascist and National Socialist Dictatorships* (Cambridge, 2007).

17 See particularly the notes kept by one of the senior Reichsheer generals who participated in the lengthy discussions with the new chancellor: "Aufzeichnung Liebmann," *Vierteljahrshefte für Zeitgeschichte*, 2(4) (October 1954).

18 This massive rearmament program came close to breaking Germany financially, but largely through the failures of British economic policies and the fact that the Germans were able to plunder first Austria, then Czechoslovakia, and then its wartime conquests, the Reich was able to escape financial ruin. For the Reich's economic difficulties during the interwar period see Williamson Murray, *The Change in the European Balance of Power, 1938–1939: The Path to Ruin* (Princeton, 1984), ch. 1; and Adam Tooze, *The Wages of Destruction: The Making and Breaking of the Nazi Economy* (London, 2006).

Hitler had long been an admirer of Mussolini and his Fascist revolution in Italy, but given Italian attitudes toward the Germans and memories of the disastrous defeat of Caporetto at German hands in 1917, Mussolini was not initially receptive to German overtures. The *Führer's* first visit to Italy in May 1934 was anything but a success. Shortly thereafter in the summer of 1934, the brutal assassination of Austria's chancellor, Engelbert Dollfus, by Nazi thugs in an attempted coup further exacerbated tensions between the two states. Mussolini moved Italian troops up on the Brenner Pass in a signal of his willingness to defend Austria's independence. The fact that Britain, France, and Italy joined in an agreement called the Stresa Front to maintain Austria's independence in the immediate aftermath of the crisis suggested that Hitler had reached a dead end in his hopes of breaking up World War I's victorious powers.

But almost immediately the Stresa Front collapsed. Mussolini decided that the moment was ripe to avenge the late-nineteenth-century defeat of Italy's colonial forces by the Ethiopians at Battle of Adowa. Thus, with French connivance, he ordered his army to invade that primitive land. The liberal use of gas warfare against Ethiopia's tribal levies served to further underline the ruthlessness of Italian actions.[19] The Ethiopians appealed to the League of Nations, and while the French were willing to stand aside for *raison d'état*, an outraged British public forced their government to take a public stand against Italian aggression. By merely closing the Suez Canal to Italian shipping, the British could have ended Mussolini's adventure, but Britain's leaders were unwilling to take such a drastic step.[20] The result was that British strategic policy fell between two stools: on one hand, the British failed to support the Ethiopians and end the Italian aggression by military force; on the other hand, they infuriated the Italians. The diplomatic road across the Brenner Pass was now open, and Mussolini would soon prove delighted to cross it.

In summer 1936 a murderous civil war broke out in Spain, as a military junta, led by General Francisco Franco, attempted to overthrow the left-wing republic. Britain and France tried to contain the spread

---

19 For the murderous behavior of the Italian army, actively encouraged by Mussolini, see MacGregor Knox, *Mussolini Unleashed: Politics and Strategy in Fascist Italy's Last War* (Cambridge, 1984), pp. 3–4.

20 Had the British closed the Suez Canal to Italian shipping it is probable Mussolini would have launched his navy against the British, but the result would have been a disastrous defeat. The British chiefs of staff warned their government that the Italians represented a serious threat, but the minutes of their own conversations indicate that they did so as a means to push the government to increase its expenditures on defense. For British estimates see Arthur Marder, "The Royal Navy and the Italo-Ethiopian Crisis of 1935–1936," *American Historical Review*, 75(5) (1970).

of the war by limiting intervention. The dictatorships, however, rallied to the respective sides based on their ideologies. Publicly the Soviet Union supported the Republic, while the murderous thugs of its secret police hunted down Trotskiites and other deviationists from Stalin's line.

One the other side, Germany and Italy lined up to support Franco. But there was a key difference in that support. Mussolini committed his regime and military to wholehearted support for the Nationalists. Ever the clever Machiavellian, Hitler offered only limited German support with small training contingents of the army and *Luftwaffe*. In fact, as he made clear to his advisors, it was in Germany's interest that Franco not win the civil war quickly.[21] As the war continued, Europe's attention focused on the Iberian Peninsula, allowing Germany to continue its massive program of rearmament unhindered. Thus, the Germans only supported Franco in a limited fashion, while the Italians poured men and equipment into the struggle in Spain, from which they would gain virtually nothing in the long run.

In October 1936 representatives from Germany, Japan, and Italy signed the Anti-Comintern Pact, which underlined their hostility to communism and the Soviet Union. Its most important aspect besides the virulent anti-communism of the signers was the fact that Hitler had decided to drop China in favor of Japan in terms of Germany's Far East Asian policy. Throughout these early years of Nazi control, Hitler masterfully wove a web of peace in public, while massively pushing rearmament at home. In 1933 Germany left the League of Nations; in 1934 Hitler promulgated conscription and announced the creation of the *Luftwaffe*; and in 1936 came the remilitarization of the Rhineland, a step opposed by the *Führer*'s military advisors, but one that Hitler got away with when the French failed to respond.[22] Nevertheless, throughout this period, Germany's financial situation trembled on the brink of bankruptcy, as the demands for massive rearmament confronted the lack of hard currency to pay for imports of raw materials.[23]

In November 1937 Hitler met with his senior military and diplomatic advisors in a day-long conference in which he made clear his belief the Reich needed to move in the near future, given the serious economic

---

21 *Akten zur deutschen auswärtigen Politik* (hereafter *ADAP*), Series D, Doc. 19, "Niederschrift über die Besprechung in der Reichskanzlei am 5. November 1937 von 16,15–20, 30 Uhr," 10.11.37.
22 British attitudes were summed up by a comment in the House of Commons that the Germans were only moving into "their backyard."
23 For the state of the German economy and the serious financial problems the Reich confronted, see Tooze, *The Wages of Destruction*.

problems it confronted.[24] Given Hitler's intention to drive forward, it is surprising he made no serious efforts to line up foreign support for his moves until the two great crises of 1938 arrived on Europe's doorstep. Nevertheless, Italy and Nazi Germany drew steadily closer together. In fall 1937 Mussolini journeyed to the Reich to visit the *Wehrmacht*'s fall maneuvers and came away enormously impressed by the obvious tactical proficiency of the army's combat units, as were a number of other foreign observers.[25]

Three months later, in the midst of a serious internal crisis over the firing of the army's chief of staff, Colonel General Werner von Fritsch, Hitler moved against Austria. This time the Italians were solidly on the German side. Thus, Mussolini made no move to shore up the clerical-fascist regime of Kurt Schuschnigg and stood by as the Nazis savaged Italy's one-time friends.[26] In May 1938, Hitler again returned to Italy, this time far better prepared to deal with his Italian hosts. Already having determined to smash Czechoslovakia in the fall, the *Führer*'s major intention in making the journey was to sound his fellow dictator out on what kind of stance Italy would take if Czech–German relations exploded. In fact, Hitler found Mussolini more than receptive to an aggressive Nazi policy toward Czechoslovakia.

Returning to Germany, Hitler then confronted an explosive situation in which the Czechs called upon their supposed allies, the French, for help, given what they interpreted as an imminent German invasion. That made up Hitler's mind. With the help of the malicious club-footed Dr. Joseph Goebbels, the *Führer* unleashed a crisis with the aim of invading and destroying the Czech state at the end of September 1938. The diplomatic and strategic consequences of the crisis were profound, including the dismal surrender of the British and French at the Munich Conference in late September and the destruction of the balance of power in Eastern Europe.[27] Mussolini did play a major role in arranging the conference, which was to save (for the time being) both Germany and Italy from a disastrous war.[28]

24 The morning session discussed Hitler's view of the strategic possibilities, and although no minutes were kept of the afternoon session, the topic was clearly Germany's economic problems. See *ADAP*, "Niederschrift über die Besprechung in der Reichskanzlei am 5. November 1937 von 16,16–20, 30 Uhr."
25 These included the British General "Tiny" Ironside.
26 The Germans incorporated the Austrian army into the *Wehrmacht*, but 50 percent of the generals and colonels and 20 percent of the junior officers were purged. Thirty senior officers were immediately sent to Dachau, while the Gestapo murdered the secretary of war. Telford Taylor, *Munich* (Garden City, NY, 1979), p. 373.
27 For an examination of the diplomatic and strategic ramifications of the crisis see Murray, *The Change in the European Balance of Power*, chs. 6 and 7.
28 For the military aspects of what a war in 1938 would have looked like see ibid., ch. 7.

The Italians appear to have believed that the Germans were only aiming at maximizing their diplomatic gains at the expense of their weaker southeastern neighbor. Thus, Mussolini openly and boisterously supported the Germans as they ratcheted up the pressure on the Czechs. On 28 September, Mussolini's son-in-law and foreign minister, Galeazzo Ciano, went so far as to warn the British minister in Rome "that Italy's interests, honor, and pledged word required she should actively and fully side with Germany."[29] In retrospect, what is clear is that neither Nazi Germany nor Fascist Italy were ready for a major conflict in the fall of 1938. Fortunately for the dictators, Hitler drew back at the last moment from launching the *Wehrmacht* into Czechoslovakia and thus precipitating a major European conflict.

The Munich settlement robbed Czechoslovakia of its defensible frontiers, its major industrial sites in the Sudetenland, and most important its independent existence.[30] Hitler, of course, had no intention of allowing the rump state of Czechoslovakia to retain its sovereignty. In mid March 1939 the *Führer* launched his legions into what was left of the Czech state, while allowing the Slovakians to slink away and establish their own puppet state under Nazi tutelage. Hitler followed that easy triumph by seizing Memel from the Lithuanians. Not to be out done, in April 1939 Mussolini ordered his troops to occupy Albania, the last peaceful triumph the Axis would enjoy. Nevertheless, these last achievements came at a considerable cost, particularly the German occupation of Czechoslovakia, which infuriated British popular opinion and undermined entirely Prime Minister Neville Chamberlain's policy of appeasement. Those actions finally awoke the democracies to the looming threat.[31]

The succeeding six months led directly to the outbreak of World War II in September 1939, but that period also saw considerable tension among the major members of the Anti-Comintern Pact. For Hitler, the main strategic issue was clearing the decks so that the *Wehrmacht* could crush the Polish state, which had had the temerity to resist German pressure and the independence of which Chamberlain had guaranteed. The German dictator hoped that he could avoid a general European war over an invasion of Poland, if possible, but he was more than willing to

---

29 Public Records Office (hereafter PRO), FO 371/21743, C 11016/194/18, Perth to Halifax, 29.9.38.
30 For the strategic and military fallout from the surrender of Czechoslovakia by the Western Powers at Munich see particularly Murray, *The Change in the European Balance of Power*, ch. 7.
31 For the considerable period of time it took Chamberlain to recognize the implications of the German occupation of Czechoslovakia see ibid., pp. 284–86.

risk one. On the other hand, partially due to the pressure of his military and diplomatic advisors, Mussolini had finally recognized that Italy and its military forces were not ready for a major war, given her immense expenditures in the Ethiopian conflict and in supporting Franco and the Nationalists in Spain.[32] In discussions with their German counterparts in May 1939, Mussolini and Ciano received the impression that the Germans agreed with them that the two powers should not court a major war until 1944.

While these major events had been unfolding in Europe, the Japanese had been busy in Asia. In summer 1937, the Kwantung army, units of the Japanese army in Manchuria, had unleashed a disastrous war against China without coordination or permission from Tokyo. Nevertheless, the Japanese government had not only acquiesced to the invasion, but had extended the war to the environs of Shanghai along the central Chinese coast. In effect, there was no serious strategic policy-making occurring within the Japanese government, despite the Kwantung army's willful decision to start a war that no one in Tokyo approved or wanted.

Moreover, there was a schizophrenic split between the focus of the Japanese Imperial Navy and the army. The navy looked eastward and southward to the wide expanses of the Pacific and the vulnerable colonies of Southeast Asia possessed by the Americans (the Philippines), the British (Malaya, Singapore, and Borneo), and the Dutch (the Dutch East Indies), as the area where Japan should seek the raw materials needed to fuel its economy. The army looked west and north toward China and the Soviet Union as the geographic area toward which Japan needed to expand. The Japanese generals in Manchuko had launched the conflict against China for two major reasons: the first in the belief that by invading China, they could force the Chinese to end their boycott of Japanese goods; the second, in a desire to clean up the troublesome threat from north China, to provide breathing room for what its leaders believed would be the inevitable war against the Soviet Union and its communist regime.[33]

---

32 The problem with the Italian military in 1939 was more basic than its commitments in the mid 1930s. As MacGregor Knox has suggested: "The fundamental problem was the Italian general staff tradition: Custoza, Lissa, Adua, Caporetto. On those occasions the military, as yet uncontaminated by contact with Fascism, distinguished itself by the absence of the study, planning, and attention to detail that characterized the Germans and by a tendency to intrigue and confusion of responsibility among senior officers." Knox, *Mussolini Unleashed*, p. 16.

33 For the Japanese efforts to bring order to northern China as a means to prepare the strategic groundwork for the coming struggle against the Soviets see Noboru Yamaguchi, "An Unexpected Encounter with Hybrid Warfare: The Japanese Experience in North China," in Williamson Murray and Peter Mansoor (eds.), *Hybrid Warfare: Fighting Complex Opponents from the Ancient World to the Present* (Cambridge, 2012).

Thus, steadily drawn into the embrace of the tar baby of the Second Sino-Japanese War,[34] the Japanese, nevertheless, still managed to get themselves involved in major skirmishes with the Soviets along the Manchurian–Siberian frontier in 1938 and 1939. They were also watching with close attention the growing troubles in Europe. From their point of view, the connection with Hitler and Mussolini provided crucial moral support for what they believed would soon be the war they desired to fight, namely the war against the Soviet Union, as opposed to the war they were actually fighting against the Chinese.

As during the previous summer, Goebbels's propaganda machine revved up in June 1939 with bogus claims about the atrocities being committed against the German minority by the Poles. The British and French stood relatively strong against that tide. Chamberlain and many of his advisors may not have wanted to deal with the Germans, but the political climate in Britain, with an election mandated to occur in 1940, was such that there was little wiggle room for further appeasement.[35]

In May 1939, Joachim von Ribbentrop, the Reich's foreign minister, met with his Italian counterpart, Ciano, in Florence to iron out a treaty of alliance between the two dictatorships. They signed the "Pact of Steel" in Berlin later that month. For all intents and purposes, it represented an offensive alliance, although the Italians had made it clear that they would not be ready for war for at least another two years at the earliest. Ciano and Mussolini believed German assurances that Hitler was thinking in the same terms. Nevertheless, it is clear the Germans knew that they intended war in early September against the Poles whatever happened. For a short period, those German assurances entirely duped the Italians.

But one should not believe that because the Italians were not in favor of war in fall 1939, they were any less belligerent. Their own goals remained both megalomaniacal and completely unrealistic. As Mussolini told the Grand Council of the Italian Fascist Party in February 1939:

Italy is therefore in truth a prisoner of the Mediterranean, and the more populous and prosperous Italy becomes, the more its imprisonment will gall.

34 To emphasize the lack of German strategy and failure to think through the results of its policy in Asia, one need look no further than the German military mission to China, which created combat effective Nationalist divisions that emboldened Chinese leader Chiang Kai-Shek to oppose the Japanese attacks rather than give in to Japanese demands – and this while German policy in Asia was tilting toward the Japanese. See Robyn L. Rodriguez, "Journey to the East: The German Military Mission in China, 1927–1938," PhD dissertation, The Ohio State University, 2011.
35 The British did appease the Japanese as war with Germany approached. See Bradford Lee, *Britain and the Sino-Japanese War, 1937–1939* (Stanford, CA, 1973).

The bars of this prison are Corsica, Tunis, Malta, Cyprus. The sentinels of this prison are Gibraltar and Suez ... [O]ne can draw the following conclusions:

1. The task of Italian policy, which cannot have and does not have continental objectives of a European territorial nature except Albania, is first of all to break the bars of this continental prison.
2. Once the bars are broken, Italian policy can have only one watchword – to march to the ocean. Which ocean? The Indian Ocean, joining Libya with Ethiopia through the Sudan or the Atlantic, through French North Africa. In either case, we will find ourselves confronted with Anglo-French opposition.[36]

By early August 1939, it was becoming increasingly clear to Mussolini and Ciano that Ribbentrop had been economical with the truth. Germany was not going to put off the war for another three or four years, but was in fact seeking war in the immediate future. Moreover, it was also clear to Mussolini's chief advisors, including Ciano, that Italy's military forces were unprepared for war.[37] Adding to the confusion, with Europe on the brink of war, was the fact that Hitler and Ribbentrop were busily engaged in negotiating a non-aggression pact with Stalin to remove the Soviet Union from the immediate chessboard and allow the *Wehrmacht* a free hand to dispose of the Poles. Late in the evening of 23 August 1939, Vyacheslav Molotov, Stalin's foreign minister, and Ribbentrop signed the Nazi–Soviet Non-Aggression Pact, one of the most dishonest and murderous agreements ever signed in history.[38] Its signing caused an enormous uproar in Europe and removed any doubts about what the Soviet Union would do, should the *Wehrmacht* invade Poland.[39] In Britain Halifax, displaying the strategic myopia that had characterized so much of British policy-making over the past several years, commented to the members of the Cabinet that the agreement was of little strategic importance, although he did admit that its moral effect would be enormous.[40]

For the Italians the pact came as a complete surprise. On 22 August, Ribbentrop informed Ciano that he could not meet him on the Brenner

36 Quoted in Knox, *Mussolini Unleashed*, p. 40.
37 Moreover, there was considerable disarray within the Italian military. To get an accurate count of the number of aircraft the Regia Aeronautica possessed, Ciano suggested to Mussolini that the Fascist Party's prefects go out to the airfields and count the number of aircraft in the hangars and then add the numbers of aircraft at each base, instead of accepting clearly inaccurate estimates from the military. Ciano, *The Ciano Diaries*, p 147.
38 For the fallout from the pact see Timothy Snyder, *Bloodlands: Europe between Hitler and Stalin* (New York, 2010).
39 The nature of the pact was best summed up by Stalin's toast to Ribbentrop that singled Heinrich Himmler out "as the man who has brought order to Germany."
40 PRO CAB 23/100, Cab 41 (39), Meeting of the Cabinet, 22.8.39.

Pass, but preferred Innsbruck, because the German foreign minister had to fly to Moscow to sign a non-aggression pact with the Soviets. It was the first inkling the Italians had heard from the Germans of the negotiations they were having with the Soviets – so much for cooperative decision-making between allies.[41] For Ciano and those Italians with any sense, the problem was how to persuade Mussolini of Italy's unpreparedness for war and that German duplicity in promising in the spring that they had no intention of going to war in the next several years removed whatever obligation there might have been to honor the Pact of Steel. It was a tough sell, because Mussolini desperately wanted to avoid the accusation that, as with the Italian government in 1914, Fascist Italy was abandoning its German ally. Here Ciano and company received considerable help from the British government, the leaders of which went out of their way to minimize actions that might have drawn the Italians into the war.[42]

Eventually Mussolini came around. The development of a skillful diplomatic ploy helped the Italians escape their obligations; they demanded that, given their nation's unpreparedness for an immediate conflict, the Reich make up Italy's deficiencies. In a message to Hitler, Mussolini indicated that Italy would join the war if the Germans would cough up "the military equipment and raw materials to withstand the blow which France and Britain will direct predominantly against us."[43] When Hitler then asked what the Italian needs might be, the Italians provided a list that could have choked a horse: some 18,153,000 tons of coal and other scarce raw materials along with 150 batteries of anti-aircraft artillery; all of these items were already in short supply in Germany.[44] Not surprisingly, the *Führer* then released the Italians from their obligations. Adding to Italian discomfort was the fact that, as Ciano recorded in his diary: "The English communicate to us the text of German proposals [for a potential settlement to the Polish crisis] to London, about which there is a great ado, but about which *we are 100 percent in the dark*. [Italics in the original] Hitler proposes to the English an alliance or something like it. And this was without our knowledge."[45]

41 Ciano, *The Ciano Diaries*, 22 August 1939, p. 126.
42 In the end this proved to be a disastrous political and strategic mistake, because the Italians eventually entered the war at the worst possible moment for the Western Powers. Had the Italians entered the conflict at Germany's side in September 1939 the results could well have been serious for both the Axis powers, because disasters in the Mediterranean would probably have forced the Germans to launch the invasion of the west prematurely. For a further discussion of these issues, see Murray, *The Change in the European Balance of Power*, pp. 314–21.
43 Quoted in Knox, *Mussolini Unleashed*, p. 43.
44 Ibid., p. 41.
45 Ciano, *The Ciano Diaries*, p. 130.

If the Italians found themselves annoyed at their treatment at the hands of the Germans, the Japanese were furious. After all, they had made the alliance with the Germans and the Italians because of their implacable hostility toward communism and the Soviet Union in particular. Moreover, the China venture had rested on the desire of a number of Kwantung generals to remove the Chinese threat to Manchuko, so that they could get on with the more important business of fighting Soviet military forces in China. Thus, the Japanese viewed the Nazi–Soviet Non-Aggression Pact with considerable anger, since it undercut the basis of their strategy.

Astonishingly, given the commitment of troops and military forces to what the Japanese so blithely termed the "China incident," in summer 1939 the Kwantung army created a major incident with the Soviets in the far reaches of Manchuria along the southeastern border of Mongolia.[46] The confrontation escalated throughout the summer. In late August, immediately before the signing of the Nazi–Soviet Non-Aggression Pact, Soviet forces, consisting of some of the most modern in the Red Army and commanded by the competent General Gregori Zhukov, destroyed the reinforced Japanese 23rd Division. The Japanese, as they would do throughout the upcoming war in the Pacific, fought to the last man, but outnumbered and possessing inferior equipment, they were slaughtered. Fortunately for its future opponents, the Kwantung army suppressed the extent of the disaster and thus there was no substantial examination of the weaknesses in Japanese tactics and equipment against a first-class opponent as opposed to the Chinese.[47] Nevertheless, the fierceness of the confrontation added to the Japanese feeling that the Germans had betrayed them by signing the non-aggression pact with the Soviet Union.

The first war year: September 1939 to September 1940

And so with their invasion of Poland, the Germans went to war without allies. Nevertheless, they were to receive considerable help from their friends, both old and new. Mussolini spent most of the Phony War – the period between the fall of Poland and the opening of German offensive operations against Scandinavia – in bemoaning Italy's lack of preparation

---

46 The most thorough history of the fighting at Nomonhan, or Khalkhin Gol as it is known to the Russians, is to be found in Alvin D. Coox, *Japan against Russia, 1939* (Stanford, CA, 1990).

47 Had the Japanese done a lessons-learned analysis that was then distributed throughout the army, they might have performed better in their later battles against the Americans in the Pacific. The same thing was to happen after the Battle of Midway, when the Japanese navy suppressed the extent of that defeat and thus prevented any major rethinking within the navy of its approach to the growing American threat.

for war as well as calculating the best moment for the intervention of Italian forces into the struggle.[48] British blockade measures, aimed at Germany, but which also affected Italy, did nothing to better *il Duce*'s mood. Crucially, Mussolini's fundamental aim had not changed: it was to replace Britain and France as the dominant power in the Mediterranean. Meanwhile, the Soviets, the Reich's new-found friend, had begun shipping vast amounts of raw materials to Germany in early 1940.[49]

Meanwhile, through their lack of action the Western Powers allowed the Germans to husband their economic resources, while repairing the considerable deficiencies in the *Wehrmacht* that had appeared in the fighting during the Polish campaign.[50] The period of the Phony War also involved considerable planning for the great campaign to come in the west. The first move came on 9 April with the attack by German air, naval, and ground forces on Denmark and Norway. With considerable irony Ciano noted in his diary:

They [the Germans] did not march in the direction of Romania [as the rumors emanating from Berlin had suggested]. A secretary of the German embassy, who came to my house at two o'clock in the morning ... asked to be received at seven o'clock in the morning. Nothing else. He arrived at six-thirty, pale and tired, and communicated Hitler's decision to occupy Denmark and Norway, adding that decision had already been acted upon.[51]

The Germans were no more forthcoming about their planned invasion of France and the Low Countries. At 0400 on 10 May the German ambassador in Rome informed Ciano that the German offensive in the west had begun.[52] By this point in dealing with the Germans, the Italians were not surprised. As the battle in the west began, they expected that the fighting in France would prove a long drawn-out affair, during which they could prepare for a future intervention while at the same time maximizing their price for joining. As one of the Italian generals informed Ciano, the "French defense will prove absolutely unbreakable."[53]

As the French defenses crumbled, and it became increasingly clear the Germans were going to win a swift and decisive victory, the Italians

---

48 For Mussolini's difficulties in accepting a seat on the sidelines during the Phony War, see Knox, *Mussolini Unleashed*, pp. 44–86.
49 For Soviet shipments of raw materials to the Reich see Ferdinand Friedensburg, "Die sowjetischen Kriegslieferungen an das Hitlerreich," in *Vierteljahrshefte zur Wirtschaftsforschung*, 4 (1962): 331–38.
50 For German problems see Williamson Murray, "The German Response to Victory in Poland: A Case Study in Professionalism," *Armed Forces and Society*, Winter (1981).
51 Ciano, *The Ciano Diaries*, pp. 233–34.
52 Ibid., pp. 246–47.
53 Ibid., p. 247.

scrambled to assemble an effective military and strategic response. What they soon discovered was that German eagerness to have the Italians join in the conflict decreased markedly as the German successes accumulated. But Mussolini was determined to have his way. There was considerable toing and froing as the Italians attempted to settle on a date to initiate hostilities against the Allies. Initially, the Italians selected 5 June; then the Germans asked for a delay; and finally the two governments settled on the 10 June.

But the Germans were distinctly unhappy, because the entrance of the Italians into the war would complicate the business of making a swift end to the conflict. Nor were the Germans particularly enthusiastic about dividing up the booty with the Italians, who, from Hitler's point of view, had displayed a distinct unwillingness to join the struggle when there was serious fighting to be done. Italian performance in the opening days lived up to the pessimistic expectations of the Germans. As the panzers mopped up the remnants of the French army, the Italians launched an offensive into the Alpine regions along the French border, which failed at a heavy cost in Italian lives with no discernible gains.

For Hitler, the war in the west was now over. For much of June he toured the French countryside, visiting Paris and the World War I battlefields over which he had fought. For the Italians, instead of a clear strategic goal, there was a multiplicity of goals: Malta, Greece, Yugoslavia, North Africa were all on Mussolini's hit list, but in what order and when *il Duce* had not a clue.[54] Instead, during the summer months he considered all of the various possibilities. Part of his problem was that his senior military officers were dead set against launching any major offensive against the British in the Mediterranean and Middle East. At least Ciano seems to have recognized that British leadership had undergone a significant shift; shortly after the Royal Navy had attacked and damaged a significant portion of the French battle fleet at Mers-el-Kebir, he noted: "For the moment it proves that the fighting spirit of His British Majesty's fleet is quite alive, and still has the aggressive ruthlessness of the captains and pirates of the seventeenth century."[55]

While the Italians were attempting to make up their minds, the Germans were already moving in a substantially new direction. At the same time that the *Luftwaffe* was deploying its air fleets and their support structure

---

54 Knox is particularly good on the shambles that characterized Italian strategic decision making. See Knox, *Mussolini Unleashed*, pp. 134–88.

55 Ciano, *The Ciano Diaries*, p. 273. In the same entry for 4 July 1940, the Italian ambassador returning from London to Italy told Ciano that the British people were united across classes to resist any air or amphibious offensive the Germans might launch against their nation.

to the northwestern coasts of France, preparatory to launching its air offensive against the United Kingdom, Hitler and the army's senior leaders were discussing the possibility of invading the Soviet Union.[56] At the beginning of July, the army's commander, Walter von Brauchitsch, soon to be promoted to field marshal, and the chief of the general staff, Franz Halder, had already ordered that planning for an invasion of the Soviet Union begin even before they received orders from Hitler.[57] At the end of the month they met with the *Führer*, who indicated his belief that the only reason the British had refused to make peace was a result of a belief that the United States and the Soviet Union would come to their aid. Therefore, his conclusion: destroy the Soviet Union in a rapid and decisive operation and the British would fold. Thus began the massive effort to plan an invasion of Russia to begin in spring 1941.[58] This represented a crucial turn in Nazi strategy. From this point, Hitler's focus as well as that of the Third Reich would remain fixed on what would soon be codenamed Operation BARBAROSSA. At the same time that these massive preparations were underway, the Germans failed to inform their major allies, Italy and Japan, of what was afoot.[59] This failure to keep their allies informed about their intentions would have serious strategic consequences for the German conduct of the war in 1941.[60]

Thus, while the Germans were moving forward in preparing to move against the Soviet Union in the east, events were occurring elsewhere that would play an important role in the war's course. The Italians for their part were considering major operations in the Balkans, but in early August Berlin discerned what was going on in Rome. The last thing that

---

56 The Italians did supply a small air contingent that arrived in September 1940 to support the aerial assault on the British Isles. It achieved nothing except to lose a considerable number of aircraft and to underline for both the Germans and the British how far behind the Italians were in the capabilities of their aircraft.

57 Horst Boog et al., *Das Deutsche Reich und der Zweite Weltkrieg*, IV: *Der Angriff auf die Sowjetunion* (Stuttgart, 1983).

58 Initially Hitler had suggested a fall 1940 date for the invasion, but the army's leaders, even given their overestimation of German military strength, had serious doubts about invading Russia with winter immediately around the corner. Thus, they persuaded Hitler to wait until the following spring.

59 They would, however, inform the Finns and the Romanians of what they were planning for the first half of 1941, because both of those small powers had important roles to play in the upcoming military operations against the Soviets in terms of their geographic position.

60 There was some justification for the German unwillingness to inform the Italians about BARBAROSSA, given the fact that the Italians were less than discreet about what was happening in Rome and elsewhere. The irony, of course, was that had the Germans informed the Italians about the upcoming invasion of the Soviet Union and that information had leaked, most probably Stalin would have disregarded the intelligence, as he did all the other warnings that made their way through to Moscow.

Hitler wanted, now that major preparations were already underway for an invasion of the Soviet Union, was a major blow up in the Balkans that would upset his intentions. As Ciano records, Ribbentrop made clear "that it is necessary to abandon any plan to attack Yugoslavia [and] that an eventual action against Greece is not at all welcome in Berlin. It is a complete order to halt all along the line."[61] Not surprisingly, the peremptory nature of the German order did not sit well with the Italians, especially since the Germans failed to inform them of the larger strategic issues lying behind their demand, namely their preparations for invasion of the Soviet Union.

The Italians were not the only ones scrambling to join in to hunt for loot occasioned by the defeat of France and the eagerly awaited collapse of Britain. In early summer Spain's Franco was eager to join in the conflict against the British. But at the time the Germans, believing the war won and with no desire to share the spoils with latecomers like the Spanish, showed little interest in the offer. Equally significant was the fact that Spain was desperately short of food, as the civil war had destroyed much of Spain's countryside and industry. In the glow of victory, the Germans had no desire to make good Spanish deficiencies in this regard.[62] Nevertheless, Hitler intended to promise the Spaniards everything they wanted, regardless of whether he could make good on the offer.

But Hitler, never sensitive to the feelings of others, overplayed his hand by demanding that the price for the Reich's supporting the Spanish war effort and sharing the spoils would be one of the Canary Islands.[63] In a meeting with Franco in mid-October 1940 on the French–Spanish border, Hitler was now interested in having the Spanish join the war, since British resistance had proven more tenacious than expected. The two dictators agreed that Spain would eventually join the war, but the price the Germans attempted to extract infuriated Franco to the point that the Spaniards decided they would not join the war until absolutely sure the British were defeated. Such an outcome did not appear to be the case in fall 1940. As for meeting with Franco again, Hitler commented that discussing strategic matters with the Spanish dictator was worse than having his teeth pulled.[64]

While the Germans were ordering the Italians to halt in August 1940, the locals in the Balkans were on the brink of starting a major war over

---

61 Ciano, *The Ciano Diaries*, p. 285.
62 On Spanish eagerness to join the Axis assault on Britain see Paul Preston, *Franco, A Biography* (London, 1993), pp. 375–400.
63 Weinburg, *A World at Arms*, p. 207.
64 Preston, *Franco*, p. 399.

the disputed province of Transylvania. Relations between the Romanians and Hungarians had reached the boiling point and by mid-August 1940 both states were on the brink of mobilizing and declaring war. At that point the Germans and Italians stepped in to force a settlement, the Hungarians receiving much of Transylvania at their neighbor's expense. The settlement resulted in a collapse of the Romanian government, a state of affairs which offered inviting prospects to the Soviets. But Hitler was not about to allow Romania to embrace Soviet overtures, given the importance of its oil to the *Wehrmacht*. As a result the Germans, without informing Mussolini, sent a "military mission" to retrain the Romanian army and stabilize the political situation. By December 1940 the German military "mission" had grown to include the 13th Motorized Infantry Division (reinforced), the 16th Panzer Division, two fighter squadrons, one reconnaissance squadron, and two flak regiments.[65] In retrospect, Hitler's move also aimed to stabilize the southern flank of what would be the invasion of the Soviet Union in spring 1941.

The German move into Romania had disastrous consequences for Hitler's alliance with the Italians, as the latter decided to pursue a "parallel war" in the Balkans without consulting their German allies. Ciano's diary entry for 12 October 1940 underlines Mussolini's furious reaction:

But above all he is indignant at the German occupation of Romania. He says that this has impressed Italian public opinion very deeply and badly, because ... nobody had expected this to happen. "Hitler always faces me with a *fait accompli*. This time I am going to pay him back in his own coin. He will find out from the papers that I have occupied Greece. In this way the equilibrium will be established."[66]

Sixteen days after Ciano recorded *il Duce*'s remarks, Italian forces in Albania invaded Greece. Mussolini only bothered to inform Hitler of the invasion on the morning of the latter's arrival in Florence.

The Italian effort was a disaster as the Greeks refused to break. Italian forces in Albania barely equaled Greek forces across the border *before* Greek mobilization; logistically the Italians could not support additional forces in Albania; and to top it all off, the Italians had just demobilized the bulk of their army.[67] Marshal Rodolpho Graziani, who led the invasion of Egypt in September, had summed up the army's approach to war

---

65 As enunciated by Field Marshal Wilhelm Keitel, the mission's responsibilities were to "protect the oil districts ... prepare the Romanian armed forces ... in accordance with German interests [and] ... prepare ... for the employment of German and Romanian forces in case the Soviets force a conflict [on the Reich]." *ADAP*, Series D, vol XI, Document #84.

66 Ciano, *The Ciano Diaries*, p. 300.

67 For the disastrous Italian invasion of Greece see Knox, *Mussolini Unleashed*, pp. 231–38.

in a remark made in June: "When the cannon sounds, everything will fall into place automatically."[68]

The disaster along the Albanian–Greek frontier, which had nothing to do with the bravery of the Italian soldiers and everything to do with the incompetence of the Italian officer corps, heralded a string of defeats for Fascist Italy. On 12 November 1940 British Swordfish aircraft flying off an aircraft carrier, HMS *Eagle*, attacked and sank three Italian battleships in the harbor at Taranto.[69] In December, the British attacked the Italian units that had advanced into Egypt, and what had initially started out as a raid soon blossomed out into a major offensive that drove the Italians far back into Libya.

The deep strategic and operational difficulties that the Italians had gotten themselves into in turn forced the Germans to intervene with substantial military forces. These events provided a considerable lift to the British, who were suffering under the pounding of the nighttime German Blitz. In the immediate aftermath of these defeats, there was relatively little the Germans could do. They began the deployment of substantial additional forces into Romania and pressured the Bulgarians to provide access for the forces they would deploy in the spring to clean up the mess the Italians had made of the Balkans. In February 1941, Erwin Rommel and the troops that would form the *Afrika Korps* began arriving in Libya to restore the situation in North Africa after the devastating defeats the Italian army had suffered in that theater. In the end, the Germans managed to impose heavier losses on the British than they themselves suffered in the fighting in North Africa, but in the long run most probably they could not afford those losses, while the British – at least after American intervention in the conflict in Europe – could.

As far as the Balkan campaign of spring 1941 went, the initial judgment of historians was that it delayed BARBAROSSA by approximately six weeks. In fact, the spring of 1941 had been a wet one in Eastern Europe and conditions were not suitable to begin operations until late June in any case. Moreover, the equipping of a significant number of the *Wehrmacht*'s motorized infantry and panzer divisions was not completed until mid June.[70] Nevertheless, the wear and tear on those divisions that had participated in the Balkan campaign and which had then been hustled back to participate in the invasion of the Soviet Union was con-

---

68 Ibid., p. 121.
69 A success that the Japanese were to replicate thirteen months later at Pearl Harbor. They clearly paid attention to the British success; their future opponents in the Pacific obviously did not.
70 See Boog et al., *Das Deutsche Reich und der Zweite Weltkrieg*, IV, pp. 183–88.

siderable. These divisions formed a significant portion of the motorized strength of Army Group South, a fact that helps to explain why that army group was to have greater difficulties in its advance than the other two army groups to its north.

The larger point in understanding the failures of the Italo-German alliance is that the two powers and their leaders displayed only minimal levels of actual cooperation, while their consistent failure to inform each other of their intentions only served to exacerbate their lack of coordination. At 0300 hours on 22 June, exactly one half hour before the German offensive against the Soviet Union began, the German ambassador delivered to Ciano "a long missive from Hitler for the Duce [explaining] the reasons for his move [the invasion of Russia]." By this point in the war Mussolini's "parallel war" had disappeared into the dustbin of history. For all intents and purposes Fascist Italy had become a German satellite, perhaps receiving favored treatment from Hitler, but with virtually no ability to act on its own. Once again, the Germans had failed to inform their allies about a major operation. Nevertheless, Mussolini's response was to offer up an expeditionary corps to fight on the Eastern Front in spite of the fact that his military forces were already stretched to the breaking point with the commitments to the war in the North African desert.

The Tripartite Pact

On 27 September 1940 Nazi Germany, Imperial Japan, and Fascist Italy signed the Tripartite Pact in which they agreed to declare war on any nation that attacked one of them. The Germans had already informed the Soviets that the pact was not aimed at them and the visit of the Soviet Foreign Minister Vyacheslav Molotov the following December was partially motivated by the Soviet desire to explore the possibility of joining the pact. While, as suggested above, the Japanese had been infuriated by the Nazi–Soviet Non-Aggression Pact, the collapse of France and Britain's desperate situation in the early summer of 1940 served to whet Japanese appetites for further expansion, in this case to the south against the great colonial empires that the European powers had amassed in Southeast Asia.

Almost immediately after the representatives of Vichy France had signed the armistice with Nazi Germany, the Japanese demanded that the French governor of Indo-China allow the Japanese military to occupy the northern half of Vietnam. The newly appointed Japanese prime minister, Konoe Fumimaro, had a complex set of objectives, few of which had the approval of the emperor, but the key point was his aim to take full advantage of the fall of France by pushing south to grab Malaya and the Dutch East Indies. Konoe wished to avoid war with the United States if possible, but if the move against the British and Dutch required it, so be it. In this view such a strategic approach also required a neutrality pact with the Soviet Union and an alliance with the Third Reich. By the end of July after considerable discussions, the members of the new government had agreed with Konoe's strategy.

The Tripartite Pact's strategic aim was specifically to keep the United States out of the war. Here the unmentioned aims and plans of the Japanese and the Germans were substantially different and, in the long run, counter-productive. Japan's foreign minister, Matsuoka Yosuke, a thoroughly unbalanced individual, achieved the desired aim of removing the Soviet threat from Manchuria by negotiating a non-aggression pact with Stalin that was signed in Moscow in April 1941.[71] By removing the Japanese military threat in Siberia, however, the pact was to assist the Soviet Union in resisting the German invasion once it came in June.

Even though the Germans were planning to invade the Soviet Union in two months, Hitler found no reason to dissuade the Japanese from taking that action. His reasoning seems to have been the belief that Japan with its great fleet represented a major counterweight to the United States. An aggressive Japanese policy in Southeast Asia would keep the Americans focused on Asia rather than on Europe. The key component in Hitler's thinking was that the invasion of the Soviet Union was going to prove to be an easy matter, with Stalin's regime collapsing like a house of cards.[72] Thus, from the *Führer*'s point of view, Japanese military action in the distant reaches of Siberia would be of little use in a campaign that was going to last a matter of weeks. Better then to have the Japanese focus on the Anglo-American powers in Southeast Asia and the Pacific.

That attitude would begin to change in late summer and early fall 1941 as it became clear that the Soviets were putting up substantially greater opposition than the Germans had expected. However, by that point the Japanese had made up their minds to go after the oil, rubber, and raw materials of Southeast Asia.[73] Given their experiences at the hands of the Red Army at Nomonhan, the Japanese may well have decided to wait until the Germans had destroyed most of the Red Army before moving

71 In a meeting in May 1941, the navy minister, Admiral Oikawa Koshiro, actually queried as to whether Matsuoka was sane. Weinberg, *A World at Arms*, p. 252.

72 For German overconfidence see Williamson Murray and Allan R. Millett, *A War to Be Won: Fighting the Second World War* (Cambridge, MA, 2000), pp. 114–20.

73 Helping the Japanese make that decision was the fact that a Soviet special operations team managed to blow up one of the main Japanese fuel and ammunition dumps in Manchuria in August 1941. Weinberg, *A World at Arms*, p. 1003, n. 323.

north into Siberia. In July 1941 the Japanese, with the connivance of the Vichy-French authorities, moved into southern Vietnam. They thereby acquired the bases, especially the magnificent fleet anchorage of Cam Ran Bay, from which they could launch their air, naval, and amphibious forces against Malaya, Borneo, and the Dutch East Indies.

This move clearly represented a direct challenge to the United States and its allies. President Franklin Roosevelt immediately replied by freezing Japanese assets in the United States and embargoing the export of oil to Japan. The British and Dutch followed suit within a matter of days.[74] There was no doubt now that the Pacific powers were on the brink of war, even though fitful diplomatic negotiations continued into December. As the Japanese gathered their forces for war, significantly, the army, deep in the morass of the seemingly endless war in China, made relatively few divisions available for the navy's war against the United States. Those forces proved sufficient to overwhelm the Allied defenders of the colonial empires in Southeast Asia, but it was conquest on a shoestring, the Japanese victories enormously aided by the gross incompetence of their enemies.

The Japanese offensive began with the tactically successful, but strategically disastrous attack on Pearl Harbor. Not surprisingly, the Japanese failed to inform the Germans of their intentions until after the fact, but the Germans had no reason to complain given their past treatment of their purported allies, including the Japanese. Hitler's reply was not short in coming. On 11 December 1941 the *Führer* honored the Tripartite Pact and before an enthusiastic Reichstag declared war on the United States. It certainly proved to be the most gratuitously disastrous strategic mistake the Germans would make in 1941, which is saying a great deal.

There appears no rational explanation for Hitler's decision, except perhaps the fact that the disastrous situation on the Eastern Front, with the *Wehrmacht* trembling on the brink of complete collapse, exacerbated Hitler's desire to strike out when he ran into difficulties. His decision rested also on the fact that he, as most Germans, completely underestimated the Americans and the immense power they were going to be able to bring to the war.[75] Of course, the defensive terms of the Tripartite

---

74 It is worth noting that this same month, the House of Representatives renewed the draft by a single vote, an indication that the present irresponsibility of that body represents nothing new in American history.

75 Gerhard Weinberg has pointed out on several occasions that since Hitler and most Germans explained the defeat of 1918 on the belief that communists, socialists, and Jews had stabbed the army in the back, then in their view obviously the arrival of millions of American troops on the Western Front in the last half of 1918 had played little role in the Reich's defeat.

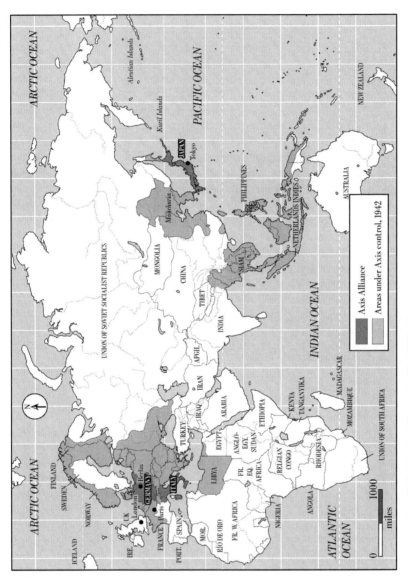

Map 12.1   The Axis Powers in World War II

Treaty did not obligate the Third Reich to follow the Japanese attack on the Americans with a declaration of war on the United States. By so doing, Hitler removed a particularly difficult political problem that was confronting Roosevelt: namely, how to declare war on Nazi Germany given that the Japanese, not the Germans, had attacked Pearl Harbor.

One might have thought that the Germans could have extracted something in return from the Japanese in return for their declaration of war on the United States; certainly, they might have requested that the Japanese close off the Sea of Japan from Soviet shipping, which would at a minimum have stopped much of the flow of Lend-Lease to the Soviets.[76] In fact, the Japanese would have probably refused, because of the vulnerability of their cities to aerial attack from Soviet bases in eastern Siberia. But the Germans never tried.

The Tripartite Pact in action, 1941–1945

It is hard to find any substantive inter-allied cooperation among the Axis powers in the conduct of the global war. Part of the problem had to do with the hard reality that strategic and geographic myopia characterized the leadership of all three powers. When told of the Japanese attack on Pearl Harbor, Hitler gathered together his military staff to celebrate the success of their "Aryan" brothers. In the midst of the toasts to the Japanese, Hitler asked his military staff where Pearl Harbor was. Not a single one of the forty-odd assembled officers knew where the great American base in the Pacific was located – and these were people planning on conquering much of the world.[77]

At the strategic level, cooperation between the Germans and the Italians now meant Hitler declaiming and Mussolini listening. For all intents and purposes, the Mediterranean represented a minor theater from the German point of view, confronted as they were by the massive bloodletting and drain the Eastern Front represented from its onset. For the 1942 offensive that would end up in the Caucasus and Stalingrad, the Germans needed allied armies to cover their growing flank to the

---

76 During the course of the war 50 percent of Lend-Lease to the Soviet Union would move across the Pacific in Liberty ships flying the Hammer and Sickle to unload the cargoes in Vladivostok.

77 One of the major aspects of the background and intellectual preparation of German, Japanese, and Italian leaders was how little they knew of the world outside of their own nations. This was, of course, a major factor in their consistent underestimation of American industrial strength, not to mention the ability of the Americans to create substantial and effective military forces. The incident described above was related to me by Dr. Horst Boog of the Militärgeschichtliches Forschungsamt.

north of the advance toward Stalingrad. As he had the year before, Mussolini stepped in to provide a major contingent of Italians to join the Romanians and Hungarians, all of whom were ill-equipped and ill-prepared for the rigors of fighting against the Red Army.

The Germans were to pay a terrible price for their overestimation of the military capabilities of their allies. In November 1942 the Romanian divisions would collapse on the flanks of Stalingrad and thus open up the German Sixth Army to catastrophic defeat. One month later, the Red Army would destroy the Hungarian and Italian armies, thereby ending German attempts to reach the beleaguered garrison at Stalingrad.[78] The Italian troops destroyed in the Soviet Union were not available to defend Italian interests in the Mediterranean or to protect the homeland.

In North Africa Rommel managed to do more than just contain British and Dominion forces, despite the fact that he and his Italian allies were considerably outnumbered and confronted enormous logistical difficulties not only in moving supplies from Italian ports to North Africa, but in then moving those supplies to the battlefront across the vast distances of Libya and western Egypt.[79] Those logistical difficulties represented a considerable hurdle with which neither the Italians nor the Germans were prepared to deal. Thus, it is unlikely that additional German forces would have been able to achieve greater success.

The one point at which the Axis forces might have considerably improved their strategic situation in the Mediterranean came in mid June 1942, immediately after Rommel had won a series of devastating successes against a wretchedly led Eighth Army along the Gazala Line.[80] The strategic question then was whether the *Afrika Korps* should pursue the fleeing British to Cairo and the Nile Delta, or to halt it and use Axis strength against Malta. Rommel was clearly in favor of the former, as were Mussolini and Hitler. *Il Duce* was dreaming of riding into Cairo, while Hitler had more megalomaniacal dreams of having Axis forces drive through the Middle East to meet up with those of Army Group South pushing through the Caucasus – an impossible task given the lack

---

78 There was a good deal of contempt (to a considerable degree racially motivated) at all levels of the German military for the performance of their allies on the battlefield, but what the Germans largely missed was how badly equipped and trained their allies were for the conditions of modern industrial warfare.

79 For those logistical difficulties see Martin Van Creveld, *Supplying War: Logistics from Wallenstein to Patton* (Cambridge, 1980). The breaking of the German Enigma cipher played a considerable role in the success of Allied attacks on Italian convoys to North Africa, which only served to exacerbate the logistical problems confronting Axis forces in that theater.

80 For a short discussion of the disastrous defeat suffered by British forces in the Gazala battle see Murray and Millett, *A War to Be Won*, pp. 268–70.

of logistical wherewithal and another indication of the inability of Axis leaders to understand geography. Hitler also seems to have justifiable doubts as to the viability of an airborne assault on Malta in view of the heavy losses German paratroopers had suffered on Crete in 1941, as well as his fear that the Italian navy would fail to show up after the German and Italian paratroopers had landed.

Throughout the North African campaign, Axis commanders on the ground displayed a predisposition not to cooperate. Rommel was perhaps the greatest offender with his general unwillingness to entrust his allies with major military tasks.[81] But his troops were equally at fault; after the collapse at El Alamein, the Germans commandeered Italian trucks and left their allies to be rounded up by the victorious British and Dominion troops. On the other hand, the Italian Commando Supremo provided scant useful guidance on how Axis forces were supposed to work together. The restoration, resupply, and reinforcement of the Eighth Army, along with the exceptional leadership provided by the arrival of General Bernard Law Montgomery, soon ended Axis dreams of conquering Egypt and the Nile Valley.

El Alamein heralded the end in North Africa and it was soon followed by Operation TORCH, the Allied invasion of French Morocco and Algeria. Only Rommel drew the correct conclusion that militarily Axis forces in North Africa were now in a hopeless position, and the sooner the remnants of the *Afrika Korps* and Italian troops were pulled back to Europe the better. Rommel argued correctly that Allied air and naval superiority was going to make the holding of North Africa a hopeless task, and that the Allies in the end would destroy whatever forces the Axis allies deployed to Tunisia. But Hitler and Mussolini, with the support of Field Marshal "Smiling" Albert Kesselring, decided otherwise.[82] The reason behind the decision lay in fears, particularly on Hitler's part, that the Fascist regime in Italy would fall if North Africa were abandoned.

Placed in a hopeless position, where it faced overwhelming superiority in numbers and materiel and suffered from tenuous supply lines, the remnants of the *Afrika Korps* and the last remaining effective units of the Italian army went down to defeat and surrender in May 1943. It was an even more inexcusable defeat than Stalingrad had been, because the

81 Rommel's attitude toward the Italians was undoubtedly reinforced by his experiences during the Battle of Caporetto in 1917, when with half a battalion he captured more than 10,000 Italian prisoners.
82 Kesselring was perhaps the most overrated commander in World War II, his headquarters a center for the optimistic reporting that Hitler loved to hear. Significantly, he was the only field marshal promoted in July 1940 still to be on active duty at the war's conclusion.

Germans were to flow substantial military forces into what was clearly a dangerously isolated pocket, with their logistical lines subject to constant air and naval attacks by the allies. Moreover, by sacrificing several hundred thousand soldiers, the German and Italian high commands ensured that there would be insufficient forces to defend Sicily and that in the end Mussolini's Fascist regime would collapse in July 1943.

Meanwhile, the Japanese had continued their war in the Pacific with little reference to their European allies. In April 1942 a great Japanese carrier task force sortied into the Indian Ocean, where it launched a series of attacks on the Royal Navy's bases and shipping in the area. Some historians have suggested that the Japanese possessed a unique opportunity at the time to destroy Britain's position in India and perhaps even to cut the supply lines to British forces in the Middle East.[83] In 1942 there were fears, particularly among some military planners in Washington, that the Axis powers were planning coordinated operations to cut the British off in the Middle East.[84] Supposedly Rommel's forces would meet up with the German drive through the Caucasus and the Japanese coming by sea to cut off the sea routes through the Indian Ocean.

In fact, such a possibility was never in the cards. The Japanese army remained solidly stuck in China and refused to make available any additional divisions to push into Southeast Asia or on into the Indian Ocean.[85] But the larger problem was one of logistics. The Imperial Japanese Navy quite simply did not possess the logistical capabilities to support sustained military operations in the Indian Ocean. Unlike the US navy, it had not thought seriously about at-sea replenishment, nor did it possess the ability to resupply its carrier forces, even if it were to capture bases, perhaps in Ceylon. Thus, it would have been almost impossible for the Japanese to maintain sustained military operations on the western side of the Indian Ocean. The larger issue was that as long as the US carrier fleet remained a direct threat to Japanese bases in the Central Pacific, the

---

83 The various possibilities open to the Japanese in the Indian Ocean are discussed in Weinberg, *A World at Arms*, pp. 322–28.

84 This fear most probably reflected the admiration that American staff officers held for the Germans as consummate military professionals. As such the Americans may have believed the Germans had developed the requisite logistical capabilities for such drives. We now know how sloppy the Germans were in matter of logistics, and so such fears were groundless.

85 One of the major factors in helping the American 1st Marine Division hang on to the airfield on Guadalcanal was the fact that the Japanese army supplied the counterattack forces in dribs and drabs, never at any one time providing sufficient forces to overwhelm the beleaguered marines. Meanwhile, there were over fifty divisions in China, Manchuria, and Korea. But then the army regarded the war in the Solomons and the islands of the Central Pacific as the Imperial Navy's responsibility.

Japanese could not afford to launch anything more than raids into the Indian Ocean, which is precisely what the April attack on Indian Ocean shipping was. The Battle of Midway ended the possibility of further Japanese incursions into the Indian Ocean.

On the other hand neither Rommel nor Army Group South possessed the logistical capabilities to support such far-flung operations as driving deep into the Middle East. Rommel barely reached El Alamein before his supplies ran out, and he found it almost impossible to support his forces once there.[86] His position represented the farthest limit of logistical capability for Axis forces. Similarly, Army Group South's logistical tether reached only as far as Stalingrad and the northern Caucasus. There was no possibility the Germans could have supported military forces across that mountainous region and then through Iran and Turkey to meet up with Rommel or the Japanese.

Once the tide turned in the last half of 1942, there was little the Germans and Japanese could do to help each other militarily. There were long-range submarine journeys back and forth, but even those disappeared in 1944 as national disaster enveloped the three powers. The Italians attempted to quit the war in early September 1943, but the Germans ensured that the damage inflicted on the Italian nation was as injurious as if the Italians had fought on. Having sown the whirlwind, the two main powers in the alliance went down to final defeat in 1945, inflicting untold suffering on much of the civilized world before their final collapse.

Conclusion

There was among the members of this "alliance" little sense of the "other." Thus, the leaders of all three powers felt few qualms about taking on not only the Soviet Union, but the United States as well.[87] Moreover, even with the immense distances between Germany and Japan, the two powers found substantial reason to be suspicious of one another. Gerhard Weinberg has brilliantly caught the nature of their relationship in his masterful study of the political and strategic levels of the terrible war that lasted from 1939 to 1945:

The Germans and Japanese were in any case finding it difficult to cooperate; the troubles of the Western allies with the Russians and with each other were harmony

---

86 Van Creveld's *Supplying War* is particularly good on the difficulties that the Italians and Germans had in supplying their forces in North Africa.
87 While the Japanese did not find themselves fighting the Soviets until July 1945, it is well to remember that their focus and planning throughout the 1930s had aimed at a showdown with the Soviets.

itself compared with the frictions between the Germans and the Japanese. The Japanese did not want any German economic or other presence in their newly won empire, and they resisted all efforts, whether by private firms or by government agencies, to restore or expand German activities and interests of any kind in Southeast Asia. Frictions, suspicions and anxieties resulted; and even Hitler's ruling that there was to be no German interference in the economic affairs of Southeast Asia never completely calmed the troubled waters.[88]

Inevitably, alliances and coalitions demand a certain level of honesty and good faith among their participants. Some level of transparency is an absolute prerequisite. Alliances also demand a willingness among their members to contest major strategic and operational issues in the making not only of grand strategy but of military strategy as well.[89] The creation of strategy by effective coalitions is a messy business, just like the making of sausages. As Rick Atkinson has noted about the Anglo-American alliance during World War II in the aftermath of the TRIDENT Conference in Washington:

> Perhaps the greatest achievement of the men meeting at TRIDENT was not the sketching of big arrows on a map but rather the affirmation of their humanity. This was their true common language: the shared values of decency and dignity, of tolerance and respect. Despite the petty bickering and intellectual fencing, a fraternity bound them on the basis of who they were, what they believed, and why they fought. It could be glimpsed ... in Churchill's draping of a blanket on Roosevelt's shoulders and in their great determination to wage war without liking it.[90]

In no fashion could one say such words about the Axis alliance and its leaders. The Axis Powers were bandits in the night, delighted to take advantage of a world deeply affected by the dark memories of World War I and the terrible impact of the worldwide depression. Their aims were entirely selfish, their view of the world hateful and narrow-minded, and their willingness to cooperate even with their allies virtually nil. The Axis was a murderous gathering of thieves without the slightest glimmering of common goals. And without common goals there could not be a real alliance even in the narrow spectrum of military strategy. In the end their divergent and ill-thought-out approaches to strategy minimized rather maximized their assault on the world balance of power. In other words, the whole was less than the sum of its parts.

---

88 Weinberg, *A World at Arms*, p. 345.
89 For the making of grand strategy see Williamson Murray, Richard Hart Sinnreich, and James Lacey (eds.), *The Shaping of Grand Strategy: Policy, Diplomacy, and War* (Cambridge, 2011).
90 Rick Atkinson, *The Day of Battle: The War in Sicily and Italy, 1943–1944* (New York, 2007), p. 24.

13 The Gulf War, 1990–1991
A coalition of convenience in a changing world

Richard Swain

Without Iraq's invasion and occupation of Kuwait, there would have been no Gulf War and no Gulf War Coalition. This strange collaboration of bedfellows, as different as the United States and Syria, was in every way a *coalition of convenience*, an ad hoc assemblage of otherwise unaligned regional and global states that came together for a specific purpose, first to defend Saudi Arabia, then to liberate Kuwait.[1] The American–Saudi-led coalition reversed the Iraqi occupation of Kuwait in seven months. Then, successful in achieving its common goal, the coalition withered away as the emergent postwar situation imposed its own logic on the volatile region. Saddam remained a regional inconvenience, requiring continued US presence and action. It was ten years before his provocations instigated longer-term policy arrangements, the wisdom of which remain a matter of serious debate at the time of this writing.

Because the invasion altered significantly the distribution of world energy resources, there was bound to be an immediate global reaction to Saddam's actions. The fact that the events of August 1990 occurred in the midst of a revolutionary readjustment of the global balance of power brought on by the end of the Cold War and the imminent collapse of the Soviet Union helped shape that response. Circumstances made possible a degree of US–Soviet cooperation that would have been unlikely before 1989.[2] China too was unusually tolerant of US actions in the Gulf. Neither Soviet nor Chinese acquiescence were unlimited, however. Indeed, the opposition of conservative Soviet "Arabists" within the USSR Foreign Ministry was a continual drag on actions favored by

---

1 The term "coalition of convenience" is taken here to represent a collaboration between what Raymond Aron refers to as "occasional allies," partners like the United States and the Soviet Union during World War II, united only by a common enemy. Raymond Aron, *Peace and War: A Theory of International Relations*, trans. Richard Howard and Annette Baker Fox (Garden City, NY, 1966), p. 28.
2 George [Herbert Walker] Bush and Brent Scowcroft, *A World Transformed* (New York, 1998), p. 303.

the more agreeable Chairman Mikhail Gorbachev and Foreign Minister Eduard Shevardnadze.[3]

Above all, the central role of the US president was decisive in forming and sustaining the Gulf War coalition. President George H. W. Bush decided to reverse the occupation, then pieced together a coalition of global and regional states to achieve this goal under auspices of the United Nations. Through his actions and personal contacts, Bush established the credibility to overcome the unwillingness of normally xenophobic Arab states to permit an armed Western presence in the region. He also demonstrated the skill and wisdom necessary to harmonize the efforts of the coalition members; asking them for no more than they were able to deliver, and limiting US ambitions to the boundaries of what was acceptable. All of this was done within the management of the greater global threat of the moment, the historical collapse of a nuclear armed superpower, and a reordering of the global balance of power.

Believing himself the leader of the wider Arab nation, Saddam Hussein was not without grievances against his smaller neighbors.[4] The failure of Kuwait and the United Arab Emirates (UAE) to adhere to agreed oil production quotas cut deeply into Iraq's anticipated oil revenues. Professors Lawrence Freedman and Efraim Karsh account for the Gulf War thus: "There were very particular reasons why Saddam Hussein seized Kuwait, not least a chronic indebtedness, but his calculations were shaped by his understanding of the meaning of these larger changes *for the stability of his regime*."[5] (Emphasis added.) In brief, the interminably long war with Iran (1980–1988) had bankrupted Iraq. International credits were drying up. Moreover, there were signs that the Iraq military, which had not been demobilized at the end of the war, was restive.[6]

Saddam opened his campaign of intimidation against Kuwait in February 1990 with a demand for cancellation of outstanding debts incurred during the war with Iran and an immediate infusion of

---

3 James A. Baker III with Thomas M. DeFrank, *Politics of Diplomacy: Revolution, War & Peace, 1989–1992* (New York, 1995), pp. 281–82, 285–86, 293.

4 On Saddam's state of mind see Kevin M. Woods, "Iraqi Perspectives Project Phase II: Um Al-Ma'arik (The Mother of All Battles): Operational and Strategic Insights from an Iraqi Perspective" (Revised May 2008), IDA Paper P-4217 (May 2008), vol. I, pp. 49–63 (http://oai.dtic.mil/oai/oai?verb=getRecord&metadataPrefix=html&identifier=ADA484530).

5 Lawrence Freedman and Efraim Karsh, *The Gulf Conflict, 1990–1991: Diplomacy and War in the New World Order* (Princeton, NJ, 1993, 1994) p. xxx. "Notwithstanding the complex mix of grand strategies, conspiracy theories, and regional animosities, the dispute between Iraq and Kuwait finally came to a head in 1990 over money." Woods, Iraqi Perspectives Project Phase II: *Um Al-Ma'arik*, p. 77.

6 Freedman and Karsh, *The Gulf Conflict*, pp. 29–30, point to three assassination attempts originating in the armed forces.

$30 billion.[7] Shortly thereafter, he went to Riyadh to demand that the Gulf States adhere to their oil production quotas. He reiterated this demand at an Arab Summit in May, equating deviation from the quotas as an act of war. Kuwait resisted the Iraqi bluster. On 15 July, Iraqi forces began to concentrate on the Kuwait border.[8] The other regional actors attempted mediation and, with the exception of the UAE, resisted external intervention.[9] President George H. W. Bush raised concerns about Iraqi actions publicly, but Arab leaders privately assured him that this was a regional Arab problem that required an Arab solution.[10] The Americans withheld their hand.

The United States had been a prominent actor in the Gulf since the Nixon administration. In his 1980 State of the Union Address, President Jimmy Carter declared the security of the Persian Gulf a US vital interest. He subsequently created a joint military headquarters, later US Central Command, to prepare plans for Gulf Security. US policy generally aimed at guaranteeing the territorial integrity of Saudi Arabia, balancing Iraq and Iran, and maintaining free passage through the Straits of Hormuz into the Gulf.[11] The end of the Cold War meant that, just when Saddam Hussein decided to demonstrate his power to his neighbors, the United States found itself in possession of significant armored forces capable of responding. Still, the combination of tough economic times and post-Cold War taxpayer fatigue meant that the president would have to be creative in funding any US reaction.[12]

Once the Iraqi armed forces invaded Kuwait, there was a brief period during which states looked to their own interests. Heads of government and foreign offices communicated with one another to assess what had happened, what might follow, and what might be done about it. President Bush spoke to Prime Minister Margaret Thatcher face-to-face in Aspen, Colorado, on 2 August. Thatcher reported she had

---

7 Ibid., p. 45.
8 Ibid., pp. 47–51.
9 The UAE requested symbolic US participation in a scheduled defense exercise. Ibid., p. 51. See Richard N. Haass, *War of Necessity – War of Choice: A Memoir of Two Iraq Wars* (New York, 2009), p. 56. Haass was senior director for the Near East and South Asia on the staff of the National Security Council (NSC) during the George H.W. Bush administration. As such, he held the NSC portfolio for the Persian Gulf region.
10 Baker, *Politics of Diplomacy*, pp. 271–74; Bush and Scowcroft, *World Transformed*, pp. 307–10.
11 Haass, *War of Necessity – War of Choice*, pp. 19–31, 37–38, 45–59; Jimmy Carter, The State of the Union Address Delivered before a Joint Session of the Congress, 23 January 1980.
12 Andrew Bennett, "Sheriff of the Posse: American Leadership in the Desert Storm Coalition," in Andrew Bennett, Joseph Lepgold, and Danny Unger (eds.), *Friends in Need: Burden Sharing in the Gulf War* (New York, 1997), pp. 48–53.

spoken with President Francois Mitterrand of France and noted that her Cabinet was discussing trade sanctions. She had also talked to Jordan's King Hussein, whom she found unhelpful. Bush talked by phone with President Hosni Mubarak and King Hussein, who were together in Alexandria, Egypt, preparing for the king to travel to Baghdad and meet with Saddam. Mubarak said he had talked to the Saudis. Bush called King Fahd later in the day. Fahd reported he had talked to Saddam and would meet with an Iraqi envoy the next day. Fahd was clearly offended by the Iraqi acts, but he declined an American offer of combat aircraft intended to deter any further aggression.[13] At the same time, Secretary of State James Baker was in Mongolia, where he spoke with Soviet Foreign Minister Shevardnadze. Shevardnadze returned to Moscow to consult with General Secretary Gorbachev, while two of Baker's subordinates worked with their Soviet counterparts to craft a joint Soviet–American statement on the crisis. The statement was issued when Baker followed Shevardnadze to Moscow.[14]

As the United States began to act, powers with fewer means or less immediate concerns were drawn into various partnerships for their own and common interests. There was no standing alliance or integrated military command in place comparable to NATO and SHAPE. There never would be. In the words of Ambassador Gordon S. Brown, then US Central Command political advisor, the Gulf War coalition was "little more than a set of interlinking groups, connected through bilateral diplomacy and the broad policy objectives established in the U.N. Security Council resolutions."[15] Still, a US-sponsored collective strategy began to emerge.

Almost immediately, Bush took two defining actions that avoided the appearance of US unilateralism. First, he began using the United Nations Security Council as the key international forum and tool to legitimize and mobilize support for a global effort to put increasing pressure on Iraq.[16] Second, and just as critically, the US government began

13 Bush and Scowcroft, *World Transformed*, pp. 318–21; Freedman and Karsh, *The Gulf Conflict*, pp. 74–75.
14 Baker, *Politics of Diplomacy*, pp. 5–16; Bush and Scowcroft, *World Transformed*, p. 319; Freedman and Karsh, *The Gulf Conflict*, pp. 78–80.
15 Gordon S. Brown, *Coalition, Coercion and Compromise: Diplomacy of the Gulf Crisis, 1990–91* (Washington, DC, 1997), p. 2. Gordon Brown was a career Foreign Service officer. He served as political adviser to General H. Norman Schwarzkopf during the Gulf War and was subsequently US ambassador to Mauritania.
16 Bush and Scowcroft, *World Transformed*, p. 303. UN Ambassador Pickering characterized the first resolution, 660, as a "block which had to be checked," rather than reflection of long-term diplomatic strategy. Arguably, it was the decision to continue to pave the way for action through Security Council resolutions that underpinned Bush's diplomatic strategy. Susan Rosegrant and Michael D. Watkins. *The Gulf Crisis: Building a Coalition for War* (Cambridge, MA, 1994), p. 13.

to structure its efforts to restore Kuwait within a *partnership* with the Kingdom of Saudi Arabia.

Operating under United Nations' authority provided a foundation for soliciting political, military, and financial support from abroad and allowed for a heterogeneous and global alliance . Seeking international authorities was one thing; going further and accepting international supervision or direction was quite another. There was no US interest in the latter goal. A Soviet suggestion that the Military Committee of the Security Council should be revived was accommodated but allowed to have no practical effect on the course of events.[17]

Saudi partnership was essential for economic, geographic, financial, and cultural reasons. Economically, the independence of Saudi oil supplies was a vital interest that extended beyond the United States. More immediately, the Saudis had the ability to increase oil production to moderate the effects of the loss of Iraqi and Kuwaiti oil supplies. Geographically, the kingdom provided an essential regional base from which US and other forces could get at the Iraqi forces in Kuwait. Financially, the Saudis (and the Kuwaiti government in exile) had deep pockets. They were able to mobilize money to underpin the coalition in the same way the United States could mobilize soldiers. Even they could not bear the entire burden, but they offered critical working funds, and the Kingdom of Saudi Arabia was generous in providing resources in kind, not least of which were bases and fuel to sustain coalition military actions. Culturally, Saudi partnership provided legitimacy for entry of a large US military force into the Arab-Islamic world, a normally closed and xenophobic region. The Saudi and Egyptian governments both took care to promote this legitimacy with their respective Islamic authorities.[18]

Because the United States would provide the bulk of offensive military capabilities for the war effort, the actions of the US government, particularly those of the American president, would quickly dominate coalition strategy. Because it would take some time to deploy US military forces in numbers, coalition strategy was measured and progressive.[19] The first step was to protect Saudi Arabia and isolate Iraq, both regionally

---

17 Baker, *Politics of Diplomacy*, p. 282. The idea was also suggested by George W. Ball, "The Gulf Crisis," *The New York Review of Books*, 6 December 1990 (www.nybooks.com/articles/archives/1990/dec/06/the-gulf-crisis/). Mr. Ball was a Democratic Party "gray beard," former UN Ambassador and Undersecretary of State. He had been the principal contrarian in President Lyndon Johnson's court in the strategic decisions leading up to the war in Vietnam.

18 Fouad Ajami, "The Summer of Arab Discontent," *Foreign Affairs*, Winter (1990/91), 6 (www.foreignaffairs.com/print/46256).

19 The most succinct description of US strategy is in Baker, *Politics of Diplomacy*, p. 277.

and through the United Nations. Bush brought economic pressure to bear through an international embargo. Increasing coalition military power ratcheted up the pressure. When that proved inadequate, the coalition employed force to remove Iraqi troops from Kuwait.

Because Saddam did not follow-up his invasion of Kuwait with an invasion of Saudi Arabia, US strategists and other coalition leaders could think forward in time to build political will and assemble a coalition. The six-month buildup of forces provided more than background noise to diplomacy. It gave clear evidence of growing regional and global commitment, and it changed, inexorably, the balance of military power against Saddam Hussein. Its presence and strength increased pressure on Iraq to comply with UN resolutions and, no doubt, ultimately contributed as well to pressure on the alliance to take military action to punish the intransigent aggressor. As one US participant notes, "We did not have unlimited time... since whatever military stability our presence in Saudi Arabia provided, would gradually be offset and more by the political instability it would generate."[20]

Bush made it clear from the start that the restoration of Kuwaiti sovereignty was non-negotiable.[21] He appears to have been sincere in his willingness to accept a positive resolution short of war, though there was no doubt he was willing to fight if it came to that.[22] As costs rose, Saddam's reckless behavior – over hostages and diplomatic immunities, not to mention the ruthless Iraqi occupation of Kuwait – became apparent. Withdrawal without punishing the aggressor became less acceptable.

A significant part of US strategy involved building the political and military coalition against Iraq, assuaging Soviet sensitivities, encouraging regional and Western states to provide practical and symbolic support, and raising funds to build and sustain the coalition. Financial support was essential to reward supporters by offsetting the costs of the trade embargo, to underwrite various military efforts, and, particularly, to limit US direct expenses to ease congressional concerns about the cost of operations in the Gulf. Much of the American secretary of state's effort involved what he called "tin-cup" trips to pay for the buildup, and eventually the war.[23]

While there was general agreement among the coalition partners about ultimate ends, there were important differences as to means,

20 Haass, *War of Necessity – War of Choice*, p. 80.
21 Ibid., p. 69. Bush announced his line in the sand thusly, "This will not stand, this aggression against Kuwait."
22 Bush comments to Baker at Helsinki Summit with Gorbachev. Baker, *Politics of Diplomacy*, p. 293.
23 Ibid., pp. 287–99, 369–78.

particularly the necessity to resort to force to eject Saddam's forces from Kuwait. These differences led to independent efforts by France and the Soviet Union, both of whom had strong domestic pro-Baghdad lobbies, to achieve an acceptable result without resort to war. In consultation and collaboration with key international partners, the United States and its allies carried out a progressive strategy of isolation and persuasion, the evolution of which one can follow in the series of United Nations Security Council Resolutions that constituted the legal framework for intervention.[24]

US strategy was framed largely in a series of National Security Council (NSC) meetings during the first five days of the crisis, then reviewed and adjusted in subsequent meetings of an inner group consisting of the president, vice president, secretary of state, secretary of defense, chairman of the joint chiefs of staff, national security advisor, White House chief of staff, and the deputy national security advisor.[25] Their work was documented and supported by a smaller group from the NSC deputies committee, called the gang of six.[26] This group was composed of senior representatives from the department of state, the department of defense, the joint staff, and the CIA. Richard Haass served as the secretary. The gang of six drafted two key strategy documents, National Security Directive 45, dated 20 August 1990, "U.S. Policy in Response to the Iraqi Invasion of Kuwait," and National Security Directive 54, "Responding to Iraqi Aggression in the Gulf," dated 15 January 1991.[27] When they were issued, these documents reflected extended institutional dialog and presidential decisions.

The first NSC meeting took place on the morning of 2 August. It served mainly to provide initial impressions of developing events. By the time the NSC meeting convened, the UN Security Council had passed Resolution 660 condemning Iraq's invasion and demanding its unconditional withdrawal from Kuwait and the restoration of Kuwaiti sovereignty. The Soviet Union had supported US Ambassador Thomas Pickering's resolution, as had almost the entire Security Council. Only Yemen abstained, due to their ambassador's lack of instructions from his government. The situation in the Gulf was still unclear, but the United States was communicating with other states to stop arms shipments to

24 United Nations Security Council, "The Situation between Iraq and Kuwait" (www. un.org/en/sc/repertoire/89-92/Chapter%208/MIDDLE%20EAST/item%2022_Iraq-Kuwait_.pdf).

25 Haass, *War of Necessity – War of Choice*, pp. 127.

26 Ibid., pp. 92–93.

27 Ibid., pp. 85, 115. Both directives are available at The George Bush Presidential Library (http://bushlibrary.tamu.edu/research/nsd.php).

Iraq, to join in measures to cut off Iraqi overseas funds, and to protect Kuwaiti assets from liquidation by Iraq.

The chairman of the joint chiefs of staff, General Colin Powell, and the commander of US Central Command, General H. Norman Schwarzkopf, briefed the initial NSC meeting about the US regional military posture and alternatives for action. Introduction of US Air Force fighters into the Arabian Peninsula was the most responsive military option, but the Saudis, so far, were unwilling to accept them. A US Navy carrier task force was on the way to the Gulf from the Indian Ocean.

Nicholas Brady, the Treasury Secretary, pointed out Iraq's real strength was in its oil. If the flow of oil were cut off, he said, Iraq would be in dire straits financially. Secretary of Defense Richard (Dick) Cheney pointed out the combination of Iraqi and Kuwaiti assets made Saddam the major Middle East oil power. Cheney also expressed concern about whether the Saudis would stand up to Saddam. National Security Advisor Brent Scowcroft pointed to an oil embargo as the most immediate coercive option available. The president decided that the United States should immediately enact economic sanctions and Ambassador Pickering should move on securing a corresponding resolution from the Security Council. Scowcroft reflects that he was disappointed with the lack of focus at the first meeting. The president, he says, agreed with his assessment.[28]

Regional diplomacy remained focused on finding an Arab solution to the crisis.[29] In his conversation with Mubarak, Bush noted that he would give the Arabs two days to find a way out. King Fahd, the president relates, was agitated and disgusted with Saddam. "I believe nothing will work with Saddam but the use of force," he said.[30] But, the king was still not ready to accept US F-15 fighters, which the president again offered. Fahd appeared to favor a regional solution via an Arab summit brokered by Mubarak. "[T]he king's reluctance to accept aircraft had me concerned," Bush records. "We couldn't have a solo U.S. effort in the Middle East. We had to have our Arab allies with us, particularly those who were threatened the most – the Saudis."[31] An Arab League ministerial meeting condemned the invasion, but it also opposed "external interference in the crisis."[32] It proposed a meeting of heads of state following an Iraqi withdrawal. Opposition to Iraq within the region, coalescing around Egypt, Syria, and Saudi Arabia, was already moving beyond such tame options.

---

28 Bush and Scowcroft, *World Transformed*, pp. 315–18.
29 Freedman and Karsh, *The Gulf Conflict*, pp. 69–72.
30 Quoted in Bush and Scowcroft, *World Transformed*, pp. 320–21.
31 Ibid., p. 321.
32 Freedman and Karsh, *The Gulf Conflict*, pp. 70–71.

When the NSC convened again on 3 August, the discussion turned more decisively toward the seriousness of the invasion and the requirement for firmness in reversing it. Afterwards, Scowcroft met with the Saudi ambassador, Prince Bandar bin Sultan. Scowcroft shared the US assessment of the Iraqi threat to Saudi Arabia. He told Bandar the United States was disposed to offer significant military forces to assist in defense of the kingdom. Bandar responded that the Saudis were dubious about whether they could rely on the United States over the long term. To persuade Bandar, Scowcroft arranged for Cheney to brief him on current US intelligence and contingency plans for responding to Iraq's threat. Convinced of the seriousness of American intentions, Bandar agreed that a high-level US team should travel to the kingdom to brief the king.[33] The president continued to work the phones, calling President Turgut Özal of Turkey (who had just spoken with Fahd), Mitterrand, German Chancellor Helmut Kohl, and Japanese Prime Minister Toshiki Kaifu. In Moscow, Baker and Shevardnadze issued their joint declaration condemning the Iraqi invasion.[34]

The next day the president met with his national security team at Camp David. General Schwarzkopf was present with his air component commander, Lieutenant General Chuck Horner, to present a proposed military response to defend Saudi Arabia. Initially a massive air force, reinforced by three carrier task forces, would act as a deterrent in support of the Saudi armed forces. Ground units would arrive more slowly, but army airborne and marine forces would offer immediate evidence of the US commitment. Schwarzkopf emphasized the time required to deploy a substantial ground force: three months for a defensive force, eight to ten months for a force capable of taking the offensive. Saudi cooperation and their ports and airfields were essential for a deliberate buildup.[35]

Scowcroft and Bush then turned their attention to getting the Saudis to agree to the deployment of US forces to the kingdom. The president spoke to the king, who remained reluctant, but Fahd agreed that the ultimate goal must be restoration of the emir to Kuwait. Afterwards, the president offered to send a team, led by the secretary of defense, to meet with the king and offer substantial US military forces for Saudi Arabia's defense. The Saudis were told the team would come only if the decision to accept military forces had already been made. The king accepted these

33 Bush and Scowcroft, *World Transformed*, pp. 324–26; Dick Cheney with Liz Cheney, *In My Time: A Personal and Political Memoir* (New York, 2011), pp. 186–87; Colin Powell with Joseph E. Persico, *My American Journey* (New York, 1995), p. 465.
34 Bush and Scowcroft, *World Transformed*, p. 326.
35 H. Norman Schwarzkopf with Peter Petre, *It Doesn't Take a Hero: The Autobiography* (New York, 1992), pp. 349–50.

terms. The following day a US delegation, led by Cheney, with Deputy National Security Adviser Robert Gates, Schwarzkopf, and other military and political officials, departed to meet with Fahd.[36]

On 5 August, both Turkey and Saudi Arabia agreed to close the Iraqi oil pipelines passing through their territory. Özal wanted NATO backing against potential Iraqi retaliation, and Saudi Arabia wanted to wait until UN action on implementation of an economic embargo.[37] In the event, the UN embargo halted transactions at the end of the pipelines and both were closed at the request of the Iraqis.[38] Bush told the press that he viewed the situation very seriously. "This will not stand," he concluded, "this aggression against Kuwait."[39]

The Cheney delegation met with the Saudi king and his advisors early 6 August and, after some discussion, the king accepted the offer of US military forces.[40] Deployment of the defensive force, Operation DESERT SHIELD, began the next day. Bush announced the decision on 8 August after the press had noted and observed obvious preliminaries to troop movements.[41] US air and naval forces headed for the Gulf. US ground forces began a protracted deployment, emplacing defensive positions around oil fields behind Saudi troops deployed forward along the Kuwait border. Eventually, US forces would be deployed in a corridor from the Gulf to Riyadh. Parallel US-Saudi military commands were established in the Saudi Ministry of Defense.

Cheney, meanwhile, was traveling home via Egypt and Morocco, seeking Arab military contributions to balance the US forces.[42] Secretary of State Baker tried to convey the news of the deployment in a way that would not ruffle Soviet feathers. In this he was only partly successful. In his discussions, he offered the Soviets a place in the multinational force. This offer came as a surprise to the US diplomatic community as well as to the national security advisor. In the end, the Soviets declined to send forces, giving as their reason the political reverberations surrounding their recently concluded Afghanistan adventure.[43]

36 Bush and Scowcroft, *World Transformed*, pp. 329–30.
37 Freedman and Karsh, *The Gulf Conflict*, pp. 82–83; Bush and Scowcroft, *World Transformed*, pp. 335, 337.
38 Freedman and Karsh, *The Gulf Conflict*, p. 83.
39 Bush and Scowcroft, *World Transformed*, pp. 332–33; Haass, *War of Necessity – War of Choice*, p. 69.
40 Cheney, *In My Time*, pp. 189–91; Schwarzkopf, *It Doesn't Take a Hero*, pp. 351–55.
41 Bush and Scowcroft, *World Transformed*, p. 340.
42 Ibid., p. 335.
43 Baker, *The Politics of Diplomacy*, pp. 282–83; Bush and Scowcroft, *World Transformed*, p. 338.

On 6 August, the UN Security Council passed Resolution 661, imposing economic sanctions on Iraq. Britain, Australia, and Canada committed military forces, and Bush called the leaders of the smaller Gulf States
with assurances of support. Scowcroft observed:

Everyone wanted some sort of 'cover' to protect themselves against any backlash.
Özal [Turkey] hoped his moves would be cloaked by NATO. Fahd did not wish
to be the only Arab state opposing Iraq. Hawke [Australia] didn't want to be the
single Commonwealth country joining the coalition. Even we needed to demonstrate that this action was not a solo U.S. effort against an Arab state.[44]

Three days after the Security Council approved the embargo, Baker
traveled to Turkey, a front-line state bordering Iraq. Cutting the Iraqi oil
pipeline passing through Turkey carried both economic costs and risks of
Iraqi retaliation. Moreover, the United States wanted to have use of the
NATO base at Incirlik if war were to break out. Baker told Özal that the
United States was committed to finding the money to offset the loss of
pipeline revenues and, as an additional source of relief, had arranged with
the World Bank for loans of $1 billion and $1.5 billion for the next two
years. He had also confirmed with NATO that the alliance would stand
with Turkey in the event of attack by Iraq. Özal, for his part, emphasized
his belief that getting rid of Saddam should be a key objective of the military effort.[45]

On 10 August, with US forces already arriving in Saudi Arabia, the
Arab League Summit in Cairo voted 12:9 to send "a pan-Arab force to
defend Saudi Arabia." Egyptian and Moroccan troops began to arrive in
Saudi Arabia the next day.[46] On 17 August, Cheney returned to the Gulf
to visit the Saudis and the smaller Gulf kingdoms of Bahrain, the Arab
Emirates, Oman, and Qatar to seek additional basing rights and to foster
additional public Arab support for the operation.[47]

On 16 August, Bush received Jordan's King Hussein and Prince Saud
al-Faisal, the Saudi foreign minister, separately. King Hussein, caught
between his longtime Western supporters, his pro-Saddam Palestinian
subjects, and his Iraqi neighbor upon whom he was dependent for oil,
still attempted to act as a mediator. The Saudis came speaking, they said,
for Egypt and Syria as well as their king. What they wanted, according
to Richard Haass, was not only Saddam's evacuation from Kuwait but

---

44 Bush and Scowcroft, *World Transformed*, p. 342.
45 Baker, *The Politics of Diplomacy*, pp. 283–85. According to Rosegrant and Watkins,
   the United States also increased the import quota for Turkish textiles. Rosegrant and
   Watkins, *The Gulf Crisis: Building a Coalition for War*, p. 20.
46 Bush and Scowcroft, *World Transformed*, p. 344; Cheney, *In My Time*, pp. 192–93.
47 Cheney, In *My Time*, pp. 194–96.

sufficient damage to his military machine so that he would no longer represent a threat. Failing this, should Saddam withdraw voluntarily from Kuwait, they wanted a peacekeeping force to remain on the Kuwait–Iraq border. Returning to the status quo, they said, was no longer satisfactory.[48]

Three issues challenged the emerging coalition almost immediately. The first involved the use of force to enforce the economic embargo of Security Council Resolution 661. The second involved hostages. The third was Saddam's linkage of Israeli occupation of Palestinian territories with his occupation of Kuwait. Resolution 661 imposed a comprehensive embargo against Iraq and established a Security Council committee to monitor its progress. The resolution said nothing, however, about enforcement. On 12 August, the emir of Kuwait sent a letter to the United States requesting enforcement of the embargo.[49]

The British, Bush, Scowcroft, and Cheney believed that the use of force was justified by Section 51 of Article VII of the UN Charter, which addresses the right of self-defense and extends the right to use force to countries coming to the aid of the party attacked.[50] Opposed to this view were the Soviet Union, France, and Canada. They argued that use of force required a further sanctions-enforcement resolution.[51] Baker argued for seeking UN authority, not because he doubted a case could be made for Section 51, but to respond to the political imperative to maintain Soviet and other nations' support of the coalition.[52]

On 18 August, the issue of embargo enforcement became critical when Iraqi tankers were sighted headed toward Yemen. Bush reluctantly supported Baker and agreed to allow General Secretary Mikhail Gorbachev to make an appeal to Saddam before using force. Saddam, in one of his many shortsighted inspirations, chose to ignore the Soviet intervention. Meanwhile, the secretary of defense had issued authority to US Central Command to proceed with enforcement of a blockade. In the absence of clear guidance, and cognizant that the UN resolution did not authorize use of force, Schwarzkopf declined to fire on an empty ship intercepted by the US Navy. Admonished for this decision, fourteen hours later he authorized the USS *Reid* to fire two warning shots across the bow of a loaded tanker headed to Yemen. The tanker did not stop, but the Pentagon again called, revising the more recent orders in light

---

48 Bush and Scowcroft, *World Transformed*, pp. 348–49; Haass, *War of Necessity – War of Choice*, pp. 79–80.
49 Bush and Scowcroft, *World Transformed*, p. 345.
50 Ibid., pp. 345, 351–53; Baker, *The Politics of Diplomacy*, pp. 286–87. For a fuller discussion, see Freedman and Karsh, *The Gulf Conflict*, pp. 145–50.
51 Bush and Scowcroft, *World Transformed*, p. 345.
52 Baker, *The Politics of Diplomacy*, p. 286.

of ongoing diplomacy. They then ordered that the Iraqi ship's captain be warned his ship would be sunk if he did not comply. By that time, darkness had fallen in the Gulf. The Iraqi ship proceeded on its way to Yemen, and diplomacy took its course.[53]

On 20 August, Bush signed National Security Directive 45, "U.S. Policy in Response to the Iraqi Invasion of Kuwait." In spite of ongoing diplomatic initiatives, the directive relied on Article 51 and Resolutions 660 and 661 for justification, and the president ordered that "all imports and exports, except medicines and food for humanitarian purposes ... bound to and from Iraq and Kuwait be intercepted immediately." The document also authorized discussions in the military staff committee and, if the Soviets requested it, approved their participation in coalition efforts.[54]

On 25 August, the Security Council passed Resolution 665 authorizing the use of "such measures commensurate to the specific circumstances as may be necessary under the authority of the Security Council to halt all inward and outward maritime shipping, in order to inspect and verify their cargoes and destinations and to ensure strict implementation of the provisions related to such shipping laid down in resolution 661 (1990)." The particular words were selected to accommodate the Soviets and Chinese.[55] The resolution also referred to use of the military committee of the Security Council for coordination, "as appropriate."

Third-country hostages seized by Iraq in Kuwait and Iraq proved to be another wedge Saddam attempted to use to manipulate the growing threat. Although the hostage question raised the level of anxiety, and a number of official and unofficial efforts to free the hostages doubtless sowed some inter-allied suspicion, the issue rebounded against Saddam in the long run. For whatever reason, the Iraqi dictator ended up releasing the captives before testing his enemy's willingness to go forward with bombing in face of the risks imposed on their citizens.[56]

The US alliance with Israel was the Achilles heel of America's policy with its Arab partners; less, perhaps, because of its influence on Arab leaders, than for its long-standing resonance on the Arab street. The US–Israel relationship, on the one hand, and the possibility of unilateral military intervention by Israel in response to Iraqi provocation,

53 Schwarzkopf, *It Doesn't Take a Hero*, pp. 372–74.
54 The White House, "National Security Directive 45, SUBJECT: U.S. Policy in Response to the Iraqi Invasion of Kuwait," 20 August 1990.
55 Freedman and Karsh, *The Gulf Conflict*, p. 149.
56 Ibid., pp. 131–42.

on the other, remained the proverbial "elephant in the room" for the allies. Saddam would play on both concerns by trying to link, and indeed subordinate, resolution of the Kuwait occupation with an end to the Israeli occupation of occupied Palestinian land, and then, when the war began in January, by launching rockets against Israeli targets, sorely trying the Israeli instinct to strike back. Following a bloody Israeli response to Palestinian stone-throwers on the Temple Mount in October, the question of the US–Israel connection would force the pace on the decision to apply a military solution to resolve the occupation before the US–Israel relationship disrupted the fabric of the US–Arab coalition.

Another major strategic challenge for the Bush administration involved mobilizing financial resources to pay for the war. In his presidential memoir, Bush reflects:

While I believed the United States must be prepared to bear the brunt of the military burden, I thought it only just that other countries with interests at stake should contribute ... We also had to find ways to bolster the coalition by offsetting the economic hardships upon not only those injured by the sanctions, such as Egypt and Turkey, but also Jordan and some Eastern European nations which depended on Iraqi or Kuwaiti oil.[57]

Following a NSC meeting on 30 August, the president dispatched Baker and Secretary of the Treasury Nicholas Brady on fundraising trips. Again, the president paved the way with personal phone calls. Baker began his trip with the Saudis. The Saudis, he reflects, "were the most aggressive member of the coalition ... they were always advocates for the massive use of force."[58] Baker asked them for $15 billion. The following day Prince Saud and Bandar told him to ask for as much from the Kuwaitis. The emir readily agreed. The secretary of state's next stop was Egypt. Egypt required financial support for its role in the coalition. Bush had promised to forgive Mubarak's $7.1 billion debt in a phone call on 1 September. US interlocutors also prevailed upon other creditor nations to forgive additional Egyptian debts.[59]

At approximately the same time he dispatched Baker and Brady on their journeys, Bush scheduled a meeting with Gorbachev to be held in Helsinki, Finland, on 9 September.[60] The Soviets sought to sustain their

57 Bush and Scowcroft, *World Transformed*, p. 359; Rosegrant and Watkins, *The Gulf Crisis: Building a Coalition for War*, pp. 19 –20.
58 Baker, *The Politics of Diplomacy*, pp. 289–90. Schwarzkopf did not find the next level of the Saudi hierarchy with whom he worked as uniformly aggressive. See Schwarzkopf, *It Doesn't Take a Hero*, p. 408.
59 Baker, *The Politics of Diplomacy*, pp. 290–91; Bush and Scowcroft, *World Transformed*, p. 360; Rosegrant and Watkins, *The Gulf Crisis: Building a Coalition for War*, p. 20.
60 Bush and Scowcroft, *World Transformed*, p. 361.

great power role, in denial of growing evidence of their rapid economic decline. The US administration supported them in this, because of larger concerns about continuing stability of a nuclear armed superpower, and in recognition of the value of US–Soviet collaboration in wider and more enduring global questions. Five days before the scheduled summit meeting, Shevardnadze appeared to take up Saddam's attempt to link solution of the Kuwait issue with that of the Palestinians, a measure the White House strongly opposed.[61]

Baker joined the president and Scowcroft in Helsinki. The American goal was to follow-up on the initial US–Soviet unity on the Kuwait question with a statement reflecting continuing firmness and an intention to go further if the economic sanctions did not work. The Soviet delegation was divided. Gorbachev pressed Bush hard, linking the conflict over Kuwait with the Palestinian problem and apparently searching for a face-saving way out for the Iraqi leader.[62] Soviet Arabists were on the ascent. The Americans resisted the attempt to create any explicit linkage with the Israel–Palestinian dispute, though Bush was afraid that, to gain US–Soviet unity, he might have to give in. Baker found Shevardnadze more forthcoming and persuaded the president to continue to resist. The results validated Baker's instincts. The two heads of state eventually issued a statement indicating common determination to see the occupation of Kuwait end unconditionally. They agreed to consider further steps if the current initiatives were inadequate. Privately, the United States committed to a regional Middle East conference after Iraq left Kuwait. Three days later, in Moscow at the signing of the documents ending the post-World War II occupation of Germany, Gorbachev asked Baker to intervene with the Saudis for some ready cash. The Saudis responded with a $4 billion line of credit, "to get the Soviets through the winter."[63]

On 10 September, Baker briefed the NATO Ministers on the Helsinki Summit and the progress of his journey. During the discussions, he apparently alluded to the value of allied armored ground forces for the growing coalition. The British responded by sending their 7th Armored Brigade from Germany.[64]

---

61 On Shevardnadze, see Francis X. Clines, "Confrontation in the Gulf; Soviets Suggest Conference Combining Issues of Mideast," *The New York Times*, 5 September 1990.
62 Baker, *The Politics of Diplomacy*, pp. 291–95; Bush and Scowcroft, *World Transformed*, pp. 361–68.
63 Baker, *The Politics of Diplomacy*, p. 295.
64 On commitment of British 7th Armored Brigade, see Freedman and Karsh, *The Gulf Conflict*, pp. 113–14, and Joseph Lepgold, "Britain in Desert Storm: The Most Enthusiastic Junior Partner," in Andrew Bennett, Joseph Lepgold, and Danny Unger (eds.), *Friends in Need: Burden Sharing in the Gulf War* (New York, 1997), pp. 69–89.

Baker's next stop was Damascus. Syria had been part of the anti-Saddam wing of the Arab response from the outset, not least because of long-standing personal animosity between Syrian President Hafez al Assad and Saddam, nominally fellow Ba'athists. Assad had already promised the Saudis a division, while the Saudis promised to underwrite its costs. Baker went to Damascus to gain a sense of how far the Syrian commitment went, if it were to come to offensive action, and to build a relationship that might be useful for dealing with postwar initiatives. Assad, whose nation bordered Iraq on the west, was non-committal about offensive operations, but he promised to contribute at least 10,000 troops to defend Saudi Arabia.[65]

Baker finished his trip with stops in Italy and Germany. Italy agreed to send a squadron of planes to the Gulf. Germany, forbidden then by its Basic Law from overseas military operations, offered what military actions it could to bolster NATO's defense of the eastern Mediterranean and Turkey. In addition, Germany contributed $2 billion of assistance, significant support equipment, transport for the Egyptian forces, and increased military and economic aid to Turkey.[66] The total contributions of the four largest donors, Saudi Arabia, Kuwait, Japan, and Germany, were not finalized until after the US initiation of a military solution in January.[67] Ultimately, the coalition received $70 billion in burden-sharing pledges, including $54 billion to defray US military costs and $16 billion to underwrite the costs of other states, principally Egypt, Turkey, and Jordan.[68]

France was among the first to respond to Saddam's invasion of Kuwait by freezing Iraqi and Kuwaiti assets on 2 August. On 8 August Mitterrand spoke forcefully against the invasion and occupation. The following day, though, he said France would not be associated with the gathering coalition, but would take independent steps.[69] Mitterrand resisted sending military forces to Saudi Arabia, though he reinforced naval forces already in and near the Gulf, and dispatched the French carrier *Clemenceau* to the region, albeit without an offensive air component. Although eventually an active participant in the military action to liberate Kuwait, France,

65 Baker, *The Politics of Diplomacy*, pp. 295–98.
66 Ibid., pp. 298–99.
67 Bennett, "Sheriff of the Posse," p. 38.
68 Ibid., p. 51; Leonard Silk, "Economic Scene; The Broad Impact of the Gulf War," in the Business Day Section of *The New York Times*, 16 August 1991. The Congressional Research Service totaled up figures as of March 1991 in Stephen Daggett and Gary J. Pagliano, "CRS Issue Brief, Persian Gulf War: U.S. Costs and Allied Financial Contributions," Washington, DC Congressional Research Service, Foreign Affairs and National Defense Division, 26 March 1991.
69 Riding, "Confrontation in the Gulf."

like the Soviet Union, sought to posture itself globally as an independent mediator between the United States and Iraq. Like the Soviet Union, France had been a long-time European sponsor and weapons supplier of Saddam's regime. Moreover, Mitterrand was expected by many of his colleagues to maintain the established tradition of Gaullist separatism within the Atlantic community.

Like Gorbachev, Mitterrand had internal constituents to deal with, most notably his defense minister, Jean-Pierre Chevènement. Chevènement was a founding member of the Iraqi–French Friendship Association. He had visited Saddam in Baghdad as recently as January 1990.[70] Chevènement took his own line more than once. In the end he resigned from office on 29 January during the air campaign against Iraq, when the French president rescinded restrictions Chevènement had announced on the participation of French forces in the conflict.[71]

Still, France supported US diplomacy in the UN Security Council and, indeed, took the lead in demanding extension of the embargo to air traffic after Iraq violated the French embassy grounds in September.[72] After the Iraqis seized the French embassy in Kuwait City, France landed a detachment of helicopters from the *Clemenceau* at the western Red Sea port of Yanbu, across the peninsula from the growing American presence in Saudi Arabia. These were shortly reinforced by 4,200 ground troops.[73] Initially, French forces were placed under the operational command of the Saudi joint forces command, though, according to one account, Mitterrand told his defense minister that "in the event of military action French forces would be under American command, and operating at the front rather than the rear."[74]

Mitterrand entertained some substantive disagreements over tactics and goals, which many of his actions and comments reflected.

70 Freedman and Karsh, *The Gulf Conflict*, p. 38.
71 Alan Riding, "French Defense Chief Quits, Opposing Allied War Goals," *The New York Times*, 30 January 1991.
72 Freedman and Karsh, *The Gulf Conflict*, pp. 114–18.
73 Isabelle Grunberg, "Still a Reluctant Ally? France's Participation in the Gulf War Coalition," Andrew Bennett, Joseph Lepgold, and Danny Unger (eds.), *Friends in Need: Burden Sharing in the Gulf War* (New York, 1997), p. 114; Freedman and Karsh, *The Gulf Conflict*, p. 117; Youssef M. Ibrahim, "Confrontation in the Gulf; Paris Adding 84,000 [sic] to Force in Gulf; Bonn's Aid to Rise," *The New York Times*, 16 September 1990. The number 84,000 is clearly an error, as the text refers to a total regional commitment of 13,000 soldiers, 14 ships, and about 100 anti-tank helicopters.
74 Freedman and Karsh, *The Gulf Conflict*, p. 118. Freedman and Karsh reference Josette Alia and Christine Clerc, *La Guerre de Mitterrand: la dernière grande illusion* (Paris, 1991). For initial command arrangements see General Khaled bin Sultan with Patrick Seale, *Desert Warrior: A Personal View of the Gulf War by the Joint Forces Commander* (New York, 1995), p. 219.

On 24 September, addressing the UN General Assembly, he appeared to link Iraqi withdrawal with settlement of other Middle East disputes. Mitterrand also indicated a reluctance to restore the Kuwaiti ruling family, suggesting instead, and apparently extemporaneously, that there be "the democratic expression of the Kuwaiti people's will." This brought a sharp diplomatic reproof from the White House, though Bush took pains to paper over the dispute in his memoir.[75]

The American president would seem to have attempted to disarm the linkage issue when he spoke to the General Assembly on 1 October. He outlined the policy of the US government as seeking Iraq's immediate and unconditional withdrawal from Kuwait, but then added that: "In the aftermath of Iraq's unconditional departure from Kuwait, I truly believe there may be opportunities for Iraq and Kuwait to settle their differences permanently, for the states of the Gulf themselves to build new arrangements for stability, and for all the states and the peoples of the region to settle the conflicts that divide the Arabs from Israel."[76] That same day in Paris, the French Foreign Ministry denied talking with Iraq unilaterally about settlement of the crisis and commented that, "Any useful discussion with Iraq can only take place under two clear conditions: that is to say the evacuation of Kuwait by Iraqi troops and the release of all hostages ... These are still the rules for France."[77] In December, following adoption of a deadline for Iraqi withdrawal, the French government increased its troop commitment to approximately 10,000 ground troops.[78] These were ultimately employed under US operational command to secure the Iraqi road junction at As Salman on the left flank of the US–British offensive.

If Bush's remarks to the General Assembly appeared to resolve the tension about linking Iraqi withdrawal from Kuwait with other Middle East issues, the US–Israeli vulnerability was thrown into harsh relief within a week of Bush's remarks. On 8 October, Israeli security forces at the Temple Mount responded with live ammunition against Palestinian rock-throwers attacking Jews worshiping at the Western Wall below. At least nineteen Palestinians were killed and more than one hundred wounded.[79] The

75 Bush and Scowcroft, *World Transformed*, pp. 375–76.
76 George [Herbert Walker] Bush, Address Before the 45th Session of the United Nations General Assembly in New York, 1 October 1990 (www.presidency.ucsb.edu/ws/index. php?pid=18883).
77 Youssef M. Ibrahim, "France Denies Talking with Iraq over Settlement of the Gulf Crisis," *The New York Times*, 2 October 1990.
78 Steven Greenhouse, "Standoff in the Gulf; France Increases its Forces in Gulf," *The New York Times*, 12 December 2012.
79 Sabra Chartrand, "19 Arabs killed in Battle with Jerusalem Police," *The New York Times*, 9 October 1990.

US administration quickly found itself with a volatile issue capable of undermining the ongoing collaboration with Arab partners.

On 9 October, Bush criticized Israel for its lack of restraint, while insisting he would not allow the incident to distract attention from the Kuwait crisis. The United States asked the Security Council to approve a resolution condemning Israel for excessive use of force.[80] The *New York Times* observed that, "Not since the Israeli invasion of Lebanon in 1982 has the United States endorsed a resolution directly criticizing Israel or one which does not balance such criticism with some criticism of Palestinian actions."[81]

Four days later, King Hassan II of Morocco asserted the existence of a "moral linkage" between the Iraqi seizure of Kuwait and the Arab–Israeli issue. In contrast, Mubarak deflected direct linkage as likely to prevent action on either.[82] On 18 October, Margaret Thatcher cabled Bush that "she was deeply concerned about how much longer we could hold the coalition together." Later, the president reflected, "I agreed we did not have the luxury of waiting for sanctions to work, but I believed it was better politically to work through the U.N. rather than act on our own."[83]

All of this commotion seems to have had the effect of persuading the US administration of the inherent fragility of the Western–Arab coalition and convincing the president that matters would have to be brought to a head before the effects of the embargo were likely to achieve the desired outcome of unconditional Iraqi withdrawal from Kuwait. The pace of US deployment offered the occasion for consideration. In his memoirs, Powell notes that he told the president in August that the chairman would come to him in October for a decision whether the president wanted to expand the defensive force to support an offensive military option or, alternatively, cap the troop flow in December and adopt a rotation policy to sustain it over the long term.[84] Powell says it seemed to him even in August the president was skeptical the embargo could work.

On 24 September, the day Mitterrand spoke to the General Assembly, Powell says he spoke to Cheney to express concern that the president, who appeared increasingly impatient for offensive action, be fully briefed on the sanctions regime as an alternative to war, reminding Cheney of the

80 Thomas L. Friedman, "Bush Assails Israeli Lack of 'Restraint,'" *The New York Times*, 10 October 1990.
81 Paul Lewis, "U.S. Presses the U.N. to Condemn Israel," *The New York Times*, 10 October 1990.
82 Alan Cowell, "Morocco, a U.S. Ally, Links Gulf Crisis and Israel," *The New York Times*, 14 October 1990.
83 Bush and Scowcroft, *World Transformed*, p. 385.
84 Powell, *My American Journey*, pp. 470–71.

approaching need for an October decision for the building an offensive capability.[85] Cheney portrays Powell arguing the case for longer reliance on sanctions, which Cheney opposed, but nonetheless the secretary of defense arranged for Powell to present his argument to the president.[86] Powell, who was sensitive to Bush's impatience and susceptibility to air-power enthusiasts, says he was only ensuring that the president was fully aware of all alternatives, not promoting a particular course of action.[87] The outcome was that, two days after the Temple Mount debacle, the president asked for a briefing on an offensive option, apparently with the forces then in hand. He received the briefing on 11 October.

By all reports the president found the presentation unsatisfactory, in large measure because of what was considered an unimaginative ground-attack plan. In fairness, the ground forces Schwarzkopf had in place did not yet represent even the projected defense force. As important, the US force was structured for defense, and so lacked the logistical and transportation resources required for far-ranging operational maneuver. Moreover, there were concerns about the trafficability of desert terrain, which still had to be resolved.[88]

The upshot was that Powell went to the Middle East to work out with Schwarzkopf what an offensive force would look like. When he returned, Cheney supported Schwarzkopf's request, which almost doubled the US ground force. Meanwhile, the planners at US Central Command began working out a new concept, Operation DESERT STORM. It would open with a six-week air offensive against targets in Iraq and Kuwait, followed by a frontal attack across the Kuwait border by US Marines and Arab forces and a wide US–UK armored envelopment wheeling through southern Iraq to destroy surviving Iraqi ground forces south of the Euphrates River.

In Washington on 19 October, the president received Soviet Diplomat Yevgeny Primakov, an Arabic-speaking academician and member of Gorbachev's presidential council. Gorbachev had sent Primakov to Baghdad two weeks earlier to discuss the freeing of Soviet citizens. Primakov portrayed an isolated Saddam, unwilling to withdraw from

85 Ibid., pp. 478–80.
86 Cheney, *In My Time*, p. 198.
87 Powell, *My American Journey*, pp. 478–80. Powell argues against what he perceived as the Cheney version presented in Bob Woodward's *The Commanders*. Haass, *War of Necessity – War of Choice*, pp. 96–97, follows Powell. James Baker's account of a mid-October meeting with Powell are also relevant. Baker, *The Politics of Diplomacy*, pp. 301–3.
88 Cheney, *In My Time*, pp. 198–99; Powell, *My American Journey*, pp. 484–85; Schwarzkopf, *It Doesn't Take a Hero*, pp. 414–21; Bush and Scowcroft, *World Transformed*, pp. 380–81, 383.

Kuwait unless forced out. Equally troubling, Primakov had discussed with the Iraqis withdrawal in terms of possible follow-on, face-saving actions. The president objected to Gorbachev, but this was only the first effort by Primakov to find a face-saving solution for the Soviet Union's former client. "The Primakov conversation," Bush records, "reinforced my pessimism about finding any solution to the crisis short of the use of force."[89]

Bush spent the next ten days pondering possibilities for using force in discussions with Scowcroft, Sununu, and Baker, as well as with British Prime Minister Thatcher. The president, Scowcroft says, was looking for a provocation to which he might be justified to respond with force. The Iraqi closing of embassies to Kuwait looked like a possibility. There were, however, differences about the need to go back to the United Nations for authority to use force. Thatcher argued against such a move; Baker argued in favor, observing it was necessary to separate justification for response to a provocation from conditions for a deliberate attack. Scowcroft seems to have persuaded the president that it was important to secure international support for any ground offensive.[90]

Scowcroft turned the US strategy process to framing war aims. The UN resolutions established the coalition's political goals. Scowcroft aimed at setting the US military goals to achieve these. "Foremost among these," he writes, "was to reduce the Iraqi military as much as possible, starting with an air campaign ... The trick here was to damage his offensive capability *without weakening Iraq to the point that a vacuum was created*, and destroying the balance between Iraq and Iran, further destabilizing the region for years."[91] (Emphasis added.) Whether such a balance point even existed is a matter of legitimate doubt and, unlike the liberation of Kuwait, it was impossible to judge either on the battlefield or in the White House when the ceasefire was finally declared. Scowcroft set the deputy's committee "gang of six" to this task. The result was National Security Directive 54, "Responding to Iraqi Aggression in the Gulf," which Bush signed on 15 January when the air offensive was initiated.[92]

The critical meeting on preparations for use of force took place on 30 October, after a particularly contentious session with Congressional leaders.[93] Scowcroft proposed going to the Security Council for one more resolution, essentially an ultimatum to Iraq, requiring full unconditional withdrawal and hostage release by a date certain. The window

---

89 Bush and Scowcroft, *World Transformed*, pp. 377–78.
90 Ibid., p. 387.
91 Ibid., pp. 383–84.
92 Ibid.; Haass, *War of Necessity – War of Choice*, pp. 93–94, 115.
93 Bush and Scowcroft, *World Transformed*, pp. 391–92.

for this effort would be the period the US held the rotating UN Security Council presidency in November.

Baker was already scheduled to meet with the several key coalition partners to ensure their commitment to proceed. Scowcroft suggested putting three questions to them: "Whether they supported the use of force … what they would do if Israel responded to an Iraqi attack … [and] whether they would allow our forces to strike at Iraq from their territory and were prepared to accept command arrangements that would place operational authority of their forces in US military hands."[94]

While an ultimatum coinciding with a further troop buildup and marshaling of the coalition was discussed, the president made only two immediate decisions: doubling of the deployed US forces (in line with Schwarzkopf's request) by 15 January, and sending Baker out to consult with the allies. The US public, about to go to the polls for a mid-term election, was to be told only that "our forces are continuing to move but there have been no decisions."[95] Announcement of the troop increase came on 8 November after the election and after Baker had a chance to inform the Saudis and secure their agreement. The announcement came while Baker was in the Soviet Union.[96] Announcement of troop increases and creation of an offensive option focused Congressional opposition in the United States, requiring the president and his lieutenants to expend considerable energy in November and December in efforts to convince Congress that it was in the US interest to fight a war in the Middle East.

Baker traveled to eighteen countries on three continents, meeting with the heads of state or foreign ministers of each of the Security Council nations and the coalition partners, "in an intricate process of cajoling, extracting, threatening, and occasionally buying votes. Such," he writes, "are the politics of diplomacy."[97] The secretary of state began his trip in the Middle East, meeting first with the emirs of Bahrain and Kuwait. Support from Bahrain was unconditional. The Kuwaitis were uneasy about an Israeli response, but replied that since the effort was their liberation, they would accept it.[98]

Baker then went to see King Fahd in Jeddah. He met first with Schwarzkopf concerning command arrangements, then with Saudi

94 Ibid., pp. 392–93. Baker, *The Politics of Diplomacy*, p. 306, indicates that the questions he asked were about the acceptability of US command, the acceptability of bombing Iraq, and allied determination to see it through if Israel retaliated against Iraqi attacks.
95 Bush quoted in Bush and Scowcroft, *World Transformed*, pp. 395–96.
96 This proved to be something of a coordination glitch for the secretary of state. Haass, *War of Necessity – War of Choice*, p. 98; Bush and Scowcroft, *World Transformed*, p. 396.
97 Baker, *The Politics of Diplomacy*, p. 305.
98 Ibid., p. 306.

Foreign Minister Prince Saud and Bandar. Baker asked Schwarzkopf what command arrangements were required. The general replied that he had written out a formulation: "Command and control: should military operations commence a joint command as currently exists will continue; however, the commander of the U.S. forces will have final approval authority for all military operations."[99] Baker gave the draft to the king. Schwarzkopf reports that even this formulation proved unsettling to the Saudi defense minister and commander.[100]

King Fahd endorsed the idea of a Security Council resolution on the use of force. He also accepted doubling of US forces in the kingdom and US operational command of Saudi forces once war began. To everyone's surprise, he was undisturbed by the issue of Israeli response to Iraqi attack. Baker asked for more financial aid, to which the king agreed as well. "There is a now a cancer in the region," Fahd replied. "For everyone's sake, we must eliminate it."[101] Baker then flew to Cairo to see Mubarak. The Egyptian president's response to the critical questions was positive, but he was unsure he could increase the Egyptian force from two to three divisions as Baker requested. (He did not.) He was also unsure he could allow air strikes to originate in Egypt, pointing to the sensitivity of the Egyptian people over attack of a fellow Arab country.[102]

While in Cairo, Baker met with the Chinese foreign minister, who was on his way to see Saddam. Foreign Minister Qian Qichen told Baker he intended to tell the Iraqi leader that the best course was to accept the Security Council mandate and leave Kuwait. He was noncommittal, however, about supporting a Security Council resolution on the use of force. Baker promised to begin coordination for a high-level visit to China if the Chinese voted for the resolution, while making sure it was clear that a veto would set back US–Chinese rapprochement.[103]

From Cairo, Baker flew to Turkey to visit Özal. The Turkish president believed that sanctions would work but promised to support the resolution on the use of force. He agreed to consider sending an armored brigade to Saudi Arabia (he did not) and to accept additional planes on Turkish airfields, but he was reluctant to authorize strike missions originating in Turkey.[104] From Ankara, Baker flew to Moscow where, on 7 November, he had meetings with Shevardnadze and Gorbachev. The general secretary remained unconvinced that it was time to threaten

---

99 Schwarzkopf, *It Doesn't Take a Hero*, p. 434.
100 Ibid., pp. 434–35.
101 Baker, quoting King Fahd, in *The Politics of Diplomacy*, p. 308.
102 Ibid.
103 Ibid., pp. 308–9.
104 Ibid., p. 309.

force and proposed two resolutions, one setting a deadline, and a second, later, authorizing force.[105] Baker then flew to the United Kingdom and France, where both Thatcher and Mitterrand agreed to support the US resolution, notwithstanding the objections Mitterrand rehashed again for Baker.[106]

After a brief break in the United States, Baker resumed his journeys. He conferred with Prime Minister Joe Clark of Canada, then continued on to the smaller Security Council members, Ivory Coast (which he promised to include in the G-7 debt forgiveness plan), and Angola. On 18 November Baker was in Paris for a meeting of the Conference on Security and Cooperation in Europe (CSCE). He met with the Romanian foreign minister, to whom the US had contributed $80 million in humanitarian assistance the previous December. He also spoke again to the Chinese foreign minister. Then Baker met with Shevardnadze, who had come for the meeting with Gorbachev. Shevardnadze said the Soviet Union would support the resolution, which had been rephrased to incorporate Soviet concerns.[107]

Bush had also come to the CSCE meeting in order to emphasize to Gorbachev the importance of maintaining a common front. The American president had responded to the two-resolutions idea, explaining that the scheme would not work because it put at risk the second and more important action resolution, which would come after the US gave up the presidency of the Security Council at the end of November.

On the way to Paris, Bush stopped off to meet with President Václav Havel of Czechoslovakia. Havel warmly supported the US position on Kuwait. Bush then went on to Germany, where Helmut Kohl, facing a tough election on 3 December, was proposing to send his own envoy to Saddam. Germany stood with the coalition, he said, but he warned against raising the use of force during public discussions in Germany. Willy Brandt, the leader of Kohl's opposition, had just returned from a trip to Baghdad with 120 freed hostages.[108]

From Germany, Bush flew to Paris where he met with Mitterrand and Thatcher. The French president agreed to work with the US on the proposed deadline. Thatcher agreed to send another armored brigade, a division headquarters, and additional Royal Navy minesweepers. Despite disagreeing about the necessity for the resolution, she promised Britain would back it. While Thatcher was at the conference, she lost her position as leader of the Conservative Party, which would lead to her replacement

---

105 Ibid., pp. 309–13.
106 Ibid., pp. 313–15.
107 Ibid., pp. 316–17.
108 Bush and Scowcroft, *World Transformed*, p. 406.

as prime minister by John Major. During the conference, Iraq announced the release of all German hostages because, Saddam said, Chancellor Kohl had made some "helpful" statements.[109]

Bush was more successful with Gorbachev. The secretary general gave way on the notion of two resolutions and agreed to the form of "all necessary measures" as the euphemism for the use of force. Asked by Bush when he thought the ultimatum should become effective, Gorbachev said mid January. Shevardnadze and Baker hammered out the wording of a draft resolution, which proposed to become effective on 1 January.[110] Bush also saw Turkish President Özal and received a call from Mubarak urging the American president to see Syrian President Assad on his way back from the Middle East visit that was to finish his trip.

Bush flew to Saudi Arabia where he met with Fahd. He urged the Saudi king to warn his Arab brothers to be careful about public statements of intent. Both Mubarak and Assad had made public statements expressing reluctance to take the offensive – Assad that his troops would not leave Saudi Arabia, and Mubarak that Egyptians would not enter Iraq.[111] After visiting US troops, Bush flew to Cairo and asked about these statements. Mubarak replied that Syria would be there when it came to war, and Egypt would do whatever was necessary. A subsequent discussion with Assad in Geneva was tougher. The Syrian leader wanted to discuss the issues surrounding Israel, and bristled when Bush replied with concerns over terrorism and civil rights. Bush raised his difficulties with Syrian statements opposing participation in the use of force to free Kuwait. He asked Assad to discuss the matter with Mubarak.[112]

While Bush dealt with Mubarak and Assad, Baker visited the remaining Security Council members, Yemen, Columbia, and Malaysia, and then returned for a final push at the United Nations. Gorbachev proposed to move the deadline to 31 January. Mitterrand suggested 15 January. That became the date. On 29 November, the Security Council passed

---

109 Ibid., pp. 407–8.
110 Ibid., p. 409, says that initially Gorbachev gave mid January as his preference for a deadline. Baker's account of UN deliberations gives 1 January for the original draft, which Gorbachev countered at UN with 31 January. Mitterrand, then, is credited with proposing that they split the difference at 15 January. Baker, *The Politics of Diplomacy*, p. 321, which is supported by the general discussion in Bush and Scowcroft, *World Transformed*, p. 414.
111 Bush and Scowcroft, *World Transformed*, p. 412. The Egyptians and the other Arab forces attacked into Kuwait, so did not enter Iraq. Elements of Syrian forces were part of the Arab offensive into Kuwait. See Khaled bin Sultan, *Desert Warrior*, pp. 230–31, 397. Khalid, Schwarzkopf's Saudi counterpart, says flatly that no Arab forces, including his, were prepared to enter Iraq, as opposed to Kuwait.
112 Bush and Scowcroft, *World Transformed*, p. 412.

Resolution 678, with twelve members in favor, Cuba and Yemen voting against, and China abstaining. The resolution demanded that Iraq comply with Resolution 660 (immediate and unconditional withdrawal) and "all subsequent relevant resolutions."[113] The resolution called the period leading up to the deadline a "pause of goodwill," to permit orderly compliance. Then it authorized "Member States co-operating with the Government of Kuwait, unless Iraq on or before 15 January 1991 fully implements ... the above-mentioned resolutions, *to use all necessary means* [emphasis added] to uphold and implement resolution 660 (1990)... and to restore international peace and security to the area."[114] On 6 December, one week after the UN Resolution, Saddam began releasing the remaining hostages held in Iraq and Kuwait.

While the Security Council had voted to authorize the use of force, Bush also had to convince the US Congress to follow suit, and perhaps convince himself that no alternative to combat had been left untried. To this end, two days after passage of Resolution 678, Bush proposed a meeting of the Iraqi foreign minister with the US President and coalition ambassadors, to be followed by another between Secretary of State Baker and Saddam.[115]

Baker writes that the meeting with Tariq Aziz, the Iraqi foreign minister, "brought out the contradictions between the needs of the international coalition and a domestic consensus for peace."[116] Scowcroft suggests that the offer of a meeting "[shook] the coalition to its core, just as the U.N. resolution had seemingly cleared away the last hurdle to taking action."[117] Baker defends the move as helping the effort to convince undecided members of Congress to authorize the use of force, to reassure the French and Soviets that diplomacy was still being tried, and to maintain control over the diplomatic momentum between 29 November and 15 January. Baker also agrees that the Saudis and Kuwaitis, in particular, had to be reassured that the offer did not represent a backing off by the coalition's military leader.[118]

The meeting between Baker and Tariq Aziz was held in Geneva, Switzerland, on 9 January. The Iraqi foreign minister was accompanied

113 United Nations Security Council, Resolution 678 (1990) of 29 November 1990, in United Nations Security Council, The Situation between Iraq and Kuwait (http://fas.org/news/un/iraq/sres/sres0678.htm).
114 Resolution 678.
115 Baker, *The Politics of Diplomacy*, pp. 346, 349; Bush and Scowcroft, *World Transformed*, pp. 420–21.
116 Baker, *The Politics of Diplomacy*, p. 351.
117 Bush and Scowcroft, *World Transformed*, pp. 420–21.
118 Baker, *The Politics of Diplomacy*, pp. 350–55.

by Saddam's half-brother Barzan al-Takriti, probably as a minder. There were no negotiations, simply a clear statement of US intentions to drive Iraq out of Kuwait if Saddam did not comply with UN resolutions. Baker presented a note from Bush to Saddam laying out US and coalition intentions and capabilities to enforce the UN Resolutions. Aziz refused to convey the message to Saddam and left it on the table. In addition, Baker warned the Iraqis against use of chemical, biological, or nuclear weapons and gained the personal promise of the Iraqi foreign minister that US diplomats remaining in Baghdad would be permitted to leave by 12 January. Intentionally paraphrasing Thucydides, Baker wrote that "what made the invasion of Kuwait inevitable – and the war to redress it – was the decline of Soviet power, the ascension of American power, and the fear that this caused in Saddam."[119]

The US Congressional debate began the same day. The vote on 12 January was close in the Senate, but the measure passed the House of Representatives by a wide margin. Congressional authorization avoided a likely Constitutional crisis had the president decided to go forward without Congressional authorization, or in the face of its denial.[120] Others made last-ditch attempts for a peaceful resolution. The UN secretary general went to Baghdad, to no avail. Gorbachev, rapidly losing power at home, swung to his right, to the old apparatchiks. Shevardnadze had resigned, suddenly, on 20 December. Primakov returned to Baghdad, while Aziz went to Moscow. Gorbachev tried to mediate a postponement of military action beyond 15 January, and later tried to delay the looming ground offensive. Each Soviet breakthrough with Iraq was conditional, and therefore unacceptable. After Bush read an Amnesty International Report on Iraqi misconduct in Kuwait and Saddam began destroying the Kuwaiti oil fields, no possibility of avoiding the destruction of Iraqi forces in Kuwait remained, except headlong flight.[121] The simple fact was that, by January 1991, there really was nothing the leader of the rapidly disintegrating Soviet Union could do to derail the coalition's strategy.

Before and after the Geneva meeting, Baker visited most major coalition partners for one last time. He visited the British first, then continued on to Spain where he obtained basing and employment rights for US B-52s at Torrejón. Then he visited the French. Mitterrand gave good advice about the wording of the president's letter to Saddam. Most

---

119 Ibid., p. 365.
120 Bush and Scowcroft, *World Transformed*, p. 446. The vote tally was 52 for with 47 against in the Senate and 250 for with 183 against in the House.
121 Ibid., pp. 427–28, 475.

importantly, the French president did not object to placing French forces under US operational direction once ground operations began, but he remained reluctant to commit French forces to US command of air operations. Kohl did not commit to the requested donation in support of offensive operations, but promised to do something. The Italians reiterated their support of any offensive.[122]

After the Geneva meeting, the Saudis responded positively to Baker's request for additional financial support, in spite of what US Ambassador Freeman called a liquidity shortage. Baker also asked Fahd for help with the Syrians. The Syrians, equipped with Soviet equipment like the Iraqis, remained reluctant to attack into Kuwait, where they might be fired on by US forces. In the end, they accepted a role as a follow-on reserve. The emir of Kuwait again provided funding equivalent to that of the Saudis, including money for Turkey and Eastern Europeans suffering from higher oil prices.[123] Baker then flew on to Cairo and Damascus. Mubarak was fuming over his latest exchange with Saddam and promised to intervene with the Syrians. In Damascus, Assad still resisted a commitment to any offensive action, though ultimately his forces did enter Kuwait, well to the rear of the Egyptians. NATO allies Turkey, Britain, and Canada continued to be supportive. Australia objected on the timing of advance notification, withheld for reasons of security.[124]

On 15 January, Bush signed National Security Directive 54, which provided strategic guidance for the conduct of offensive operations against Iraq. The directive listed four strategic goals and six military objectives. Consistent with the Saudi's early concern with postwar security, the document singled out destruction of the Republican Guard as a military objective.[125] A separate paragraph directed that: "Should Iraq resort to using chemical, biological, or nuclear weapons, be found supporting terrorist acts against U.S. or coalition partners anywhere in the world, or destroy Kuwait's oil fields, *it shall become an explicit objective of the United States to replace the current leadership of Iraq.*"[126] (Emphasis added.) Starting on 21 January, the Iraqis destroyed the Kuwaiti oil fields, but neither the US nor the coalition followed up as the directive indicated. Indeed, Bush, Scowcroft, and Baker all argued against such action, pointing to the logical consequences: disruption of the coalition,

---

122 Baker, *The Politics of Diplomacy*, pp. 369–72.
123 Ibid., pp. 372–75.
124 Ibid., pp. 375–77.
125 The White House, Washington, DC, National Security Directive 54, 15 January 1991 (http://bushlibrary.tamu.edu/research/nsd.php).
126 Ibid.

fragmentation of Iraq, sectarian civil war, and prolonged, costly, US occupation – all contributing to regional instability.[127]

As Aziz was leaving the Geneva meeting site, he was asked by the press if Iraq would attack Israel in the event of war. He replied, "Yes. Absolutely, yes."[128] The DESERT STORM air campaign began on 16 January. True to their word, the Iraqis fired the first Scud rockets at Israel the next day. The Israelis wanted to strike back, but there was no viable way for them to do so without overflying either Jordan or Saudi Arabia, and neither would countenance such an operation. The Israelis persisted in demanding the United States create conditions by which they could retaliate, either by deconflicting airspace or by providing friend-or-foe identification codes, requests which were refused. If they came anyway, that left the Israelis with the probability of detection as intruders in the ongoing coalition air offensive. Israel then demanded an Israeli presence in the theater command structure, which American leaders also denied.[129]

Ultimately, the president sent Patriot missile batteries, Deputy Secretary of State Lawrence Eagleburger, and Assistant Secretary of Defense Paul Wolfowitz to appease the Israelis. Moreover, Schwarzkopf diverted significant air resources to Scud hunting, and US and UK special operations forces went into western Iraq to try and find the elusive Scud batteries. The Americans informed the Israelis there was nothing Israel could do which the United States was not already doing and that any Israeli move might well disrupt the coalition fighting their common enemy. With great reluctance, the Israelis bowed to the logic of circumstances.[130]

A critical event occurred on 12 February when a US strike on an Iraqi command and control bunker in Baghdad killed a number of civilians who were using the bunker as an air-raid shelter. The international press, urged on by Saddam's minions, immediately sped images of the carnage around the globe. Sensitivity to the impact of the coverage led to curtailment of bombing in Baghdad. Bush notes that "One immediate consequence to this tragedy was additional public questioning of the length of the air war."[131]

127 Baker, *The Politics of Diplomacy*, pp. 436–38; Bush and Scowcroft, *World Transformed*, pp. 433, 464, and 489; Freedman and Karsh, *The Gulf Conflict*, pp. 342–43; Schwarzkopf, *It Doesn't Take a Hero*, p. 521.
128 Baker, *The Politics of Diplomacy*, p. 364.
129 Bush and Scowcroft, *World Transformed*, pp. 456.
130 Ibid., pp. 452–57. Freedman and Karsh assert there was a contingency plan to open a corridor for the Israelis, if the persisted. They were not informed of this and did not press the issue. Freedman and Karsh, *The Gulf Conflict*, p. 335.
131 Bush and Scowcroft, *World Transformed*, p. 470; Schwarzkopf, *It Doesn't Take a Hero*, pp. 504–5; Freedman and Karsh, *The Gulf Conflict*, pp. 324–29.

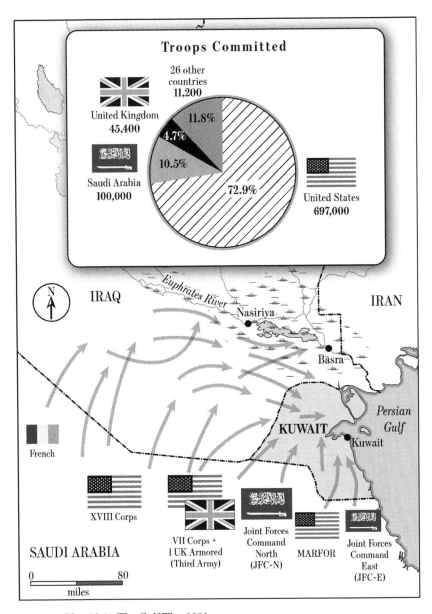

Troops Committed

26 other countries 11,200

United Kingdom 45,400

Saudi Arabia 100,000

11.8%

4.7%

10.5%

72.9%

United States 697,000

IRAQ

Euphrates River

Nasiriya

Bāsra

IRAN

Persian Gulf

KUWAIT

Kuwait

French

XVIII Corps

VII Corps + 1 UK Armored (Third Army)

Joint Forces Command North (JFC-N)

MARFOR

Joint Forces Command East (JFC-E)

SAUDI ARABIA

0   80
miles

Map 13.1   The Gulf War, 1991

Primakov revisited Baghdad, which led to another qualified offer to withdraw from Saddam. The coalition rejected the offer. The Iraqis and their Soviet sponsors continued efforts to avoid a ground attack. Finally, Bush issued an ultimatum that Iraq must accept the mandates of the United Nations without reservation and withdraw unconditionally, or accept the consequences. While the ultimatum was being drafted, Saddam began the destruction of Kuwaiti infrastructure. The president informed his allies, and issued his final ultimatum on 22 February.[132] The ground attack began on 24 February, two days after the arrival of the last US combat unit.[133] There was a minor contretemps in the Arab Joint Forces Command on 26 February, when the emir of Kuwait announced without coordination that his Crown Prince had assumed command of all allied forces operating in the kingdom.[134]

The war ended on 28 February with the Iraqis driven out of Kuwait. The decision to terminate offensive action was taken the evening of 27 February in the White House by President Bush. Bush records that he was under no pressure from his allies and appears to have made no special effort to consult with them or his military commanders on the spot about the decision before he made it.[135] The decision appears to have been made based partly on optimistic estimates of damage done to the Republican Guard, but primarily for humanitarian reasons, as well as to observe strictly the UN mandate, which limited military action to the purpose of reversing the Iraqi occupation.[136] The war had, nevertheless, liberated Kuwait and restored its government.

The subsequent ceasefire and peace process were ragged and the peace unsatisfying.[137] Much of the Republican Guard survived. The United States began withdrawing its forces immediately, perhaps with undue haste, leaving a temporary UN separation force in place to protect Kuwait.[138] Non-Saudi coalition forces also departed. In spite of the extent of his defeat Saddam too survived, but only barely and then only through the most ruthless of measures, including the use of airstrikes against ill-trained rebels.

---

132 Bush and Scowcroft, *World Transformed*, pp. 473–77.
133 Schwarzkopf, *It Doesn't Take a Hero*, p. 516.
134 Ibid., p. 539; Khaled bin Sultan, *Desert Warrior*, pp. 413–17.
135 Bush and Scowcroft, *World Transformed*, p. 485.
136 Ibid., pp. 485–86.
137 Ibid., pp. 483–92; Schwarzkopf, *It Doesn't Take a Hero*, pp. 542–69; Khaled bin Sultan, *Desert Warrior*, pp. 421–38. Khaled titles his chapter, "Failure at Safwan."
138 Bush and Scowcroft, *World Transformed*, p. 490. On the rapid withdrawal, see Schwarzkopf, *It Doesn't Take a Hero*, p. 549.

Scowcroft's balance point of leaving Saddam sufficient force to deter Iran, yet not enough to threaten his neighbors, was not achieved. The unstable peace, rather than recreating a regional balance, demanded a continuing US presence. It was necessary almost at once to impose no-fly zones to provide some protection for the Kurds and Shi'ites, and then to conduct a major relief operation in northern Iraq to avoid a human catastrophe from spilling over into Turkey. Small US ground forces rotated into Kuwait as a deterrent. Meanwhile, during the immediate postwar period, Saddam Hussein played cat and mouse with UN nuclear inspectors.

In 2003, when President George W. Bush exploited the post 9–11 political unease to overthrow the Iraqi regime, he was unable to duplicate the coalition his father had built. Furthermore, the American experience in Iraq from 2003 onward confirmed most of the concerns Bush Sr., Scowcroft, and Baker had forecast a decade before. In any event, such an action by the first Bush administration would have been beyond the UN mandate and was dependent on Saudi complicity, mainly because of the reliance on fuel provided by the kingdom to US forces and delivered largely in Saudi trucks. There is little evidence the king would have been willing to underwrite such an effort had it been proposed.

Conclusion

A number of factors combined to make the Gulf War coalition a success. First of all, the leaders of the principal participating states knew one another and proved remarkably capable of coordinating their diplomatic and military actions through frequent personal communication. Second, the global situation, marked by the precipitous decline of the Soviet Union, created conditions in which the old Cold War certainties of Soviet sponsorship of client states in the Middle East were collapsing. Globally, there was a sense that a new world order was emerging, and leading nations outside the region wished to influence its development. Participation in the coalition effort provided a voice in that process. Somewhat unusually, military resources were plentiful since the post-Cold War military drawdown had not yet taken hold. Finally, as the focal point of coalition efforts, Saddam Hussein was an invaluable adversary. He upset the regional balance within the Arab world in a way that both irritated fraternal comity and threatened the immediate security of his neighbors. His threat to the stability of the global oil supply was compounded by his seizure of Western hostages, the latter tactic sufficiently ill-managed to serve as a rally point for international opposition without producing any long-term inhibiting effect on his principal opponents.

In the end, Saddam's forces remained too long in Kuwait in face of every incentive to depart.

The good faith and commitment of the two leading nations, the United States and Saudi Arabia, cannot be underestimated. The willingness of the Saudi Royal Family to accept and underwrite a major Western army in their territory is indicative of their perception of the threat Saddam represented to their regime. Their forbearance, matched by the corresponding sincerity of the US military command to respect host-nation sensitivity, solidified the common effort. The ultimate US military dominance of the coalition ensured unity of effort and made it possible to ask no more of the allies than each was willing to give. The unstinting support of the Saudis and Kuwaitis, and the generous contributions of the major global economic powers, underwrote the significant US military contributions to the coalition, while the dependence of allied forces on Saudi fuel and logistical support provided the Saudis assurance of continuous consultation and a reasonable degree of control over developing military affairs.

In the end, the decisive element appears to be the mutual forbearance of the principal coalition partners. Neither the US nor the Saudis overreached. Coalition goals were established by continuous dialog and documented in UN resolutions. When the established goals were achieved with the liberation of Kuwait, the coalition halted military operations and then dispersed as measures were put in place to preserve the peace, however tenuous it was to prove. The Bush administration returned to the greater problem of managing the Soviet collapse. A decade later another Bush, less skilled as a diplomat and less attuned to ambiguity, would choose to cut the Gordian knot in Iraq, an impulsive act by no means a necessary consequence of the 1991 settlement.

14 Conclusion
Alliances and coalitions in the twenty-first century

Peter R. Mansoor

What we have tried to accomplish in this survey of alliances and coalitions from the ancient to the modern world is to examine the difficulties of alliance politics in war and explain why political and military leaders have managed to succeed or fail to achieve their goals by working with, competing against, or simply ignoring their allies in practice. A great deal of social science and historical literature deals with alliance formation and termination, including theories and examples of balancing and bandwagoning, entrapment and abandonment, the impact of ideological solidarity, and the importance of state reputation.[1] Much less deals with the realities of alliance management in practice, especially over the broad sweep of history.[2] This study is intended to add to the academic literature in this regard, and provide policy makers and military leaders with historical context on alliances and coalitions that will help guide their decisions in the future.

As US policy makers consider the formulation of a grand strategy to guide the fortunes of the American people in the twenty-first century, they should consider the fate of other great powers that have wrestled with similar challenges. Of primary concern to Washington today is the rise of China and the impact of its nascent power, both regionally and

---

1 A few of the many works on alliances include George Liska, *Nations in Alliance: The Limits of Interdependence* (Baltimore, 1962); Hans Morgenthau, Kenneth Thompson, and David Clinton, *Politics Among Nations* (New York, 1993), ch. 12; Stephan Walt, *The Origins of Alliances* (Ithica, NY, 1987); John Mearsheimer, *The Tragedy of Great Power Politics* (New York, 2001); Jonathan Mercer, *Reputation and International Politics* (Ithica, NY, 1996); Gregory Miller, *The Shadow of the Past: Reputation and Military Alliances before the First World War* (Ithica, NY, 2012); and Fotini Christia, *Alliance Formation in Civil Wars* (New York, 2012).
2 For several such efforts, see Glenn Snyder, *Alliance Politics* (Ithica, NY, 1997); Barry Rubin and Thomas A. Keaney (eds.), *US Allies in a Changing World* (London, 2001); Robert S. Rush and William W. Epley (eds.), *Multinational Operations, Alliances, and International Military Cooperation: Past and Future* (Washington, 2006); and Melissa P. Yeager and Charles Carter (eds.), *Pacts and Alliances in History: Diplomatic Strategy and the Politics of Coalitions* (London, 2012). The latter volume was also a product of a conference (in 2010) at the Mershon Center for International Security Studies.

globally. The recent and ongoing rebalancing of US military capabilities towards Asia is a response to those challenges. The United States, however, lacks the economic and military power to contain a potentially belligerent China without the assistance of allies. For a brief period of time at the end of the Cold War, American strategists enjoyed a unipolar moment which seemed to allow them the latitude to determine their foreign and defense policies without significant input from partner states. After two lengthy wars and the worst economic turndown since the Great Depression, those heady days are over. The United States confronts an uncertain future in a rapidly changing and increasingly multipolar global environment. Any viable grand strategy demands restoration of the economy at home and the strengthening of alliances abroad.

Recent debates concerning US strategy in Asia, however, have largely focused on anti-access/area-denial challenges to the projection of power. More to the point, discussions of "Air-Sea Battle" and the development of US air and naval capabilities to project power into contested areas fail to explain how such an operational concept – even if successful – could achieve victory in a potential conflict with China.[3] Commentators usually mention America's allies in Asia, if they are discussed at all, in the context of basing for air and naval units. US strategy has seemingly ceded land power on the Asian mainland to Chinese dominance. Indeed, proponents of offshore balancing and maritime strategies believe US ground forces should not play a major role in future conflicts, leaving messy ground fighting to regional allies absent a wholesale breakdown in the balance of power.[4] "America's comparative strategic advantages rest on naval and air power, not on sending land armies to fight ground wars in Eurasia," states one proponent of offshore balancing. "Thus the United States should opt for the strategic precepts of Alfred Thayer Mahan (the primacy of air and sea power) over those of Sir Halford Mackinder (the primacy of land power)."[5] As Williamson Murray has examined in his chapter on blue-water versus continental strategies, history suggests otherwise. In fact, nearly every time maritime powers such as the United States have

3 For a brief discussion of the concept of Air-Sea Battle, see John Callaway, "The Operational Art of Air-Sea Battle," Center for International Maritime Security, 18 July 2014 (http://cimsec.org/operational-art-air-sea-battle/11913).

4 For a discussion of a grand strategy based on offshore balancing see Christopher Layne, "From Preponderance to Offshore Balancing: America's Future Grand Strategy," *International Security*, 22(1) (Summer 1997), 86–124 and John Mearsheimer, "A Return to Offshore Balancing," *Newsweek*, 30 December 2008 (www.newsweek.com/return-offshore-balancing-82925).

5 Christopher Layne, "The (Almost) Triumph of Offshore Balancing," *The National Interest* (January 27, 2012) (http://nationalinterest.org/commentary/almost-triumph-offshore-balancing-6405).

attempted to prosecute a war against other great powers but without allies, they have lost. Furthermore, the cohesiveness of alliances rests not just on shared objectives, but shared risk. The Pacific is without a doubt the greatest maritime theater in the world, but Murray's essay convincingly hypothesizes that US national interests there cannot be realized without the commitment of ground forces to bolster America's regional allies.

This study, therefore, provides a crucial context largely lacking at present from the debate over US grand strategy. It suggests that despite the preponderance of American power, alliances will matter a great deal to US national security in the twenty-first century. Elizabeth Sherwood-Randall posits four reasons why alliances are necessary for the United States going forward: "To generate capabilities that amplify American power; to create a basis of legitimacy for the exercise of American power; to avert impulses to counterbalance American power; and to steer partners away from strategic apathy or excessive self-reliance."[6] Alliances and the diplomacy and institutions that surround them are the most influential way in which the United States can wield its power in a constructive manner in a globalized world. Alliances afford America the addition of combined military capabilities, access to overseas bases, shared intelligence, counterterrorism and cyber defense cooperation, and other resources that serve to enhance its influence and magnify its power. Rather than shackling the United States, alliances are in America's national interest.

The United States prosecuted the wars of the past decade in conjunction with both ad hoc coalitions (in the case of Iraq) and formal alliances (in the case of NATO in Afghanistan). But these ventures were fraught with difficulties. The US Joint Staff examination of the lessons from the wars of 9/11 includes this finding: "Establishing and sustaining coalition unity of effort was a challenge due to competing national interests, cultures, resources, and policies. Critical challenges when operating with coalition partners included national caveats, interoperability, training and TTP [tactics, techniques, and procedures], resources, national interests, culture, and information sharing and inclusion in planning."[7] The US military performed poorly in alliance management initially because professional education about the importance of alliances and training opportunities with potential alliance partners was lacking in the decade following the end of the Cold War. It should have come as no surprise,

6 Elizabeth Sherwood-Randall, *Alliances and American National Security* (Carlisle, PA, 2006), p. v.
7 Joint and Coalition Operational Analysis (A division of the Joint Staff J7), *Decade of War*, I: *Enduring Lessons from the Past Decade of Operations* (Washington, 2013), p. 29.

then, when US military leaders encountered difficulties in shaping and managing alliances in practice.

These problems existed in part because the United States sought partners as much to lend international political legitimacy to these ventures as it did to strengthen the coalitions in a military sense. The result was a patchwork of national caveats that made force management difficult at best. Aircrews operating in Afghanistan, for instance, had to negotiate a labyrinth of rules concerning which national forces they could support under various conditions.[8] In Iraq, national contributions ranged from those with few caveats on employment (US and British forces), to those that could only conduct defensive operations (Polish troops, for example), to those that could only conduct humanitarian operations (Thai, Korean, and various others).[9] Even if employed jointly, coalition forces often had difficulties operating with one another due to different procedures and command and control systems. Coordination was best among Western allies using NATO procedures, a tangible benefit of the decades-long military alliance aimed at the defense of Western Europe. Officers educated and trained to NATO standards, and often in the same schools, made a significant difference in the functioning of the coalitions in Iraq and Afghanistan.[10] On the other hand, over-classification of data led to the creation of stovepiped digital command and control systems, which in most cases meant that US forces could not share critical information and intelligence with other coalition forces.[11]

On the whole, the challenges of coalition management identified in the past decade are not new. As this study has shown, they are inherent in the nature of coalitions and alliances going back to the ancient world. Alliances are stronger when allies need each other, either to stave off defeat or to secure victory. Alliances that include countries as mere political window dressing will invariably be weak creations of major powers with hesitant buy-in from reluctant allies. On the other hand, the creation of effective alliances among unequal powers is possible, but the most

---

8 Ibid.
9 For an example of the impact of national caveats on the fighting in Iraq, see Peter R. Mansoor, *Baghdad at Sunrise: A Brigade Commander's War in Iraq* (New Haven, CT, 2008), ch. 10.
10 During my brigade's operations in Karbala, Iraq in the spring of 2004, we worked closely with a brigade of Polish forces. The operations went much more smoothly because the executive officer of the Polish brigade was a graduate of the US Army War College and the Polish unit used NATO procedures (including the use of English in communications) to command and control its task force, which included units of multiple nationalities.
11 Joint and Coalition Operational Analysis, *Enduring Lessons from the Past Decade of Operations*, p. 30.

powerful alliance member needs to be willing to accommodate the interests of lesser powers to ensure alliance harmony. In successful alliances the great powers involved avoided the danger of mirror-imaging their allies, and instead allowed them to fill those missions for which they were best suited. American policy makers must consider these examples as they fashion current and future alliances.

Alliance management occurs on three levels: political, military, and technical (finances, industrial resources, sharing of technology, etc.). Of these three areas, the political basis for an alliance is clearly the most important. The current effort by the United States to fashion an alliance to fight the Islamic State of Iraq and al-Sham in Iraq and Syria exemplifies this truth. While American policy makers have trumpeted the participation of more than sixty states in the alliance, serious strategic differences among various alliance partners have jeopardized its coherence.[12] But this is not to say that the other areas are unimportant; indeed, coordination of military forces and sharing of resources are critical to the success of combined ventures in peace and war. Not all alliances reach the relatively smooth functioning of the Grand Alliance in World War II or the North Atlantic Treaty Alliance in these regards, but when they do, they are all the more effective for doing so.

The political goals underpinning alliances – whether defense against shared threats, a collective attempt to balance other powers, a mutual desire to conquer, the maintenance of the existing economic and security order, or other objectives – trump all other factors in determining their durability. This fact has always been the case with alliances since the ancient world, and it will not change in the twenty-first century. In the years since the terrorist attacks of 9/11, the United States has attempted to create alliances and coalitions based on a shared desire to combat the global scourge of terrorism. But this objective has proven to be thin gruel on which to feed a continuing desire to cooperate in international affairs. The perceived legitimacy of the cause compelling alliance creation matters more in an era dominated more by mass politics than Cabinet diplomacy, a factor that played a large role in the eventual fracturing of the coalition assembled by the administration of President George W. Bush to wage the war against Iraq beginning in 2003. Although the North Atlantic Treaty Organization cooperated in peacekeeping operations in Bosnia and Kosovo, in counterinsurgency operations in

---

12 Craig Whitlock and Karen DeYoung, "Serious Disagreements Remain in U.S.-led Coalition Battling the Islamic State," *Washington Post*, 14 October 2014 (www.washingtonpost.com/world/national-security/serious-disagreements-remain-in-us-led-coalition-battling-the-islamic-state/2014/10/14/69772516-53cd-11e4-809b-8cc0a295c773_story.html).

Afghanistan, and most recently in operations in Libya, its future is uncertain absent the Soviet threat that was for decades the *sine qua non* of its existence. For the time being, the constituent members still find enough value in membership to keep the alliance intact.[13]

Coordination of military forces in alliances and coalitions requires judicious leadership and the development of effective coordination mechanisms to manage operations, preferably before a crisis emerges. Alliances that do not work in peacetime will perform no better (and probably worse) in wartime, when the pressure on policy makers and military leaders increases by an order of magnitude. The professional military education system must take this reality into account and do more to prepare US military leaders to work within multinational environments. Those leaders who take the time to understand the political and military cultures of allied nations will be most effective in fashioning a cohesive bond among them. As the examples in this volume have shown, relationships based on blood, friendship, honor, and professional respect can help to smooth relations among allies.

Perhaps the most important take-away from this study of alliances and coalitions is that they have and will in the future make a huge difference in grand strategy. In today's interconnected, globalized world, unilateralism is a recipe for catastrophe. In this century, US policy makers would be well advised to remember the words of Benjamin Franklin upon the signing of the Declaration of Independence, "We must, indeed, all hang together, or assuredly we shall all hang separately."

13 Melissa Yeager and Michael McCoy posit "inertia and vested interests" as potential reasons for the durability of the North Atlantic Treaty Organization even after the breakup of the Soviet Union. Yeager and Carter, *Pacts and Alliances in History*, p. 212. As recent NATO operations in Afghanistan and Libya have shown, however, the alliance still performs a useful military function not replicated in other institutions in Europe.

Index

Adams, John, 259
Adenauer, Konrad, 175, 180, 194
Aegospotomi, Battle of, 8
Afghanistan, Soviet invasion of, 184
Alcibiades, 23, 208, 211, 214
Alexander I of Russia, 74, 81, 93
  Congress of Vienna and, 101, 106
  "Crisis of Troyes" and, 97
  operations, interference in, 81, 83,
    90, 93
  peace negotiations and, 96, 99, 107
Alexander the Great, 24
alliances, 107, 253, 284
  aims of, 3, 4, 6, 9, 14, 214, 284, 313
  allies, understanding of, 9, 253, 313, 380
  ambitions, control of, 5, 107
  assumptions and, 285
  chance, matters of, 10
  cohesion of, 74, 284, 378, 380
  contentious discourse and, 313, 342
  cultural sensitivity and, 253
  defeat, salvaging of, 7, 74
  definition of, 3, 3n7
  elements for success of, 9
  enemies, understanding of, 9
  external factors and threats to, 6, 8
  geography, influence of, 5, 9
  global balance of power and, 20
  grand strategy, role of, 20
  history, knowledge of, 9
  ideological regimes and, 10, 214
  independent forces within, 13
  leadership and, 9, 107, 214, 381
  management of, 379, 380
  maritime/island powers and, 20
  military capabilities and, 9
  operations, conduct of, 6, 381
  politics and, 4, 5, 13, 15, 74, 105, 227,
    253, 380
  post-conflict durability of, 8
  shared success and, 253
  strategic culture and, 9

  transparency and, 10, 12, 106, 314, 342
  trust and, 240, 253
  unity of command and, 13
  unity of effort and, 14
  victory, approach of, 7, 74
  world views and, 9
Alsace-Lorraine, 287
American Revolutionary War, 31, 71,
    262, 281
  Amity and Commerce, Treaty of, 260
  British leadership and, 31
  British naval disadvantage and, 264
  British strategy in, 9, 281
  Camden, Battle of, 268
  Capes, Battle of the, 6, 273
  Caribbean Basin theatre and, 262
  European theatre and, 262
  France, British view of, 256
  France, early intervention and, 256
  India and, 262
  Newport, French occupation of, 266
  Saintes, Battle of the, 275
  Saratoga, Battle of, 32, 256, 258
  Spanish intervention and, 257, 260,
    261, 262
  Yorktown, siege of, 275
Amiens, Battle of, 133
Andrassy, Julius, 286, 288
Andrews, Admiral Adolphus, 12n34
Anglo-Burgundian alliance. *See also*
    Hundred Years War
  Agincourt, Battle of, 222
  aims of, 220, 223
  Arras, Treaty of, 246
  Brittany, alliance with, 232
  Burgundian expansion and, 226, 236
  Burgundian security and, 226
  cohesion of, 226, 227, 229, 233n41,
    236, 238, 242, 249, 251
  collapse of, 226, 246, 251
  cooperation and, 222, 227, 234,
    238, 246

Made in the USA
Middletown, DE
30 July 2019